AP Biology For Dummies®

Cheat Sheet

Atoms, Molecules, and Biochemistry

Here are some important concepts to remember about atoms, molecules, and biochemistry:

- Water is highly polar. Water's properties give it a large heat capacity, high surface tension, and cause it to drive the formation of phospholipid membranes.
- Proteins are built from amino acids. Nucleic acids are built from nucleotides. Polysachharides are built from monosacharride sugars.
- Enzymes are biological catalysts. They speed up chemical reactions without altering the reactants or products, and without being consumed in the reactions.
- $pH = -\log[H^+]$
- DNA acts as a template for RNA during transcription. RNA acts as a template for protein during translation.

Cells and Cell Cycles

Keep these facts about cells and cell cycles close at hand and constantly review them — you never know — you may end up memorizing them all:

- Prokaryotes lack membrane-bound organelles, are single-celled, and usually have cell walls. Eukaryotes have membrane-bound organelles, can be single- or multicellular, and only have cell walls in special cases like plants and fungi.
- Cell membranes are selectively permeable. Transport across membranes can be passive (diffusion) or active (requires an input of energy).
- Chloroplasts perform photosynthesis: Light (energy) + $6\ H_2O$ + $6\ CO_2 \rightarrow C_6H_{12}O_6$ + $6\ O_2$
- Mitochondria perform cellular respiration: $C_6H_{12}O_6$ + $6\ O_2 \rightarrow 6\ H_2O$ + $6\ CO_2$ + energy
- Aerobic respiration yields 36 ATPs per molecule of glucose. Anaerobic respiration yields 2 ATPs per molecule of glucose.
- Interphase consists of G_1, S, and G_2 phases (growth 1, synthesis, and growth 2). M phase consists of mitosis (prophase, metaphase, anaphase, and telophase) and cytokinesis. Mitosis results in the division of a parent cell into two genetically identical daughter cells.
- Meiosis consists of meiosis I and meiosis II. Crossing over occurs during prophase I. Independent assortment occurs during metaphase I. During meiosis I, cells move from diploid to haploid states. Meiosis results in the division of a single parent cell into four haploid cells that will become gametes.

For Dummies: Bestselling Book Series for Beginners

Plants and Animals

We've picked some of the more challenging info on plants and animals to include in the following list as you'll likely need to refer to these often:

- Vascular plants have roots, shoots and stems, each of which arises from dermal, vascular, and ground tissues. Apical meristems elongate root and stem tips. Lateral meristems thicken existing roots and stems.

- Xylem conducts water and dissolved nutrients from roots upward. Phloem conducts dissolved sugars from sugar sources to sugar sinks.

- Phototropism is growth towards light. Gravitropism is upward growth. Thigmotropism is growth in response to contact. Photoperiodism is growth is response to periodic changes in light.

- Gymnosperm plants are either male or female. Angiosperm plants produce flowers that contain both male and female reproductive parts.

- Oxygen and carbon dioxide exchange between circulatory systems and respiratory systems. These dissolved gases diffuse down concentration gradients between cells and capillaries, and between capillaries and alveoli.

- Nerves conduct electrical signals to allow for rapid communication between specific sites. Hormones move through body fluids to allow for slower, more distributed communication.

- Skeletal muscles contract to create movement about skeletal joints. Cardiac muscle contracts to force blood through vessels. Smooth muscle contracts slowly and for longer periods. Skeletal and cardiac muscles are striated because they contain sarcomeres.

- Mechanical digestion occurs by chewing and by churning of the stomach. Chemical digestion occurs via enzymes, stomach acid, and bile, especially in the duodenum. The small intestine absorbs many digested nutrients though vili. The large intestine absorbs water.

- Nonspecific immunity initially fights off infection and buys time for the onset of specific immunity. Specific immunity includes humoral and cell-mediated immunity. Humoral immunity involves the production of antibodies, and is organized by B-lymphocytes. Cell-mediated immunity is carried out by T-lymphocytes.

- Zygotes develop into blastulas, which develop into gastrulas. Gastrulas give rise to endoderm, mesoderm and ectoderm layers. Further development is spurred by induction.

Wiley, the Wiley Publishing logo, For Dummies, the Dummies Man logo, the For Dummies Bestselling Book Series logo and all related trade dress are trademarks or registered trademarks of John Wiley & Sons, Inc. and/or its affiliates. All other trademarks are property of their respective owners.

AP Biology

FOR

DUMMIES®

AP Biology
FOR
DUMMIES®

by Peter Mikulecky, PhD
Advanced Science Teacher, Fusion Learning Center

Michelle Rose Gilman
Founder/CEO Fusion Learning Center

Brian Peterson
Science Department Chair, Fusion Learning Center

WILEY

Wiley Publishing, Inc.

AP Biology For Dummies®

Published by
Wiley Publishing, Inc.
111 River St.
Hoboken, NJ 07030-5774
www.wiley.com

WILEY

About the Authors

Peter Mikulecky: Peter Mikulecky grew up in Milwaukee, an area of Wisconsin unique for its high human-to-cow ratio. After a breezy four-year tour in the Army, Peter earned a BS in biochemistry and molecular biology from the University of Wisconsin – Eau Claire and a PhD in biological chemistry from Indiana University. With science seething in his DNA, he sought to infect others with a sense of molecular wonderment. Having taught, tutored, and mentored in classroom and laboratory environments, Peter was happy to find a home at Fusion Learning Center and Fusion Academy. There, he enjoys persuading students that biology and chemistry are in fact fascinating journeys, not entirely designed to inflict pain on hapless teenagers. His military training occasionally aids him in this effort.

Michelle Rose Gilman: Michelle Rose Gilman is most proud to be known as Noah's mom (Hi Munch!). A graduate of the University of South Florida, Michelle found her niche early and at 19 was already working with emotionally disturbed and learning disabled students in hospital settings. At 21 she made the trek to California, and there she found her passion for helping teenage students become more successful in school and life. What started as a small tutoring business in the garage of her California home quickly expanded and grew to the point where traffic control was necessary on her residential street.

Today, Michelle is the Founder and CEO of Fusion Learning Center and Fusion Academy, a private school and tutoring/test-prep facility in Solana Beach, California, serving over 2,000 students per year. She is the author of *ACT For Dummies, Precalculus For Dummies,* and other books on self-esteem, writing, and motivational topics. Michelle has overseen dozens of programs over the last 20 years, focusing on helping kids become healthy adults. She currently specializes in motivating unmotivatable adolescents, comforting their shell-shocked parents, and assisting her staff of 35 teachers.

Michelle lives by the following motto: "There are people content with longing; I am not one of them."

Brian Peterson: Brian remembers a love for science going back to his own AP Biology high school class. At the University of San Diego, Brian majored in Biology and minored in Chemistry, with a pre-med emphasis. Before embarking to medical school, Brian took a young-adult-professional detour and found himself at Fusion Learning Center/Fusion Academy, an independent private school, where he quickly discovered a love of teaching. Years later, he finds himself the Science Department Head at Fusion and oversees a staff of 11 science teachers. Brian, also known as "Beeps" by his favorite students, is committed to encouraging the love of science in his students by offering unique and innovative science curricula.

Dedication

We would like to dedicate this book to all the students who motivate us to be better teachers, and to everyone who has waited patiently for us while we wrote this book: We are now ready to play!

Authors' Acknowledgments

Thanks to Bill Gladstone from Waterside Productions for being an amazing agent and for not only giving us the opportunity to write *this* book but believing enough in us to continue giving us more. You're a brave man, Bill! Thanks to our Wiley editors, Stacy Kennedy and, especially, Jennifer Connolly for her constant humor, compassion, and salt lick.

Publisher's Acknowledgments

We're proud of this book; please send us your comments through our Dummies online registration form located at www.dummies.com/register/.

Some of the people who helped bring this book to market include the following:

Acquisitions, Editorial, and Media Development

Project Editor: Jennifer Connolly

Acquisitions Editor: Stacy Kennedy

Copy Editor: Jennifer Connolly

Technical Editor: Barry Ludvik

Senior Editorial Manager: Jennifer Ehrlich

Editorial Supervisor: Carmen Krikorian

Editorial Assistants: Erin Calligan Mooney, Joe Niesen, Leeann Harney, David Lutton

Cover Photos: © David Chasey/Getty Images

Cartoons: Rich Tennant (www.the5thwave.com)

Composition Services

Project Coordinator: Kristie Rees

Layout and Graphics: Claudia Bell, Carrie A. Cesavice, Reuben W. Davis, Stephanie D. Jumper

Proofreaders: Laura Albert, Susan Moritz, Evelyn W. Still

Indexer: Galen Schroeder

Publishing and Editorial for Consumer Dummies

Diane Graves Steele, Vice President and Publisher, Consumer Dummies

Joyce Pepple, Acquisitions Director, Consumer Dummies

Kristin A. Cocks, Product Development Director, Consumer Dummies

Michael Spring, Vice President and Publisher, Travel

Kelly Regan, Editorial Director, Travel

Publishing for Technology Dummies

Andy Cummings, Vice President and Publisher, Dummies Technology/General User

Composition Services

Gerry Fahey, Vice President of Production Services

Debbie Stailey, Director of Composition Services

Contents at a Glance

Table of Contents

Introduction

*W*ait, how did you get here?

That's a reasonable question. Take a seat, unfurl your map, and review what you know:

- ✔ You're smart. Maybe you forgot about that. Let the title of this book roll off your back like water from a duck in a raincoat. You wouldn't be anywhere near the AP Biology exam if you didn't have the goods. Believe it.

- ✔ You're a little nervous. The College Board sits atop Mount Olympus, hurling thunderbolts at you, sneering at your hubris:

    "So you think you're going to get college credit? First you must pass a little test we have devised for you . . . bwah-hah-hah-hah!"

    Peals of laughter thunder down from the summit. Gulp.

- ✔ You have — or soon will have — a plan. Your AP Biology course is part of it. This book is another part. Ignore the thundering laughter, and put one foot in front of the other. Sure, eventually you'll have to face the judgment of the Board. But a lot is going to happen between now and then. By the time you have to fight for your Five, you'll be ready. In the meantime, stick to your plan.

Remember, the Board may be a jealous and vengeful god, but biology is your friend. Biology just asks reasonable questions, like:

Wait, how did I get here?

About This Book

Like biology, we are your friends. No matter how you got here, or how this book came to you, we're here to help. We've broken things down into sections that correspond to just the kind of content and questions you'll see on the AP Biology exam. We've emphasized those things on which you're more likely to be tested, and tread lightly over those things that you probably won't see on test day. You have enough on your plate.

Each chapter reviews big ideas, and highlights those nitty-gritty, rubber-meets-the road details that tend to pop up in test questions. Although you may want to start at the beginning and soldier your way through to the end, that's not absolutely necessary. Based on your experiences in the AP Biology course, you've probably got a pretty good idea of your strengths and weaknesses. Feel free to pick and choose.

Maybe you don't know what your weaknesses are. That's okay, too. Each chapter is accompanied by a follow-up chapter that summarizes the most important points and provides questions to help you figure out where you stand. If you're using this book as you go through the AP Biology course, you'll find it easy to flip to the topic of the moment. Please do.

And when you begin to hear the thunder from the summit, we've got you covered. We've included two full-length practice tests. Use them to make final adjustments to your plan, and to ensure that by the time you sit down for the real thing, you'll have done it all before. Twice.

Foolish Assumptions

Yes, we made some assumptions about you while we wrote this book. If you're reading this you probably fit into one or more of the following assumptions:

- ✔ **We assume that you're probably planning to take the AP Biology exam.** Otherwise, you'd probably have better ways to pass the hours than, well, preparing for the AP Biology exam. But maybe you're just deciding whether or not to take the AP Biology course. Or maybe you're taking the course, but haven't decided whether to take the exam. This book will help you with those decisions.

- ✔ **We do *not* assume that you have aced all of your previous courses in math and science.** Whatever math and chemistry you really need to know is presented within. Don't sweat it. We've got your back.

- ✔ **We assume that you don't like being bored or judged.** Neither do we. This book is designed to be a streamlined, practical companion that doesn't take things more seriously than necessary — in short, a good traveling partner.

How This Book Is Organized

Because the AP Biology exam is a standardized test, it tests more than just biology. It tests your ability to take tests. True story. We've accounted for that, and included a handy primer on how to prepare for the test-taking experience. Once you're primed, you're ready to fling yourself into the biological fray; the bulk of the book reviews the biology emphasized on the exam, in the proportions described by the College Board's AP Biology syllabus. Each chapter of new material is followed by a chapter that summarizes the key points, provides practice questions, and gives a concise review of any AP Biology labs associated with that material. Finally, there are the practice tests. They're not going anywhere, so just take them when you feel ready.

Part I: Doing Your Best for the Test

Should I even take the AP Biology exam? What's it like? How do they score it? Will they try to trick me? What can I do to defend myself? Are vomit bags provided? These are the sober questions of a scientific mind, and we take them seriously.

Part II: Molecules and Cells

Start at the source, and things seem simpler. Biology may cover millions of species, but they begin to look more and more alike when you put them under a microscope. By starting with the small stuff — the *really* small stuff — differences in the bigger bits just seem to make a whole lot more sense. Back when the earth was steamy and soupy, when biology was just waking up and taking a look around, life was a story of molecules and cells. The tricks of the trade that evolved back then still apply now.

Part III: Living Large — Organisms and Populations

Once you've got a handle on what cells do with molecules, you already understand the basics behind what organisms do with organs. Things take a turn for the dramatic when you start talking about what organisms do to each other. This section is thick and rich, because the AP Biology exam dwells on these topics at great length. You might want to dally a bit longer in this part, too.

Part IV: Inheriting and Evolving

Whether we're talking cells or stegosauruses, the name of the game is evolution. It's really the only rule by which biology plays. What evolution looks like depends on how far back you stand and how much you squint your eyes. By the time you get through with this Part, you may feel a warm sense of kinship with bacteria.

Part V: Putting It All into Practice, or, Practicing What Has Been Preached

Oh, right — there was something about a *test*, wasn't there? This Part contains two full-length, timed practice tests, modeled on the actual AP Biology exam. And even if you guess on a lot of the questions, we won't leave you guessing. We provide full answer keys with explanations. And remember, there are two tests; if you crash and burn on the first, there is room for redemption.

Part VI: The Part of Tens

Wouldn't it be nice if there were some sort of really nice summary of the big ideas and the must-know bits? Yes, it would be. That is the purpose of this Part. It contains three concise, ten-part summaries of the pithy good stuff.

Icons Used in This Book

Every now and then, you may catch a glimpse of something in the margins. We meant to do that. Included throughout the book are helpful icons, little pointers that help you navigate through the material.

The remember icon is a subtle but strong suggestion that you file the indicated material in that separate folder of your brain reserved for things you'll have to use later.

This icon flags information that may help you save time, prevent mistakes or generally make life easier on yourself.

When you see this icon, relax. The material you're reading may seem particularly involved or esoteric. That's because it is. If it interests you, please dig in, but if not, feel free to move on.

This icon is just what it says. It flags the kind of information that you ignore at your own peril. If we could make it our own peril, we would. But we can't, so we use this icon.

Where to Go from Here

Start with the first two chapters. They'll help you to figure out where you stand with respect to the AP Biology exam, and to formulate your plan of action.

Then, flip through the biology review to regain a sense of what you already know, what you've never seen, and what you've long since forgotten. Let yourself glide through the material that's easy for you, saving time and energy for the parts that make you close your eyes, massage your temples, and curse the Board that sits atop Olympus.

However you start, remember that this book is not an assignment — it is a tool. Use it in the way that helps you the most. Follow your plan. After the smoke of the AP Biology exam clears to reveal your stellar score, you'll regard that plan with affection, thinking, "Ah yes, *that's* how I got here."

Part I
Doing Your Best for the Test

The 5th Wave · By Rich Tennant

"There'll be an additional question on the science portion of the test. It has to do with the digestive tract of a dog who has just eaten an entire can of pink Play-Doh."

In this part . . .

Put a picture in a different frame, and the picture looks different somehow. The same is true of biology — frame it within an AP exam, and it somehow seems a little different. Before you take that AP Biology exam out for a drive, you might want to kick the tires, pop the hood, and see how it's put together. Think of this part as AP Exam Mechanics 101. You want to be so familiar with the ins, outs, and idiosyncrasies of the exam that by the time you take it you don't notice anything but the biology. You want to see the picture, not the frame.

In this part, we delve into the structure of the exam and how you can use that structure to your advantage. What's more, we give you tips and strategic pointers on how to pace your preparation. Proper pacing will ensure that you review what you need when you need it, without burning out and without scrambling at the last minute. By following the well-scheduled plan we'll help you create, you'll have calm, quiet confidence when you need it most. When the sun rises on test day, you'll feel its warmth — not its shadow.

Chapter 1

Dissecting the AP Biology Exam

. . . .

In This Chapter

▶ Understanding why you take this exam

▶ Breaking down the exam into all its parts

▶ Guessing or not

▶ Getting the skinny on the scores

▶ Packing your bags: What to take and not take to the test

▶ Preparing for unusual circumstances: What to do if you need special assistance

. . . .

*Y*ou really didn't know what the insides of the frog looked like before you opened it up, did you? Well, consider this first chapter the dissection of the AP Exam. As we slice and cut through the test, you will begin to get familiar with why you should (or shouldn't) take this test, the test's structure, how you will be scored, what's allowed on test day and what to do if you require special assistance. Many students are intimidated by the AP tests, but the Wizard of Oz was also scary before the curtain flew open! So sit back, relax, get your scalpel out, and open this thing up!

We do a lot of talking in this chapter about the AP Exam, but if you're taking AP Biology now or getting ready to, keep in mind that while this book can be a great support throughout your course, the AP Exam is the end game, so you need to know this info, too!

Proving Your College Prowess

Taking the AP test is basically telling those good folks at any college that you can already think and perform on the college level. Although taking an AP Biology course is not required to take the AP test (although we highly recommend you do), your high score on the test (see the skinny on the scoring information below) signifies that you understand advanced material and already possess what it takes to be successful in college. Go you! By getting a high score, you also have the opportunity to receive credit or advanced standing at most universities around the country. You should take this test if Biology is "your thing" and you want the world to know.

If you received poor grades in Biology in high school and could care less about what's inside a cell, you might want to consider spending your time on a subject you truly enjoy. Those smart AP creators have AP tests in a variety of different subjects, so if you're not sure about your dedication to this particular test, you might want to visit their Web site and glance at the other subjects offered. If you're just taking an AP Biology class and don't plan on taking the exam at the end, then that's cool too. This book will definitely help you succeed in an AP Biology class.

Because you bought this book, however, we will assume you are a natural Biologist and that after studying this book you will bust out of your high school body and become your true self: the college student that you were meant to be!

Getting to the Guts of the Exam

The AP Biology Exam takes three hours and includes two parts: an 80-minute, 100-question multiple choice section; a 100-minute writing period broken down into a 10-minute reading period, and a 90-minute four-question, free-response section. After you complete the multiple choice section you get a short break.

You can't return to the multiple choice section after you hand it in, so make certain you are satisfied before you stretch your legs!

The multiple-choice questions

We have a feeling that the AP bigwigs couldn't agree on what types of problems and questions to include in the multiple choice section. As a result, they just decided to throw in everything. The multiple choice questions that you will encounter cover a broad range of topics. You can expect to answer basic factual information as well as heavy-duty, thought-provoking problems. You have basically 48 seconds per question on the multiple-choice section, and to get a great score on the exam, you need to correctly answer around 60 questions or more (more information on tackling these types of questions in Chapter 2).

The free-response questions

The second section of the exam is the writing section. Of 100 minutes you read for 10 minutes, after which you get 90 minutes to complete an essay period. You're given four broad essay questions. On average, one essay covers material relating to molecules and cells, one essay covers heredity and evolution, and — lucky you — you get two essays covering organisms and populations. Remember that at least one of the essays will ask you to analyze experimental data and perhaps design an experiment. So pay close attention when we talk about the labs in each chapter (more information on tackling these types of problems in Chapter 2).

Ticking through the Topics Covered

Before writing the AP exam, a few Biology geniuses studied the Biology curricula of many of the nation's best colleges. They came away from the study with a clear understanding of which high-level concepts were being taught to Biology college students around the country. From their research they decided that the AP exam should cover three main areas. But because you deserve to know everything, we break these three areas down even further, outlining every subheading in the test, as well as the percentage of the test attributed to it:

- **Molecules and Cells** (25 percent of test):
  - **Chemistry of Life:** Water, organic molecules in organisms, free energy changes, enzymes (7 percent)
  - **Cells:** Prokaryotic and eukaryotic cells, membranes, subcellular organization (10 percent)
  - **Cellular Energetics:** Coupled reactions, fermentation, and cellular respiration (8 percent)
- **Heredity and Evolution** (25 percent of test):
  - **Heredity:** Meiosis and gametogenesis, eukaryotic chromosomes, inheritance patterns (8 percent)

- **Molecular Genetics:** RNA and DNA structure and function, gene regulation, mutation, viral structure and replication, nucleic acid technology and applications (9 percent)

- **Evolutionary Biology:** Early evolution of life, evidence for evolution, mechanisms of evolution (8 percent)

✔ **Organisms and Populations** (50 percent of test): As you can see, Organisms and Populations covers half the test. So, when studying, you know where to place your attention.

- **Diversity of Organisms:** Evolutionary patterns, survey of the diversity of life, phylogenetic classification, evolutionary relationships (8 percent)

- **Structure and Function of Plants and Animals:** Reproduction, growth and development, structural, physiological and behavioral adaptations (32 percent)

Notice that 32 percent of the test is Structure and Function of Plants and Animals. That's a big chunk, so when studying later, make sure to pay careful attention to this section.

- **Ecology:** Population dynamics, communities and ecosystems, global issues (10 percent)

Trying to Decide: To Guess or Not to Guess

Here's our advice on guessing: Guess and don't guess. Not the answer you wanted? Let us explain. The test folks don't take away points for answers left blank, but they do remove a portion of points for wrong answers (we get into more of the scoring of the test in the section, "Getting the Skinny on Scoring"). If you can whittle away the obvious wrong answers and make a really good *educated* guess, then we say go for it. Never, we repeat, never answer a question if you have absolutely no idea where to begin. You don't get dinged for leaving a blank answer, but you do suffer the point loss for the wrong answer. If you have *some* knowledge of the question and can eliminate two to three obvious wrong answers, informed guessing is definitely to your advantage.

Getting the Skinny on Scoring

After all is said and done, you end up with a final composite score between 1 and 5. Those smart AP folks did a lot of researching to figure out how to score you. They periodically compare the performance of AP students with that of college students tested on the same material. Basically, a grade of 5 on the AP test is comparable to a college student earning an A in their college level Biology course. A grade of 4 on the AP test is like receiving a B in a college level class, and so on. An AP score of 3 or higher would qualify you for college credit because it would be the equivalent of earning a middle C or higher if you were to take that class in college. The College Board likes to put it this way:

5: Extremely well qualified

4: Well qualified

3: Qualified

2: Possibly qualified

1: No recommendation

Before you receive a composite score, however, a lot of calculating goes on to get that number. Take a look at the breakdown in the following sections.

Tabulating the multiple-choice section

Chapter 2 discusses the multiple choice and free response questions at length. This section is all about the final numbers. Once you know the scoring and then get the skinny on how to tackle the questions in Chapter 2, we feel strongly that you will score high and feel great!

The multiple choice section is scored by a computer. The computer counts the amount of wrong answers and subtracts .25 points for each wrong answer from the amount of right answers. Any question that you didn't answer is counted as 0. So basically, the formula for scoring this section is:

Multiple-choice score = Number of correct answers – (number of wrong answers × .25)

Adding up the free-response section

Your essays are read by top-secret, highly trained professionals — think "secret service" of the College Board. No one knows the identity of these professionals. Isn't this getting exciting? Your four essays are read by four different secret people — that's four, highly trained, hidden, underground readers just for you! Each scorer is trained to score just *one* essay question on the exam. They truly become experts in that *one* question. Each essay is scored on a scale from 1 to 10. The secretive AP leaders assure us that they have ample check-double-check systems in place to ensure that all essays are scored fairly.

Reaching the composite score

Okay, after you have two sets of scores (one score for the multiple-choice section and one score for the free-response section) they're put together to get your composite score and your final number. The highest composite score for the AP Biology test is 150. The multiple-choice score makes up 60 percent, or 90 points, of the 150 total. The free-response section is 40 percent, or 60 points, of the 150 total. There is no definitive composite score range that is consistent from year to year or even from subject to subject. So we can't give the exact formula used to determine your score. But we *can* take a look at a prior year's range of scores and get a hint as to where you might find your score.

In a recent year composite scores between

108 to 150 received a 5

93 to 107 received a 4

72 to 92 received a 3

43 to 71 received a 2

0 to 42 received a 0

This range changes every year. Why, you ask? Well, the answer the College Board gave to us is more difficult to interpret than the essay section of the test, so the fact remains: The range changes every year, and that's that!

Packing Your Tools for the Test

When packing to go on vacation, you don't want to forget your favorite piece of clothing or that hair product you can't live without. Packing for the test is the same thing, albeit not as fun. Although all of the following aren't mandatory to bring to the test, we highly encourage you bring all of them. It's always better to pack more, not less. Here we list what's important to make sure you bring with you to the test site:

- **Pencils with erasers:** Pencils with erasers are best for the multiple-choice test.
- **Black pens:** Black is a better choice because it is a bolder color.
- **Your social security number:** This identifies you.
- **Photo ID:** Take this in case they think you paid your best friend to take the test for you!
- **A watch:** You need to pay close attention to the time.
- **Snacks and drinks:** Quiet snacks are better than loud snacks. Go with soft snacks that won't disrupt others, like chewy granola bars. Water is a better choice than popping a loud soda.
- **Your knowledge:** 'Nuff said.
- **Appropriate clothing:** Bring a light jacket in case there's an arctic freeze in the test center.
- **Something to wipe your nose if you should drip:** You don't want to be leaving every ten minutes, and nobody wants to be distracted by sleeve wipes or sniffing. Bring tissues!

We said over-packing for a vacation is a good thing, but remember that there are usually luggage restrictions on planes. You can't bring *everything*. The following items are definite no nos. You will even be thrown out of a test site for bringing some of these. So, leave 'em home, or in your car. Here we list what not to bring to the test:

- **Scratch paper:** The good folks at AP thought of that already. You get what you need at the test center.
- **Notes, books, dictionaries, highlighters, cheat sheets:** Keep that all at home.
- **Electronic devices like cell phones, beepers, mp3 players:** Sorry, but you can't take the test while listening to The Black Eyed Peas.
- **Your best friend to take the test for you:** They frown on that.
- **Computers or calculators:** Nope, sorry.
- **Your parents for moral support:** Leave the folks at home.

Requesting Special Modifications

Not everyone takes the AP test under the same conditions. You may have a special circumstance that can allow you to change the date of the test or the way you take the exam. Here is a brief list of special circumstances and how they affect your AP test:

- **Learning disabilities:** If you have a diagnosed learning disability, you may be able to get special accommodations. You may have extended time, large print, a reader, frequent breaks, among other things, but you must specifically request this on your application form. You should make sure that your school has a SSD (Services for Students with Disabilities) Coordinator's Form on file with the College Board. You must fill out this form and send it to the College Board. Allow seven weeks for the pros at College Board to review your request. Please note that in order to get special testing, you must have been formally diagnosed with a learning disability by a professional and must have a current, individualized plan at school. In most cases, the evaluation and diagnostic testing should have taken place within five years of the request for accommodations. You must also describe the comprehensive testing and techniques used to arrive at the diagnosis, including test results with subtest scores. Your best bet is to log onto the College Board Web site to see all the up–to-the-minute requirements for accommodations.

- **Physical disabilities:** If you have a physical disability, you may be allowed to take a test in a special format — in Braille, large print, or on an audiocassette or CD. Follow the same instructions detailed above and contact the College Board for more information.

- **Religious obligations:** If your religion prohibits you from taking a test on a specific day, you may test on an alternate date. Again, the College Board folks can guide you in the right direction for alternate dates.

- **Military duty:** If you're an active-duty military person, you don't need to complete the normal registration form. Instead, ask your Educational Services Officer about testing through DANTES (Defense Activity for Nontraditional Educational Support).

Chapter 2

Strategies, Suggestions, and Schedules

. . . .

In This Chapter

▶ Creating a study schedule

▶ Taking care of yourself

▶ Acing the questions with confidence

▶ Reviewing stress busters for D-Day

. . . .

You already know a ton about Biology. You've probably spent the past year in an intensive AP Biology course. Full comprehension of the material is mandatory when trying to ace this exam, but it's only one part of the puzzle (albeit a really big one). In this chapter, we introduce you to the other important things you can do to help boost your score that have absolutely nothing to do with studying Bio. So dive right into the superb suggestions, the super strategies, and the stupendous scheduling.

Training For a Marathon, Not a Sprint

Studying for the AP exam is not the same as cramming the night before a test, and then promptly forgetting the information. As much as you might want to sprint to the finish line, the AP test is a process that should evolve over a lengthy period of time. Taking the full year-long AP Biology class is not a requirement to take the exam (College Board wants everyone to have access to AP, like home-schooled students, for example), but to get the highest score, and receive those coveted college credits, we are going to give you a schedule over the course of two semesters to make sure that you are well prepared for this test:

✔ **September:** Enroll in an AP Biology class at school. If your school doesn't offer one, speak with your counselor to see if you can get your hands on an AP Biology book you can use. Or perhaps there is an AP class offered at a nearby school that your counselor will allow you to enroll in. As much as this book will assist you in understanding the biological concepts addressed on the test, nothing ever really takes the place of a passionate teacher teaching you face to face.

✔ **November:** After familiarizing yourself over the last few months with the concepts of AP Biology, take a diagnostic test. You can use one of the sample tests in this book, or you can go to *www.Collegeboard.com* and find some there. This will help you pinpoint your strengths and weaknesses and assist you in guiding you through the rest of the schedule.

✔ **December:** Begin reading this book from the beginning. You will find that being in the classroom over the last four months has provided you a wealth of information. You should already be familiar with many of the concepts covered in the first third of this book.

✔ **January through March:** Continue using this book, and take another practice test in early March. You still have two months until D-Day, so your score on this test will guide the rest of your studying. Review the material in which you feel you need the most assistance.

✔ **April:** Take another practice test around mid-May. Make this your last practice test. Whatever you do, do not take a practice test the week of the real test. Like a long distance swimmer who has been swimming and practicing all year, she doesn't do the race right before the race! If she's been pacing herself and practicing regularly, she's ready for the win!

✔ **The night before the test:** We really recommend that you not study too hard this night. You might be tempted to pull an all-nighter, but our experience has shown that if you don't know the material the night before, any more studying for this type of test isn't going to help. We also recommend that you relax your head the night before. Read a good book, watch some TV, go out to dinner, and enjoy yourself. If it eases your anxiety to take a peek at Bio, maybe just look over some notes, glance through this book one last time, but please do not attempt to cram. You'll just exhaust yourself right before you exhaust yourself!

✔ **The morning of the test:** Eat breakfast, please. You may be nervous and your appetite might be low, but your brain needs the fuel.

✔ **Test day:** Take the test.

✔ **June:** Wait patiently, very patiently for your score.

Taking Care of Yourself Before the Test

Just like a long distance swimmer, you are in training for a long period of time. The swimmer doesn't just swim in order to prepare for the race, she takes care of her body, too. Believe it or not, taking care of your body is just as essential to your success as it is for any athlete.

Staying active

You can't just be a bookworm for the year before the exam. You must remember that there are parts other than the brain that still need to be used. Exercise helps all parts of the body, including the brain. The more you exercise, the more oxygen gets to your brain. More oxygen to the brain means clearer thinking. So get moving people!

Eating well

Just like exercising, the right food contributes to sustained attention and clear thought. You want to avoid sugar highs that eventually lead you to come crashing down. Forget those energy drinks that combine huge amounts of caffeine and sugar to get you to a state of heightened paranoia. They might tell you that you will focus better when you drink those, but you will only be reading and writing at a superhuman speed and your recall will be nada after you come down. Your mom was right: Eat your veggies, fruit, and an overall well-balanced diet. Your brain will be nourished, and in turn will thank you with a score of a 5.

Learning to relax

We have seen students who are so overextended and overachieving that they don't have any time for pleasant relaxation. They get stressed out, take anti-anxiety pills, have trouble sleeping and concentrating, get panic attacks, and generally exhaust themselves and get sick. Stop for a minute, get in a comfy position, and read this next sentence carefully and slowly: Relaxation is not a luxury; it is a requirement for a well-balanced life.

You're a multifaceted human. You're not a work and study robot. Relaxation comes in many different forms for all kinds of people. Some people are relaxed when they are with friends, some read books for enjoyment and play music they like, others do Yoga, meditate, or paint. There is only one requirement when choosing what relaxation tool to use and that's making sure that your brain is not running 100 miles an hour. The whole purpose of relaxation is to give your brain a rest. Your poor brain needs that rest to function properly when called to duty. So find a relaxing activity you enjoy, thank your brain by telling your brain it can take some time off, and whether you choose to "oooomm" or paint tulips, make it peaceful.

Staying away from artificial study aids (drugs)

We're gonna come clean right here: We've pulled all-nighters with the assistance of either a keg of coffee or some over-the-counter caffeine pills, and it wasn't pleasant. The only thing that uppers, stimulants, and amphetamines do is make you feel like you could clean every kitchen in your neighborhood. And you probably could, except these drugs backfire when it comes to studying. Although they aid in staying awake for longer periods of time, stimulants make it hard to retain and recall information. They will leave you jittery, anxious, agitated, and restless. There are some situations when taking stimulants is required, like if you've been diagnosed with ADHD and require them in order to concentrate. But for the rest of us these drugs just do the opposite. They make you think you are concentrating and studying really hard, but the reality is that you won't remember too much of what you've studied. If you've been diligent in the studying schedule (see, "Training For a Marathon, Not a Sprint," earlier in this chapter), pacing yourself through Biology, then no kind of drug is needed to help you study harder or better.

Acing the Questions

There are no surprises. Every question on the AP test is based on fundamental knowledge of the material. If you don't know the material, the AP folks will know. The AP folks aren't trying to trick you. They just want to make sure that you know your stuff. Following the basic guidelines in the following sections will help you to tackle the multiple-choice and free-response sections of the exam.

You have been studying and preparing for this test for a long time. You know more than you think you do. Even if you fail to remember every detail of every concept, you know at least something about it. If you come to the test feeling completely insecure and doubting yourself, take a moment to remember that we told you that you know more than you think. If you find a question that makes your heart stop with dread, turn that immediately around and say, "I can do this, I will do this, and I feel good about this question."

The multiple-choice questions

There are one hundred multiple choice questions covering molecules and cells, heredity and evolution, and organisms and populations. The list below outlines a few general rules to stick by:

1. **Answer all questions that you can on the first attempt, but if you can't answer the question, *skip it and move on!***

2. **Use leftover time to check your answers.**

3. **First answers are normally the correct ones — go with those.**

4. **Use guessing to your advantage.**

As a rule of thumb, go through and answer the types of questions you feel comfortable with first. Everyone is different, and everyone should follow their own gut.

The multiple choice questions are broken up into the following categories:

- ✓ **Basic-knowledge questions,** which include traditional multiple-choice and elimination-type questions

- ✓ **Elimination-type questions,** which are actually a subset of basic knowledge questions (see bullet above)

- ✓ **Data-interpretation questions,** which include graphs and figures

- ✓ **Category questions,** which involve a group of statements in which one, more than one, or none, is true

Basic-knowledge questions

The basic-knowledge questions are just what they claim to be. They're testing your knowledge of the subject. Each question touches on a different Biology topic. For a traditional multiple-choice question, usually there is a small piece of information given at the beginning of the question, such as

1. Given a DNA strand of the sequence, 5'-GAC TCA CCA TAA-3', what would be the sequence of the corresponding mRNA strand, assuming no introns?

You would be given a list of possible answers. In case you were wondering, the answer to this question is 3'-CUG AGU GGU AUU-5'.

Elimination questions

To approach an elimination question, read the question and think about what you know about the topic presented. Then read the choices, eliminating false statements as you go. It might look something like this:

1. Which of the following is true about enzymes?

   I. They speed up the rate of a reaction.

   II. They are used up in the reaction.

   III. They are usually proteins.

  (A) I only

  (B) II only

  (C) III only

  (D) I and III only

  (E) I, II, and III are all true

The answer is D, in case you were unsure.

Data-interpretation questions

The data interpretation question gives you either a graph, diagram, data table, or mini experiment. Check out the picture first to give you a sense of what the questions might be asking of you. Then check out the questions. It might look something like this:

The following question refers to the Figure 2-1.

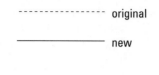

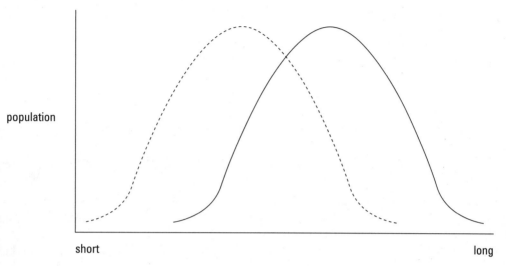

Figure 2-1:
Type of
selection.

1. What type of selection does this figure represent?

(A) Bimodal

(B) Directional

(C) Stabilizing

(D) Disruptive

This one hard? The answer is B.

Category questions

A category question gives you four to five vocabulary words of a specific category, followed by the questions which define or describe the given vocabulary terms. It might look like this:

(A) Commensalism

(B) Parasitism

(C) Predation

(D) Mutualism

1. Relationship between two organisms in which one benefits and the other is harmed

2. Relationship between two organisms in which one benefits and the other is neither helped nor harmed

3. Relationship in which both organisms benefit

The answers are, respectively, B, A, and D.

The free-response questions

The free-response questions consist of four essays, one covering molecules and cells, one covering genetics and evolution, and two covering organisms and populations. One of the four is based on labs.

First, it is important that you make sure you answer the question. You don't have much time: Ninety minutes for four essays. So, here are some tips to keep in mind when responding to the essays:

✔ Start by checking for key-question words, such as *explain, describe,* and *contrast.*

✔ Make sure that you plan out your response. Keep in mind that this has to be an essay — it has to demonstrate that you know your stuff — fill your answer with facts that adequately answer the question.

✔ It may be appropriate to draw diagrams in your response, however you must remember to refer to them in your essay.

✔ Don't worry about grammar and spelling, this is a Biology exam and not an English exam. Grammar problems will not be counted against you.

✔ Each of the main questions has two or three sub-points that the AP Bio folks are looking for. Don't spend too much time on any one sub-part. Address every single portion of the question, equally.

✔ Be sure to check out the sample free-response questions at the end of this book.

The lab essay question typically has you design an experiment. Be sure to include all of the key elements of a good scientific experiment. Define your:

✔ Hypothesis

✔ Control group

✔ Dependent and independent variable(s)

✔ Controlled variables

✔ Data collection

✔ Equations or calculations

✔ Results

✔ Proposed conclusion

Four Stress-Busters to Help You Survive During the Test

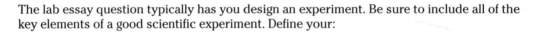

We know that you are going to feel nervous the day of the test. Everyone does. Research has shown us that a little anxiety is actually good for the brain. Anxiety helps the brain stay ultra-focused and attentive, tells the brain, "Hey, this must be important if I'm feeling this way, so I better stay alert," and a little anxiety helps to make sure you get to the test center on time. However, *excess* anxiety does the exact opposite. High levels of fear make the brain go into fight-or-flight mode. So, if you're feeling too much anxiety during the test, use the stress-busters in the following sections to calm your nerves.

Counting to four

Breathing is grossly underrated. Breathing is good. Take a deep until your belly expands, hold it in four counts, and then expel the air for four counts. Try not to take shallow breaths, which can cause you to become even more anxious because your body is deprived of oxygen.

Stretching

Rotate your head around to stretch out and relax your neck muscles. We suggest keeping your eyes closed so the proctor doesn't think you are trying to cheat. Hunch and roll your shoulders to help relax your back and spine. You'll be sitting for quite some time, so maintaining good posture is crucial. Shake out your hands like you have writer's cramp. Imagine that all your tension and stress is going out through your fingertips. Extend and push out your legs like you're pushing something away with your heels. Point your toes back toward your knees and hold that position for a count of three.

Practicing visualization

Don't do this during the test — you just waste time and lose concentration. However, right before the exam or during a short break, practice visualization. Close your eyes and imagine yourself in the test room cheerfully looking at questions that you know the answer to, filling in the answers, finishing early, and double checking your work. Picture yourself leaving the exam room all uplifted, then getting your score and rejoicing. Think of how proud of you your parents are (if thinking about them stresses you out leave this one alone). Imagine not having to take early Biology in college. Picture yourself driving a fire-engine-red Ferrari ten years from now, telling the *Time* magazine reporter in the passenger seat that your success started with your excellent score on your Biology AP test. The goal is to associate the AP exam with good feelings.

Thinking positively

Any time you feel yourself starting to panic or thinking negative thoughts, make a conscious decision to say to yourself, "Stop! Don't dwell on anything negative." And then switch over to a positive track. Suppose you catch yourself thinking, "Why didn't I pay more attention to polar covalent bonds?" Change that script to, "I've got most of this right, maybe I'll get this right, too. No sense worrying now. Overall, I think I'm doing great!"

Part II
Molecules and Cells

The 5th Wave   By Rich Tennant

IRONICALLY, THE LAST THING PROF. CARUTHERS REMEMBERED WAS EXPLAINING HOW ENERGY IS PRODUCED WHEN MOLECULES COLLIDE.

In this part . . .

One of the overarching themes of biology is that cells use energy to arrange matter in useful ways. To really "get" what's going on with living things, you need to know something about matter and about how cells use energy to transform it. That's what this part is about.

We start by reviewing the kinds of matter you find in cells and the important ways that matter is arranged — and re-arranged. This busy shuffling about of the matter within cells sometimes goes by the name biochemistry. Cells are professional biochemists. Cells expertly assemble molecules into elaborate structures called organelles. Organelles are nature's way of dividing labor. Each organelle contributes some specific, critical function to a cell. We tour the major kinds of cells with an eye to the organelles, seeing how they all conspire towards life.

The function of an organelle results from its structure. This is a second overarching theme: function derives from structure. Things do what they do because of what they are. That is why cells use energy to re-arrange matter. We close this part by reviewing the grand dialogue between photosynthesis and respiration, the two opposing sides to life's energy conversation.

Chapter 3

Biochemistry: The Little Things That Count

C ells are masters of efficiency. The daily business of a cell includes taking in nutrients, breaking them into useful parts, building things from these parts, recycling anything handy, and only throwing away a bare minimum. All this busy efficiency requires a lot of specialized parts and pieces. It requires molecules. How molecules change from one kind to another is chemistry. How cells use chemistry is biochemistry, which is what we focus on in this chapter.

Matters of Matter: Biology Emerges from Chemistry

Here's a bit of good news. You don't need to understand a great deal of chemistry in order to gain a much deeper insight into life at the molecular level. Many biochemical reactions are just variations on a few simple themes. In other words, a small investment in chemistry pays huge dividends in biology.

This chapter begins with a review of how atoms come together in order to make molecules, through the formation of different kinds of bonds. All the important categories of biochemical molecules (carbohydrates, lipids, proteins, and nucleic acids) and other compounds (like electrolytes) are simply bonded groups of atoms.

Because cells are largely made up of water, you will not be surprised to discover that the chemical properties of water are vital to biochemistry. Water helps to give cells and big biological molecules their unique shapes, and helps cells keep things running smoothly. You will find out how.

With the basic understanding of atoms, bonds, molecules, and water we give you in the following sections, you'll be prepared to launch into the rest of the chapter, which shows how cells build big molecules by linking together many smaller ones. These big molecules are the key to the marvelous efficiency with which cells handle information, matter, and energy.

An elegance of elements

You remember what an atom is, right? *Hint:* a positively charged nucleus of protons and neutrons, enveloped by shells of negatively charged electrons. Different elements have different numbers of protons, and even atoms of the same element can have slightly different numbers of neutrons or electrons. Atoms with the same number of protons but differing numbers of neutrons are *isotopes* of the same element.

It turns out that some atoms are "happier" (in other words, more stable) when they alter the number of electrons in their shells. Such atoms have a tendency to either gain, lose, or share electrons with other atoms. When they do so, these atoms form bonds. The three major types of bonds in biology are

- ✔ Ionic
- ✔ Covalent
- ✔ Hydrogen bonds

When one atom gives up one or more electrons, it's good news for other atoms that are seeking additional electrons. This happy situation results in the complete transfer of electrons from one atom (or group of atoms) to another. Electrons have negative charges, so giving up electrons leaves an atom with a positive charge. Accepting electrons leaves an atom with a negative charge. Charged atoms are called *ions*. Because "positively charged ion" and "negatively charged ion" are phrases with far too many syllables to be convenient, shorter names exist for them: *cations* (positive) and *anions* (negative).

Because opposite charges attract, cations are drawn to anions. When oppositely charged ions cozy up to one another, we say that they are held together by "ionic bonds." For reasons that will be discussed shortly, water molecules are very good at undoing ionic bonds, separating cationic and anionic partners. These separate anions and cations can move about freely in water, carrying their ionic charges with them. Freely moving ions are called *electrolytes*, and help cells use electrical energy.

Giving up electrons isn't always an all-or-nothing process. Sometimes, atoms *share* electrons. When they do, these atoms form *covalent bonds*. Each covalent bond consists of two shared electrons. Atoms can share two, four, or six electrons to form single, double, and triple covalent bonds.

Not all atoms share their electrons equally. Some atoms are more willing than others to donate their electrons to a covalent bond. When covalent bonds are formed between atoms that don't share equally, we say that those bonds are polar. When the atoms share equally, the bonds are nonpolar. Figure 3-1 shows some common types of polar and nonpolar covalent bonds. As you'll soon see, the polarity of a molecule greatly affects how that molecule interacts with water.

Figure 3-1:
Types of covalent bonds common in organic molecules and their polar character.

$C-C$	Nonpolar
$C-H$	Nonpolar
$C-O^-$	Polar
$^-O-H^+$	Polar
$C\overset{O^-}{\underset{}{\diagup\!\!\!\diagup}}OH^+$	Polar

Biology likes to use lots of weak bonds because they can be easily made and broken according to the needs of the moment. Hydrogen bonds are a type of weak bond found nearly everywhere in biochemistry. Hydrogen bonds can form when a hydrogen atom is engaged in a polar covalent bond with another atom — one that doesn't like to share electrons (oxygen, for example). In this scenario, since the hydrogen has less than its fair share of electrons, it carries a partial positive charge. The electron-greedy oxygen carries a partial negative charge. Imagine now that another oxygen atom enters the picture, carrying its own partial negative; this new oxygen will be attracted to the partially positive hydrogen, since opposite charges attract. So, the two oxygens will line up with the hydrogen between them, making a sort of negative-positive-negative sandwich. Large biological molecules (*macromolecules,* such as proteins and nucleic acids) use hydrogen bonds to knit themselves together into beautiful, functional shapes. With its two polar oxygen-hydrogen bonds (H_2O, remember?), water is the hydrogen-bonder par excellence, as shown in Figure 3-2.

Think of hydrogen bonds, nonpolar covalent bonds, polar covalent bonds, and ionic bonds as lying along a spectrum of electron-sharing, ranging from the least shared (hydrogen bonds) to the completely transferred (ionic bonds).

Previous scholarship of *Star Trek* may have informed you that we humans are carbon-based life forms. So are bacteria. So is all other terrestrial life. What this means is that biochemistry is largely organic chemistry, involving the making and breaking of bonds with carbon.

If you remember one thing about carbon, remember that it likes to form four covalent bonds. Any carbon atom engaged in more or less than four covalent bonds is highly unstable, and therefore, highly improbable. Really. If you see one on a test, be suspicious.

Other atoms frequently bond with carbon. These atoms include hydrogen, oxygen, nitrogen, and phosphorous. Between these four atoms and carbon, you can account for most of the matter in anything that lives. Certain bonded groups of these atoms occur repeatedly in organic molecules. These popular groups are good at certain chemical jobs, and we call them functional groups.

The importance of being wet

Aaah, the water molecule . . . so simple, yet so powerful! Just one oxygen atom covalently bonded to two hydrogen atoms — what's the big deal? Look a little more closely. Each hydrogen atom engages in a very polar covalent bond with the oxygen. This polarity, combined with the "Mickey Mouse" shape of the molecule means that water is a *dipole,* with two distinct positive and negative regions. Since water is nearly everywhere in cells, we might wager that its properties have profound impact on biology. We'd win that wager, thanks to water's ability as a solvent, to its adhesive/cohesive properties, and to its temperature stability.

Water is the solvent of life. If you doubt it, just try not drinking any for a week. Swarms of water surround and interact with other molecules in cells, such as ions, lipids, carbohydrates, proteins, and nucleic acids. Because it is so polar, water happily hangs out with other polar molecules. Polar molecules tend to be charged or to have many polar covalent bonds. Since they work and play well with water, we call these molecules *hydrophilic,* which means water-loving. Water nicely dissolves hydrophilic molecules, allowing them to move freely through the watery cellular environment. On the other hand, *nonpolar* molecules don't get along so well with water. We call these molecules *hydrophobic,* which means water-fearing. In water, hydrophobic bits tend to cluster together in order to minimize their contact with water (see Figure 3-3). Because cells are so watery, being hydrophilic or hydrophobic largely defines the lifestyle of any biological molecule.

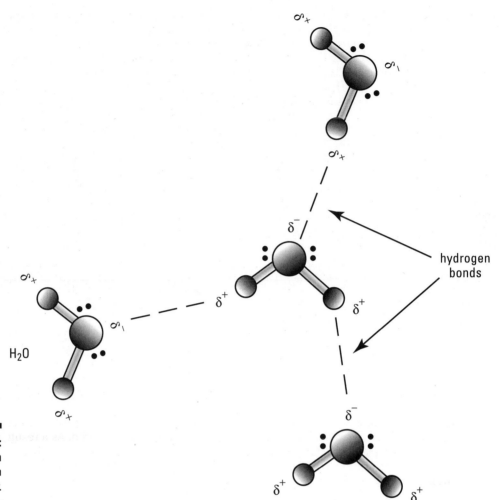

H₂O

Figure 3-2:
Hydrogen
bonding in
water.

hydrogen
bonds

Don't let this hydrophilic/hydrophobic business scare you. It all boils down to Italian salad dressing. Ever notice how a bottle of dressing separates into two layers after it has been stored for a while in the refrigerator, and you have to shake it before pouring it on your salad? The two layers consist of oil and water. Oil and water don't mix. Oil is hydrophobic. Think of nonpolar molecules as "oily."

If you're up for some hydrogen-bonding, water will meet you halfway. And if you're not willing, water is perfectly happy to have hydrogen bond with itself, as you can see from Figure 3-2. Water-water hydrogen bonding is what gives water its "cohesive" properties — water's tendency to stick to itself. Cohesion gives water its high-surface tension. That's right: Spiders creepily walk across ponds because of water-water hydrogen bonds. Hydrogen bonding between water and *other* polar molecules explains water's *adhesive* properties — water's tendency to stick to other things. The combination of cohesion, adhesion, and a thin tube results in *capillary action.* Water can pull itself easily through small tubes (as in, capillaries) by hydrogen bonding with polar surfaces on the inside of the tube and with itself.

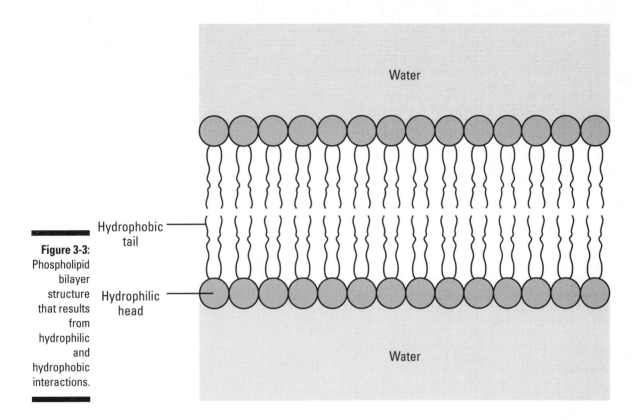

Water

Hydrophobic tail

Hydrophilic head

Water

Figure 3-3:
Phospholipid bilayer structure that results from hydrophilic and hydrophobic interactions.

Each of the countless hydrogen bonds flickering into and out of existence within the watery guts of a cell serves as a little bin in which heat energy can be stored. As a result, water has a high heat capacity. Water — and therefore, cells —can gain or lose a lot of heat without changing temperature very much. By helping maintain a stable temperature, water creates a friendly environment for biochemistry.

The Power of Carbohydrates

Biology uses carbohydrates to store and transport energy. In addition, carbohydrate molecules are the bricks in plant cell walls. Though they occur in numerous forms, the basic formula for all carbohydrates is $(CH_2O)_n$. Any carbohydrate molecule is built from multiples of carbon and water — hence the term *carbo-hydrate*. Cells use enzymes to change carbohydrates from one form to another and to break them down or build them up, according to the needs of the moment.

Sweet! Sugars for life

The simplest kind of carbohydrate is the sugar. More complicated carbohydrates are built up from sugars. A one-sugar carbohydrate is called a monosaccharide. Link two monosaccharides together and you've got yourself a disaccharide. Link a whole mess o' monosaccharides together and you have a polysaccharide.

Monosaccharides are named according to the number of carbon atoms they contain. Monosaccharides containing three, four, five, or six sugars are called *trioses, tetroses, pentoses,* and *hexoses,* respectively. Sugary cousins that share a common molecular formula, but in which the precise molecular structure differs, are called *isomers.* Sugars can exist in both linear and circular (cyclical) forms, as shown in Figure 3-4.

(a)

(b)

Figure 3-4: Alternate forms of the monosaccharide glucose: (a) linear, and (b) cyclic.

Monosaccharides are reversibly built up into polysaccharides or broken down from them by enzymes. These enzymes speed up "dehydration" and/or "hydrolysis" reactions, depicted in Figure 3-5. When monosaccharides are linked together by dehydration, a water molecule is removed in order to form a covalent bond. This same bond can be broken in a hydrolysis reaction by adding water across the bond, reversing the linkage.

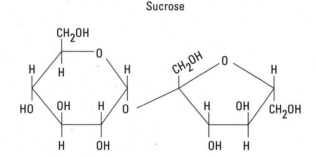

Figure 3-5:
Dehydration
reaction
linking
glucose and
fructose
monomers
into the dis-
accharide
sucrose.

Storing fuels for later

Cells store energy in the form of sugars by forming polysaccharides. Starch and glycogen are polysaccharides, built of repeating glucose units. Though they each use glucose monosaccharides as building blocks, starch and glycogen differ in the exact linkages between glucose molecules. When cells have access to plenty of food, they store glucose as starch or glycogen as a hedge against leaner times. When nutrients are scarce, cells break down starch or glycogen, freeing up glucose molecules to harvest their stored energy. In other words, cells are responsible little citizens, saving their sugars for rainy days.

Another important glucose-based polysaccharide is cellulose, which is formed in plant cells. Although cellulose is not used like starch or glycogen for energy storage, it is an important building material in plant cells.

Amino Acids, Proteins, and Enzymes

Proteins are workhorses of the cell, sticking their amino acid fingers into nearly every bit of cellular business. Cells use proteins for catalysis, regulation, structure and other roles. This section focuses on two things: how protein catalysts — enzymes — run cellular metabolism, and on the ingenious structures (from amino acids through large protein assemblies) that enable proteins to perform their many functions.

Running metabolism

Simply put, metabolism is the complete set of chemical reactions occuring within an organism. You're right, that covers a lot of ground. Cells are always breaking things down to get materials and energy, and then using those materials and energy to build up new, more useful things. All this deconstruction and reconstruction occurs through chemical reactions. Most of these chemical reactions involve special kinds of proteins called enzymes.

Enzymes *catalyze* reactions; this means that they speed up reactions, but are not themselves changed or used up in the process. One enzyme can repeatedly catalyze the same reaction. Moreover, the enzyme does not alter the reactant or product of the reaction — it simply makes the reaction go faster. As you can see in Figure 3-6, enzymes speed up reactions by lowering the *activation energy,* the energetic hill a reacting molecule must climb in order to undergo the reaction. Think of an enzyme as a sort of gymnastics coach, "spotting" molecules as they vault through reactions.

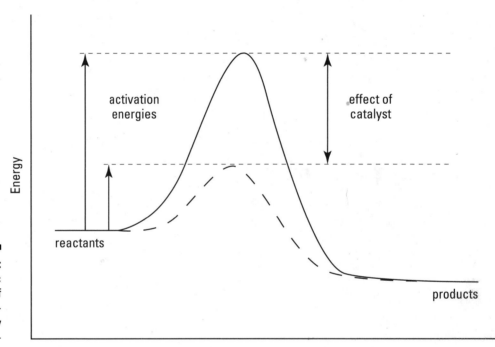

Figure 3-6:
Enzymatic
reduction of
the activa-
tion energy
of a chemi-
cal reaction.

Enzymes bind their substrates (as in, reacting molecules) within an *active site,* a pocket where all the chemistry takes place. Binding can occur in a number of ways. In *lock-and-key binding,* the substrate slides snugly into a perfectly pre-formed active site. *Induced-fit binding* features a flexible active site; when the substrate binds, the active site changes shape to achieve a better fit. Either way, once bound in an active site, the substrate is in an environment uniquely tailored for the reaction. After the reaction has occurred, an enzyme releases its product(s), and is free to bind another substrate. The overall process is shown in Figure 3-7.

Reaction:

A + B ────────────► C

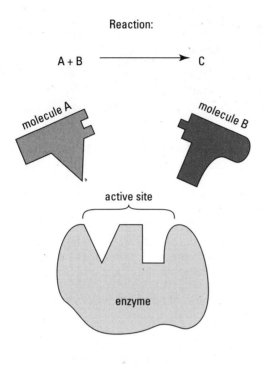

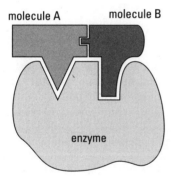

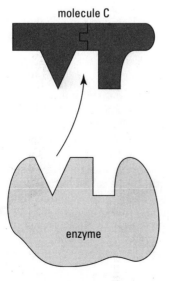

Figure 3-7:
An enzyme
facilitates a
reaction
by binding
substrates,
catalyzing
chemistry,
and
releasing
products.

Some of the general types of reaction catalyzed by enzymes are:

- ✔ **Hydrolysis:** Adding a water molecule across a covalent bond in order to break that bond.

- ✔ **Dehydration:** The reverse of hydrolysis. Forming a new covalent bond by the removal of a water molecule.

- ✔ **Oxidation-reduction (Redox):** A reaction in which electrons are transferred between reactants.

- ✔ **Exergonic:** A reaction that releases energy, and therefore occurs spontaneously.

- ✔ **Endergonic:** A reaction that takes up energy, and therefore will not proceed unless that energy is provided.

Many factors can affect enzyme "activity," or just how much enzymes speed up reactions. Some of these factors are general, affecting the activity of most enzymes. Others are specific, affecting only one or a few types of enzyme. General factors include temperature, pH, and concentration. More specific factors include "activators" or "inhibitors," molecules that increase or decrease the activity of specific target enzymes.

Increasing temperature tends to increase the speed of enzyme-catalyzed reactions, up to a point. Beyond that point, excessive temperature destroys an enzyme's intricate structure.

Changes in pH (the acidity or basicity) of the environment can also modify enzyme activity, especially in the case of reactions that involve the transfer of hydrogen ions. Recall that pH = $-\log [H^+]$, so that a pH change of one unit (say, from 7.5 to 6.5) corresponds to a tenfold change in the concentration of hydrogen ions. Enzymes often have optimum activity at a certain pH, which tapers off in more acidic or more basic conditions.

Because enzyme activity can be so sensitive to pH, cells have an interest in maintaining stable internal pH conditions. To promote a constant pH, many cellular solutes act as pH *buffers*, releasing or taking up hydrogen ions as needed to keep the overall hydrogen ion concentration constant. Different chemicals have differing tendencies to release or take up protons. These differing tendencies can be measured by a quantity called the pK_a, or acid dissociation constant. The pK_a is the pH at which one half of a chemical species is in an H^+-bound form (*conjugate acid*), and the other half occurs in a form without bound H^+ (*conjugate base*). Solutions with a high concentration of solute at a given pK_a tend to maintain pH at that pK_a value, buffering the solution against pH changes. The relationship between pH and the concentrations of conjugate acid and base of a given solute are expressed by the *Henderson-Hasselbach equation* where $[A^-]$ and $[HA]$ are the molar concentrations of conjugate base and conjugate acid, respectively. Notice that when the conjugate acid and base are present in equal concentration, the pH of the solution equals the pK_a of the buffer solute:

$$pH = pK_a + \log ([A^-]/[HA])$$

Perhaps the most straightforward way to alter enzyme activity is to change the concentrations of enzyme and/or substrate. Increasing the concentration of either causes more collisions to occur between enzymes and substrates. Each collision has a chance of leading to binding and reaction. Decreasing concentrations have the opposite effect.

Finally, specific molecules can bind to enzymes in ways that increase or decrease enzyme activity. Molecules whose binding increases activity are called activators. Molecules whose binding decreases activity are called inhibitors. *Competitive inhibitors* bind enzymes at the active site; this blocks the binding of substrate and prevents catalysis. *Noncompetitive inhibitors* bind enzymes at locations other than the active site, but alter the enzyme's structure. These changes in enzyme structure reduce the ability of the enzyme to bind substrate or to catalyze a reaction.

Building the blocks of life

Proteins must be annoying to other types of molecules. How can proteins do so many things so well? As numerous and diverse as they are, proteins are built from a humble inventory of parts: twenty amino acids, common to all known organisms. A covalently linked chain of these amino acids comprises a polypeptide, and polypeptides "fold" into the functional structures known as proteins. Proteins can have four distinct levels of structure: primary, secondary, tertiary, and quaternary.

Amino acids are the building blocks of proteins. Genes, written in DNA, code for the identity and sequence of the amino acids that make up a protein. As helpfully suggested by their name, each amino acid contains amine ($-NH_2$) and carboxylic acid ($-COOH$) functional groups, attached to a central carbon. Also attached to that carbon are a hydrogen atom and a unique sidechain. Differences among the sidechains are what make the amino acids an interesting cast of characters. Different sidechains have different properties. They may be large or small, hydrophobic or hydrophilic, positively or negatively charged, or uncharged.

As shown in Figure 3-8, individual amino acids are covalently bonded via a dehydration reaction. This reaction removes a water molecule to join the amine group of one amino acid to the carboxylic acid group of the next. This kind of covalent bond is called a *peptide bond*. A long chain of amino acids linked in this way is a bit like a charm bracelet, decorated with different sidechains. The exact sequence of sidechain "charms" defines a protein's primary structure.

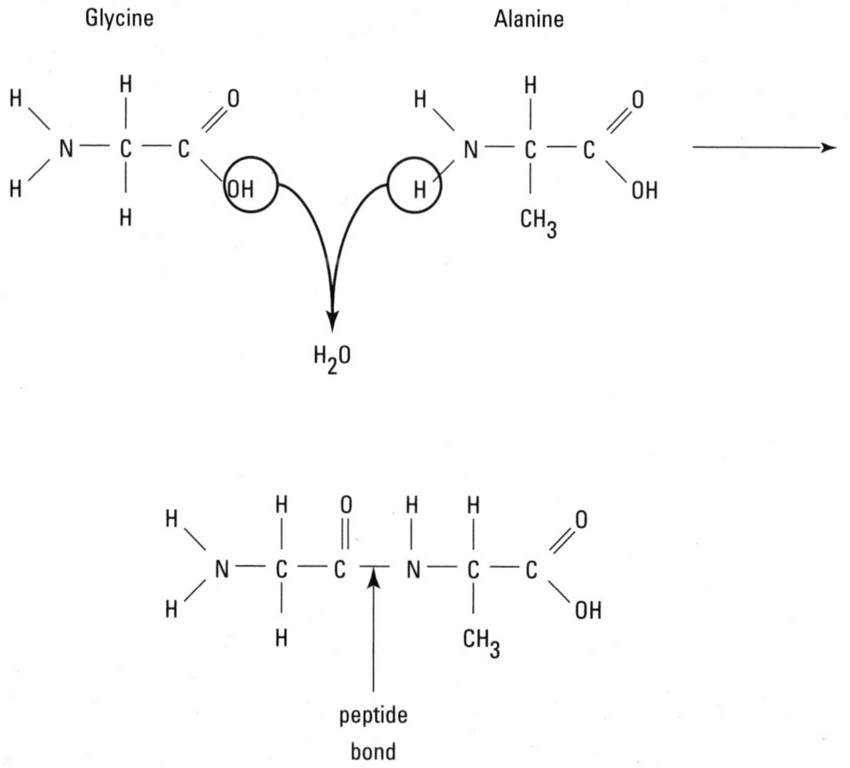

Glycine

Alanine

H_2O

Figure 3-8: Dehydration reaction to form a peptide bond between two amino acids.

peptide bond

When amino acids are linked into a chain, the peptide bonds between each amino acid pair form a long backbone. Peptide bond backbones can hydrogen bond with themselves to form regular, repeating structures such as helices (spirals) and undulating strands. These spiraling or wavy patterns are the secondary structure of a protein. Secondary structures occur in two major forms, α-helices and β-strands. β-strands associate with themselves to form β-sheets. Both the spiraling α-helices and the wavy β-sheets display their amino acid sidechains to the outside, where they can interact with each other or with water. Sometimes, several polypeptides that have only secondary structure can associate to form "fibrous" proteins.

The amino acid sidechains that protrude from α-helices and β-sheets can interact closely with each other, packing into compact shapes called tertiary structures. Typically, hydrophobic sidechains end up on the inside of the structure, away from water, while hydrophilic sidechains tend to cover the outer surface. These kinds of compact structures are typical of "globular" proteins. Figure 3-9 shows the structure of a typical globular protein, where it is clear how the secondary structures (the α-helices and β-sheets) have packed together to form the tertiary structure.

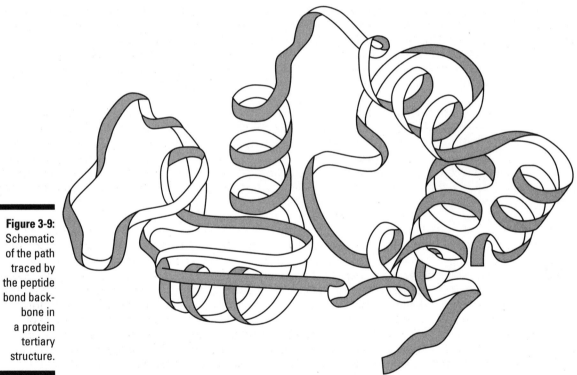

Figure 3-9:
Schematic of the path traced by the peptide bond backbone in a protein tertiary structure.

Sometimes one polypeptide just isn't enough to do the job. Many proteins function within larger assemblies of proteins. These assemblies are held together by noncovalent bonds, and can vary widely in size and in the number of proteins involved. Quaternary structure refers to the noncovalent association of multiple proteins.

Parts and Processes of Nucleic Acids

Nucleic acids are all about information. Genetic information is stored in the form of deoxyribonucleic acid, or DNA. Working copies of that stored information are made from DNA's less stable cousin, ribonucleic acid, or RNA. The major use of genetic information is to direct the building of proteins. This section describes the structures of DNA and RNA, how enzymes make copies of these structures, and how they use those copies to make proteins.

Forming RNA and DNA

Like proteins and polysaccharides, nucleic acids are polymers. Compared to the twenty common amino acids used to build proteins, however, the inventory of parts used to build nucleic acids is far less diverse. DNA and RNA are each composed from a tiny alphabet of four nucleotide bases.

Whether DNA or RNA, a nucleotide consists of three parts: a base, a sugar, and a phosphate group. *D*NA employs a *d*eoxyribose sugar, while *R*NA uses *r*ibose. Ribose is nearly identical to deoxyribose, but contains an extra hydroxyl (i.e., –OH) group. This hydroxyl causes RNA strands to be far less stable than DNA. It makes sense, then, that DNA is used for long-term storage of genetic information, while RNA is used to make short-term, working copies of that information.

The bases of DNA are adenine (A), thymine (T), guanine (G), and cytosine (C). RNA uses the same bases, with the exception that in RNA, uracil (U) is used in place of thymine. Bases A and G are larger molecules, called *purines*. Bases T (or U) and C are smaller molecules, called *pyrimidines*. As shown in Figure 3-10, nucleic acid strands are composed of a sugar-phosphate backbone and a linear sequence of bases. Each strand has a defined direction; by convention, the strands are said to run in the 5' to 3' direction, in reference to numbered carbons of sugars at the strand tips.

Both DNA and RNA can form *double helices.* An example of a DNA double helix is shown in Figure 3-11. Two strands, running in opposite directions, come together to form a structure resembling a spiral staircase with nucleotide "steps" stacked one atop the next. The two *antiparallel* strands (as in, parallel, but in opposite directions) are held together by hydrogen bonds between bases. Each base on one strand bonds with its "complementary" base on the opposing strand. Purines pair with pyrimidines, and vice-versa. Bases A and T (or U) form two hydrogen bonds, while the slightly stronger interaction between G and C consists of three hydrogen bonds. Here's a helpful feature of base-pairing: Knowing the sequence of one strand in a double helix means you know the sequence of the complementary strand. In the cell, DNA is almost always found as a double helix, whereas RNA frequently exists in single-stranded form. Complementary strands of DNA and RNA can base-pair to form hybrid double-helices.

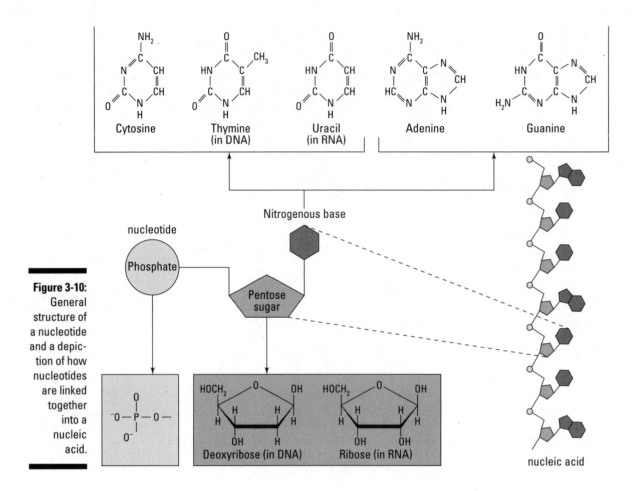

Figure 3-10:
General structure of a nucleotide and a depiction of how nucleotides are linked together into a nucleic acid.

Although DNA is used mostly to store genetic information, RNA is used in many roles. RNA is used to transmit genetic information (as messenger RNA [mRNA]). RNA is also used in structural and even catalytic roles (as transfer RNA [tRNA], ribosomal RNA [rRNA] or small nucleolar RNA [snRNA]).

Using the genetic code to make proteins

All proteins begin as but a twinkling in the eye of a gene. That twinkling is genetic information, encoded within DNA, the "Master Molecule." This section is devoted to understanding how genetic information is copied and transmitted within cells. In DNA replication, the genes of a cell are copied in order to pass the information on to new cells. To make proteins, the information in DNA is *transcribed* (copied within the same language) and *translated* (converted into a different language). In eukaryotes, *processing* (editing of the language) occurs between transcription and translation. Replication, transcription, processing, and translation are all carried out by groups of highly specialized enzymes.

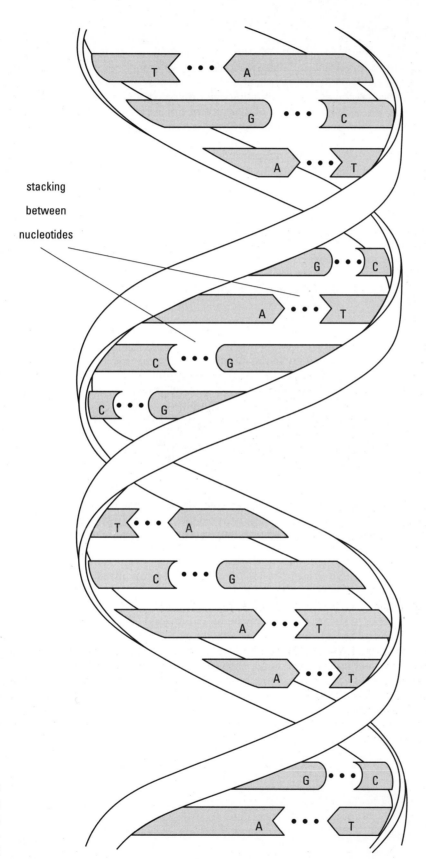

stacking
between
nucleotides

Figure 3-11:
The DNA
double helix.

Replicating DNA

All cells come from other cells. The DNA in every newly born cell is inherited from its parent cell. In order for both parent and daughter cells to have complete copies of DNA, the DNA must be *replicated* (copied). DNA replication is a *semi-conservative* process, meaning that each daughter cell receives DNA containing one original strand from the parent, and one new, complementary strand — think of it as a dowry of sorts. The details of replication, summarized in Figure 3-12, make clear just how this happens.

Perhaps poetically, before DNA can reproduce it must unzip. Unzipping is performed by an enzyme, helicase, that separates complementary strands of the DNA to be copied. Helicase opens up a region of unpaired DNA, the strands of which join at the replication fork. The separated strands each serve as a template for making new strands. An enzyme called DNA polymerase makes the new strands, one nucleotide at a time. To begin, the polymerase requires a short RNA primer, provided by the enzyme primase. Once primed, DNA polymerase moves along the template strand in the 3' to 5' direction, making a new complementary strand, 5' to 3'. Nucleotides are selected for incorporation in the new strands based on their ability to pair with their complements on the template strand. So, if the template strand displays a G, DNA polymerase adds a C; if the template strand displays an A, DNA polymerase adds a T. And so on.

DNA polymerase chugs along templates in one direction only, 3' to 5', making new strands 5' to 3'. This task is straightforward with one template strand, the *leading strand,* but more complicated with the complementary template, the *lagging strand.* On the lagging strand, DNA polymerase continually bumps up against the replication fork. DNA polymerase must make the new strand discontinuously, in short stretches called Okazaki fragments. Refer to Figure 3-12 to convince yourself of this. Each Okazaki fragment requires its own RNA primer, and the fragments must be joined together by another enzyme, DNA ligase. Ligase also substitutes DNA bases for the RNA bases of the primers. All the enzymatic busywork necessary with the lagging strand takes time, and this explains why the leading strand leads the lagging strand.

Transcribing DNA

DNA is chock-full of genetic secrets that the cell needs to know. Fortunately for the cell, DNA wants to blab. This blabbing begins with the process of transcription. During *transcription,* the information written into the DNA of a gene is copied in a slightly different form: its RNA complement, called messenger RNA (mRNA). While the genes themselves must remain safeguarded in the stable form of DNA, these mRNA transcripts can be made whenever the cell requires a certain protein to be built, and degraded when the protein is no longer required. In eukaryotes, transcription occurs in the nucleus, where the DNA resides. The mechanism of transcription has three major steps: initiation, elongation, and termination. As you read through the details of these steps, it may be helpful to consult Figure 3-13.

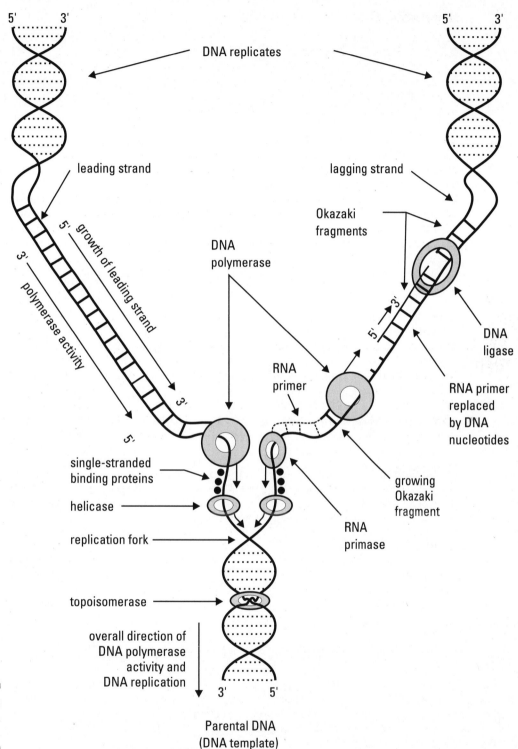

DNA replicates

5' 3'

5' 3'

leading strand

lagging strand

Okazaki fragments

growth of leading strand

DNA polymerase

5'

polymerase activity

3'

3'

DNA ligase

5' 3'

RNA primer

RNA primer replaced by DNA nucleotides

5'

single-stranded binding proteins

helicase

RNA primase

growing Okazaki fragment

replication fork

topoisomerase

overall direction of DNA polymerase activity and DNA replication

3' 5'

Figure 3-12:
DNA replication.

Parental DNA
(DNA template)

Here's how each major step of transcription works:

- **Initiation:** Transcription begins with initiation. An enzyme called RNA polymerase recognizes and binds to a "promoter" region that precedes a gene within the DNA sequence and "promotes" or encourages the transcription of the gene. Promoters often contain the DNA sequence TATA. Proteins called transcription factors may help RNA polymerase to bind the promoter. Once bound, RNA polymerase begins to unwind the DNA to allow transcription of the template DNA strand, starting at a specific signal called the "initiation site."

- **Elongation:** Once initiated, transcription of mRNA enters the elongation phase. During elongation, RNA polymerase moves along the template DNA strand, 3' to 5', making the complementary mRNA, 5' to 3'. Elongation is similar in this way to DNA replication, except that in the case of transcript elongation, the new strand is composed of RNA, not DNA. The ability of RNA to form hybrid base-pairs with DNA is critical to elongation. If the template DNA displays a G, RNA polymerase adds a C; if the template DNA displays an A, RNA polymerase adds a U. And so on.

- **Termination:** Elongation continues until the RNA polymerase reaches a signal sequence called the *termination site*. After this site is reached, RNA polymerase and the mRNA transcript are released from the DNA, and another round of transcription can begin.

Processing RNA

Eukaryotic genes are more complicated buggers than their prokaryotic counterparts. In eukaryotes, messenger RNAs must undergo "processing" before they can be sent from the nucleus into the cytoplasm, where the messages will be translated in order to build proteins. Steps of processing as shown in Figure 3-13 are:

- **Splicing:** Eukaryotic mRNAs consist of alternating stretches of sequence, called introns (*int*ervening sequences) and exons (*ex*pressed sequences). During splicing, a large molecular machine called the *spliceosome* removes introns and splices together exons.

- **Capping:** The 5' end of the mRNA is capped with a guanosine triphosphate (GTP) nucleotide. Capping protects the mRNA from degradation at the 5' end, and eventually helps the mRNA to bind the ribosome, another molecular machine. *Ribosomes* use mRNAs to direct the building of proteins.

- **Polyadenylation:** The 3' end of the mRNA receives a long "tail" of adenosines, roughly 30 to 200 "A" bases in length. This addition is often called the *polyA tail*. This tail protects the mRNA from degradation at the 3' end, and is required before the mRNA can be sent out of the nucleus to be translated.

What's the point of having introns?

All the effort expended by eukaryotic cells to snip out introns and splice together exons may seem like a waste of time and energy. Why have introns in the first place? It turns out that intron sequences may serve many functions at both DNA and RNA levels.

At the level of DNA, introns may serve important roles in evolution and regulation. The proteins for which DNAs code often consist of modular chunks that have useful individual functions. Introns may facilitate a mix-and-match form of evolution called *exon shuffling*, in which DNA coding for modular protein parts can be recombined to form new proteins. Alternately, intron sequences in

DNA may help to regulate how often an mRNA is transcribed, either by acting as a sort of extra promoter or by coding for small, nonmessenger RNAs that announce to the cell, "I've just been transcribed!"

At the level of the mRNA, introns make it possible for cells to engage in *alternative splicing*. By splicing out introns and joining exons in alternative ways, cells can generate several useful variants of a protein from a single gene. Finally, since mRNAs cannot leave the nucleus until splicing has occurred, introns may help the cell to regulate when mRNAs are translated.

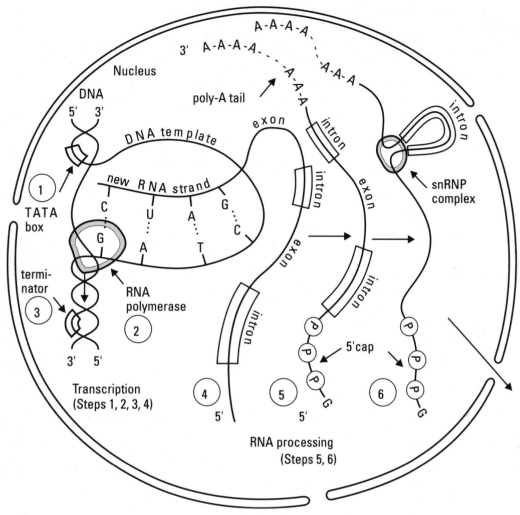

Figure 3-13: Transcription and processing of mRNA.

Translating RNA

This is the homestretch of the journey of genetic information. The messages of genes in the Master Molecule, DNA, are inherited (imperfectly) over countless generations through replication. The messages flow from DNA into mRNA during transcription, are edited during processing, and are finally expressed as proteins during translation.

Translation takes place within the ribosome, a large molecular machine built of two subunits (one small, one large). An mRNA feeds through an "active site" within the ribosome, and the message is decoded there. The decoded message directs the linkage of amino acids into a polypeptide chain. Like transcription, translation consists of three steps: initiation, elongation, and termination. Do yourself a favor, and keep an eye on Figure 3-14 as you read the details of each step:

✔ **Initiation:** An mRNA, the small ribosomal subunit and a special molecule called the *initiator tRNA* assemble into a large complex. This complex makes friends with the large ribosomal subunit, who joins the party to make a complete ribosome. An mRNA "message" is written with three-base "words" called *codons*. The message reads in the 5' to 3' direction. Each codon corresponds to a specific amino acid. One codon in particular (AUG, which codes for the amino acid methionine) marks the site where translation begins, and is the site recognized by the initiator tRNA.

tRNAs are like linguists, translating from mRNA-speak into protein-speak. Each tRNA is covalently bonded to a unique amino acid, and contains an "anticodon" that recognizes the mRNA codon specific to that amino acid. Codons and anticodons are both made of RNA, so they can recognize each other through complementary base-pairing. The enzymes responsible for bonding the correct amino acid to each kind of tRNA are called *aminoacyl-tRNA synthetases*.

✔ **Elongation:** Within the ribosome, tRNAs step through three distinct sites: the acceptor, peptidyl and exit (or A, P, and E) sites. At the beginning of elongation, the "initiator tRNA" sits in the P site. In the A site, an appropriate tRNA, carrying its amino acid payload, binds to the next codon of the mRNA. When a correct codon-anticodon match is made in the A site, the ribosome acts as an enzyme, catalyzing the covalent bonding of amino acids attached to the A site and P site tRNAs. As this bonding takes place, the mRNA and the tRNAs ratchet through the ribosome exactly one codon; this ratcheting movement is called *translocation*. Translocation shifts the A site tRNA into the P site, and shifts the P site tRNA into the E site, where it is released from the ribosome. This cycle of recognition, catalysis, translocation and release is repeated for each codon as the mRNA feeds through the ribosome like film through a projector. The product is an elongating chain of covalently linked amino acids. The sequence of the amino acids is directed by the mRNA.

✔ **Termination:** At the end of the mRNA message, a *stop codon* signals that translation should stop. There are three stop codons:

- UAA

- UAG

- UGA

The stop codon is recognized by a release factor. This event triggers release of the newly translated polypeptide chain. Like late-night stragglers after a party, the ribosome subunits, tRNAs and mRNA, go their separate ways. The journey of genetic information is thereby completed and can start again with another gene.

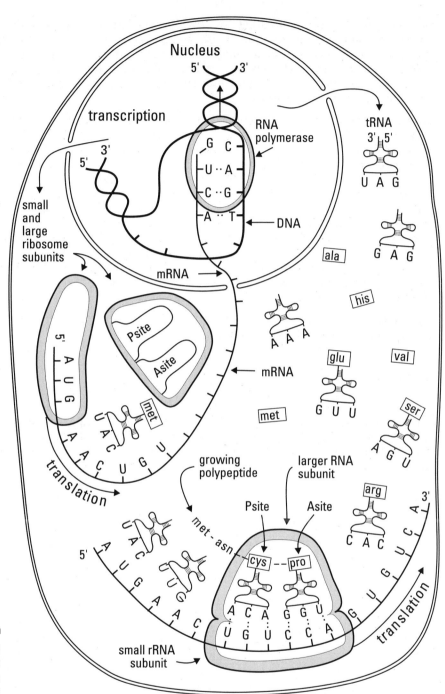

Figure 3-14: Translation of protein from an mRNA template.

Protein Synthesis

Chapter 4

Answering Questions on Biochemistry

• •

In This Chapter

▶ Getting some pointers for practice

▶ Testing your knowledge

▶ Hitting the labs

▶ Checking your work

• •

This section will help you understand the material in the previous chapter, Biochemistry: The Little Things that Count, by highlighting the most important concepts and details. Multiple choice and free-essay response questions will test your ability to apply what you know to the kinds of questions you'll find on the exam. In addition, you'll find summaries and explanations for two biochemistry-related labs of the AP Biology curriculum.

Pointers for Practice

The main points of this chapter are:

✔ **Atoms come together to form compounds by forming bonds.** Ionic bonds are formed by completely transferring electrons, while covalent bonds are formed by sharing electrons. Depending on how equally the electrons within covalent bonds are shared, those bonds can be polar (not equally shared) or nonpolar (equally shared). Organic molecules common in biochemistry are based on a covalently bonded carbon skeleton. Carbon forms four covalent bonds.

✔ **Water is a very polar molecule.** Water makes an excellent solvent because its poles interact with other polar species (ionic compounds and polar molecules), surrounding them and allowing them to move freely. Water helps form bilayer membranes and directs the shape of proteins by driving nonpolar groups to the inside of structures, while interacting directly with polar groups on the outside. Water is excellent at hydrogen-bonding, and this trait gives water its cohesive/adhesive properties and its large heat capacity.

✔ **Carbohydrates have a basic formula of $(CH_2O)_n$.** Carbohydrates can be divided into three main categories: monosaccharides, disaccarhides, and polysaccharides, composed of one sugar, two sugars, and many sugars, respectively. Monosaccharides can be assembled into polysaccharides or broken down from them by enzymes that facilitate dehydration/hydrolysis reactions.

✔ **Proteins are built from an inventory of twenty common amino acids, linked together by peptide bonds.** The primary structure of a protein is the sequence of amino acids. Hydrogen-bonding between peptide backbones gives rise to regularly repeating secondary structures, which in turn pack into tertiary structures. Multiple proteins can associate into quaternary structures.

✔ **Enzymes are an important class protein catalysts that speed up chemical reactions.** Enzyme activity is affected by temperature, pH (=-log [H⁺]), concentrations of enzyme and/or substrate, and the presence of activators or inhibitors.

✔ **Nucleic acids are used to store and transmit genetic information.** DNA and RNA are two types of nucleic acids. DNA forms double-helices, while RNA is mostly single stranded. The bases that make up DNA are A, T, G, and C; the bases of RNA are A, U, G, and C. Purines A and G form complementary base-pairs with pyrimidines T/U and C, respectively.

✔ **DNA replication is semi-conservative.** The following enzymes facilitate DNA replication: helicase, DNA polymerase, primase, and DNA ligase.

✔ **During transcription, an RNA "working copy" is made from a DNA template.** During RNA processing, introns are cut out and exons are spliced together; the 5' end is capped and the 3' end receives a polyA tail. During translation, a polypeptide is built from amino acids in a sequence directed by codons on an mRNA.

Testing Your Knowledge

This section contains multiple choice, free-essay response and laboratory sections to test your knowledge of the material in Chapter 3.

Answering multiple-choice questions

Directions: Each question is followed by five possible answers. Choose the best answer.

1. Ionic bonds are formed between which of the following:

    (A) Atoms sharing electrons

    (B) Ions of opposite charge

    (C) A partially positive hydrogen and a partially negative atom

    (D) Two anions

    (E) Two cations

2. All of the following are characteristics of water EXCEPT

    (A) It is a polar molecule

    (B) It is an excellent solvent

    (C) It has a high heat capacity

    (D) It has high surface tension

    (E) It interacts well with nonpolar molecules

3. All of the following are carbohydrates EXCEPT

    (A) Glucose

    (B) Cellulose

    (C) Polypeptides

    (D) Starch

    (E) Glycogen

4. Enzymes do all of the following EXCEPT

   (A) Speed up reactions

   (B) Respond to specific inhibitors

   (C) Get consumed during reactions

   (D) Bind substrates within an active site

   (E) Release products

5. What scenario best describes a hydrolysis reaction?

   (A) A water molecule is added across a covalent bond, breaking that bond.

   (B) A new covalent bond is formed by the removal of a water molecule.

   (C) Electrons are completely transferred between reactants.

   (D) Amino acids are linked together with peptide bonds.

   (E) Water molecules surround and separate ionically bonded atoms.

6. All of the following are nitrogenous bases of DNA EXCEPT

   (A) Guanine

   (B) Adenine

   (C) Thymine

   (D) Cytosine

   (E) Uracil

7. All of the following are characteristics of RNA EXCEPT

   (A) It is mostly single-stranded

   (B) It contains the nitrogenous base uracil

   (C) It employs a ribose sugar

   (D) It is very chemically stable

   (E) It acts as a messenger during protein synthesis

8. What is the product of translation?

   (A) Carbohydrates

   (B) Nucleic acids

   (C) Polypeptides

   (D) Water

   (E) Cellulose

9. Which of the following statements about pH is true?

   (A) The pH of water is 8.

   (B) Bases have pH < 7.

   (C) Enzymes are usually sensitive to pH.

   (D) Acids have pH > 7.

   (E) A solution with 0.001 moles/liter H^+ has a pH of 4.

10. All of the following occur to mRNA before it leaves the nucleus EXCEPT

    (A) The addition of a 5' cap

    (B) The addition of a polyA tail

    (C) Excision of introns

    (D) Splicing together of exons

    (E) Binding to the small ribosomal subunit

11. Choose the correct DNA complement to this DNA strand:

3'-ACCGTGACT-5'

    (A) 3'-TGGCACTGA-5'

    (B) 5'-CAATGTCAG-3'

    (C) 5'-ACCGTGACT-3'

    (D) 5'-TGGCACTGA-3'

    (E) 5'-UGGCACUGA-3'

Answering free-essay response questions

Directions: Answer the following questions in essay form, not in outline form, using complete sentences. Diagrams may be used to supplement answers, but diagrams alone are not adequate.

1. Describe the transformation of genetic information from gene to protein.

2. Discuss the process of DNA replication.

Lab on diffusion and osmosis

Every year an osmosis question appears on the exam.

To better understand this lab, first master a few key terms:

- ✔ **Diffusion** is the movement of particles from an area of high concentration to one of low concentration.

- ✔ **Osmosis** is the diffusion of water across a selectively permeable membrane.

- ✔ **Hypotonic** solutions have a concentration of dissolved substances lower than that found within the cell; this means that the water concentration of the solution is higher than it is within the cell.

- ✔ **Hypertonic** solutions have a concentration of dissolved substances greater than that found within the cell; this means that the water concentration of the solution is lower than it is within the cell.

- ✔ **Isotonic** solutions have a concentration of dissolved substances equal to that found with the cell, so the water concentrations are also equal.

In this lab you observe the effects of diffusion and osmosis. In the first experiment, a length of dialysis tubing is filled with a solution of glucose and starch. The tubing serves as a semi-permeable membrane, one that allows passage of small molecules like water and glucose, but blocks passage of large molecules like starch. When the filled tubing is immersed in a beaker of water, glucose diffuses out of the membrane until its concentrations within and outside the membrane are equal. Starch is prevented from diffusing, due to the small pore size of the tubing. The presence of starch and glucose is detected using various chemical reagents.

In the second experiment, several bags of dialysis tubing are filled with varying concentrations of sucrose, a molecule that cannot diffuse through the tubing. The solution-filled bags are immersed in beakers of water. The water is hypotonic compared to the bags filled with sucrose solution. Bags filled with higher concentrations of sucrose experience a greater amount of osmosis, as water molecules diffuse across the membrane in order to equalize water concentrations within and outside the membrane, leading to isotonic solutions. The extent of osmosis is measured by weighing the bags before and after immersion in water.

Lab on enzyme catalysis

Review your lab manual and notes on the enzyme catalysis lab. Be sure to understand the effects of temperature, pH substrate concentration, enzyme concentration, and activators or inhibitors.

Enzymes are biological *catalysts*. Catalysts speed up chemical reactions by lowering *activation energy*. Each type of enzyme works best at an optimal temperature and an optimal pH, and works less well at other temperatures and pH values. Enzyme activity will increase with added substrate, but will eventually level off as all the available enzyme active sites are filled. Enzyme activity will increase with added enzyme up to the point where all substrate molecules have an available enzyme active site. *Activators* and *inhibitors* are molecules that help or prevent specific enzymes from doing their thing. Enzyme activity is usually measured under conditions where the concentration of substrate greatly exceeds the enzyme concentration. Under these conditions, you can measure the amount of product made as time passes. At early time-points, the graph of product made versus time will be linear, as shown in Figure 4-1. The slope of this line is the *initial rate*.

In this lab you measure the initial rate of an enzyme-catalyzed reaction under different conditions. Depending on the enzyme you are studying, you might measure the initial rate directly, by measuring the *appearance of product,* or indirectly, by measuring the *disappearance of substrate.* By comparing initial rates measured at different temperatures, pH value, and concentrations of enzymes, substrates, or activators/inhibitors, you discover how each of these factors impacts the activity of your particular enzyme. Different enzymes respond differently changes in these variables.

One tool used to analyze enzyme activity is a *Lineweaver-Burk plot*. In this kind of plot, the inverse of an enzyme's rate (1/V) is plotted versus the inverse of the concentration of added substrate (1/[S]). By plotting enzymatic rates measured in the presence of different concentrations of substrate and/or inhibitor, you can figure out the way an inhibitor interacts with the enzyme. The three major kinds of inhibition are competitive, non-competitive and mixed. *Competitive inhibitors* bind directly to an enzyme's active site, blocking substrate from binding there. *Non-competitive inhibitors* bind the enzyme at locations other than the active site. *Mixed inhibitors* bind away from the active site, but still affect binding of substrate. Adding high enough concentrations of substrate can overcome competitive inhibition and can partially alleviate mixed inhibition, but has no effect on non-competitive inhibition, as depicted by the Lineweaver-Burk plots in Figure 4-2.

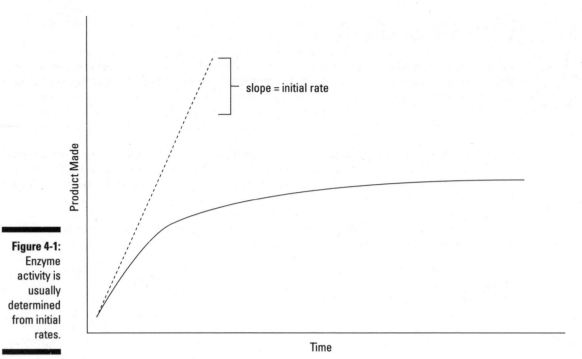

Figure 4-1:
Enzyme
activity is
usually
determined
from initial
rates.

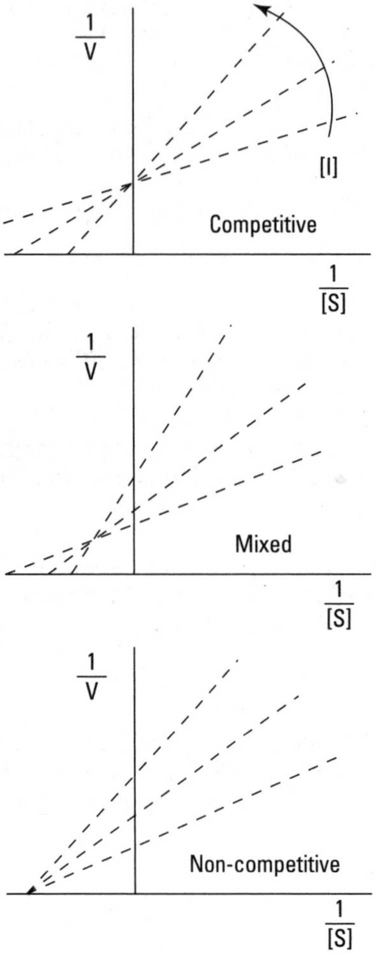

Figure 4-2:
Lineweaver-
Burk plots
showing
competitive,
mixed and
non-com-
petitve inhi-
bition. The
inverse
of the
observed
enzymatic
rate is plot-
ted as 1/V.
The inverse
of the added
substrate
concentra-
tion is plot-
ted as 1/[S].
The con-
centration
of inhibitor
is indicated
by [I].

Checking Your Work

Even if you think you knew the answers to the multiple-choice and free-essay response questions, it might pay to read this section. You can learn from mistakes you *haven't* made as well as those you have.

Answers and explanations for the multiple choice questions are:

1. (B) Ionic bonds are formed between ions of opposite charge. Anions have negative charge and cations have positive charge. Answer (A) describes covalent bonds. Answer (C) describes hydrogen bonds. Answers (D) and (E) are wrong because ions of like charge do not bond, but repel each other.

2. (E) Water interacts much more favorably with polar substances than with nonpolar substances. All of the other choices are characteristics of water.

3. (C) Polypeptides fold to form functional proteins. Glucose, starch, and glycogen are all carbohydrates.

4. (C) Enzymes are biological catalysts. Catalysts speed up reactions without themselves getting altered or consumed.

5. (A) Hydrolysis is the breaking of a covalent bond by the addition of a water molecule across that bond. Answers (B) and (D) describe a dehydration reaction. Answer (C) describes a redox reaction. Answer (E) describes dissolution of an ionic compound.

6. (E) Uracil is used in RNA, not DNA. The DNA equivalent is thymine.

7. (D) Compared to DNA, RNA is easily broken down. This is a useful property of RNA, because it means that mRNAs can be kept around only as long as they are needed.

8. (C) Translation occurs on the ribosome, where the information in mRNA directs the linkage of amino acids into polypeptides.

9. Answer (C) is true. Answer (A) is wrong because water is neutral, with a pH of 7. Answers (B) and (D) have the situation reversed; acids have pH < 7 and bases have pH > 7. Answer (E) is wrong because pH = -log $[H^+]$. Thus, if $[H^+]$ = 0.001 moles/liter, or 10^{-3} moles/liter, then pH = 3.

10. The answer is (E). Binding of the small ribosomal subunit occurs in the cytoplasm. Answers (A) through (D) all occur in the nucleus, and in fact *must* occur before the mRNA is allowed to depart for the cytoplasm.

11. (D) is the correct answer. Answer (A) has the right sequence but the wrong 5'-3' direction. Answers (B) and (C) don't follow correct base-pairing rules. Answer (E) shows a correct RNA complement, but the question calls for a DNA complement.

Models for the free-essay response questions are:

1. Genetic information flows from DNA through RNA into protein. The move from DNA into RNA involves a process called transcription. The move from RNA into protein involves a process called translation. In eukaryotes, an additional step, called processing, occurs between transcription and translation.

Genes are encoded within the DNA, using an alphabet of four bases: adenine, thymine, guanine and cytosine (A, T, G and C). Each base has a complementary partner. In a DNA double helix, for example, A pairs with T, and G pairs with C. RNA uses a similar base-pairing system, with the exception that RNA uses uracil (U) instead of thymine. During transcription, the message of a gene is "transcribed" or rewritten in the form of a messenger RNA (mRNA), using the ability of RNA bases to pair with DNA bases.

In eukaryotes, transcription occurs in the nucleus. While still in the nucleus, mRNAs undergo processing. Processing includes the cutting out of introns (*inter*vening sequences) and the splicing together of exons (*ex*pressed sequences). In addition, mRNAs receive a 5'-cap and a polyA tail, each of which protect the mRNA from degradation and allow it to be sent out of the nucleus.

Once an mRNA has left the nucleus, it is ready to be translated into protein. Translation occurs on the ribosome. The ribosome has two main jobs:

- ✔ To decode the information written into the mRNA
- ✔ To use that information to link together amino acids, thereby building a protein

In other words, the ribosome must "translate" information from the language of DNA and RNA into the language of protein. The "linguists" that help the ribosome with this task are the transfer RNAs (tRNAs). Each tRNA recognizes a particular, three-base "word" within an mRNA sequence. These "words" are called codons. Every tRNA carries with it an amino acid corresponding to the codon it recognizes. As an mRNA feeds through the ribosome, tRNAs enter in order to recognize codons and to hand off the correct amino acids. The ribosome links together these amino acids, forming a "polypeptide" chain. The sequence of amino acids in this chain corresponds to the sequence of bases within the DNA of a gene. Fully assembled polypeptides are released from the ribosome and go on to be proteins, completing the journey of genetic information from DNA through RNA into protein.

2. DNA replication is the copying of genetic material in a cell so that each of two daughter cells may receive a complete copy once the parent cell has divided. The process of DNA replication is semi-conservative; this means that each daughter cell receives one original DNA strand from the parent, as well as one newly made strand. Replication involves unwinding the DNA double helix and using the exposed single strands as templates for new copies. Replication is performed by a team of specific enzymes. Because DNA strands have direction, also known as polarity, the copying process is more complicated for one strand (the "lagging strand") than the other (the "leading strand").

Replication begins when an enzyme called helicase starts to unwind the DNA double helix at the site where copying is to start. This unwinding creates a "bubble" region in which single DNA strands are exposed. The single strands rejoin at a point called the replication fork. Within the exposed bubble, one strand of DNA runs 5' to 3', while the other runs 3' to 5'. An enzyme called DNA polymerase binds to individual DNA strands in order to perform the actual process of copying. To start copying, DNA polymerase needs a short stretch of RNA called a "primer". The enzyme primase provides the primer. Once "primed", DNA polymerase scans along the DNA single strand, 3' to 5', adding one DNA base at a time. The bases are chosen by their ability to base-pair with the bases on the template strand. The new strand is made 5' to 3'.

Because DNA polymerase moves along template strands 3' to 5', replication is more complicated for one strand of the "bubble" than it is for the other strand. On the "leading strand", DNA polymerase can move along smoothly, and replication occurs quickly. On the "lagging strand", DNA polymerase keeps bumping into the replication fork, and must wait for helicase to continue unwinding. As a result, DNA polymerase makes a series of short, disconnected DNA pieces. These pieces are called Okazaki fragments. Each fragment needs its own RNA primer. The primers of neighboring fragments must be replaced with DNA, and the DNA fragments must be joined. These tasks are carried out by the enzyme ligase. Making and joining all these separate fragments takes time, which is why lagging strand replication is so slow. In the end, what started as two exposed template strands becomes two new double helices. Each helix contains one original strand and one new strand.

Chapter 5

The Cell's Structure: Factories at Work

*E*ver since the first eyeball peered through a microscope to gaze at a cell, biology has never been the same. Cells are the basic units of life. Cells are the smallest bits of an organism that can take in nutrients, extract and use energy, give off wastes, and reproduce. Living organisms are built from as few as one to as many as trillions of cells. For all the diversity of life, from bacteria to blue whales, there are striking similarities at the level of the cell. Because all cells come from other cells, this makes a certain amount of sense. All cells have membranes, store genetic information in DNA, and have specialized parts for specialized jobs. Those special parts are the focus of this chapter.

Categorizing Cells

Nobody likes to be labeled. But in biology, labels can be pretty useful. For example, simply by knowing that a particular cell bears the label "prokaryote" or "eukaryote," you automatically know a lot about that cell's structure. Or, you will soon, anyway.

Poking around prokaryotes

If you were told that the word *prokaryote* literally meant "before the kernel," you might not be impressed. But if you were told that "kernel" was a sort of poetic shorthand for "nucleus," well, then you might have learned something. *Prokaryotes* are predominantly single-celled organisms with no distinct nucleus. This group has ancient evolutionary origins, and includes two major groups:

✔ Bacteria (the majority)

✔ Archaea (the minority)

Both bacteria and archaea tend to be smaller and simpler than their more recently evolved cousins, the eukaryotes (to be discussed in the following section). For all their simplicity, the prokaryotes are a spectacularly successful group of organisms, accounting for most of the species on the planet. Small and sleek, prokaryotes are the sports cars of the cellular world.

You, a eukaryote

If prokaryotes are sports cars, eukaryotes are luxury sedans. Eukaryotic cells have all the bells and whistles, to include a membrane-bound nucleus which stores the cell's DNA. In addition to this nucleus, eukaryotic cells contain a small fleet of other membrane-bound organelles absent from prokaryotes. There is much diversity among the eukaryotes. For example, single-celled yeasts and all plant and animal cells are eukaryotic. Though there are many differences among different kinds of eukaryotic cell, the eukaryotes as a group are generally larger and more complicated than the prokaryotes. In addition to all this internal complexity, eukaryotic cells have evolved into highly specialized multicellular assemblies. These specialized groups form tissues, and the tissues in turn are organized into organs.

Powerhouse Parts: Cell Structures

Every cell in existence is the finely honed product of billions of years of evolution. As a result, each structure within a cell is uniquely tailored to perform a useful function. So, by examining the collection of structures within cells, you get a really good idea of how cells work.

In the sections that follow, you get introduced to the concept of *homeostasis,* or the maintenance of stable conditions within the cell. For such a simple notion, a great deal of cellular parts and energy are devoted to the task. If you think about it for a second, it only makes sense: Cells are busy little cities, carrying out countless chemical reactions at any given moment. All these reactions require starting materials and generate products. Many of the starting materials have to be continually imported, and many of the products are wastes, which must be exported. You can explore these cell cities and their structures in the sections that follow.

Prokaryotic cell structure

Like all cells, prokaryotic cells (see Figure 5-1) are enclosed by a plasma membrane. Since the vast majority of prokaryotes are single-celled, it would make sense for them to have evolved some protection beyond a simple plasma membrane. This is in fact the case, as nearly all prokaryotes have outer cell walls. The cell walls are made up of carbohydrate and peptide building blocks, and most often are built from a cross-linked material called *peptidoglycan.*

Bacterial cells with a single outer layer of peptidoglycan are called gram-positive, while bacteria with a second layer of phospholipid membrane enveloping the peptidoglycan layer are called gram-negative. Gram-positive and gram-negative cells can be distinguished under a microscope by their ability to take up red and purple Gram stains. Gram-positive bacteria stain red, while gram-negative bacteria stain purple.

In addition to the cell wall, some prokaryotes secrete a sticky, outermost layer called a capsule. Capsules provide further protection and can help the cell stick to surfaces. Other structures on the exterior of prokaryotic cells include pili and flagella. A pilus is an arm-like structure that some prokaryotes use to stick to surfaces or to other cells. Flagella are long, whiplike structures that prokaryotes use like boat propellers to move around in fluid environments. Flagella may be scattered all around the outer surface or concentrated at one end.

The interior of a prokaryotic cell contains the cytoplasm. Suspended in the cytoplasm are many ribosomes, ready to make proteins. The genes that code for proteins are found in the DNA of the prokaryotic chromosome. Prokaryotic chromosomes usually consist of one large loop of double-stranded DNA, entangled into a mass called the *nucleoid.*

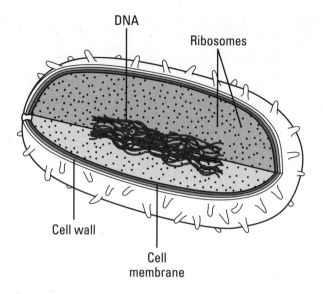

DNA

Ribosomes

Cell wall

Cell
membrane

(a) prokaryotic cell

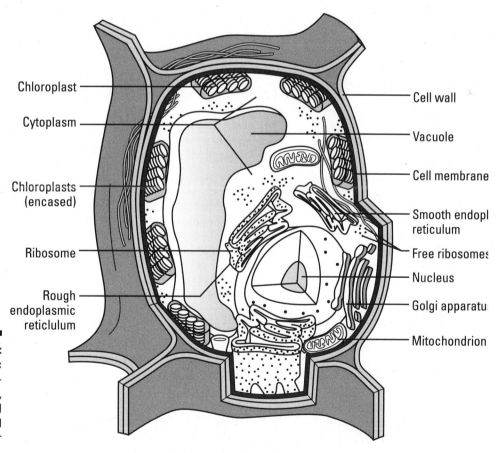

Chloroplast

Cytoplasm

Chloroplasts
(encased)

Ribosome

Rough
endoplasmic
reticlulum

Cell wall

Vacuole

Cell membrane

Smooth endopl
reticulum

Free ribosomes

Nucleus

Golgi apparatu:

Mitochondrion

Figure 5-1:
Prokaryotic
and eukary-
otic cells,
sectioned
to reveal
their inner
contents.

(b) eukaryotic cell (plant cell)

Eukaryotic cell structure

Eukaryotic cells are all about division of labor. As seen in Figure 5-1b, these cells have many organelles, microscopic structures that perform specialized functions. Most of these organelles are enclosed within their own membranes, which help to ensure that only those substances relevant to the organelle's function are allowed inside. The organelles are suspended in a jellylike fluid called the cytosol.

Remember, organelles are quite literally tiny organs; just as the heart, lungs, and brain perform specific functions for the body, each organelle performs a specific function for the cell. What follows is a brief summary of the most important eukaryotic organelles, with descriptions of their particular functions in the cell:

- **Plasma membrane:** The plasma membrane encloses the cell, making it distinct from other cells and from the outside environment. In plant cells, the plasma membrane is itself enclosed by a rigid cell wall, built largely of the carbohydrate polymer, cellulose. The plasma membrane is vital to the process of homeostasis, or the maintenance of a stable, steady internal environment. The plasma membrane enables this stability because it is selectively permeable. This simply means that the membrane controls what can enter or exit the cell. Useful nutrients are selectively allowed entrance while waste materials are selectively allowed to leave. As you can see in Figure 5-2, the plasma membrane is largely made up of molecules called phospholipids. Each phospholipid has a phosphate head and lipid tails. The head portion is *hydrophilic,* meaning that it interacts well with water. The tails are *hydrophobic,* avoiding contact with water. As a result, the phospholipids organize themselves into a phospholipid bilayer, with heads pointing outward and tails hidden away from the watery cytosol or extracellular (outside-the-cell) environment. Phospholipid membranes are fluid structures, similar in consistency to cooking oil. Cholesterol molecules embedded in the bilayer help to maintain this fluidity. Also embedded within the bilayer are membrane proteins that act as gatekeepers, enforcing the selective permeability of the membrane. This description of the plasma membrane, with membrane proteins moving freely along the expanse of the membrane, is called the fluid mosaic model (see Figure 5-2).

- **Cytoskeleton:** The cytoskeleton is a network of protein fibers that extends like scaffolding throughout the cytosol, giving shape and structure to the cell, assisting in the transport of materials, and enabling cell motility (as in, self-directed movement). The fibers are built from many smaller protein subunits, and can quickly grow or shrink to meet the needs of the moment by adding or shedding these subunits from the fiber tips. The cytoskeleton consists of three main types of fibers: microtubules, microfilaments, and intermediate filaments. Microtubules are the major building blocks of another type of organelle, called the centriole. Found within animal cells, centrioles organize other bunches of microtubules called spindle fibers during the process of cell division.

- **Nucleus:** The nucleus is the information center of the cell, and is separated from the cytosol by a membrane called the nuclear envelope. The genes of the cell are found within the nucleus, encoded in DNA. DNA takes different forms at different points during the cell's life cycle. When the cell is rapidly growing and needs quick access to the genes, the DNA exists in a loose, unraveled form called chromatin. When the cell is preparing to divide or is dividing, the DNA is neatly wrapped up into distinct chromosomes, so it can be cleanly divided between daughter cells, which avoids any sibling rivalry. Working copies of the genetic information, called messenger RNAs (mRNAs), are transcribed from the DNA genes, processed, and sent out of the nucleus to be translated into proteins. Each nucleus contains a separate compartment called the *nucleolus.* The nucleolus is a factory for making parts that eventually assemble into another kind of organelle, called the ribosome.

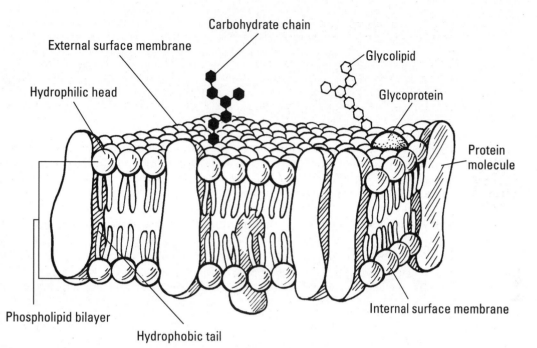

External surface membrane

Carbohydrate chain

Glycolipid

Glycoprotein

Hydrophilic head

Protein molecule

Figure 5-2:
Fluid mosaic model of the plasma membrane.

Phospholipid bilayer

Hydrophobic tail

Internal surface membrane

✔ **Ribosome:** Ribosomes are the molecular machines that make proteins. Ribosomes are made of RNA and protein parts, and consist of a large and a small subunit. Ribosomes are found both free within the cytosol and attached to an organelle called the endoplasmic reticulum (see the next bullet). Together with other RNA molecules called transfer RNAs, ribosomes decode the information within messenger RNAs (originally encoded in the DNA) and use that information to chemically link amino acids into long chains called polypeptides. Polypeptide chains fold up into precise protein structures.

✔ **Endoplasmic reticulum:** Sometimes referred to simply as ER, the endoplasmic reticulum is a many-layered membrane structure. The stacked membrane layers of the ER enclose an interconnected network of channels that are separated from the cytosol. The ER exists in "rough" and "smooth" forms. Rough ER, which extends directly from the nuclear envelope, is studded with attached ribosomes, each dedicated to making proteins that will be transported elsewhere in the cell or will become membrane proteins. Proteins destined for transport are packed into spherical membrane sacs called vesicles. Smooth ER lacks ribosomes, but houses enzymes that produce lipids for the cell, among other things.

✔ **Golgi apparatus:** The Golgi apparatus is the warehouse and distribution center of the cell. Products enter the Golgi, are modified, addressed and then sent off to their final destinations. In particular, the Golgi receives "raw" protein products from the rough ER and applies any necessary finishing touches. In addition, the Golgi assists in the distribution of lipids and in the production of organelles called lysosomes. Finished products are packed into vesicles, and each vesicle is tagged with a molecular "address," specifying the location to which the vesicle must be sent. Some vesicles are sent to other locations inside the cell, while other vesicles are sent to the plasma membrane where they release their payloads to the external environment (secretion).

✔ **Lysosome:** Lysosomes are membrane-bound digestive centers, containing enzymes that specialize in breaking down large molecules. The internal space of a lysosome is very acidic (has low pH), which aids in the digestive process. Worn out or faulty cellular parts, large chunks of nutrients and unwanted invaders like viruses and bacteria all meet their end within lysosomes. All these materials are broken down into smaller components that can be recycled according to the needs of the cell.

✔ **Mitochondrion:** Mitochondria are the power plants of the cell. Mitochondria specialize in converting the energy stored in "food" molecules (like sugars and fats) into energy in the form of ATP, which can be readily used by the cell. Mitochondria have both an inner and an outer membrane, and the two membranes are separated by an intermembrane space. The interior of a mitochondrion is filled with a fluid called the matrix. The membrane and fluid regions of the mitochondrion each play specific roles in the process of energy production, called "cellular respiration."

✔ **Chloroplast:** Found in plant cells, chloroplasts are organelles that capture energy from light and convert it into chemical energy, stored within molecules of the sugar, glucose. Like mitochondria, chloroplasts have inner and outer membranes. The interior of the chloroplast is filled with a fluid called the stroma, and houses stacked membrane discs called the thylakoid. The thylakoid and stroma each play specific roles in converting light energy into chemical energy, in a process called *photosynthesis*.

✔ **Cilia and flagella:** Cilia and flagella (shown in Figure 5-3) are long, slender structures built from microtubules. Each serves a variety of roles, but all these roles have to do with moving about (motility), sensation or helping to transport materials. Cilia and flagella use ATP to power whipping or waving motions. Unlike prokaryotic flagella, these eukaryotic organelles are encased by the plasma membrane, and so are actually within the cell, even though they project outwards from the main cellular body.

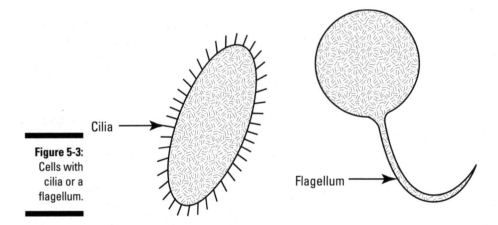

Figure 5-3:
Cells with cilia or a flagellum.

Cilia →

Flagellum →

Crossing the Border: Six Ways to Transport

All this importing and exporting makes for busy borders. In cells, the borders are membranes, and materials are constantly being shipped one way or another across membranes. At any given moment, a particular substance may exist in higher or lower concentrations on one side of the membrane versus the other. Such a difference in concentration is called a *gradient*. The particular type of transport used for a particular substance depends on the direction of its concentration gradient, and on its size. The major types of transport are:

✔ **Diffusion:** Shown in Figure 5-4, diffusion is the movement of a substance from an area of higher concentration to one of lower concentration (down a gradient), and occurs on its own without the input of energy. Think of a drop of ink spreading throughout a glass of water, and you'll understand diffusion. Many waste materials exit the cell through diffusion because that is their natural direction of movement as they build up within the cell.

✔ **Osmosis:** Osmosis is simply the diffusion of water, but it holds the distinct honor of having its own name because water is so important to life. Solutions with higher amounts of dissolved substances have lower concentrations of water, and water will diffuse across membranes in order to minimize the difference in concentration.

✔ **Facilitated diffusion:** Most kinds of materials can't easily diffuse across the plasma membrane unless an opening is provided for them. Cells can support and control the diffusion of these materials by means of membrane proteins. Specific membrane proteins allow passage across the membrane to specific ions or molecules, but not to others. This pickiness is a big source of the selective permeability of the plasma membrane. As long as the appropriate membrane protein is present and open, a given ion or molecule can diffuse through the protein, across the membrane, along its concentration gradient. This kind of transport is called facilitated diffusion, and is depicted for sodium ions in Figure 5-4. Although facilitated diffusion requires a protein tunnel through the membrane, it is still diffusion, and requires no added energy.

✔ **Active transport:** Sometimes, much-needed nutrients or harmful substances must be transported across the membrane against a concentration gradient. In these cases, the cell must provide energy in order to move the material against the direction of diffusion. This kind of energy-requiring transport is called active transport and, like facilitated diffusion, uses membrane proteins. Often, these proteins cleave ATP in order to obtain the needed energy. Other proteins use the energy released from the diffusion of one substance to power the active transport of another substance.

✔ **Exocytosis:** Membrane proteins are fine for channeling the movement of ions and small molecules, but for transporting large molecules, a different strategy is required. When cells need to send large molecules (like proteins) outside their plasma membrane borders, they turn to exocytosis. Sizable cargo is loaded into spherical membrane vesicles. These vesicles move towards the plasma membrane and fuse with it, exposing the vesicle interior to the outside of the cell and releasing its contents.

It's easy to remember the meaning of *exo*cytosis, because it involves the *exit* of materials from the cell.

✔ **Endocytosis:** Sometimes cells have cause to import large molecules. For this challenging task, the solution is endocytosis. Endocytosis is essentially exocytosis in reverse, as you can see in Figure 5-5. Molecules to be imported contact the exterior surface of the plasma membrane, triggering the membrane to fold inwards, enveloping them. The infolded membrane pinches off into a vesicle containing the imported molecules, which can be further transported to their eventual destination within the cell.

Liposomes: Versatile vesicles for drugs

Biomedical researchers have taken a cue from nature when it comes to finding ways to deliver therapeutic drugs to cells in sick patients. Some of the key challenges to drug-based therapies are getting enough of the drug into cells, or getting the drug to the *right* cells. By using a tool called the liposome, researchers address both these challenges.

Liposomes are essentially vesicles, small membrane structures that enclose a watery internal environment. Liposomes are exciting candidates for drug delivery because they offer so many ways to accommodate the specific properties of different drugs and to ensure effective delivery to target cells within patients. Hydrophilic

(water-soluble) drugs can be loaded into the interior space of liposomes, and the interior environment (pH, ion concentrations, and so on) can be tailored to enhance the efficacy of the drug. Hydrophobic (non-water-soluble) drugs can be incorporated into the membrane of the liposome. A single liposome can even carry combinations of multiple drugs!

The outer surface of the drug-toting liposome can be decorated with molecules that target the liposome for delivery to only certain cell types. Once at the target cell, liposomes can effectively deliver drugs into the cell interior simply by undergoing the normal process of endocytosis.

(a) Simple Diffusion

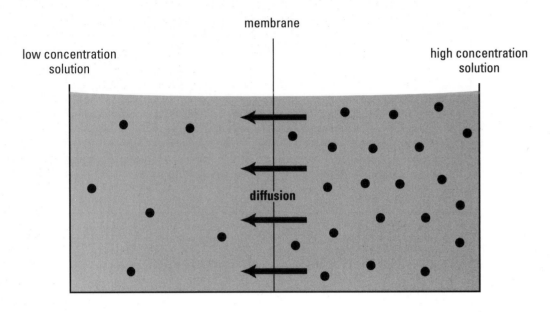

membrane

low concentration
solution

high concentration
solution

diffusion

(b) Facilitated Diffusion

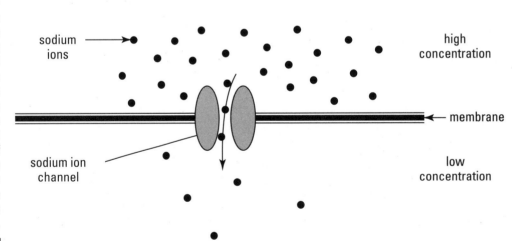

sodium
ions

high
concentration

membrane

sodium ion
channel

low
concentration

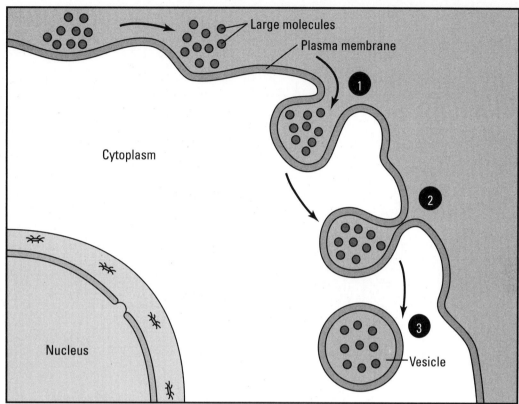

Figure 5-5:
The transport process of endocytosis.

Endocytosis

Chapter 6

Answering Questions about Cell Structure

· ·

In This Chapter

▶ Taking in test-taking tips

▶ Trying your hand at some questions

▶ Seeing how your answers match up

· ·

*Y*ou've taken a tour of the cell, discovering the arsenal of organelles within, each with its own specialized task. Now it's time to impress yourself with what you've learned. The questions in this chapter focus on the material covered in Chapter 5: The Cell's Structure: Factories at Work. Multiple choice and free-essay response questions and answers are provided.

Pointers for Practice

The most important points covered in Chapter 5 are:

✔ **Cells are the fundamental units of life, able to ingest nutrients, use energy, release waste, and reproduce.**

✔ **All cells are enclosed by plasma membranes, store genes within DNA, and use specialized organelles to perform specific tasks.**

✔ **Prokaryotes are small, relatively simple cells with ancient evolutionary origins.** The two main groups of prokaryotes are bacteria and archaea, the vast majority of which are single-celled organisms. Prokaryotic DNA exists within the cytoplasm in a dense tangle called the nucleoid. Prokaryotic cells usually have protective cell walls that enclose the plasma membrane.

✔ **Eukaryotic cells are typically larger and more complicated than prokaryotic cells.** Eukaryotes range from single-celled organisms to all the varieties of plants and animals on the planet. Eukaryotes store DNA within a membranous nuclear envelope, and possess a wide variety of specialized organelles.

✔ **The fluid mosaic model of the plasma membrane features an oily phospholipid bilayer, within which are embedded various membrane proteins.** These membrane proteins help the cell to maintain homeostasis by selectively controlling the passage of materials across the membrane.

✔ **The cytoskeleton consists of several types of protein fibers.** These fibers provide structure, enable cell movement and transport of materials, and coordinate events during cell division.

✔ **The nucleus houses the DNA, wherein the genetic blueprints for proteins are stored.** Transcription and processing of mRNAs occurs in the nucleus. The nucleus also contains a structure called the nucleolus, which specializes in building ribosomes, the machines that translate proteins by using information from mRNAs.

✔ **The endoplasmic reticulum (ER) is a many-layered membrane structure involved in producing proteins and lipids for the cell.** Rough ER contains ribosomes; smooth ER does not.

✔ **The Golgi apparatus is a large, membranous organelle in which proteins are processed and packaged for delivery within vesicles.** The Golgi also helps form lysosomes. Lysosomes are vesicles with an acidic interior; they contain digestive enzymes that break down large molecules for recycling.

✔ **Chloroplasts and mitochondria are organelles dedicated to converting energy into different forms.** Chloroplasts perform photosynthesis, capturing energy from light and converting it into chemical energy within sugar. Mitochondria perform cellular respiration, releasing energy from sugars and converting it into energy stored within ATP. Most eukaryotic cells contain mitochondria; chloroplasts are found within plant cells and algae.

✔ **Cilia and flagella are long structures that engage in whipping or waving motions.** These organelles are involved in cell movement, sensation, and transport of materials.

✔ **Materials are constantly transported across membranes within cells.** Differences in the concentration of a substance across a membrane are called gradients. Movement down a gradient (towards lower concentration) is called diffusion, and occurs without input of energy. Diffusion of water is called osmosis. Diffusion through a membrane protein is called facilitated diffusion. Movement up a gradient (towards higher concentration) requires energy and is called active transport.

✔ **Large molecules are transported across the plasma membrane within vesicles.** Release of molecules within a vesicle to the exterior of the cell is called exocytosis. Import of molecules from the exterior into a vesicle within the cell is called endocytosis.

Testing Your Knowledge

This section contains multiple choice and free-essay response sections to test your knowledge of the material in Chapter 5.

Answering multiple-choice questions

Directions: Each question is followed by five possible answers. Choose the best answer.

1. Which of the following structures are present in prokaryotic cells?

   I. Plasma membrane

   II. Nucleus

   III. Ribosomes

   (A) I only

   (B) II only

   (C) III only

   (D) I and II only

   (E) I and III only

2. In the course of fighting off a virus that has infected the cell, which organelle is most directly involved in digesting viral proteins?

   (A) Chloroplast

   (B) Golgi apparatus

   (C) Lysosome

   (D) Cytoskeleton

   (E) Smooth ER

3. You have purified a protein and embedded it within a synthetic phospholipid bilayer in order to study the protein's ability transport materials across membranes. You add different combinations of substances (glucose, urea and ATP) to one side of the membrane, and then measure any changes in the concentrations of those substances. You make the following observations per Table 6-1.

Table 6-1		Observations of Changes in Concentrations			
Trial	Initial Concentration of Glucose	Initial Concentration of Urea	Final Concentration of Glucose	Final Concentration of Urea	ATP added?
1	High	High	High	High	No
2	Low	Low	Low	Low	No
3	High	Low	High	Low	Yes
4	Low	High	Low	Low	Yes
5	High	Low	High	Low	No
6	Low	High	Low	High	No

Given these data, what is the most likely function of the protein?

   (A) Facilitates diffusion of glucose

   (B) Facilitates diffusion of urea

   (C) Actively transports glucose

   (D) Actively transports urea

   (E) Data provide no clues to the protein's function

4. Using an electron microscope, you study the structures of cells grown in rich media (plenty of nutrients) and minimal media (few nutrients). Compared to the cells grown in minimal media, the cells grown in rich media possess much larger versions of a many-layered structure that is "peppered" with dark spots. What is the most likely interpretation?

   (A) The cells grown in rich media have larger mitochondria

   (B) The cells grown in minimal media cannot build full-sized mitochondria

   (C) The cells grown in rich media produce more proteins within the ER

   (D) The cells grown in minimal media have a defective Golgi apparatus

   (E) The cells grown in rich media have more genes

5. Cells lining the inner surfaces of the Fallopian tubes help sweep fertilized egg cells into the uterus at the beginning of a pregnancy. Which organelles are probably most directly involved with this important "sweeping" function?

    (A) Lysosomes

    (B) Cell walls

    (C) Cilia

    (D) Nucleoli

    (E) Ribosomes

6. Certain cells of the immune system, called plasma cells, produce large numbers of special proteins, called antibodies, which are important in fighting off infections. The plasma cells make large numbers of these antibody proteins and "secrete" them, releasing them outside the cell via exocytosis. Which organelle(s) is/are most likely to be highly developed in plasma cells?

    I. Rough ER

    II. Golgi apparatus

    III. Mitochondria

    (A) I only

    (B) II only

    (C) III only

    (D) I and II only

    (E) II and III only

7. Cyanide ion (CN^-) is a lethal poison. The ion binds to an enzyme called cytochrome c oxidase, disabling it entirely, which prevents cells from producing ATP. Which organelle does cyanide most directly cripple?

    (A) Nucleus

    (B) Ribosome

    (C) Cytoskeleton

    (D) Mitochondrion

    (E) Smooth ER

Questions 8 through 12 refer to the following list:

    (A) Active transport

    (B) Facilitated diffusion

    (C) Simple diffusion

    (D) Endocytosis

    (E) Exocytosis

8. Low-density lipoproteins (LDL) are removed from the bloodstream when they bind to outer surfaces of cells and are folded into vesicles within the cell.

9. Oxygen inhaled into the lungs moves across the plasma membranes of alveolar cells, into oxygen-poor blood.

10. Some bacteria are grown in a broth containing very high concentrations of the sugar, maltose. Maltose enters the bacterial cells by passing through maltoporin, a protein that spans the outer bacterial membrane.

11. Cells within the pancreas store the hormone insulin within vesicles, and release it to the outside of the cell when glucose is detected in the bloodstream.

12. An enzyme called the sodium-potassium pump cleaves ATP to drive the export of three sodium ions from the cell for every two potassium ions that enter.

Answering free-essay response questions

Directions: Answer the following question in essay form, not in outline form, using complete sentences. Diagrams may be used to supplement answers, but diagrams alone are not adequate.

1. The plasma membrane is a selectively permeable barrier that controls the flow of nutrients and wastes into and out of the cell. As the size of a cell increases, its internal volume grows much more rapidly than its surface area. Using these facts, explain one reason why it might be necessary that cells are so microscopically small.

Checking Your Work

Check to see how much of the information in Chapter 5 passed through the selectively permeable barrier surrounding your brain. Whether you answered each question correctly is less important than your understanding *why* you got each question right or wrong.

Answers and explanations for the multiple choice questions are:

1. The answer is (E). All cells have a plasma membrane and ribosomes. Only eukaryotic cells possess a nucleus. Prokaryotic DNA is stored in a nucleoid region, which has no nuclear membrane.

2. (C) is the correct answer. Lysosomes digest large molecules, as are found in foreign particles like viruses and bacteria, or in worn out organelles or other cellular debris.

3. The answer is (D). Answers (A) and (C) cannot be right because the concentration of glucose remained unchanged, whether or not ATP was added. (B) is a tempting answer, because the concentration of urea did change in trial 4; however, high urea concentrations did not decrease in trials 1 and 6, where no ATP was added. The overall picture is of a protein that has no effect on glucose, but has the ability to pump urea across a membrane as long as ATP is present as an energy source. This suggests that the protein is an active transporter of urea. After sifting through all this evidence, (E) is clearly incorrect.

4. Answers (A) and (B) are wrong because, although it might be plausible that the nutrient conditions affect the mitochondria, the description of a "many-layered structure, peppered with dark spots" simply doesn't match a mitochondrion. Answer (E) is obviously wrong, because there is no reason to expect a large difference in the number of genes between exactly the same types of cell. Both (C) and (D) describe "many-layered" organelles that are involved in protein production and processing, processes we would expect to increase in the rich-media batch of cells. However, the dark spots are a dead giveaway that we are observing the rough ER, with its coat of protein-producing ribosomes. Thus, (C) is the correct answer.

5. The answer is (C). "Sweeping" motions that transport materials are the classic domain of cilia.

6. The key to this question is to notice that the plasma cells are 1) making a lot of proteins, and 2) secreting those proteins. Secreted proteins tend to be made in the rough ER and sent to the Golgi apparatus to be packaged into vesicles prior to export. Therefore, (D) is the best answer. If you absolutely had to pick just one organelle, then the Golgi, (B), would be your best bet, due to its central role in secretion of protein-loaded vesicles.

7. You picked (D), right? The clincher is that cyanide directly impairs ATP production, which occurs in mitochondria.

8. Go with (D). Large particles like proteins entering a cell from the outside are a prescription for endocytosis. Count on it.

9. (C) is the answer. A small molecule like oxygen, moving down a concentration gradient, with no mention of a carrier protein...it just smacks of simple diffusion.

10. The answer is (B). The question strongly implies that maltose moves down a concentration gradient, into the cell, but requires a membrane protein passageway. That sounds like diffusion, guided by a membrane protein: facilitated diffusion.

11. The answer is (E). Products stored in a vesicle, then released to the outside of the cell? That's pure exocytosis.

12. The transport process requires the cleavage of ATP, using the released energy; it is therefore active transport. That's why the answer is (A).

Here is a model answer for the free-essay response question:

1. Nutrients necessary for cellular life must be imported across the plasma membrane. Waste products must be eliminated from the cell by export across the plasma membrane. Proteins are embedded within the plasma membrane, whose vital job it is to regulate which substances are imported and which are exported. Since all this import/export activity is restricted to the surface of the plasma membrane, the total capacity of the cell to import nutrients and export wastes is limited by the total surface area of the plasma membrane.

The majority of nutrient-consuming, waste-producing biochemistry occurs within the inner volume of the cell, which contains the cytoplasm and the organelles. As a cell increases in volume, the amount of nutrient consumption and waste production increases with it. Since a given increase in cell size results in significantly greater rise in volume than in surface area, larger and larger cells would quickly outgrow their capacity for importing nutrients and exporting wastes.

Chapter 7

Dividing Cells and Conquering the Processes

• •

In This Chapter

▶ Seeing the "big picture" in which life continues by the division of cells

▶ Understanding mitosis

▶ Getting a handle on meiosis

• •

*P*erhaps a house cannot stand divided, but cells, the little Houses of Life, must divide in order for life to continue. Most cells continually move through a cycle, alternately preparing to divide into new cells or actually dividing. Each new cell inherits two complete sets of DNA copied from its parent cell, and the process of organizing all this DNA during division is a major event in any cell's life. The products of this cyclic division, in eukaryotes called *mitosis,* are two new daughter cells. But the dividing doesn't end there. Although most of the cells in eukaryotic organisms divide through mitosis, a small subset of cells divide to form sex cells, or *gametes,* in a process called *meiosis.* Meiosis both mirrors and differs from mitosis. In particular, whereas mitosis provides two complete sets of the DNA to each daughter cell, the function of meiosis is to divide the genetic material so that each gamete only gets one complete set. When a male gamete combines with a female gamete during fertilization, two complete sets are reformed (. . . it's romantic . . . in a molecular sort of way). As we show you in this chapter, meiosis is a major means by which new combinations of genes are created, allowing evolution to occur within species. If you aren't yet convinced that mitosis and meiosis are central processes of life, then simply focus on the fact that you'll see plenty of them on the AP exam.

Stages and Phases: The Cell Cycle

Because all cells come from other cells, it makes sense that cells are, in some sense, always preparing to divide — or dividing. For this reason, the circular path of the cell cycle moves between two major phases: *interphase* (life between divisions) and *M phase* (division). Interphase itself is split into three sub-phases: Growth 1 (G_1), Synthesis (S), and Growth 2 (G_2). M phase consists of mitosis (the source of the "M" in M phase) and cytokinesis, the physical separation of the parent cell into two daughter cells. Mitosis is a ballet of the chromosomes, consisting of four acts: prophase, metaphase, anaphase, and telophase (think P-MAT). As with all dramatic forms, the individual acts are best understood in light of the larger story. So, as you take in the following sections, always connect the details of these processes with their function in the big picture: How does each step help fulfill the parent cell's ultimate task of passing on two complete sets of the DNA to each daughter cell?

Checkpoints

Before copying all the DNA during S phase, or passing on the DNA to daughter cells during M phase, doesn't it seem like a good idea to make sure all that precious DNA is in ship-shape condition? Rest assured, your cells think it's a good idea, too. Cells have evolved checkpoints to guard against the passage of damaged DNA to succeeding generations.

Fleets of enzymes guard entry into S phase and M phase. At the end of phases G_1 and G_2, the cell deploys specific enzymes to scan the DNA for signs of damage and to inspect the cellular machinery for the upcoming phases.

If those inspector enzymes find anything out of place, attempts are made to repair the damage. If repair is successful, signals (molecular "thumbs-up" signs) are sent to allow passage to the next phase. If, sadly, the damage is beyond repair, other signals (molecular "thumbs-down" signs) are sent that cause the irreparably damaged cell to . . . ahem . . . commit suicide. The price for imperfection is death. This may seem severe, but failures in these checkpoint systems can result in cancer. Like Spock, cells understand that the good of the many outweighs the good of the one.

Between phases of cell divisions: Interphase

Cells may divide rapidly (within less than half an hour after having divided from a parent cell) or they may divide only once every several years. The vast majority of cells lie on a timeline somewhere in between. Whatever it is that a particular kind of cell does *between* divisions occurs within interphase.

Of course, different types of cells do different types of things, but eukaryotic interphase generally breaks down into the following phases:

- ✔ **G_1 phase:** Immediately after daughter cells divide from their parent, the new cells enter G_1 phase. During the freshly concluded division, a lot of routine biochemical business has been put on the back burner. During G_1, this business resumes. Newly divided cells are only half the size of their parents, so a lot of biochemical building must be done as the daughter cells grow up. In G_1, cells have two complete sets of DNA (i.e., they are *diploid*), but only one copy of each set. Some cells exit the cell cycle at this point, never to divide again — or at least not for a very long time; we say that these cells have entered G_0 phase.

- ✔ **S phase:** S phase involves the synthesis of DNA. A lot of DNA. In fact, an entire second copy of each of the two sets of DNA is made during S phase. Note that, although the cell concludes S phase with twice the total bulk of DNA, no new genetic information has been added. Cells depart S phase in a diploid state, just as they entered it. So, why would the cell go to all the trouble of copying its DNA? Because the cell will eventually divide, and must pass on an identical DNA inheritance to each daughter. If only human parents were all so evenhanded.

- ✔ **G_2 phase:** After the DNA has been copied, the cell enters a final period of rapid growth in preparation for the exciting business of cell division. This preparatory burst is dubbed G_2 phase. Much of the action in G_2 involves the construction of long, cytoskeletal proteins called microtubules. During the fast-approaching M phase, these microtubules will associate into spindle, ropelike fibers that coordinate the distribution of DNA among the daughter cells. DNA copied, microtubules made, the stage is set: The curtain opens on M phase.

Splitting into Two: Mitosis and Cytokinesis

Just as the separate phases of interphase make perfect sense in light of the big picture of cell division, the events of M phase — much dreaded among biology students — seem only natural and logical when viewed from the perspective of the dividing parent cell. The key concern for the parent is that each daughter cell receives the right allotment of DNA. Mitosis, the chromosomal ballet of a dividing cell, addresses this concern. Before the ballet begins, let's take a moment to examine the dancers — the chromosomes.

Within eukaryotic cells, DNA tends to exist in one of two forms: as chromatin or within chromosomes. As detailed in Figure 7-1, chromatin is a loose, largely unraveled state in which the DNA double helix coils around protein cores (called histones), but is otherwise accessible. DNA exists as chromatin during interphase to allow access to the genes during normal cell growth. During mitosis, however, the cell gets meticulous with its DNA, condensing the chromatin into a highly organized, multiple coiled structure called a chromosome.

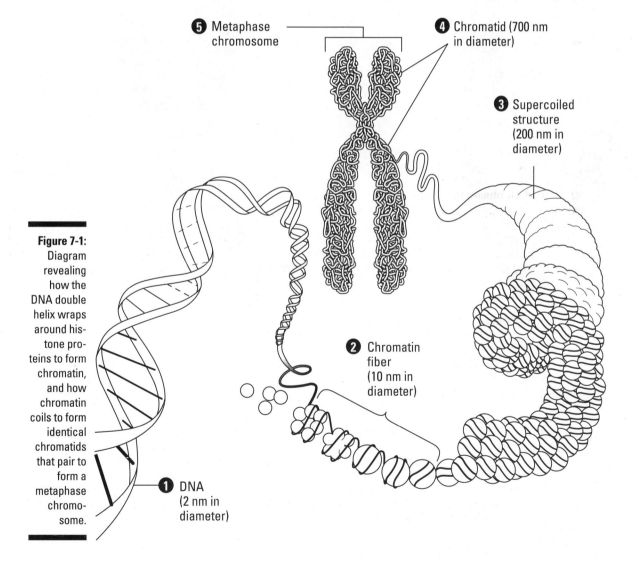

5 Metaphase chromosome

4 Chromatid (700 nm in diameter)

3 Supercoiled structure (200 nm in diameter)

2 Chromatin fiber (10 nm in diameter)

1 DNA (2 nm in diameter)

Figure 7-1: Diagram revealing how the DNA double helix wraps around histone proteins to form chromatin, and how chromatin coils to form identical chromatids that pair to form a metaphase chromosome.

Prior to S phase, when the cell has only one copy of its genome, there is only enough DNA to form one chromatid of a complete chromosome. However, mitosis occurs after S phase, so each condensed chromosome is built of two sister chromatids, identical copies of one another (see Figure 7-2). The sister chromatids join at a central structure called the *centromere,* so that a complete chromosome forms an X-shaped structure. Recall that during both interphase and M phase the cell is diploid, containing two complete sets of DNA. Each set contains the same total number of genes, but the exact versions of the genes (the *alleles*) may differ between sets. So, when the DNA condenses during mitosis, each chromosome has two equal but non-identical representatives; we call them homologous chromosomes.

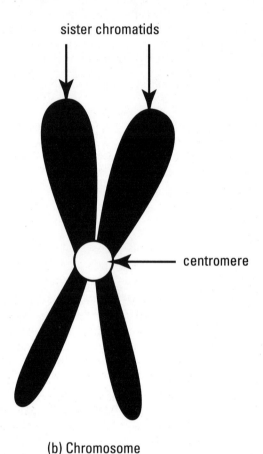

Figure 7-2:
A single chromatid, prior to DNA replication, is shown in (a). After replication, identical sister chro-matids can join at a centromere, as shown in (b).

(a) Chromosome before copying

(b) Chromosome after copying

Got it? Good. The ballet is beginning. As you read, follow the dance in the list below as well as in Figure 7-3.

✔ **Prophase:** Mitosis (and M phase) opens with prophase, which is easier to remember if you recall that "pro-" can mean "before." Prophase occurs before the other phases, and for good reason, as you will see. Several things occur during prophase that make the remainder of mitosis possible. First, the DNA condenses from chromatin into discrete chromosomes. Since the parent cell must be certain to give each daughter cell the right genetic inheritance, it only makes sense to organize the DNA into neatly wrapped packages. Second, small organelles called centrioles, initially located near the nucleus, begin to migrate toward opposite sides or "poles" of the cell. The migrating centrioles begin to organize microtubules into spindle fibers that will choreograph the movements of the chromosomes in later phases of mitosis. Third, the membrane enclosing the nucleus (the nuclear envelope) breaks down, exposing the chromosomes to the cytoplasm. Why expose the precious DNA in this way? The chromosomes must be divided among two new daughter cells — the nuclear envelope would only get in the way, and the show must go on.

✔ **Metaphase:** Following prophase, the chromosomes really begin to dance. "Meta-" here means "across," as the chromosomes become aligned across the centerline of the parent cell, called the "metaphase plate." You may also remember this phase because it sounds a bit like "middle-phase," during which the chromosomes line up across the middle of the cell. This dramatic alignment of the chromosomes is enforced by the spindle fibers. One end of each fiber is attached to a centriole, and the other is attached to the centromere of a chromosome. All those chromosomal dancers neatly aligned on the metaphase plate look poised to do something dramatic, don't they?

✔ **Anaphase:** Consider that analyzing something essentially involves taking it apart, and you will more easily remember that anaphase, the climax of the chromosomal ballet, involves splitting chromosomes into their identical, sister chromatids. In a heartrending moment, cruel spindle fibers pull twin sisters apart, their arms still outstretched towards each other as they are towed toward opposite sides of the cell. All that remains is to seal them off from one another completely. Forever.

✔ **Telophase:** The final act of the chromosomal ballet is telophase, during which the landscape of the parent cell begins to look a lot more like two daughter cells, twin sisters beginning dramatic new lives of their own. Nuclear envelopes form around the clusters of separated chromatids; the chromatids unravel into chromatin. Finally, a furrow forms at the center of the cell, darkly suggestive of a final cleavage into two separate cells as the curtain falls on mitosis (P-MAT exits, stage left).

✔ **Cytokinesis:** Mitosis concludes with telophase, but the story has an epilogue in cytokinesis (P-MAT exited, stage left; cytokinesis is the stage that was left). During this last stage of M phase, the cleavage furrow that appeared during telophase constricts along the center of the parent cell, entirely separating it into two daughter cells. In plants, cytokinesis doesn't involve the contraction of a cleavage furrow; instead, the daughter cells are separated when a slab of new cell wall, called a cell plate, forms between the two cells. In both plants and animals, each daughter cell has an identical, diploid set of chromosomes, though each daughter has only one copy of this set. After division, each daughter cell enters interphase, and the cycle renews itself.

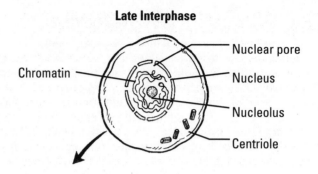

Late Interphase

Chromatin

Nuclear pore

Nucleus

Nucleolus

Centriole

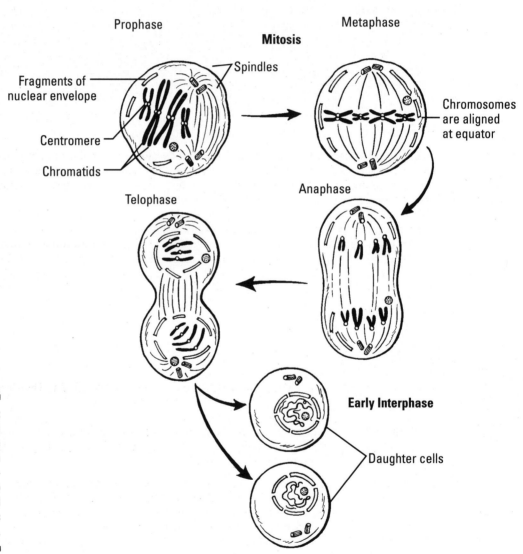

Prophase

Metaphase

Mitosis

Spindles

Fragments of
nuclear envelope

Centromere

Chromatids

Chromosomes
are aligned
at equator

Anaphase

Telophase

Early Interphase

Daughter cells

Figure 7-3:
Schematic
showing the
transition
from inter-
phase to
mitosis, and
the phases
of mitosis.

Shuffling Genetic Information

As beautiful as the chromosomal ballet of mitosis may be, there's something incomplete about the storyline. We eukaryotes aren't all identical sisters. From the earliest single-celled organisms to the present cornucopia of life, natural selection has acted upon a wondrous array of genetic variation. Genetic variation, within and between species, is necessary for evolution in response to the ever-changing conditions of life. Eukaryotic organisms have evolved powerful means to continually create new mixtures of genes from generation to generation, ensuring that whatever the conditions, at least some members of a species will prosper. The most important of these means is sexual reproduction.

Sexually reproducing organisms are created from the combination of two sets of genetic information. One set is contributed from each of two sex cells, called *gametes*. Typically, gametes come in the form of eggs (from females) and sperm (from males). Each gamete contains one complete set of genes, but the exact version of each gene may vary from one gamete to the next. During fertilization, the genes (within the DNA of the chromosomes) pool together to form a zygote, the first cell of the newly generated organism. In humans, for example, each parent contributes a gamete containing 23 chromosomes, so that the cells in the body of each new human contain 46 chromosomes — two full sets. Human cells (and other eukaryotic cells, for that matter) with two sets of chromosomes are called somatic cells, and are diploid. The sex cells, called gametes or germ cells, are haploid.

Meiosis is the process of creating haploid sex cells (gametes) from diploid cells. Meiosis is similar in many ways to mitosis, as you will see, and offers key opportunities to mix and match the combinations of genes within each gamete, helping to create the genetic variation so critical to evolutionary adaptation.

Meiosis consists of two rounds of cell division. The first round of division, meiosis I, begins with a single diploid cell and ends with two haploid cells. The second round of division, meiosis II, starts with these two haploid cells and concludes with four haploid cells, each of which goes on to become a gamete. To simplify the chromosomal bookkeeping, diploid cells are sometimes called "2n," and haploid cells dubbed "n," where "n" refers to one complete set of genes.

Meiosis 1

Meiosis I begins with a single cell, destined for sex. The cell is diploid (2n). Division proceeds through phases like those of mitosis (dust off your P-MAT):

✔ **Prophase I:** As in mitosis, the chromatin condenses into chromosomes. Once this occurs, the first grand opportunity for genetic recombination (shuffling of the genes to produce variation) promptly presents itself.

The cell is still diploid, so there are two versions of each chromosome. Such corresponding chromosome pairs are called *homologous chromosomes.* Each chromosome, in turn, consists of two identical sister chromatids, joined at a centromere. In an event called *synapsis,* homologous chromosomes line up alongside each other, forming "tetrads." Each tetrad (group of four) consists of four chromatids, two sister chromatids per homologous chromosome. And here is where the first act of genetic recombination within meiosis takes place, in a process called *crossing over.* During crossing over, nonsister chromatids (from opposing homologous chromosomes) exchange genetic information, as shown in Figure 7-4. Exchange occurs at precisely corresponding spots on each chromatid, resulting in clean, tit for tat swaps. Crossing over recombines genetic information between chromosomes, leaving each with a complete set of genes, but an entirely different combination of alleles.

Following crossing over, prophase I moves on largely as in mitosis; the nucleoli and nuclear envelope break down, centrioles migrate toward opposite poles of the cell, and the spindle begins to assemble.

✔ **Metaphase I:** Again, as in mitosis, pairs of homologous chromosomes line up at the centerline of the cell, called the metaphase plate. Here, the second grand recombination takes place. The two chromosomes of a homologous pair are destined for opposing sides of the dividing cell. One half of all the chromosomes were inherited from a male parent, and the other, homologous half were inherited from a female parent. But these historical distinctions between the chromosomes fall away during metaphase I, in a process called *independent assortment.* At the metaphase plate, each pair of homologous chromosomes lines up randomly, to one side or the other, independently of the other pairs. Just as the combinations of alleles within chromosomes were shuffled during crossing over, the combinations of maternally- versus paternally-inherited chromosomes are shuffled during independent assortment.

✔ **Anaphase I:** Spindle fibers span the space between centrioles at either pole of the cell and the metaphase plate, connecting to the independently assorted chromosomes aligned there. The spindle contract, segregating the pairs of homologous chromosomes, one complete set to a side.

✔ **Telophase I:** As the spindle disassembles, a nuclear envelope forms around the single set of chromosomes at either side of the dividing cell. A cleavage furrow constricts at the center of the cell, beginning to physically separate the two sides. In most cases, the division proceeds all the way through cytokinesis, although there are exceptions in which cytokinesis doesn't occur until the end of the second round of division. In plant cells, cell wall formation takes the place of cleavage furrows and cytokinesis. In either case, meiosis I concludes here, with two haploid cells, each containing one recombined set of chromosomes. Each chromosome consists of two sister chromatids. For now.

Meiosis II

Meiosis II splits the sisters, yielding four haploid cells bearing one chromatid apiece:

✔ **Prophase II:** Once more, chromatin condenses, nuclear envelopes disappear, centrioles migrate and spindle forms.

✔ **Metaphase II:** Chromosomes align at the metaphase plate, connected by spindle to centrioles at the poles.

✔ **Anaphase II:** The centromeres of the chromosomes are cleaved, and sister chromatids are segregated to opposing sides of the dividing cell.

✔ **Telophase II:** Again, the spindle dissolves, nuclear envelopes form, chromosomes uncoil, and cytokinesis (or cell wall formation) occurs. Four haploid cells now stand, where once there was but a single diploid cell. The overall progress through both rounds of meiosis is summarized in Figure 7-4. After meiosis II is complete, the four haploid cells go on to develop into gametes, eventually to fuse with other gametes during fertilization. The diploid zygote produced from this union will possess a unique combination of genes, thanks to crossing over, independent assortment, and the all-too-familiar unpredictability of male-female pairing.

If you're a cynical, glass-is-half empty sort, you may be thinking to yourself that with all the complicated machinery involved in two rounds of meiosis, something is bound to go wrong every now and then. Well, sure, it happens. In particular, things can go wrong during the anaphase stages of meiosis I or II. During anaphase I, when one homologous chromosome should be segregated to each cell, both chromosomes may end up in one cell, leaving the other cell with nothing. This kind of mishap is called *nondisjunction.* Nondisjunction can also occur during anaphase II, yielding one cell with both sister chromatids and another cell with neither sister. The results of nondisjunction during either round of meiosis are shown in Figure 7-4. Nondisjunction is a rather serious sort of monkey wrench in the works of sexual reproduction. Having too many or too few chromosomes is . . . well . . . *bad.* Cells unlucky enough to find themselves in this kind of situation usually die. Occasionally, however, the cells do not die, but go on to form gametes. If nondisjunctive gametes are fertilized, and the resulting zygotes are viable, they can go on to produce organisms with serious genetic disorders, several of which are summarized in Table 7-1. For example, trisomy 21 is a serious genetic disease in humans who possess three copies of chromosome 21 (instead of the normal diploid set of two). Trisomy 21 results in Down syndrome, a condition associated with problems in mental and physical development as well as accelerated aging. A brief inspection of Table 7-1 reveals that many of the chromosomal number disorders involve additional or missing sex chromosomes, such as in Klinefelter's, Turner, Jacob and Triple-X syndromes. It turns out that cells are better able to survive abnormal numbers in the sex chromosomes than in the autosomes, so sex chromosome nondisjunction is more likely to produce viable offspring. In the case of the Y chromosome, this situation is easiest to explain, because that chromosome contains fewer genes (about 300) than the other chromosomes do. In the case of X chromosome abnormalities, it may be that there are mechanisms available that help to regulate gene expression in such a way that the effects of the change in chromosome number are reduced. Fortunately, evolution has selected for cells that deal excellently with the intricacies of meiosis, so the glass is usually half full.

Table 7-1	Genetic Disorders Associated with Nondisjunction
Disorder	*Chromosomal Abnormality*
Down's syndrome	Three copies of chromosome 21 (trisomy 21).
Edward's syndrome	Extra copy of chromosome 18 (trisomy 18)
Klinefelter's syndrome	Extra X chromosome in a male (XXY)
Turner syndrome	Missing X chromosome in a female (X)
Jacob syndrome	Extra Y chromosome in a male (XYY)
Triple-X syndrome	Extra X chromosome in a female (XXX)
Pallister-Killian syndrome	Four copies of chromosome 12 (tetrasomy 12)
Patau syndrome	Three copies of chromosome 13 (trisomy 13)

A. Crossing Over

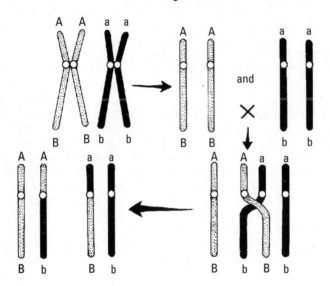

B. Normal Meiosis

Meiosis I

Meiosis II

C. Abnormal Meiosis

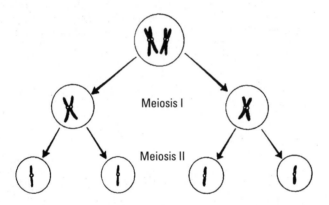

Or

Figure 7-4: Crossing over (a). Normal progress through meiosis I and II. (b) Abnormal meiosis (nondisjunction) during meiosis I or II (c).

Chapter 8

Answering Questions about Cell Functions

Apparently, cells divide not only to continue the wondrous pageant of life, but also so that you can be tested on the details of those divisions. The questions in this chapter focus on the material covered in Chapter 7. Multiple choice and free-essay response questions and answers are provided. In addition, you'll find a summary of a two-part lab on mitosis and meiosis that is part of the AP Biology curriculum.

Pointers for Practice

The main points of Chapter 7 are:

✔ **Eukaryotic cells participate in a circular pattern of life-stages, alternately growing and dividing into identical daughter cells.** The growth stages of this "cell cycle" occur during interphase, and are G_1, S, and G_2 (growth 1, synthesis of DNA, growth 2). The division stages occur during M phase, which follows G_2, and consists of mitosis (chromosome division) and cytokinesis (physical separation of cells).

✔ **Mitosis is the process of dividing a cell's genetic information into two identical copies, to be passed on to genetically identical daughter cells.** Cells are diploid at both the beginning of mitosis and after its completion. Mitosis proceeds through four phases: prophase, metaphase, anaphase, and telophase.

The phases of mitosis can be remembered with the mnemonic "P-MAT" or "Put My Answer There."

✔ **Meiosis is the process of converting a diploid cell, through two successive rounds of division, into four, non-identical haploid cells.** These haploid cells go on to become gametes (haploid sex cells). Each of the two rounds of meiosis consists of prophase, metaphase, anaphase, and telophase.

Meiosis is in many ways like two successive rounds of mitosis, without pausing for interphase (most importantly, without an intervening S phase).

✔ **Different processes during the first round of meiosis contribute greatly to genetic variation between gametes.** This variation is crucial to the process of evolutionary adaptation. During prophase I, homologous chromosomes undergo synapsis and crossing over, in which corresponding portions of non-sister chromatids exchange genetic information. During metaphase I, homologous chromosomes align at the metaphase plate, sorting independently of one another to one side or the other of the plate. Consequently, at the end of the first round of meiosis, each new cell contains a random mixture of maternally- and paternally-inherited chromosomes.

✔ **Very occasionally, homologous chromosomes or sister chromatids may be sorted improperly during either round of meiosis, resulting in one cell with too many chromosomes/chromatids and one cell with too few.** The name for this phenomenon is nondisjunction. Nondisjunction usually results in cell death, but it can also be the source of faulty gametes that, if fertilized, may go on to produce organisms with severe genetic disorders.

Testing Your Knowledge

This section contains multiple choice and free-essay response sections to test your knowledge of the material in Chapter 7, and also includes a summary of the AP Biology lab on mitosis and meiosis.

Answering multiple-choice questions

Directions: Each question is followed by five possible answers. Choose the best answer.

1. Which of the following cell types are haploid?

    I. Gamete

    II. Zygote

    III. Germ cell

    (A) I only

    (B) II only

    (C) III only

    (D) I and II only

    (E) I and III only

2. Klinefelter syndrome is found in males with two copies of the X chromosome and one copy of the Y chromosome. The occurrence of this syndrome most likely implies an error in which of the following processes?

    (A) Mitotic anaphase

    (B) Meiotic prophase

    (C) Cytokinesis

    (D) Meiotic anaphase

    (E) Mitotic telophase

Questions 3 through 7 describe cells most likely found in one of the following processes:

(A) Mitosis

(B) Meiosis I

(C) Interphase

(D) Cytokinesis

(E) Meiosis II

3. Endothelial cell that is replicating its DNA

4. A haploid spermatocyte (developing sperm cell) in a seminiferous tubule of the testes

5. A cell within an aggressive, malignant brain tumor, with chromosomes aligned at the center of the cell

6. An immature oocyte within a follicle of an ovary, just beginning the process of developing into an egg cell

7. Two closely connected skin cells, each half the size of a normal skin cell

Questions 8 through 12 refer to the following experiment:

Different cells are isolated from different tissues of the same species of eukaryotic organisms. The total DNA content of each cell is measured, with the results in Table 8-1.

Table 8-1	DNA Content Results
Cell Sample	*Total DNA Content, in nanograms*
#1	5.1 ± 0.2
#2	2.4 ± 0.1
#3	6.7 ± 0.1
#4	9.8 ± 0.2
#5	2.7 ± 0.2

Each isolated cell was one of the following types. (*Hint:* Consider *all* the data within the table before answering questions 8 through 12.)

(A) Skin cell in G1 phase

(B) Lung cell in G2 phase

(C) Skin cell in S phase

(D) Mature sperm cell

(E) Mature egg cell

8. What type is cell #1?

9. What type is cell #2?

10. What type is cell #3?

11. What type is cell #4?

12. What type is cell #5?

13. Which of the following processes does *not* contribute to genetic variation?

   (A) Crossing over

   (B) Genetic mutation

   (C) Fertilization

   (D) Mitosis

   (E) Independent assortment

Answering free-essay response questions

Directions: Answer the following question in essay form, not in outline form, using complete sentences. Diagrams may be used to supplement answers, but diagrams alone are not adequate.

1. Compare and contrast the processes of mitosis and meiosis, focusing especially on the actions of chromosomes, the haploid or diploid states of the cells, and on the overall function of each process.

Lab on mitosis and meiosis

The AP Biology lab on mitosis and meiosis involves two separate parts. Each part involves the examination of prepared sample slides under a microscope. The first part focuses on cells undergoing mitosis, and the second part examines the effects of crossing over during meiosis.

In the first part, the slides contain samples of onion root tips and whitefish blastula. What these two tissues have in common is that essentially all the cells within them are undergoing mitotic division. Therefore, among the large collection of cells visible in each sample, one finds representatives at each stage of mitosis. The chromosomes are clearly visible in these samples, so it is possible to assign different cells to the various stages of mitosis based on the characteristic patterns of the chromosomes at each stage. Furthermore, each of the hundreds of cells on a slide can be considered a random sample. Therefore, by counting the number of cells in each stage, one can estimate the amount of time it takes to pass through the different stages of mitosis. For example, since a typical mitotic division in an onion root tip cell takes 24 hours (1,440 minutes), one can make the following calculation:

(percent of cells in phase) × (1,440 minutes) = minutes in that phase

In the second part of the lab, one observes the effects of crossing over during meiosis. These effects are seen in slides containing spore cells (haploid reproductive cells) from the fungus, *Sordaria*. Different haploid strains of *Sordaria* carry different genes for the color of spore cells (dark-colored versus light-colored). When "filament" structures from different strains meet, fertilization occurs, forming a diploid zygote. The zygote replicates its DNA, undergoes meiosis to form four haploid cells, each of which undergoes mitosis, resulting in eight haploid "ascospores" (Note: usually, eukaryotic cells are *diploid* when undergoing mitosis!). These eight spore cells line up within sac-like "asci" structures. Because the zygote was formed from two different haploid strains, each asci will contain ascospores of two different colors. The linear arrangement of spores within an asci reflects the progressive segregation of the zygote's chromosomes during meiosis and mitosis. Therefore, one can determine if crossing over of the spore color gene occurred during meiosis simply by examining the arrangement of spore colors within each group of eight. If the dark and light spores occur in continuous stretches of four (e.g., four dark in a row, then four light in a row), then no crossing over occurred. Any other arrangement of the spores implies that crossing over did occur, as shown in Figure 8-1.

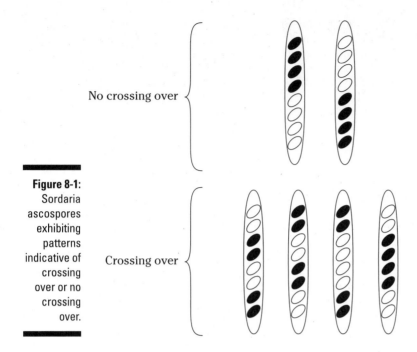

No crossing over

Crossing over

Figure 8-1:
Sordaria
ascospores
exhibiting
patterns
indicative of
crossing
over or no
crossing
over.

Checking Your Work

Check to see whether you put your haploids and your diploids in the proper places. Be sure to read through all the answers and explanations, because the AP Biology exam will be unforgiving towards those who confuse mitosis with meiosis.

Answers and explanations for the multiple-choice questions are:

1. The answer is (E). Germ cells and gametes are interchangeable terms for haploid sex cells. A zygote is the diploid product of fertilization, the fusion of two gametes.

2. The best answer is (D). Individuals with too many or too few chromosomes typically developed from a zygote that was formed with a nondisjunctive gamete. Nondisjunction is the unequal division of chromosomes or chromatids during meiosis. Although answer (B) is possible, because an error during meiotic prophase could conceivably lead to nondisjunction, answer (D) is more likely; meiotic anaphase is the step wherein chromosomes (anaphase I) or chromatids (anaphase II) are divided.

3. The answer is (C). A cell that is replicating its DNA is engaging in DNA synthesis, the defining event of S phase, which is itself a part of interphase.

4. (E) is the best answer. Sperm cells are haploid gametes, so developing sperm cells are likely undergoing meiosis. Since the spermatocyte described in the question is haploid, it must have undergone meiosis I already, and is therefore most likely to be undergoing meiosis II.

5. The most likely answer is (A). Cancerous cells, like those found within malignant tumors, are characterized by rapid, uncontrolled mitotic division. That's what makes them so dangerous. Therefore, such a cell would very likely be undergoing mitosis, and the presence of chromosomes lined up at the center of the cell strongly suggests that the cell is in mitotic metaphase.

6. The best answer is (B). Egg cells are haploid gametes, but an immature egg cell (i.e., an oocyte) that is *just beginning* the process of development into an egg cell would still be undergoing the diploid-to-haploid conversion of meiosis I.

7. (D) is the clear answer here. The facts that 1) these two cells are still connected, and 2) that they are only half the size of a normal cell, scream out to be recognized as hallmarks of cell in cytokinesis, the physical division of cells that have just undergone mitosis.

8. The answer is (A). Within error, cell #1 has half the total DNA content of the maximum content observed in any cell (5 nanograms compared to a maximum of 10 nanograms). Since the maximum DNA content most likely corresponds to a diploid cell with two identical copies of the DNA, then cell #1, with half that amount, must correspond to either 1) a diploid cell with only one copy of the DNA (i.e., in G_1), or 2) a haploid cell with two copies of the DNA (i.e., between meiosis I and II). Since *mature* gametes will have completed meiosis II, the only remaining possibility is (A), a skin cell in G_1.

9. There are two ways to be right here. Soak this up — you won't be so lucky on the AP exam. Answers (D) or (E) could both be correct. Cells #2 and #5 have the least total DNA content observed for any cell, and are within error of one another. Furthermore, they have one fourth the maximum DNA content observed for any cell. Since the maximum DNA content corresponds to a diploid cell with two copies of the DNA, a cell with one fourth the maximum is likely haploid, with only one copy. Only cells that have undergone both rounds of meiosis (e.g., gametes) are in this position. Mature sperm and egg cells are both gametes, so either answer could apply.

10. The answer is (C). Cell #3 has the only "weird" value for total DNA content, one that is not a clean multiple of the minimum content. Furthermore, cell #3 has the second highest total DNA content, intermediate between cells #1 and #4. Since we assigned cell #1 to G_1, and the maximum content likely corresponds to a diploid cell with two copies of the DNA, then cell #3 is most likely diploid, with somewhere between one and two copies of the DNA. In other words, it is probably in S phase, replicating its diploid genome.

11. Pick (B) here. Based on its maximum observed content of total DNA, and on its relationship to the other observed DNA contents, this cell is most likely diploid, with two full copies of the DNA, and therefore resides in G_2.

12. As with the answer for question #9 and for the same reasons, either (D) or (E) are correct answers here.

13. The best answer is (D). Mitosis is simply the passage of identical DNA inheritances to each of two new daughter cells. Crossing over and independent assortment are the processes occurring in meiosis I that are critical to creating genetic variation within sexually reproducing species. Fertilization also contributes to variation because it is random; any egg might be fertilized by any of millions of sperm, each with a different set of alleles. Mutation creates genetic diversity within *all* organisms.

Here is a model answer for the free-essay response question:

1. Mitosis and meiosis are both processes of eukaryotic cell division. Although they feature similarities in the movements of chromosomes and in the machinery used to perform those movements, the details of these processes and their overall functions are very different.

Mitosis is the process of cell division used for the growth and maintenance of multicellular organisms. Mitosis begins with a diploid cell containing two identical copies of the genetic information. These identical copies are stored within chromosomes, each of which consists of two identical sister chromatids. When such a diploid cell undergoes mitosis, it proceeds through four phases, called prophase, metaphase, anaphase, and telophase. The result of this progression is that the sister chromatids that make up each chromosome are separated from one another and assigned to each of two new, genetically identical daughter cells. Each new cell is diploid, but contains only one set of the genetic information.

Meiosis is the process of cell division used to produce gametes, cells that combine with other gametes to form zygotes in the process of sexual reproduction. Like mitosis, meiosis begins with a diploid cell containing two identical copies of the genetic information, stored as the sister chromatids of each chromosome. Furthermore, there are two non-identical versions of each chromosome, one from each parent, and these non-identical pairs are called homologous chromosomes. When a diploid cell passes through meiosis, it undergoes two rounds of division, meiosis I and meiosis II. Each round is similar to the single round of mitosis, in that it consists of prophase, metaphase, anaphase, and telophase. However, the details and functions of the divisions differ.

During prophase of the first meiotic division, homologous chromosomes enter synapsis, in which the chromosome pairs physically align with one another. In this state, the homologous chromosomes undergo a process called crossing over, in which corresponding non-sister chromatids from homologous chromosomes swap genetic information. During metaphase of the first meiotic division, homologous chromosomes align at the metaphase plate, with maternally-inherited and paternally-inherited chromosomes lining up randomly with respect to one another. In the ensuing anaphase, each daughter cell receives a mixture of maternal and paternal chromosomes, and is haploid. In the second round of meiosis, each of the two new haploid cells divides, separating the sister chromatids of each chromosome. The result is four haploid cells, each containing one non-identical copy of the genetic information. The processes of crossing over and of independent assortment of homologous chromosomes are vital to providing genetic variation among the haploid gametes. This genetic variation is critical to the long-term survivability of a given species, because the variation is the raw material for natural selection, allowing individuals with more favorable combinations of traits to thrive under changing environmental conditions. Because both mitosis and meiosis involve separating chromosomes between dividing cells, the two processes can both suffer from nondisjunction, the improper separation of chromosomes during division. Nondisjunction can lead to cells that have only a single copy of a chromosome (monsomy) or cells that possess three copies of a chromosome (trisomy). Most such cells die. When nondisjunction occurs during meiosis, it leads to gametes with an improper allotment of chromosomes. If these gametes survive, and go on to fertilization, they can lead to zygotes with chromosome number abnormalities. Most such zygotes die, but some can survive, yielding offspring with genetic disorders.

Chapter 9

Cell Respiration: Energized and at the Ready!

● ●

In This Chapter

▶ Following the flow of energy from light into glucose through the power of photosynthesis

▶ Finding out how cells use respiration to unlock the energy stored in glucose

▶ Introducing the cast of molecular characters that shuttle energy about

● ●

*P*reparing for the AP Biology exam takes energy. Just being alive takes energy. This chapter is all about energy — trapping it, releasing it, and making it available for use. Plants are pretty helpful in this energy business because they capture energy from light. Predictably, greedy nonplants just go ahead and steal that useful energy from plants. But we nonplants aren't all bad. We give back to plants the stuff they need to keep trapping that precious energy for us and for themselves. The whole arrangement works out nicely for everyone concerned. The details of this energy-trapping and energy-releasing exchange are many, but fortunately, they follow some easy-to-remember patterns. Muster a little energy, read on, and find out.

Powering Up

Look, there's no denying it. Trapping and releasing energy is a complex business. Even the terms for these kinds of processes (photosynthesis and cellular respiration) can make the hair stand up on the back of your neck like a whiff of H_2SO_4. Hint: a smidgen of chemistry lurks in these waters (in these H_2Os, if you like). But don't worry. A little dab of Chapter 3 will do ya'. And understanding photosynthesis will help you understand cellular respiration (and vice-versa), because the two are opposite sides of the same coin. Wade through the chemistry, but keep your eye on the big picture; the AP testing fiends like to ask free-response questions about photosynthesis and cellular respiration. Now you know. Power on.

Photosynthesis

The sun pours sugar on everyone. Okay, not exactly, but thanks to photosynthesis, it's not so far from the truth. Wrapped up into one big reaction burrito, photosynthesis is the arrow in the following chemical equation:

Light (energy) + 6 H_2O + 6 CO_2 →$C_6H_{12}O_6$ + 6 O_2

Yes, we're already speaking in chemistry. But check out those friendly reactants and products: light, water, carbon dioxide, sugar (glucose), and oxygen. And the equation echoes the literal meaning of the word photosynthesis, or "making stuff with light." Unwrap the photosynthetic burrito and you'll find two groups of reactions:

✔ **Light-dependent reactions:** The light-dependent reactions capture light (usually, sunlight) and turn it into chemical energy.

✔ **Light-independent reactions:** The light-independent reactions store this energy in chemical bonds within glucose molecules.

Photosynthesis is so important that plant cells devote an entire organelle to the job: the chloroplast. Chloroplasts are evolutionary cousins to mitochondria, as is evident from comparing their structures (and their functions — but more on that later), as shown in Figure 9-1. Chloroplasts are surrounded by an outer, double membrane. Inside the chloroplast sit stacks of membranous discs called thylakoids. These funky discs contain two kinds of colored pigments that specialize in harvesting energy from light: chlorophyll a and chlorophyll b. Chlorophyll a absorbs all colors of light except green, and gives the lush leaves of summer their green appearance. Chlorophyll b absorbs all but red light, and accounts for the fiery leaves of autumn, when chlorophyll a has left the scene. Chlorophyll is the headquarters for the light-dependent reactions. Fluid surrounding the stacked thylakoids is called stroma. The light-independent reactions occur in the stroma. See how everything has its place?

(a) Mitochondria

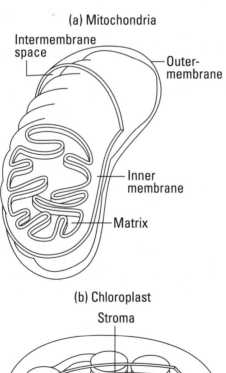

(b) Chloroplast

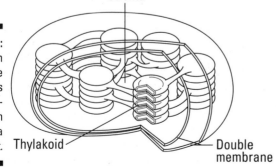

Figure 9-1:
Comparison
of the
structures
of a mito-
chondrion
and a
chloroplast.

Imagine that you are a bit of light energy that has traveled to Earth across the gaping vacuum of space from the sun, avoided rude reflection by some annoying cloud, and had the tremendous good fortune to land on a leaf. Within the bustling confines of a thylakoid disc, you burrow into a cluster of molecules called photosystem II. You zoom into a special reaction center called P_{680} that specializes in absorbing light of 680 nanometer wavelength — that's you. Waiting for you there are two lonely electrons. They're so elated to see you that they entirely absorb you, and leap into an *electron acceptor,* a sort of party zone for energized electrons. It's a wonderful welcome, but from this point on, you're basically a prisoner. Your gift of energy is mercilessly divided among a collection of energy-storage molecules who are all eager to get a piece of you. What follows is the story of how energy captured by photosystem II is taken for all it's worth in the process of photosynthesis. The whole sordid affair is depicted in Figure 9-2.

The two electrons dancing in the electron acceptor leave that joint, and are passed from one molecule to another in a series of redox reactions (check out Chapter 3). This series of reactions is called an electron transport chain (ETC). Each electron handoff releases a little bit of energy which is used to build the energy-storage molecule called adenosine triphosphate, or ATP. ATP is like the cash of the cell's energy economy; the cell can easily spend energy in the form of ATP to power important reactions. Using the energy of light to build ATP is called photophosphorylation, and it involves the bonding of a phosphate group to a molecule of adenosine diphosphate (ADP). ATP built in this way journeys from the thylakoid to the stroma, and feeds into the light-independent reactions; we'll see these ATPs again soon.

Depleted of energy now, the two exhausted electrons enter another cluster of molecules called photosystem I. Indeed, it seems backward to start from photosystem II and end up at photosystem I, but there you have it. Within photosystem I is another reaction center, P_{700}, which earns its title by absorbing light with a wavelength of 700 nanometers. When such light arrives, the electrons get another energy boost and jump up into another electron acceptor/party zone. At this point, two paths diverge in the woods. (More specifically, two paths diverge in the reaction center, within a chloroplast, within a leaf on a tree in the woods.) In cyclic light-dependent reactions, the electrons feed back into the ETC. In non-cyclic light-dependent reactions, the electrons get handed off down a shorter series of redox reactions. At the end of this shorter redox chain, the electrons are used to bond a hydrogen ion, H^+, to a molecule called $NADP^+$. The result is another kind of energy-storage molecule called NADPH. Like their ATP buddies, energy-rich NADPH molecules take a hike to the stroma to feed into the light-independent reactions.

The light-independent reactions await. But first, a few loose ends need tying. This whole business of making ATP and NADPH in the light-dependent reactions uses up electrons and H^+ ions. Where does the chloroplast get more? Simply put, it gets them from water, H_2O. Inside the thylakoid discs, more light energy is used to break apart H_2O molecules into electrons, H^+ and oxygen (O_2). This process of "splitting" water with light energy is called photolysis. The electrons and H^+ freed by photolysis keep the photosynthetic ball rolling. The freed oxygen diffuses out into the air. Conveniently, we non-plants get to breathe it. Ultimately, we use it in an eerie mirror image of photosynthesis called cellular respiration.

ATP and NADPH molecules power the light-independent reactions. These reactions form a circular pathway, and sometimes go by another, less descriptive name: the Calvin-Benson Cycle. This cycle is like a wheel, spinning in the stroma. Energy from ATP and NADPH turns this wheel in order to build glucose, a six-carbon sugar. Each glucose molecule requires six turns of the wheel. Plants get the carbon atoms for building glucose from carbon dioxide, CO_2. Remember how photolysis produced O_2 for greedy non-plants to use in cellular respiration? In a lovely turn of events, non-plants give off CO_2 as a waste product of cellular respiration. Thus, each side gets what it needs from the other. Of course, plants do cellular respiration too, but not enough to finance their photosynthesis habit. Maybe we non-plants aren't so greedy after all. Still, it's probably a good idea to talk nicely to your plants.

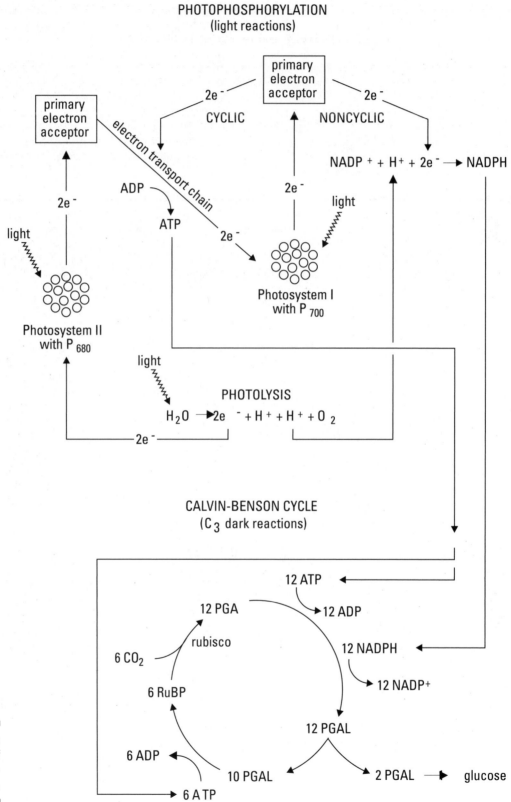

It ain't only trees, buddy

When we think of photosynthesis, many of us conjure up pastoral images of verdant glades, leafy bushes, and endless fields filled with swaying green grass. Well-informed others immediately imagine the lush green riches of the rainforests. But both these pictures are deeply incomplete.

Most of the experts agree that the majority of photosynthesis done on Earth goes on in the oceans. Don't forget that our planet is mostly covered with saltwater. These waters are teeming with algae and cyanobacteria, both of which are fully committed to the task of harvesting sunlight and converting it to chemical energy. The swimming members of marine food chains depend on these underappreciated organisms to support their energy needs. And we ungrateful humans depend on them to keep Earth's atmosphere rich in oxygen. So give a bacterium a break.

CO_2 molecules combine with a helper molecule called ribulose bisphosphate (RuBP) to form phosphoglycerate (PGA). These carbon-toting PGA molecules then draw on the energy stored in ATP and NADPH to form phosphoglyceraldehyde (PGAL). Each PGAL carries three carbon atoms that can be used to make glucose, so for every two PGAL molecules made, the plant cell racks up one molecule of glucose (ka-ching!). Guess what glucose is good for. That's right — cellular respiration.

Finally, in order to tie the ends of this reaction pathway together to make a cycle, PGAL must be regenerated into RuBP. The energy for this regeneration comes from ATP, the official energy currency of cells everywhere.

Cellular Respiration

With all that lovely energy trapped within its bonds, the glucose molecule is a valuable commodity in the cellular economy. Some animals eat plants to get at that energy. Other animals eat the plant-eaters. However organisms acquire their glucose, cellular respiration is the tool used to unlock the energy stored in that sugar. Now get this: Here's the equation that wrapped up photosynthesis into one big burrito:

$$\text{Light (energy)} + 6\ H_2O + 6\ CO_2 \rightarrow C_6H_{12}O_6 + 6\ O_2$$

When oxygen is present, this is how respiring cells eat the burrito:

$$C_6H_{12}O_6 + 6\ O_2 \rightarrow 6\ H_2O + 6\ CO_2 + \text{energy}$$

That's right, the two equations are mirror images. You can bet that all the reactions summed up in the arrows have some similarities, too. For cells with good access to oxygen, cellular respiration occurs in three steps: glycolysis, the Krebs cycle, and oxidative phosphorylation. (Respiration can also occur without oxygen, but we'll get to that later.) Where do you think respiring cells like to store the energy they get from glucose? Yup: ATP. For an overview of the pathways used in cellular respiration, take a gander at Figure 9-3, and don't be afraid to check back often.

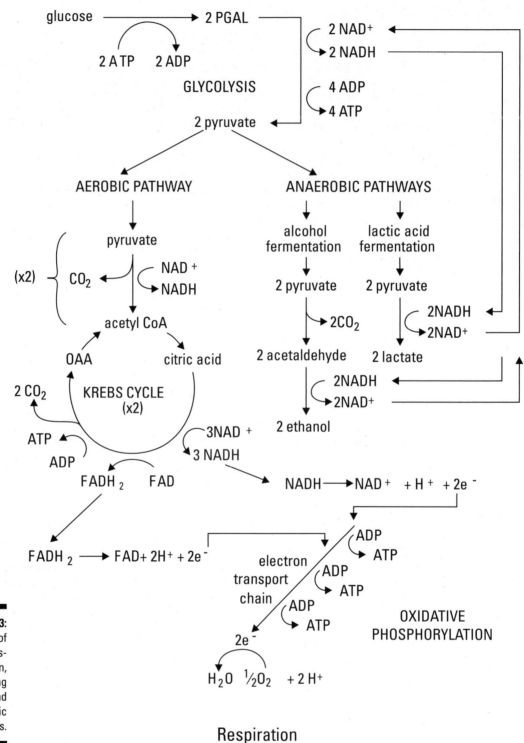

Figure 9-3:
Overview of cellular respiration, including aerobic and anaerobic pathways.

Respiration

Glycolysis

Glycolysis is another one of those chemical terms that reveals its own meaning: splitting sugar. This sugar-splitting takes place in the cytoplasm of a cell. Each glucose molecule is broken into two molecules of pyruvate, and generates a stored-energy profit of two ATPs and two molecules of NADH. NADH is very similar to its energy-storage cousin, NADPH. To realize these profits, the cell must invest two molecules of ATP at the front end of glycolysis. It's a good investment, because it makes a profit. That profit is small at this point (2 ATP, 2 NADH), but will grow tremendously later in the process of respiration, so stay tuned.

Krebs Cycle

There's a lot of energy still to be had, locked up in the bonds of pyruvate. The Krebs cycle is about getting at that remaining energy. The Krebs cycle is sometimes called the citric acid cycle; this is nice to know, because it reminds us that citric acid is one of the intermediates formed and used in the circular (cyclical) reaction pathway. The Krebs cycle takes place in the fluid inner "matrix" of an organelle called the mitochondrion. In a way, this business in the matrix is a mirror image of the Calvin-Benson cycle that took place within the fluid stroma of the chloroplast during photosynthesis.

On the trip from the cytoplasm to the mitochondrion, three-carbon pyruvate loses a carbon, in the form of CO_2. Chemically removing CO_2 is known as decarboxylation. This reaction produces one energy-storing NADH molecule, and leaves two remaining carbons in the form of acetyl-CoA. In the Krebs cycle, these remaining carbons will be similarly split off as CO_2 in order to produce other energy-storage molecules. All this CO_2 can eventually be recycled back into glucose during photosynthesis. So efficient!

Entering the Krebs cycle proper, the two carbons attached to acetyl-CoA are shuffled through a series of intermediates, including citric acid and oxaloacetate (OAA). This profitable little cycle generates a pile of energy-storage molecules: 3 NADH, 1 $FADH_2$ and 1 ATP. One the way, the two carbons depart as CO_2. At this point, the original glucose molecule is completely broken down, and its energy distributed among a fleet of energy-storage molecules. All that remains for the respiring cell is to convert the energy stored as NADH or $FADH_2$ into energy stored in the universal currency, ATP.

Oxidative phosphorylation

Take a breath, and consider the poor glucose molecule, born during photosynthesis, who has had the misfortune to end up in a respiring cell. He was cut in two during glycolysis, and completely disintegrated during the Krebs cycle. It seems that nothing remains of him — except energy. Energy from our hapless glucose friend has been handed out to a group of ATP, NADH, and $FADH_2$ molecules. The energy stored in ATP will go its merry way, to be used by the cell in powering any of countless reactions. The energy stored in NADH and $FADH_2$ awaits conversion into ATP. This conversion is what oxidative phosphorylation (adding phosphorous to ADP, with the help of oxygen) is all about. Where does oxidative phosphorylation take place? Again, we find a mirror image with photosynthesis. Just as light energy was originally captured within the thylakoid membrane of a chloroplast, that same energy now emerges in the form of ATP, in a process at the inner membrane of the mitochondrion, chloroplast's cousin. And just as the thylakoid membrane was host to an electron transport chain (ETC), so is the inner mitochondrial membrane.

At the front end of this respiratory ETC, NADH, and FADH$_2$ release their payloads in the form of high-energy electrons. These electrons descend the ETC, from one molecule to another, releasing energy as they go. Each step down the ETC is a redox reaction: One molecule gives up an electron (is oxidized), and another molecule gains an electron (is reduced). The energy freed from electrons as they step down this redox chain is used to build ATP. Building ATP with energy from electrons involves a process called *chemiosmosis*. The details of chemiosmosis are only few pages away.

The journey that began with glucose ends with ATP. But wait! We still have some electrons to deal with. You remember, the electrons that gave up their energy on the trip down the ETC. Cells can't tolerate free electrons just loitering about. What's a respiring cell to do? Hint: at the beginning of this section you were asked to "take a breath." If you did so, you imbibed a healthy dollop of oxygen, O$_2$. The point of taking in O$_2$ is to provide a home for unemployed electrons. The final step of oxidative phosphorylation is the combining of O$_2$ with electrons and H$^+$ ions to form water, H$_2$O. Hey, remember how photosynthesis split water in order to get electrons for capturing light energy? And so we finish with a final mirror image: Respiration gasps at its photosynthetic reflection, dancing on the surface of the water.

Working with oxygen

The "oxi" in oxidative phosphorylation means that the process requires oxygen. Oxygen serves as the final electron acceptor. Without it, oxidative phosphorylation and the Krebs cycle get plugged, and can't churn out ATP. Cellular respiration that uses oxygen is called "aerobic respiration." Having oxygen around to receive spent electrons is really handy, because it allows respiring cells to squeeze the most ATP out of their glucose: a net profit of 36 ATPs for each glucose molecule. But some cells live in oxygen-poor environments. And even cells that usually have plenty of oxygen sometimes have to make do. What then?

Working without oxygen

There are ways to eke out a few ATPs that don't require oxygen. We group these ways together under the banner of "anaerobic respiration." Since glycolysis doesn't require oxygen, anaerobically respiring cells still use glycolysis to cleave glucose into two pyruvate molecules. With the Krebs cycle blocked, pyruvate can enter two distinct pathways of anaerobic respiration: alcoholic fermentation or lactic acid fermentation.

Despite the earnest hopes of countless football-watching fraternity brothers, alcoholic fermentation does not occur in animal cells. However, many plants, bacteria, and fungi (most famously, yeast) do use this pathway. When three-carbon pyruvate enters the alcoholic fermentation pathway, it is split into two-carbon acetaldehyde and CO$_2$. Beer bubbles are proof of this CO$_2$. The cell then uses energy stored in NADH to convert acetaldehyde into ethyl alcohol (ethanol). Beer-drunk fraternity brothers are proof of this alcohol. By giving up its energy-rich electron, NADH is oxidized to NAD$^+$. By regenerating NAD$^+$, alcoholic fermentation drives glycolysis, because cleaving glucose requires NAD$^+$. The result is that each glucose molecule that undergoes alcoholic fermentation earns a net profit of two ATPs. It's something, but it ain't the 36 ATPs offered by aerobic respiration.

Fraternity brothers may not be able to create alcohol within their own cells while watching football, but they can certainly create lactic acid in those cells while playing football. When aerobically respiring cells are deprived of oxygen, they can shift to lactic acid fermentation as a backup pathway. In humans, this often occurs during strenuous exercise, when muscle cells simply can't get enough oxygen to maintain high rates of oxidative phosphorylation. The end product of this backup, lactic acid, accounts for the lingering burn you might feel in your leg muscles, days after a five-mile run. Lactic acid is made from pyruvate in a reaction that reduces NADH to NAD⁺. Regeneration of NAD⁺ allows glycolysis to continue, as in alcoholic fermentation, and the net result is again a mere two ATPs per glucose molecule. Not great, but it comes in handy in a pinch.

Each of the two anaerobic respiratory pathways yields two ATPs per molecule of glucose. By contrast, aerobic respiration yields 36 ATPs per glucose. Sure, oxidative phosphorylation is complicated, but do the math.

More in Stored Energy

This chapter buzzes with energy-storing molecules. Here are the important ones, so you can get a feel for who's who. You'll probably find it useful to review Figures 9-2 and 9-3 as you go through the list of players. Don't bother memorizing the full chemical names, unless you're into that sort of thing.

Storage molecules

Several molecules act as storage facilities. Here's a list of the ones you need to know:

- ✔ **ATP (adenosine triphosphate.):** ATP is the most useful form of energy within cells. Oodles of enzymes use ATP to do their catalytic thing. Most typically, energy is released from ATP by means of a hydrolysis reaction between the second and third of three phosphate groups attached to adenosine. This hydrolysis results in adenosine diphosphate (ADP) and a free phosphate group. ATP is regenerated simply by performing the reverse reaction (dehydration).

- ✔ **NADH (nicotinamide adenine dinucleotide):** Used during cellular respiration, NADH is the reduced form of a redox pair. The oxidized form of NADH is NAD⁺. NAD⁺ accepts electrons during glycolysis and the Krebs cycle. NADH gives up electrons during oxidative phosphorylation and both types of anaerobic respiration.

- ✔ **NADPH (nicotinamide adenine dinucleotide phosphate):** NADPH is just like NADH with an added phosphate. The extra "P" in the abbreviation stands for phosphate, but you might as well think of it as standing for "plant" or "photosynthesis," because that's where NADPH is used. The oxidized form of NADPH, NADP⁺, accepts electrons during the light-dependent reactions of photosynthesis. The reduced form, NADPH, gives up those electrons during the Calvin-Benson cycle.

- ✔ **FADH₂ (flavin adenine dinucleotide):** FADH₂ is similar to NADH/NADPH in overall structure, so it is unsurprising that it has a similar function: to shuttle electrons from one place to another. The oxidized form, FAD, accepts electrons during the Krebs cycle. The reduced form, FADH₂, feeds those electrons into the electron transport chain of oxidative phosphorylation.

Tapping into energy

By this point, you've been subjected to multiple rounds of applause for ATP, the universal energy currency of the cell. Okay, so how exactly is energy stored in the form of ATP? Why is ATP more "energetic" than ADP and free phosphate? Believe it or not, this question is still debated among scientists. The bond in ATP that is broken to form ADP and phosphate is a regular "phosphodiester" bond (P-O-P), and is certainly not magical. Nevertheless, the *difference* in total energy between an ATP "reactant" and the corresponding ADP + phosphate "products," depicted in Figure 9-4, is significant. Several explanations for this difference in energy have been proposed.

First, phosphate groups are negatively charged. Like charges repel each other, similar to like poles of two magnets. Pushing two negatively charged phosphates close together (during the formation of ATP from ADP and phosphate) may require an input of energy. When ATP is hydrolyzed to ADP and phosphate, this energy could be released. Second, electrons in the covalent bonds of phosphates may be able to move around more freely when they are apart than when they are confined to a phosphodiester bond. Any time electrons can move around more freely within covalent bonds, their energy is lower, so ATP hydrolysis may release this form of energy. In a similar way, the phosphate cleaved off of ATP can move more freely after cleavage, so its energy may be lower. Finally, water molecules in the environment of the cell may get along better with ADP and free phosphate than they do with ATP. In chemistry terms, getting along better means having lower energy. So, there are many ways in which energy might be stored in an ATP phosphodiester bond. Whatever the ultimate answer, it is clear that nature has selected ATP as its favorite little cubbyhole for short-term storage of energy.

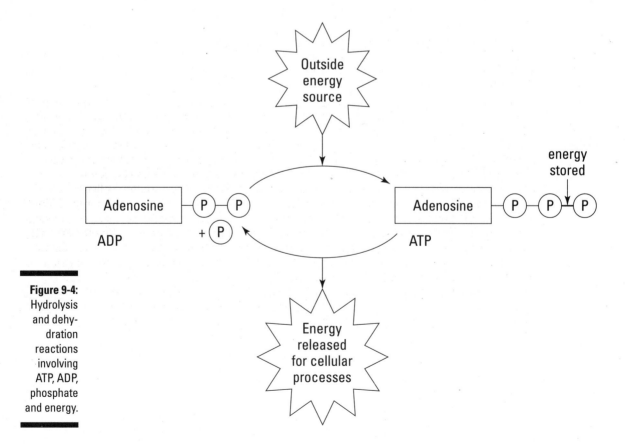

Figure 9-4:
Hydrolysis and dehydration reactions involving ATP, ADP, phosphate and energy.

Coupling Gets a Reaction

Recall for a moment the difference in ATP output achieved by aerobic versus anaerobic respiration: 36 ATPs for aerobic respiration, and 2 ATPs for each of the two anaerobic pathways. If that sounds like a big difference, that's because it is. The key features of aerobic respiration, the ones that give it its punch, are the electron transport chain (ETC) and chemiosmosis. Electrons give up their energy on the way down the ETC, and this energy is harnessed during chemiosmosis to power the production of ATP. This spectacularly effective ETC-chemiosmotic pairing deserves a closer look.

The Electron transport chain (ETC)

NADH and $FADH_2$ arrive at the inner mitochondrial membrane, fresh from the hectic front lines of glycolysis and the Krebs cycle. They carry with them precious electrons, ripped from the carcass of a poor glucose molecule who has since passed on to CO_2. Now what? Sure, they hand off the electrons to molecules of the ETC, and in turn are oxidized back into NAD^+ and FAD. But look closely: In addition to giving up electrons, NADH and $FADH_2$ give up H^+ ions when they are oxidized. As you've already discovered, energy is released from electrons as they move along the ETC, one redox reaction at a time. ETC proteins use that released energy to pump H^+ ions across the inner mitochondrial membrane, into the space between the inner and outer membranes. By the time the electrons meet their final acceptor, oxygen, all this H^+-pumping action has created a reservoir of H^+ ions in the intermembrane space. There's energy in that reservoir. Chemiosmosis taps that energy to make ATP.

Balancing act: coupled reactions and chemiosmosis

Chemiosmosis is the diffusion of ions across membranes. Fine, you say, but what is diffusion? *Diffusion* is the movement from an area of high concentration to one of lower concentration; this movement releases stored energy. By pumping H^+ ions into the intermembrane space, the ETC creates a reservoir of stored energy. And because H^+ ions have charge, creating that reservoir also creates a charge imbalance between the mitochondrial matrix and the intermembrane space. Given the opportunity, H^+ ions in the reservoir will rush back into the matrix to restore the imbalances in concentration and charge. The situation is like that of water pent up in a reservoir behind a dam. When people want to harness the energy of flowing water, they install a hydroelectric generator in the dam. To harness the energy of flowing ions, cells install their own kind of generator: ATP synthase. ATP synthase is an enzyme that spans the membrane between the matrix and the intermembrane space, as shown in Figure 9-5. The synthase contains a pore to allow H^+ ions to cross the membrane, restoring balance and releasing pent up energy. The beauty of ATP synthase is that it *couples* (joins) the released energy to the dehydration reaction that makes ATP from ADP and phosphate. The dehydration reaction requires an input of energy, so it needs to be coupled to another reaction that gives off energy. Moving H^+ across the membrane is just such a reaction. Voila!

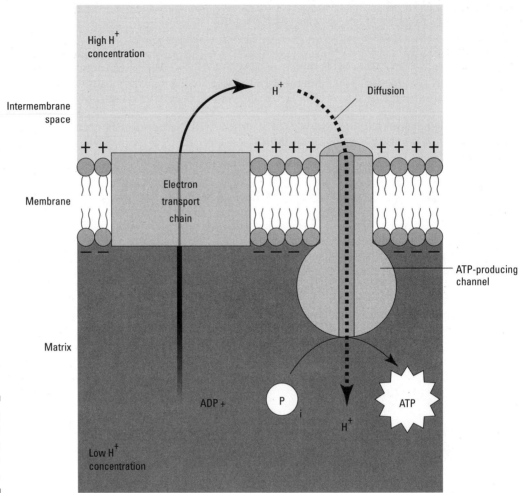

Figure 9-5:
Production
of ATP using
chemi-
osmosis.

The reactions of the electron transport chain and chemiosmosis are used by almost all
known organisms. Despite their central importance to the energy economy of cells, these
reactions have dangerous by-products. Particularly dangerous are *reactive oxygen species*,
chemical intermediates on the pathway that reduces oxygen to water during cellular respiration. For the most part, electron transfer is well-controlled within the electron transport
chain, the electrons safely hopping from one dedicated electron carrier molecule to another.
Still, some electron-carrying species are quite unstable, prone to prematurely dumping their
electrons in a phenomenon called "electron leakage." Leaked electrons can react directly
with oxygen to produce the reactive oxygen species *superoxide* and *peroxide* (see Figure 9-6).

Figure 9-6:
Reduction of molecular oxygen (O_2) to the reactive oxygen species, superoxide and peroxide. Transfer of one electron to O_2 yields superoxide, and transfer of a second electron yields peroxide.

$$O_2 \xrightarrow{\;e^-\;} O_2^{\cdot-} \xrightarrow{\;e^-\;} O_2^{2-}$$

Superoxide   Peroxide

These reactive oxygen species, and others resulting from them, can damage cells by reacting with proteins and DNA, creating faulty enzymes, genetic mutations and other undesirable molecules. Cancer and aging are two of the less palatable consequences of reactive oxygen species. To help combat these dangers, cells employ enzymes like superoxide dismutase, and antioxidant molecules like vitamins C and E. Eat your fruits and vegetables.

Chapter 10

Answering Questions about Cell Respiration

*T*ime for another Inquisition! This time, the questions focus on the material covered in Chapter 9. Multiple choice and free-essay response questions and answers are provided. In addition, an explanatory summary is given for a Lab on Cell Respiration.

Pointers for Practice

The main points of this chapter are the following:

✔ **Photosynthesis and cellular respiration are biochemical mirror images.** The reactants of one process are the products of the other:

- **Photosynthesis:** Light (energy) + 6 H_2O + 6 CO_2 → $C_6H_{12}O_6$ + 6 O_2

- **Respiration:** $C_6H_{12}O_6$ + 6 O_2 QQ → 6 H_2O + 6 CO_2 + energy

✔ **Both photosynthesis and cellular respiration involve many transfers of electrons between molecules.** Each of these transfers is an oxidation-reduction (redox) reaction. Molecules that give up electrons become oxidized, and are reducing agents. Molecules that receive electrons become reduced, and are oxidizing agents.

✔ **Photosynthesis consists of light-dependent and light-independent reactions, which take place within the chloroplast.** During the light-dependent reactions, water is split (hydrolysis) to provide electrons to chlorophyll, and this reaction releases oxygen. Within chlorophyll, these electrons absorb light energy, and release some of this energy as they proceed down an electron transport chain. NADPH receives the electrons and shuttles them to the Calvin-Benson cycle, site of the light-independent reactions. Carbon dioxide and the shuttled electrons feed into the Calvin-Benson cycle, which uses them to make glucose.

✔ **Cellular respiration breaks down glucose to harvest the energy stored in the electrons of its bonds.** In the cytoplasm, six-carbon glucose is cut in half (glycolysis), and the three-carbon pieces are fed into the mitochondrion. On the way, each piece releases a carbon in the form of carbon dioxide. The two-carbon chunks that remain are fed into the Krebs cycle. There, the remaining carbons are also released as carbon dioxide, and the energy-containing electrons are loaded onto electron shuttles, NADH and $FADH_2$. The shuttles dump these electrons onto an electron transport chain. The electrons release their energy as they descend the chain, and this energy is used to make ATP (oxidative phosphorylation). At the end of the chain, oxygen accepts the electrons and converts to water.

✔ **Oxidative phosphorylation involves chemiosmosis, the diffusion of ions across a membrane.** As electrons from glucose descend the electron transport chain, their energy is used to pump H^+ ions across the inner mitochondrial membrane. This pumping builds up a reservoir of stored energy. Like water from a dam, the H^+ ions flow back through ATP synthase, which uses the released energy to build ATP.

✔ **Although cellular respiration is far more efficient when oxygen is present to receive electrons (aerobic respiration), there are two modes of respiration that do not require oxygen (anaerobic respiration): alcoholic fermentation and lactic acid fermentation.** Aerobic respiration yields 36 ATPs per glucose. Anaerobic respiration yields only two ATPs per glucose.

Testing Your Knowledge

This section contains multiple choice, free-essay response and laboratory sections to test your knowledge of the material in Chapter 9.

Answering multiple-choice questions

Directions: Each question is followed by five possible answers. Choose the best answer.

1. Which of the following represents glucose?

    (A) $C_3H_6O_3$

    (B) $C_6H_{12}O_6$

    (C) $C_2H_4O_2$

    (D) CH_2O

    (E) $C_5H_{10}O_5$

2. All of the following do not require oxygen *except*

    (A) Alcoholic fermentation

    (B) Lactic acid fermentation

    (C) Anaerobic processes

    (D) Krebs cycle

    (E) Glycolysis

3. Where does oxidative phosphorylation occur?

    (A) Cytoplasm

    (B) Stroma

    (C) Thylakoid

    (D) Inner mitochondrial membrane

    (E) Matrix

4. Per molecule of glucose, how many ATP are generated during anaerobic respiration?

   (A) 2

   (B) 35

   (C) 36

   (D) 37

   (E) 38

5. People need to inhale oxygen, O_2, because:

   (A) Oxygen helps dissolve glucose

   (B) Oxygen combines with carbon dioxide to form glucose

   (C) Oxygen is the final electron acceptor in respiration

   (D) Oxygen transports electrons to the Krebs cycle

   (E) We take electrons from oxygen during glycolysis

6. What is chemiosmosis?

   (A) Diffusion of water across an membrane

   (B) Diffusion of ions across a membrane

   (C) Formation of ATP

   (D) Formation of glucose

   (E) Formation of pyruvate

7. Which of the following is true of ATP synthase?

   (A) Shuttles electrons to produce ATP

   (B) Uses ATP to produce lactic acid

   (C) Uses ATP to produce alcohol

   (D) Forms ATP directly from glucose

   (E) Couples the energy of ion diffusion to make ATP

   Questions 8 through 12 refer to the following list:

   (A) Chloroplast

   (B) Chlorophyll

   (C) Stroma

   (D) Thykaloids

   (E) Glucose

8. Produced during photosynthesis

9. Light-absorbing pigment

10. Membranous discs where light-dependent reactions occur

11. Evolutionary cousin to mitochondria

12. Fluid where light-independent reactions occur

Questions 13 through 17 refer to the following list:

(A) Glycolysis

(B) Krebs cycle

(C) Oxidative phosphorylation

(D) Chemiosmosis

(E) Fermentation

13. Requires investment of 2 ATP

14. Can account for "muscle-burn"

15. Releases the energy of concentrated H^+ ions

16. Process during which oxygen receives electrons

17. Generates 3 NADH, 1 $FADH_2$, and 1 ATP

Answering free-essay response questions

Directions: Answer the following questions in essay form, not in outline form, using complete sentences. Diagrams may be used to supplement answers, but diagrams alone are not adequate.

1. Compare the light-dependent reactions with oxidative phosphorylation.

2. Compare the light-independent reactions with the Krebs cycle.

Lab on cell respiration

As with all labs, it's a great idea to review your own notes and lab manual to make sure you really "get" how the procedures and measurements you performed in the lab relate to the larger concepts. Having said that, what follows is a useful summary of the main ideas and techniques of the lab on cell respiration.

This lab measures the extent of respiration in plant seeds. Both germinating (growing) and dry, nongerminating seeds are used, and seeds are grown at different temperatures. Therefore, the lab tests for the effects of cell growth and temperature on the extent of respiration. The extent of respiration is measured indirectly by measuring the amount of carbon dioxide given off during growth (or non-growth) of the seeds. During respiration, oxygen is consumed and carbon dioxide is released in a one-to-one ratio.

Seeds are grown within closed tubes, so that no gases can enter or escape. Within each tube is a small amount of potassium hydroxide, a salt that traps carbon dioxide so that it no longer contributes to the gaseous volume in the tube. Each tube is fitted with a "respirometer" that measures the change in total gaseous volume. A sketch of the setup is shown in Figure 10-1. Seeds undergoing greater amounts of respiration will convert more oxygen to carbon dioxide. Trapping the carbon dioxide decreases the total gaseous volume. Typically, the germinating (growing) seeds are shown to convert more oxygen into carbon dioxide, as one would expect. Furthermore, seeds growing at higher temperature (for example, at 25°C instead of 10°C) will convert more oxygen into carbon dioxide. Comparing the results of seeds grown at different temperatures is a bit complicated, however, because you have to correct for the expansion of gases at higher temperatures. This correction is made using the Ideal Gas Law: (pressure)(volume) = (# molecules)(gas constant)(temperature).

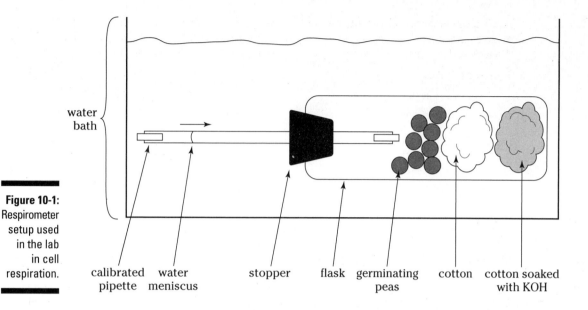

Figure 10-1:
Respirometer
setup used
in the lab
in cell
respiration.

calibrated   water   stopper   flask   germinating   cotton   cotton soaked
pipette   meniscus   peas   with KOH

With a respirometer, germinating seeds are placed within a stoppered flask along with a small amount of potassium hydroxide (KOH). The flask is fitted with a calibrated pipette, and immersed in a temperature-regulated water bath. As the seeds consume oxygen, they produce an equivalent amount of carbon dioxide, which is trapped by the KOH. The resulting decrease in pressure pulls water into the pipette, so the position of the meniscus can be used to measure oxygen consumption.

Checking Your Work

See how well you absorbed the material in Chapter 9. Be sure to read the explanations, to help seal all this new knowledge into your brain!

Answers and explanations for the multiple choice questions are:

1. (B) is the answer. $C_6H_{12}O_6$ is the molecular formula for glucose.

2. The answer is (D), the Krebs cycle. Although it does not directly consume oxygen, the Krebs cycle is directly coupled to oxidative phosphorylation, which does consume oxygen. If oxidative phosphorylation is blocked, so is the Krebs cycle. Note that glycolysis does not require oxygen.

3. The answer is (D). Answers (A) through (C) describe structures associated with photosynthesis. Answer (E) is the site of the Krebs cycle.

4. (A) is the correct answer. Remember, anaerobic respiration is far less efficient than aerobic respiration.

5. The answer is (C). During oxidative phosphorylation, oxygen accepts electrons at the end of the electron transport chain, and is converted to water.

6. (B) is the answer. Although both (A) and (B) refer to diffusion, the diffusion of water described in (A) is simply called osmosis. Chemiosmosis is specifically the diffusion of ions across a membrane.

7. (E) is the correct answer. Answer (D) is tempting, because the energy used by ATP synthase to make ATP ultimately (but not directly) derives from the electrons of glucose. However, ATP synthase directly uses the energy of diffusing H⁺ ions to do its job.

8. Glucose, (E), is one of the products of photosynthesis, along with oxygen.

9. (B), chlorophyll, is the pigment found in chloroplasts that absorbs the sun's light.

10. (D) The light-dependent reactions occur in the thykaloid membranes.

11. (A) is the answer. Both chloroplasts and mitochondria likely evolved from species of bacteria, and were incorporated into ancient cells as part of the evolution of eukaryotes.

12. The stroma, (C), is the fluid surrounding the thykaloid membranes, and is the site of the light-independent reactions of photosynthesis.

13. (A), glycolysis, makes 4 ATP but consumes 2 ATP.

14. The answer is (E). During strenuous exercise, oxygen-deprived muscle cells resort to lactic acid fermentation, a type of anaerobic respiration. The build-up of lactic acid in muscle cells contributes to the burning sensation you might feel in your muscles the day after exercise.

15. Chemiosmosis, (D), is the energy-releasing process of ions diffusing across a membrane. If you chose (C) because chemiosmosis is used to make ATP during oxidative phosphorylation, then you get smarty-pants points, because that is also correct.

16. (C) Oxygen is the final electron acceptor during the process of oxidative phosphorylation.

17. By breaking down acetyl-CoA, each turn of the Krebs cycle, (B), generates 3 NADH, 1 $FADH_2$, and 1 ATP.

Models for the free-essay response questions are:

1. The light-dependent reactions of photosynthesis are the mirror image of oxidative phosphorylation. There are parallels between these two processes, both in the individual reactions involved, and in the structures where the reactions take place.

The light-dependent reactions occur within the thylakoid membrane of chloroplasts. These reactions begin with the absorption of light by electrons within the pigment, chlorophyll. The electrons are obtained through hydrolysis, the splitting of water, which produces not only electrons but also oxygen, which is released from the cell. The energized electrons descend an electron transport chain, in which they are transferred from molecule to molecule in a series of redox reactions, releasing energy along the way. At the end of the electron transport chain, the electrons are received by NADP⁺, an electron shuttle. In short, during the light-dependent reactions, energy is captured, electrons descend a transport chain, and water is split.

Oxidative phosporylation also occurs within a membrane, the inner membrane of the mitochondrion. The reactions of oxidative phosphorylation begin when electron shuttles (NADH and $FADH_2$) deposit electrons at the beginning of an electron transport chain. The electrons descend this chain in a series of redox reactions, releasing energy along the way. This energy channeled into a reservoir of H⁺ ions, and the energy stored in this reservoir is used by ATP synthase to make ATP. The chemical energy stored in ATP is distributed throughout the cell. At the end of the electron transport chain, the electrons are received by oxygen, converting it to water. In short, during oxidative phosporylation, energy is distributed, electrons descend a transport chain, and water is reassembled.

2. The light-independent reactions of photosynthesis are the mirror image of the Krebs cycle. There are parallels between these two processes, both in the individual reactions involved, and in the structures where the reactions take place.

The light-independent reactions occur within the fluid stroma of chloroplasts. These reactions begin when the electron shuttle NADPH deposits electrons into the Calvin-Benson cycle. The function of this reaction cycle is to combine these electrons with carbon atoms obtained from carbon dioxide, all in order to make glucose. In short, during the light-independent reactions, carbon dioxide is consumed, and energy is stored within carbon-carbon bonds.

The Krebs cycle occurs within the fluid matrix of mitochondria. These reactions begin with two-carbon fragments from glucose molecules, in the form of acetyl-CoA. As these fragments move through the reaction cycle, carbon atoms are released as carbon dioxide, and energy-containing electrons are distributed to electron shuttles, NADH and $FADH_2$. In short, during the Krebs cycle, carbon dioxide is produced, and energy is released from carbon-carbon bonds.

Part III
Living Large — Organisms and Populations

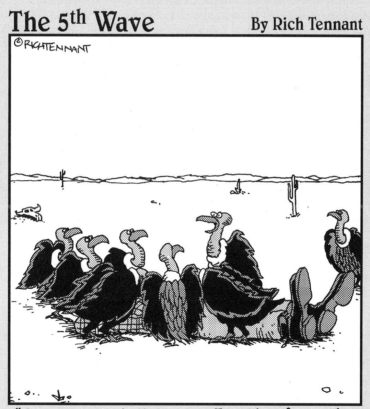

"Can anyone tell me, am I eating from the endocrine system or the nervous system? I always get those two mixed up."

In this part . . .

In this part, we lean back from the microscope and regard the larger world of plants, animals, and other fine, upstanding creatures. We ask three things: How do they work? How are they related? How do they interact? It turns out that these questions cover a lot of ground.

Your efforts in the previous parts will pay off handsomely. As you become more familiar with organisms, you'll remember what you learned about cells; you'll find yourself thinking, "Ah yes, *of course* it works that way."

Then we turn to the family of life, and we cover it from trunk to tip. You'll realize two things. First, in the grand scheme of the universe, you're much more like a fungus than you are different from one. Second, just as with humans, knowing something about an organism's family can explain a lot about the organism.

Finally, we think big. Living things don't exist in glass cases or as theoretical branches of family trees — life lives, interacting with other life and with the environment. No matter which organisms we're talking about, these interactions follow some surprisingly similar patterns. Apparently, we're all in the same boat.

Chapter 11

Rooting Through Plant Life

In This Chapter

▶ Exploring plant structures: seeing the forest for its roots, shoots, stems, and leaves

▶ Following water and nutrients on their travels through plants

▶ Understanding how similar cells develop into different plant parts

▶ Peeking under the covers of the intimate connection between plants and light

▶ Seeing how seeds and spores keep plants going over generations

*Q*uiet and green, plants are the underrated eukaryotes. Plants extend from the soil towards the sky, efficiently using resources both above and below ground. You may recall that plant cells have a few key differences from other eukaryotic cells, to include chloroplasts, vacuoles, and a rigid cell wall. In nature, structures have functions, so you can be sure that each of these differences is associated with a task unique to the lifestyle of the plant. This chapter examines that lifestyle, tying each task to the structures, large and small, that do the job. The details of this chapter dangle from a set of overall themes: What are the major parts of plant bodies? How do plants take in nutrients from their environment? How do they transport those nutrients to where they're needed? How do plants capture and use energy? How do plants coordinate all these tasks, so each happens at the right time? How do they reproduce? In other words, we'll ask all the same biological questions of plants as we do of any other type of organism.

First, a word to the wise (er . . . that's you). There are many varieties of plants, arranged within several different categories. Some varieties are more common than others, and some are much more likely to confront you on the AP Biology exam. This chapter, mercifully, focuses on those more common, most-tested types. But you should know where these common plants fit into the overall scheme of plant life. The major categories of plant are the tracheophytes and the nontracheophytes, sometimes referred to as the vascular and nonvascular plants, respectively. Vascular plants (tracheophytes) have circulatory systems in which materials are transported throughout the plant within tubes, in a way roughly similar to how nutrients are carried by the blood within our own veins and arteries. We will focus on plants which possess these vascular systems, the tracheophytes, whose members include trees, bushes, and most of the other plants you talk to in your neighborhood.

Within the tracheophytes, we find two further categories of plant: those with seeds and those without seeds. These cousins are largely similar, but reproduce in different ways. We discuss both of those ways. Among the plants that use seeds to reproduce, there are the angiosperms and the gymnosperms. Angiosperms are flowering plants, while gymnosperms are cone-producing plants (such as pine trees). Finally, the flowering angiosperms contain two separate groups, the monocots and the dicots. Monocots develop from a single cotyledon, or embryonic seed leaf; dicots develop from a pair of such cotyledons.

Got it? Excellent. Now, dive into the green.

Weeding Through Plant Parts

Roots, shoots, stems, and leaves. Those are your basic vascular plant parts, and you'll find them in Figure 11-1. Of course, there's a wealth of variety within these types or part, but it boils down to those four. Each part has distinct functions. Together, these parts reflect how vascular plants evolved to inhabit two distinct environments at the same time: the soil and the air. Why would plants do such a thing? Follow the money (where "money" actually means "nutrients and energy"). The soil offers water and vital minerals. The air offers carbon dioxide and the energy of sunlight. To forge the successful lifestyles they enjoy today, plants evolved systems to tap into all these resources, both above and below the ground. In short, plants evolved roots and shoots. Shoots, in turn, can develop stems and leaves.

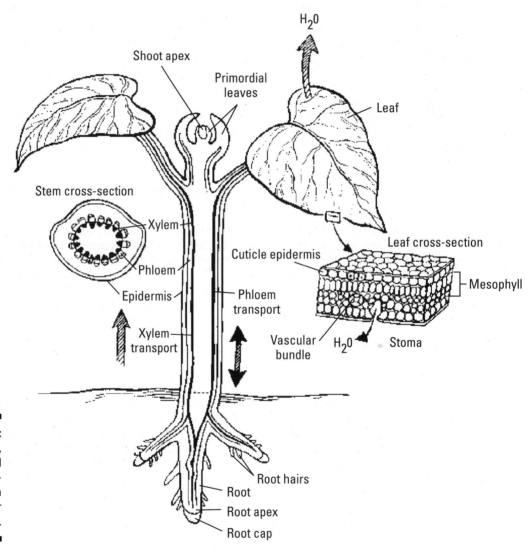

Figure 11-1: Root, shoot, stem, and leaf structures of a vascular plant.

The tissues that make up these roots, shoots, stems, and leaves fall into three categories:

- ✔ **Ground:** Ground tissues account for most of a plant, and are built from collenchyma cells, parenchyma cells, and sclerenchyma cells. Collenchyma cells provide strength and flexibility, especially to the stems and leaves, and tend to have thick cell walls. Parenchyma cells are the most common ground tissue cells and are tailored to many different functions, to include storage and secretion of nutrients and water, as well as photosynthesis. Accordingly, parenchyma cells often have large vacuoles for storage, and thinner cell walls. Sclerenchyma cells have very thick, hard cell walls that provide protective strength where it is needed, as in the coatings of seeds.

- ✔ **Dermal:** Dermal tissues make up the outer surfaces of the plant body. They help form protective barriers that prevent invaders from entering, and precious resources from exiting. They form the "skin" of the plant.

- ✔ **Vascular:** Vascular tissues come in two distinct (and highly testable) forms: xylem and phloem. Xylem and phloem are discussed in greater detail later in the chapter. For now, understand that xylem tissue consists mostly of dead cells that form a system of tubes extending throughout the plant. These xylem tubes both physically support the plant (most of wood is xylem) and provide an avenue for transporting water and other nutrients from the soil to the various hungry and thirsty cells of the plant. Like xylem, phloem tissues form a network of tubes. Phloem tubes specialize in transporting the sugar produced during photosynthesis to the plant's cells, where the sugar can be broken down and used for energy.

Roots

Roots are branched, underground structures that serve two major functions. First, somewhat obviously, roots firmly anchor the plant to a fixed spot. Once plant takes root and begins to grow in an area with good access to moisture, soil nutrients and light, it pays to stay. Second, roots serve as transport systems, allowing the plant to suck up water and dissolved nutrients from the soil to support the plant's growth. Roots have specialized parts, as we'll discuss, and these parts develop from the three major types of plant tissue: ground, dermal, and vascular.

Shoots

Shoots target the above-ground business of the plant. Very young plants may possess only simple, undeveloped shoots. As a plant grows, however, these tender shoots develop into stems and leaves. So, stems and leaves are really part of the shoot system. Stems and leaves are so different and specialized that it is worth considering them separately. Overall, the shoot system enables a plant to grow taller to gain access to energy-giving light, and allows the plant to convert that light energy into the chemical energy of sugar. Like roots, shoots develop from ground, dermal, and vascular tissues.

Stems

Stems are sturdy structures that can grow in order to give a plant a fighting chance to spread its leaves in the sun. Stem growth can add to the plant's height, broaden the area covered by the leaves, or even direct growth from a dark area towards one with more light. To provide mechanical support for a growing plant, stems need to be strong. To help move water and nutrients to the furthest reaches of the plant, stems are stuffed with little transport pipes, in the form of xylem and phloem.

Leaves

Leaves are the original solar panels, capturing energy from sunlight in a biochemical process called photosynthesis. The cells within leaf tissues are hectic with biochemistry, importing water and nutrients to support their frantic work, and exporting sugar to provide energy to the remainder of the plant. The import/export business conducted by the leaves is supported by xylem and phloem pipelines, which explains why leaves are so richly veined.

The arrangement of veins within leaves are an easy way to distinguish the two types of flowering plants, monocots and dicots. As shown in Figure 11-2, the veins within monocot leaves run parallel to each other, while the veins of dicot leaves branch outwards.

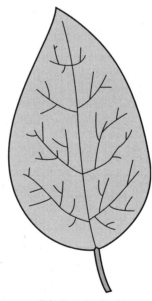

Figure 11-2:
The arrangement of veins within (a) monocot, and (b) dicot leaves.

(a) monocot leaf with parallel veins

(b) dicot leaf with branching veins

Sucking Up Nutrients: How Roots Function and Grow

Root systems are intricate and finely tailored to fulfill their functions: anchoring plants and giving them access to water and nutrients in the soil. In the next sections, we describe how roots manage these vital tasks and how their elaborate root structures develop from humble origins.

Root Systems

Just as monocots and dicots revealed themselves in the patterns of veins within their leaves, these two groups take slightly different approaches to sinking roots into the soil. The differences are summarized in Figure 11-3. Monocots employ fibrous, highly branched "bunches" of roots that cover a wide area, but don't descend too far below ground. Dicots go for depth, sending long taproots into the dirt, with smaller lateral roots branching off the central taproot. Taproots can be quite thick, and some plants use them to store sugars and starches (long sugar polymers). Sometimes these sugary taproots are edible. Sometimes they are orange. Sometimes they are nice when steamed and served with a little butter. Sometimes we call them carrots.

In both monocots and dicots, most of the crucial water- and nutrient-absorbing action occurs at the tips of the roots. These tips bristle with a fine covering of root hairs (see Figure 11-3), which serve to greatly increase the surface area of the roots in contact with the soil.

Root shafts are made up of layers within layers, each layer playing a distinct role. The outer surface of the root, called the epidermis, is the layer from which root hairs grow. Immediately within the epidermis is the cortex, which is built of parenchyma cells and is the largest part of the root. Equipped with large vacuoles, the parenchyma cells of the cortex are useful for storing starch. The most central layer of the root is the vascular cylinder, or "stele." The vascular cylinder houses the xylem and phloem pipelines, through which pass water and dissolved nutrients. To prevent leakage of these precious fluids, the vascular cylinder and cortex are separated by a thin layer of endodermis, impermeable to water.

Transpiring and thriving

Lovely as they often are, plants are nevertheless heartless. Without a muscular pump to push nutrients and water through their vascular tubes, plants require other strategies to distribute these goodies among their cells. Transpiration is one of those strategies. Transpiration teams up with a supporting cast of processes to ensure that hungry and thirsty cells are fed and watered.

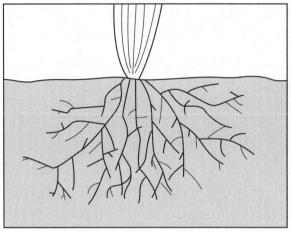

(a) bunch roots on a monocot

(b) tap root on a dicot

tap root

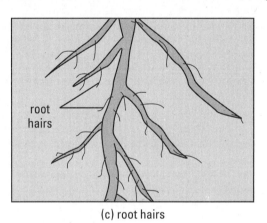

root hairs

(c) root hairs

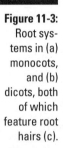

Figure 11-3:
Root systems in (a) monocots, and (b) dicots, both of which feature root hairs (c).

During transpiration, plants move water and dissolved nutrients upwards from the roots to the remainder of the plant. Because the nutrients are dissolved in water, they move as the water moves. During the day, a great deal of water evaporates from leaves via pores called stomata. The stomata are regulated by special "guard cells" that open or close depending on the temperature and other environmental factors. The stomata-bearing leaf cells are connected to the roots by a network of xylem tubes. So, as water evaporates from the stomata, more water moves along the xylem to replace the lost water. Because of its cohesive properties, water has a high surface tension (as discussed in Chapter 3). This surface tension transmits the loss of water by evaporation all the way through the xylem, down to the water-absorbing root tips.

The more evaporation, the greater the transpirational pull upwards from the roots. The watery solution moving upwards through xylem (xylem sap) carries dissolved nutrients with it. In short, evaporation sucks tasty stuff from the soil, through a xylem straw.

Chemiosmosis: Not just for respiration

You might recall that chemiosmosis, the diffusion of ions across a membrane, is a key process involved in cellular respiration (described in galling detail in Chapter 9). Since dissolved ions are important nutrients for plant cells, and since Nature is so thrifty, it's no great shock that plant cells use chemiosmosis to grab much-needed ions from the fluids transported by the xylem and phloem.

The nutrient-grabbing application of chemiosmosis begins with a hydrogen ion (H^+) pump, just as it did in cellular respiration, wherein hydrogen ions were pumped across the mitochondrial inner membrane in order to power the production of ATP by the enzyme, ATP synthase. In a subtle twist, plant cells *use* ATP to power the export of hydrogen ions outside the cell membrane. Why burn ATP fuel to kick hydrogen ions out of the cell? Because outside is where the nutrients are, like potassium (K^+) and nitrate (NO_3^-). The ATP-driven export of hydrogen ions creates a charge imbalance across the cell membrane, with excess positive charge on the outside and excess negative charge on the inside.

The inside-negative charge imbalance helps persuade positively charged potassium ions to flow into the cell through special potassium channels. Negatively charged nitrate ions simply hitch a ride with hydrogen ions, as the two ions together flow through channels into the cell; energy released from the diffusion of H^+ back into the cell drives the process.

Even sucrose, an uncharged sugar, is open for grabs by this method. Like nitrate ions, sucrose molecules ride the coattails of hydrogen ions as they diffuse back into the cell, each diffusing H^+ taking a sucrose molecule along for the ride.

At night (or when it's really hot), guard cells close the stomata, preventing the evaporation that drives transpiration. Without the "pull" of transpiration, plants resort to the "push" of root pressure. Recall from Chapter 3 that osmosis is the diffusion of water from areas where it is more concentrated to those where it is less so. At the root tips, cells in fine root hairs contact the soil. When the soil is moist (like when water is abundant), osmosis drives water into the roots. This phenomenon creates root pressure, as the higher concentrations of water now present in the roots press their way upwards, towards drier, lower pressure regions in the rest of the plant. In extreme circumstances, root pressure can result in *guttation,* in which water and nutrients are pushed through the xylem all the way out of the plant, exiting at the stomata.

Capillary action, the combination of adhesive and cohesive forces that pull water forwards through fine tubes (like those of the xylem), provides a small assist to transpiration and root pressure. Capillary action alone is insufficient to drive xylem transport, but it contributes as it can.

Nutrients from the soil may be tasty, but for a plant, they do not make for a balanced meal. True plant food is sugar, produced by photosynthesis. Since the vast majority of photosynthesis occurs in the leaves, plants have a problem: how to move sugars downwards, from the leaves to all the other hungry cells of the plant. Furthermore, plants often store sugars for safe keeping within the roots, only to move them upwards again during periods of growth. So, plants need to be able to move sugar up *and* down, as required.

To solve this up-and-down problem, plants have evolved another network of vascular tubes, called the phloem. Sugar-laden water (phloem sap) moves along this phloem network from sugar *sources* to sugar *sinks*. A sugar source is wherever sugar is in high concentration, be it a photosynthesizing leaf or a starchy root. Water tends to move by osmosis into sugar sources, increasing the water pressure within sugary cells. This pressure forces the dissolved sugars outwards, into the phloem network and towards sugar sinks.

Transpiration, root pressure, and phloem transport all occur along the largely up-and-down networks of xylem and phloem. Monocots and dicots arrange xylem and phloem a bit differently within their stems, as shown in Figure 11-4. Water and nutrients also need to be able to move side-to-side, and plant cells have devised means for them to do so. One major means is through plasmodesmata, little tunnels that bore through cell walls, directly connecting the cytoplasm of one cell to that of its neighbor.

Figure 11-4:
Organization of xylem and phloem tubes as seen in cross-sections of stems in (a) moncots, and (b) dicots.

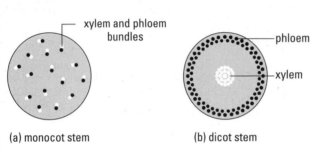

Zoned for development

Respect root growth. It starts from just a few cells, but can produce structures that crack concrete (as inspection of any sidewalk near a tree reveals). Roots grow by rapidly producing new cells within meristems. As new cells divide into existence within the meristems, older cells are pushed outward through several zones. As cells move through these zones, they grow and develop into different kinds of cells with particular functions. Roots exhibit two major types of growth. Primary growth occurs at apical meristems, and results in longer roots. Secondary growth occurs at lateral meristems, and results in thicker roots.

Apical meristems are located at root tips, and are busy regions, buzzing with mitosis as cells continually divide to provide the raw cellular building blocks for growth. The apical meristem — a vitally important structure — is protected by a root cap, a layer of cells that are constantly sloughed off and replaced as the root tip pushes through the soil. As a further insurance, the center of the apical meristem houses a quiescent center. Cells of the quiescent center divide slowly and serve as backup in case the apical meristem is damaged. Cells born within the apical meristem are quickly pushed by younger cells through the zones of cell division, elongation, and maturation.

The zone of cell division contains three distinct layers. The outermost layer is the protoderm, and is the site where cells destined to become dermal tissue are formed. The central layer, the ground meristem, gives rise to cells that will develop into ground tissue. The procambium is the innermost layer, and produces cells that will grow into vascular tissue.

In the zone of elongation, cells grow longer. Over time, this growth is what causes entire roots to grow longer. Finally, cells complete their development into specialized cell types within the zone of maturation.

Lateral meristems are found on the outer edges of roots, and are busy places, like their apical counterparts. Lateral meristems come in two major forms: the cork cambium and the vascular cambium. The cork cambium is the outermost meristem, and gives rise to the periderm, a layer of new cells that will form the epidermis (outer layer) of roots. Cell division in the vascular cambium produces secondary xylem and secondary phloem, water- and nutrient-transporting tubes that support growth in the thickening root.

Now take a breath. All the preceding detail about root growth boils down to a few core principles. Roots elongate from primary growth at apical meristems, located at root tips. Roots thicken from secondary growth at lateral meristems, located on the sides of roots. Both types of meristem produce three types of tissues: dermal, ground, and vascular. Dermal tissues develop into protective outer layers. Ground tissues develop into spongy middle layers. Vascular tissues develop into xylem and phloem.

Reaching for the Sky: How Shoots Function and Grow

Just as roots push into the earth, shoots reach for the sky. Shoot growth includes the elongation of stems and the development of new leaves. Nature is thrifty, so it will come as no surprise that the elegant system of meristems used for root growth is also used for shoot growth. This is good news, not only for the plant, but also for you, because it makes things that much simpler to remember for the exam. Shoot growth can be directed by a number of environmental factors and regulated by hormones, chemical messengers used by the plant to ensure the new growth happens at the right place and the right time. Directing and regulating growth are particularly important for plants, because their root systems fix them in place; they can't just pack their bags and ditch town if times get tough.

Shooting for the sky

As with roots, shoots engage in primary and secondary growth, which yield length and thickness, respectively. Primary growth of shoots occurs at apical meristems (at shoot tips) and axillary meristems (from stem sides). Axillary meristems become the apical meristems of new branches. These shoot meristems give rise to the same three types of primary meristem tissue: protoderm, ground meristem, and procambium. Stem protoderm develops into the epidermis, the outer layer of the stem. Ground meristem produces primary xylem and phloem, the tubes involved in fluid transport along the stem length. Procambium cells develop into the spongy inner pith of the stem.

At the stem tips, apical meristems prevent the growth of new branches in their immediate vicinity. However, once the apical meristem moves on, it leaves behind axillary meristems that are now free to split off as new branches, becoming apical meristems in their own right.

Stems grow thicker as the result of secondary growth from two types of secondary (or lateral) meristem: the cork cambium and vascular cambium (again, as with roots). In woody dicots, cork cambium cells develop into tough, protective periderm tissue. Vascular cambium gives rise to secondary xylem and phloem. Dicots make extensive use of secondary growth, while monocots lack secondary growth entirely.

Leaves arise from leaf primordia at the sides of apical meristems. This makes sense, since leaves grow from the tips of branches, right? The three types of ground tissue all contribute to leaf growth, as they do for stem and root growth. Protoderm cells grow into leaf epidermis, which covers the leaf's upper and lower surfaces. The epidermis itself is covered by a waxy "cuticle," which helps the plant prevent unauthorized water leakage. Ground meristem develops into mesophyll cells, the soft, inner cells of the leaf that perform photosynthesis. Procambium cells grow into the xylem and phloem systems that serve the leaf. All these various leaf tissues are seen in context in Figure 11-5.

The leaf epidermis is perforated by stomata, the previously described pores that allow water to evaporate in order to drive transpiration. But the stomata have other jobs as well. Guard cells flank the stomata, controlling whether the pores are open or closed. Guard cells will open to allow water and oxygen to exit the leaf, and to let carbon dioxide enter. Alternately, the guard cells may close, excluding carbon dioxide and trapping water and oxygen inside. Thus, in addition to regulating water evaporation, stomata are important sites for the exchange of oxygen and carbon dioxide, the key gases involved in the processes of photosynthesis and cellular respiration. With the stomata open, plants can perform photosynthesis, feeding the mesophyll cells with water and carbon dioxide, and allowing the oxygen byproduct to escape. On the other hand, open stomata put the plant at risk of dehydration under hot, dry and windy conditions. So, there's a certain physiological calculus involved in deciding whether to open or close the stomata.

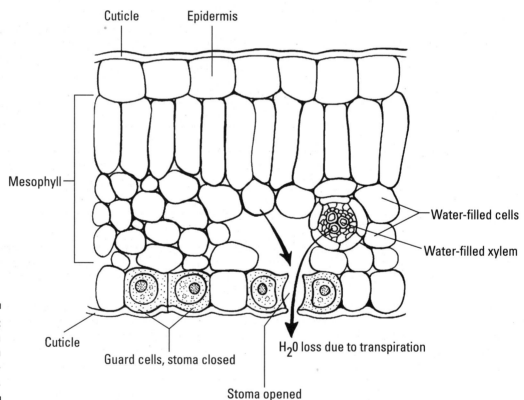

Figure 11-5:
Tissues of a leaf, seen in cross-section.

Reacting to conditions and hormones

In some ways, plants seem a bit vulnerable . . . stuck in one spot, exposed to the elements, nervously eyeing the bigger plants around them. Over a few hundred million years of evolution, however, plants have learned a few tricks that allow them to respond to their environment. Plants alter their growth in response to light, gravity, and physical contact with other objects. Plants are so dependent on light for photosynthesis that they have devised elaborate adaptations to varying light conditions, and these adaptations will be described in the following section. For the moment, we focus on other plant responses, and how they are controlled by hormones.

You've heard of hormones. As someone of the appropriate age to take the AP Biology exam, you are probably under the influence of a stiff dose of hormones this very moment. Hormones are chemical signals that travel through tissue fluids to create a response in target cells. Clinical and cold as that definition may sound, it accounts nicely for both the regulated growth of plants, and the keen interest many high school students take in the swimming unit of gym class.

Plant hormones are an active area of research. There are many more plant hormones and possible hormones than you'll be expected to know about for the exam. Focus on the following five hormone types, whose functions are listed in Table 11-1 below: auxins, gibberellins, cytokinins, abscisic acid, and ethylene.

Table 11-1	Hormone Types and Functions
Hormone	*Functions*
Auxins	Promote stem elongation, inhibit lateral branch growth
Gibberellins	Promote stem elongation
Cytokinins	Promote cell division in areas of growth
Abscisic Acid	Inhibits cell growth, promotes closing of stomata, inhibits germination (initial growth) of seeds
Ethylene	Promotes fruit ripening

One really clever use of hormones is to promote the growth of cells in specific areas of the plant in such a way that the plant grows in a specific direction. Growth in a particular direction is called *tropism.* Plants exhibit phototropism, gravitropism, and thigmotropism.

Phototropism is growth towards light, and is described in the next section. Gravitropism is growth opposite the direction of gravity, and is particularly useful for plants growing on steep hillsides, helping them to grow "up" despite the angle of the ground in which they are rooted. Auxins and gibberellins appear to be important in gravitropic growth. Thigmotropism is growth in response to physical contact. The classic example of thigmotropic growth is found in climbing vines, which reliably change their direction of growth in order to maintain contact with whatever surface they happen to be climbing.

The Rhythm of the light: Photoperiodism, phototropism, and steps in photosynthesis

The love affair between plants and light is ancient, intimate, and powerful enough to animate most of the habitable land on the planet. Plants set their clocks to the rising and setting of the sun. Plants arch towards sunlight, weaving it into their very cells, whispering oxygen into the sky. The inner details of this affair beg to be brought into the light.

Let there be light

By the sinking of their roots, plants commit themselves to a particular plot of ground. In the dark, roots tunnel towards water, but the shoots do their utmost to find light. Often, the search for light can be a real challenge because taller plants spread umbrellas of leaves overhead, and nearby plants are equally eager to get their piece of the sun. The auxin hormones guide the search in a process called phototropism, the growth of stems in the direction of light. Auxins concentrate in parts of plant stems that receive too little light. In those shady portions of stem, auxins promote rapid cell growth. Since this rapid growth is not matched on the other, well-lit side of the stem, the stem bends away from shade and towards light.

Once plants have found the light, the adaptations continue. In order to perform photosynthesis as efficiently as possible, and to flower at the right time, plants must adjust to varying light conditions as our swiftly tilting planet moves through the seasons. Plants follow the seasons by keeping track of the relative length of periods of light and darkness (i.e., "photoperiods") during each day. During summer, daylight hours are longer than during winter, and plants sense these differences precisely. Note that plants make both daily decisions and seasonal decisions based on photoperiods. The daily period is critical to deciding when to open and close stomata, and daily responses are enforced by a "circadian rhythm," a sort of built-in, daily biological clock. The seasonal period is important for deciding when to flower or perform other major life-cycle events. Photoperiodism refers to the responses a plant makes to photoperiods.

How do plants sense light? Phytochromes, light-absorbing molecules within plant cells, are an important part of the answer. Different forms of phytochrome within plants absorb different colors (different wavelengths) of light. By distributing phytochromes throughout the plant, plants can detect changes in the direction, intensity and quality (i.e., different wavelengths) of light. Changes in direction are important for phototropic growth, as discussed previously. Changes in intensity are critical for photoperiodism. The critical, threshold photoperiod for some plant responses is tied to some wavelengths more than others.

The special properties of phytochromes help them fulfill their function as meticulous accountants, keeping tabs on the changing balances in different light accounts. One form of phytochrome best absorbs light with a wavelength of 660 nanometers (nm), while another form of phytochrome specializes in absorbing 730 nm light. What's more, by the very act of absorbing light, 660 nm phytochrome rapidly *converts* to 730 nm phytochrome. Given time, 730 nm phytochrome slowly reverts back to 660 nm phytochrome. When you consider that sunlight is enriched in 660 nm light, while moonlight is enriched in 730 nm light, you begin to see how phytochromes help plants to sense shifts in their light environment, the better to tailor their activities to the changing moods of their fickle lover, the sun.

The phytochromes provide initial "training" to the circadian rhythm. Once set, however, this built-in, daily biological clock gains some independence, exerting its effects without much further input from the phytochromes. However, phytochromes may help to gently tune the circadian rhythm as the seasons change. Circadian cues open stomata during hours of daylight, allowing the free passage of water, oxygen and carbon dioxide necessary for the reactions of photosynthesis. Recall that the "light reactions" of photosynthesis consume water and produce oxygen. The "dark reactions" consume carbon dioxide. The dark reactions can proceed happily in the presence of light — they simply don't require it.

Heading to the dark side

Despite the worthwhile emphasis on light, the trigger for many important plant activities is actually *darkness*. On a daily basis, plants use circadian rhythms to close stomata during the darkest hours, restricting the flow of water and gases. Under these conditions, the light reactions of photosynthesis shut down — no great loss when there isn't much light, in any case. Enough carbon dioxide persists, however, for the plant to continue with the glucose-producing dark reactions.

Plants attune themselves to the seasonal period by means of darkness thresholds; when hours of darkness exceed a certain value (the *critical night length*), the plant initiates a pre-programmed response. This is especially true of flowering. Some plants will not flower if the critical night length isn't satisfied up to the very minute.

Sowing the Seeds: Reproduction in Plants

Plants have sex. Well, only in a sense, and not all of them. Still, most plants reproduce sexually, meaning that the genes of a new plant are a unique combination, assembled from the genes contributed by two parents. Most plants can also reproduce asexually — you can plant a hedge clipping and it will grow, for example — but sexual reproduction is preferable; new combinations of genes give species greater ability to adapt over generations.

On the AP Biology exam, you're most likely to run into questions about sexual reproduction within seed-bearing plants, and that is the specific focus of this section. For good measure, you'll also get a smidgen of knowledge about reproduction in seedless plants.

The seedy side of life

Seeds develop from zygotes, the diploid products of fertilization, in which a haploid male gamete fertilizes a haploid female gamete. If all this business of zygotes and gametes sounds terribly unfamiliar, you may wish to peruse Chapter 7. At a minimum, understand that haploid gametes have one full set of genes, but only one allele (version) for each gene. In plants, male gametes are called pollen, and female gametes are called ova. Upon fertilization, a diploid zygote is created that possesses two full sets of genes, and may have different alleles for each gene. The multitude of different combinations of alleles made possible in this way is a major strength of sexual reproduction.

Seeds harbor vital genetic information, the potential for a new plant life. The structure of a seed reflects its role. Seeds have a tough outer layer, the seed coat, which protects the inner seed contents in harsh environments. Seeds are built to be blown about by winds, exposed to icy winters, and even passed through the digestive systems of animals. At the end of a long and hazardous journey, the diploid seed embryo (developed from the zygote) may find itself in favorable conditions for growth. But until the conditions are right, the embryo sustains itself with a food supply that surrounds it within the seed.

Different types of seed seek different conditions in order to begin growing. The most important criterion is usually the presence of water. In addition, seeds may wait for appropriate temperatures, or they may simply wait for a certain duration of time. Until the right conditions are met, the seed remains dormant, or inactive. In some cases, dormancy may last for many years. If and when good growth conditions present themselves, the seed germinates; the embryo begins to grow and to put out shoots and roots.

Fertilization is different for different plants:

✔ Within the vascular plants, fertilization of an ovum by pollen can take different forms. In the gymnosperms (cone-bearing plants), entire plants are either male or female, and produce cones that contain either pollen or ova, respectively. Wind blows pollen from male cones, and some of this wind-blown pollen lands on female cones, fertilizing the ova within.

✔ In angiosperms (flowering plants), fertilization still involves pollen meeting ovum, but the process involves some interesting ecological interactions. All these interactions organize themselves around the peculiar anatomy of a flower, shown in Figure 11-6. Flowers possess both a female portion, the carpel, and a male portion, the stamen. Both carpel and stamen sit within a bed of petals, and this entire assembly rests upon the sepal.

The carpel itself has several parts. A swell at the top of the carpel, called the stigma, gathers pollen. Gathered pollen descends the length of the carpel through a tube called the style. At the base of the style lies the ovary, which in turn contains the ovum. The ovum waits for pollination.

Pollen is produced within the stamen, and in particular by a structure called the anther. The anther is held aloft by a filament, in a design intended to maximize contact with insect and animal pollinators. Pollinators? That's right, angiosperms often outsource the most critical element of their reproduction to bugs. Attracted by the colorful petals and enticing aromas of the flower, many insects and animals approach flowers for closer inspection. Within the flower they find nectar, a sugary liquid reward for their efforts. In the process of seeking nectar, pollinators brush against anthers, and in so doing pick up a cargo of pollen that they carry with them on their travels. Those travels are often in search of more nectar, so a pollen grain may well be transported to another flower. There, the pollen may be deposited upon a stigma, and make its way through carpel to the anxious arms of an ovum.

Once fertilized, the angiosperm zygote develops differently in the case of monocots and dicots. In both cases, the ovary surrounding the fertilized ovum plays a part. In monocots, the ovary grows into a protective seedpod. At an appropriate time, the seedpod bursts, releasing the seeds within to their separate destinies. In dicots, the ovaries swell with carbohydrate-rich tissue that can nurture the seeds as they begin to grow. These tissues can also nurture us, as sweet and tasty fruit.

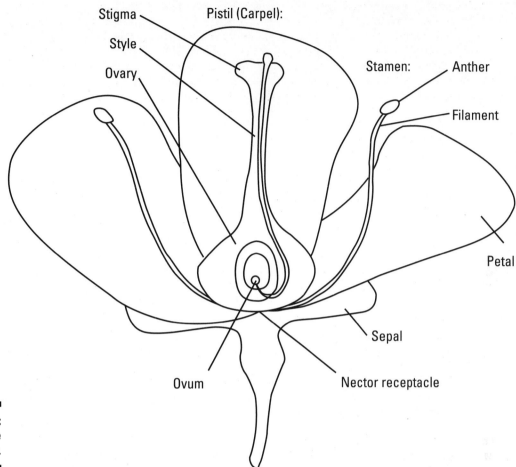

Stigma

Pistil (Carpel):

Style

Ovary

Stamen: Anther

Filament

Petal

Sepal

Ovum

Nector receptacle

Figure 11-6:
Structure
of a flower.

Seedless wonders

This chapter as a whole emphasizes tracheophytes, the vascular plants, because these are the plants on which you are most likely to be tested. Similarly, you will most likely be tested on seed-bearing plants. Even within the tracheophytes, however, there are plants that reproduce without seeds. Seedless reproduction involves an "alternation of generations." What this means is that individual gametes — instead of engaging in fertilization — develop into spores. These spores grow into entire haploid plants, called gametophytes. Fertilization occurs between gametophytes to produce diploid, sporophyte plants. Sporophyte plants in turn yield haploid spores, and the cycle continues, alternating between haploid and diploid states.

This "alternation of generations" system may seem odd, but *all* sexually reproducing organisms alternate between haploid and diploid states — even humans. The only real difference with vascular seedless plants is that their haploid states spend a little time in the sun before recombining.

Chapter 12

Answering Questions about Plant Life

See if the seeds have taken root. This chapter offers review and questions covering the material found in Chapter 11. Multiple choice and free-essay response questions and answers are provided. In addition, explanatory summaries are given for labs on plant pigments and photosynthesis, and on transpiration.

Pointers for Practice

The main points of this chapter are the following:

✔ **There are several groups and sub-groups of plants, including the following major divisions: Tracheophytes and non-tracheophytes possess or lack vascular tissues, respectively.** Tracheophytes include seed-bearing and seedless plants, which reproduce by different means. Seed-bearing plants are divided among the angiosperms (flowering) and gymnosperms (cone-bearing). The angiosperms include both monocots and dicots.

✔ **The three major parts of vascular plants are roots, shoots, and stems.** Roots anchor plants and absorb water and dissolved nutrients from the soil. Shoots develop into stems and leaves. Leaves perform photosynthesis and transpiration, which respectively provide chemical energy and a driving force for upward transport of fluids. Stems provide structural support, height, and an avenue for fluid transport.

✔ **Roots, leaves, and stems all develop from three types of germ tissue: dermal, vascular, and ground.** These germ tissues arise from two types of meristem: apical and lateral. Apical meristems produce elongation at root and stem tips. Lateral meristems produce thickening of existing roots and stems.

✔ **Vascular tissues occur in two major forms: xylem and phloem.** Xylem tubes are mostly composed of dead cells, and conduct xylem sap from the roots upward to the cells of the plant. Xylem sap consists mostly of water and dissolved nutrients, like minerals, from the soil. Xylem transport is driven by transpiration, root pressure and capillary action. Phloem tubes are made of living cells, and conduct phloem sap both upwards and downwards within the plant. Phloem sap consists largely of dissolved sugars. Phloem transport moves from sugar sources (sugar-rich areas) to sugar sinks (sugar-scarce areas). Phloem transport is driven by osmosis and pressure.

✔ **Transpiration is the pull of fluid from the roots upward, driven by the evaporation of water from stomata in the leaves.** Stomata are pores within leaves whose precise degree of opening is controlled by flanking guard cells. In addition to regulating evaporation of water, stomata control the exchange of important gases like carbon dioxide and oxygen.

✔ **Plants regulate their growth in critical ways by using hormones, chemical messages that move through fluids to alter the activity of target cells.** Hormones promote or inhibit growth in specific areas, and help control such things as stomatal opening, seed germination, and ripening. Specific hormones help plants respond to environmental stimuli, promoting growth towards light (phototropism), growth in an upward direction (gravitropism), or growth in contact with supporting structures (thigmotropism).

✔ **Plants synchronize their activities with periodic shifts in the amount and quality of light, called photoperiods.** Photoperiodism includes responses to both daily and seasonal light cycles. Daily responses, like the opening and closing of stomata, are regulated by a built-in biological clock, called a circadian rhythm. Seasonal responses, like the precise timing of flowering, rely on critical thresholds of darkness. Plants sense the direction, intensity and quality of light by means of phytochromes, pigment molecules that absorb specific wavelengths of light.

✔ **Seedless plants reproduce through an alternation-of-generations strategy, involving an alternating sequence of haploid plants (gametophytes) and diploid plants (sporophytes).**

✔ **Seed-bearing plants reproduce by means of pollen and ovum gametes.** Gymnosperms produce cone-bearing plants that are entirely male or female, with cones exclusively containing pollen or ova. Pollen is released from "male" cones, and travels to "female" cones, where fertilization takes place. Angiosperms produce flowers that contain both male and female sexual parts. Fertilization often gets an assist from pollinators such as insects or other animals. Seeking nectar, pollinators visit flowers, where they receive a dusting of pollen. Subsequent visits to other flowers lead to cross-pollination, the fertilization of an ovum by the pollen of another flower.

Testing Your Knowledge

This section contains multiple-choice, free-essay response and laboratory sections to test your knowledge of the material in Chapter 11.

Answering multiple-choice questions

Directions: Each question is followed by five possible answers. Choose the best answer.

1. All of the following arise from lateral meristems *except*

   (A) Secondary growth

   (B) Root thickening

   (C) Branch elongation

   (D) Bark development

   (E) Cork development

2. The following phenomena help cause the distribution of dissolved minerals throughout a plant:

   I. Evaporation of water from leaves

   II. Absorption of water by root hairs

   III. Guttation

(A) I only

(B) II only

(C) III only

(D) I and II only

(E) II and III only

3. Which of the following are most characteristic of dicots?

(A) Parallel leaf veins, branching root bunches

(B) Branching leaf veins, branching root bunches

(C) Parallel leaf veins, deep taproots

(D) Branching leaf veins, deep taproots

(E) Bunched leaf veins, branching root bunches

4. Which of the following accurately characterize phloem?

   I. Involved in upwards transport

  II. Relies on osmosis

 III. Built largely of dead cells

(A) I only

(B) II only

(C) III only

(D) I and II only

(E) II and III only

5. All of the following could explain the stem curvature shown in Figure 12-1 *except*

(A) Phototropism

(B) Application of auxin to stem's left side

(C) Application of abscisic acid to stem's right side

(D) Application of gibberellins to stem's right side

(E) Gravitropism

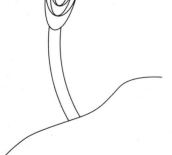

Figure 12-1:
A vascular
plant with a
curved
stem.

Select from the following choices when answering questions 6 through 10:

(A) Collenchyma cells

(B) Epidermal cells

(C) Sclerenchyma cells

(D) Guard cells

(E) Mesophyll cells

6. Tightly packed cells covering a plant's outer surface

7. Structurally supportive cells with unevenly thickened cell walls

8. Thinly walled cells that may specialize in photosynthesis

9. Regulatory cells flanking stomata

10. Thickly walled cells that provide protection and support

Questions 11 through 15 refer to the following list:

(A) 660 nanometers

(B) 730 nanometers

(C) Circadian rhythm

(D) Critical night length

(E) Photoperiod

11. Duration of daylight

12. Wavelength enriched in sunlight

13. Tunes plant activity to daily photoperiod

14. Wavelength enriched in moonlight

15. Tunes plant activity to seasonal photoperiod

Answering free-essay response questions

Directions: Answer the following question in essay form, not in outline form, using complete sentences. Diagrams may be used to supplement answers, but diagrams alone are not adequate.

1. Plants are organisms adapted to life on land, but evolved from organisms adapted to life within water. Evolving in order to inhabit a land environment requires species to make adaptations in their mode of reproduction, in physical structure and in the way in which they manage water. Discuss how angiosperms adapted to reproducing on land, physically supporting their weight on land, and staying hydrated on land.

Lab on plant pigments and photosynthesis

This two-part lab employs the techniques of chromatography and spectrometry to investigate the composition and photosynthetic activity of plant pigments. In part one, a mixture of pigments extracted from spinach leaves is separated into its component pigments based differences in those pigments physical and chemical properties. In part two, the photosynthetic activity of chloroplasts (also extracted from spinach leaves) is monitored indirectly by means of a colored indicator compound, DPIP.

Part one employs paper chromatography, a technique wherein one passes a dissolved mixture over a strip of paper, thereby separating the components of the mixture. In this lab, the mixture consists of different pigments contained within spinach leaves. Pigments are extracted from the leaves by crushing and scraping, and then are spotted along a line near the bottom of a long paper strip. The strip is placed, pigment side pointing down, within a sealed vessel that contains a shallow pool of an organic solvent, such as acetone. The very end of the paper strip contacts the acetone. Via capillary action — adhesion to the paper and cohesion with itself — the acetone progresses up the length of the strip, dissolving spinach pigments as it passes over them. The progress of the acetone up the strip can be tracked by a visible "solvent front" moving upwards.

Different pigments within the mixture possess different solubilities in acetone, and different affinities for the paper. Those pigments with the highest solubility and lowest affinity for paper travel fastest, keeping closest to the solvent front. Those pigments with the lowest solubility and highest affinity for paper move most slowly, lagging far behind the solvent front. Different combinations of solubility and paper affinity result in different rates of movement. Once the solvent front nears the top of the paper, the strip is removed, and the position of the solvent front is quickly marked. As capillary action ceases, the bands of pigment, now separated, also cease to migrate along the paper strip. Each component pigment of the mixture has a characteristic mobility that can be calculated as the retardation factor, or R_f:

Rf = (distance migrated by pigment) ÷ (distance migrated by solvent)

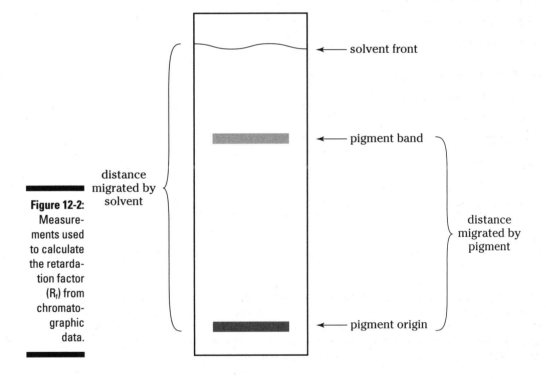

Figure 12-2: Measurements used to calculate the retardation factor (R_f) from chromatographic data.

Part two of the lab investigates the effect of light and high temperature on the photosynthetic activity of solutions of chloroplasts. Chloroplast solutions are prepared from spinach leaves, and are used to prepare several experimental samples. The amount of photosynthetic activity in each solution is determined by use of DPIP (2,6-dichlorophenol-indophenol), a chemical which is blue when oxidized (has fewer electrons) and colorless when reduced (has more electrons). As photosynthesis occurs, electrons within chloroplast pigments become energized by light; some of these energized electrons are accepted by DPIP, converting it from its blue to colorless form. This conversion is quantitatively measured by using a spectrometer, a device that measures the transmittance of different wavelengths of light.

Five samples are prepared and measured spectrometrically. The first sample, a blank, contains no DPIP, and is used to calibrate the spectrometer between readings. This calibration ensures that the various readings can be reliably compared. Another sample contains DPIP but no chloroplasts, and serves as a negative control. This negative control reveals the amount of DPIP conversion one should expect in a solution with no chloroplasts; in other words, it shows how much DPIP is reduced even in the absence of photosynthesis. Two further samples contain both DPIP and chloroplasts, and have both been exposed to an intense light source, one that would presumably drive photosynthesis. In one of these two samples, however, the chloroplasts have been boiled, a harsh treatment that disrupts the intricate protein structure of the pigment molecules. One expects photosynthesis to be diminished in the boiled sample. Finally, measurements are taken of a solution that contains DPIP and chloroplasts, but which was not exposed to intense light, presumably diminishing the amount of photosynthesis in that sample. For all samples, spectrometric measurements are taken initially, and at five minute increments up to fifteen minutes. The results are plotted to reveal differences between samples.

Lab on transpiration

This lab consists of two parts, the first consisting of measurements of transpiration by a leafy shoot under different conditions, and the second consisting of a microscopic investigation of the structure of a plant stem. The second part will not be discussed in this section, as it contains no substantive experimental content. The cell types and stem structures considered in this second part are well-discussed in Chapter 11.

Part one of the transpiration lab indirectly measures transpiration by use of a potometer — a device that measures water uptake by plants or plant structures. The simple potometer used in this lab consists of a pipette attached to a length of clear plastic tubing. The stem of a leafy shoot is inserted into one end of the plastic tubing, the other end of which is attached to a pipette. This maneuver is performed underwater, such that the entire inner volume of the potometer is filled with water, and contains no air bubbles. The stem-tube-pipette assembly is clamped into position such that the stem and pipette point upwards, with the plastic tubing forming a curved U-shape below and between them. In this way, the amount of water taken up by the plant shoot can be directly measured from the decreasing level of the meniscus along the marked gradations of the pipette. Presumably, water uptake at the stem results directly from water loss at the leaves, due to transpiration.

Several such plant-potometer assemblies are constructed, and are subjected to various conditions: the ambient (normal) conditions of the room, under the glare of a bright lamp, in the breezy path of a fan, or covered in a mist of water. Potometer readings are taken initially, and every third minute up to thirty minutes.

To allow comparison between different sets of data, the potometer readings must be adjusted to account for differences in total leaf surface area per plant. The idea here is that, all other things being equal, the amount of transpiration from a given plant is directly proportional to the amount of leaf surface area, since transpiration occurs from the surface of the leaves. Thus, the leaf surface area, in square meters (m^2), of different leaves is estimated either from tracings of the leaves in graph paper, or from measurements of leaf masses (multiplied by a factor that reflects the amount of surface area per unit mass). Potometer readings, in milliliters (mL), are converted to water losses per square meter (mL/m^2) and can then be directly compared. For each condition (room, light, fan, mist), these data are plotted versus time points to reveal differences between samples. One expects transpiration to be increased over the "room" condition in the "light" and "fan" samples, but decreased in the "mist" sample. The principle is that anything increasing evaporation of water at the leaf surface will increase uptake of water from within the potometer. Decreased evaporation at the leaf surface results in decreased water uptake. Put another way, water moves from areas of high water potential (as in, where water is in greater concentration) to areas of lower water potential.

Checking Your Work

See how well you distinguished your roots from your shoots. Here are the answers to the practice questions testing your grasp of Chapter 11. As always, reading the explanations is certain to help.

Answers and explanations for the multiple-choice questions are:

1. (C) is the answer. Elongation (i.e., primary growth) of branches and roots occurs at apical meristems. Secondary meristems produce secondary growth, which typically involves thickening already existing structures.

2. The answer is (D). Evaporation from leaves drives transpiration. Uptake of water by root hairs leads to root pressure. Transpiration and root pressure team up to power to upward flow of xylem sap, the watery liquid that contains dissolved minerals and other nutrients from the soil. Guttation, the outward flow of water from leaf stomata, does not *cause* the distribution of xylem sap, but is rather a *symptom* of high root pressure.

3. The answer is (D). Dicots are characterized by branching networks of veins within their leaves and deep, central taproots. Monocots have parallel veins within their leaves, and more shallow, bunched networks of roots.

4. The answer is (D). Although phloem is often associated with "downward" transport of sugars from the leaves to the rest of a plant, sugar can be transported different directions at different times. For example, surplus sugar stored in roots must eventually be transported "upwards" during less photosynthetically friendly times of year. Osmosis is an important component of the "pressure flow" system that results in transport of sugar from sources to sinks. Xylem, not phloem, is the vascular tissue composed largely of dead cells.

5. (D) is the answer. The stem could curve as a result of phototropic growth towards the sun. Alternately, gravitropism could account for the curvature, as the plant is growing from a slanted surface. Application of auxins to the left stem side would increase cell growth on that side, resulting in the observed rightward curve. Application of abscissic acid to the stem right side would decrease cell growth on that side, also resulting in rightward curvature. However, application of gibberellins to the stem right side would increase cell growth on that side, and should result in leftward curvature — the opposite of what is observed.

6. (B) is the answer. It may help to recall that "dermal" refers to the skin.

7. (A), collenchyma cells, is the correct answer. The unevenly thickened walls of collenchyma cells are ideal for providing structural support to young plants without restricting their growth.

8. Mesophyll cells, (E), is the answer. These cells are a specialized form of ground tissue, located within leaf interiors.

9. Guard cells are the answer, listed as (D). Pairs of these cells site bestride the pores in leaves called stomata. The guard cells respond to many different stimuli, and take up or release water in response. This water transport alters the shape of the guard cells in such a way as to either widen the stomata or close them.

10. (C) is the answer. Sclerenchyma cells specialize in strength, providing support and protection. These cells have thick, secondary cell walls. These walls can be reinforced by the structural protein, lignin.

11. A photoperiod, (E), is the relative length of the "day," the illuminated portion of the daily cycle.

12. Compared to moonlight, sunlight is enriched in light of 660 nanometers (nm), (A). Plants detect this wavelength of light by means of 660 nm phytochromes; absorption of 660 nm light rapidly converts 660 nm phytochrome into 730 nm phytochrome, acting as a sort of ledger to keep track of amounts of sunlight.

13. (C), the circadian rhythm, is a built-in molecular clock that helps plants make appropriate responses to environmental changes that occur with a daily period.

14. The answer is (B), 730 nanometers (nm). Compared to sunlight, moonlight is enriched in this lower-energy wavelength. Plants have phytochromes designed to absorb this wavelength of light. Although 730 nm phytochrome can be rapidly generated from 660 nm phytochrome, it takes 730 nm phytochrome much longer to revert back into 660 nm form.

15. Though we most often think of plants as responding to light, it turns out that critical night length, (D), is the primary determinant of when plants perform important seasonal activities, such as flowering. Interruption of "daytime" exposure by brief periods of darkness does not affect flowering, but interruption of dark "nighttime" periods by as little as a few minutes can disrupt flowering.

Here is a model for the free-essay response question:

1. Angiosperms, the flowering plants, are a highly successful group of land-based organisms. Although angiosperms are highly adapted to life on land, their evolutionary ancestors inhabited watery environments. Therefore, during the course of their evolution, the evolutionary forebears of modern angiosperms needed to address several challenges of land-based living: how to reproduce, how to support their own weight, and how to stay hydrated.

Angiosperms make use of flowers in reproduction, and the structures within flowers bear evidence of adaptations made for reproduction on land. Flowers contain both male and female reproductive parts. Chief among these parts are the gametes, which house the genetic information. In flowers, male gametes take the form of pollen, tiny, spore-like structures ideally suited for being carried on the winds and on the bodies of pollinators. Pollinators, such as insects or other animals, are enticed by the highly-evolved colors and aromas of flowers, and learn to seek the sugary nectar contained within them. Nectar-seeking trips to flowers result in the deposition of pollen onto the pollinators, who subsequently transfer the pollen to other flowers. Hence, the combination of male and female sexual parts within flowers, the multi-faceted allure of flowers, and the small size and structure of pollen combine within an evolutionary package of adaptations to reproduction on land. Furthermore, the blossoming of flowers is timed in synchrony with the seasons such that reproduction is only possible during environmentally favorable times of year.

Physical support within a watery environment is simpler than on land, because land-based organisms do not have the benefit of the large buoyant force of water. Thus, in adapting to life on land, the precursors of the angiosperms had to develop ways to support their relatively greater weight. The most obvious such adaptation is probably the stem, a sturdy structure well-designed to support the weight of shoots and leaves. At the microscopic level, specialization among cell types reflects the need for greater structural support: collenchyma cells have intermittently thickened cell walls that grant strength while still allowing flexibility for growth. Sclerenchyma cells have impressively thick cell walls that provide tremendous support. The cell wall of these and other varieties of plant cell are built of strong, interlocking cellulose chains, often reinforced by the protein lignin. Not only in the structure of their walls, but also in their interiors, plant cells are adapted for physical support: by actively transporting water into themselves, plant cells increase their turgor pressure, which provides structural rigidity.

Finally, access to that crucial solvent of life, water, is obviously more difficult on land than it is in water, so angiosperms must have addressed this difficulty throughout their evolution. The structure of roots, leaves, and the vasculature connecting them reveal how angiosperms addressed the problem of dehydration. Roots are structures that elongate into the soil, tending towards moister and moister areas. To whatever extent roots encounter moisture, they are maximally prepared to receive it, as their fine covering of root hairs provides a massive surface area over which to absorb water. Once absorbed, water may be transported throughout the plant within a system of xylem tubes whose structures are tailored for moving fluids without leakage. These xylem tubes extend all the way into the leaves, structures which themselves reflect adaptations to life on dry land. Although water loss due to evaporation (i.e., transpiration) is a necessary component of angiosperm life, as it helps to pull nutritious xylem sap through the plant, excessive transpiration would lead to dehydration. Thus, stomata, the pores in leaves through which water evaporates, are flanked by guard cells that respond to various stimuli and open or close stomata accordingly. Moreover, leaves are coated in a waxy cuticle, the physical properties of which prevent loss of water through the membranes of epidermal leaf cells. These and other leaf structures are especially evident in plants that live in arid environments, highlighting these structures as direct adaptations to a dry, land environment.

Chapter 13

Animals and Behavior

· ·

In This Chapter

▶ Understanding the flow of matter and energy through animal bodies

▶ Keeping things steady with homeostasis

▶ Surveying the systems that do our inner dirty work for us

▶ Fusing sperm and egg and watching what happens from there

▶ Distilling the themes of animal movement, communication, learning, and behaving

· ·

*I*n this chapter, we stare into our own belly buttons. No, we are not on a mission to locate lint; our mission is to understand how animal bodies — including our own — are built, and how those bodies allow animals like us to do what we do.

In a way, your belly button tells the whole story. Animals must feed, extract and use energy, and get rid of waste. They must maintain a stable internal environment. They must reproduce. Your belly button marks the attachment site of your fetal food-and-waste lifeline. You used the nutrients fed into your belly to develop your own budding body. You curled within a protective sac, one that helped maintain a stable environment as your body took form. Finally, without an act of reproduction on the part of your parents, there would have been no lifeline, no curled and developing you, and no possibility of your contemplating at this moment the belly button with which the story began.

Then, of course, you were born. Feeding, excreting, and maintaining got more complicated. But by that time you had a body chock-full of useful organs to help you with those tasks. Nicely equipped with organ systems, you were able to devote much of your day to learning. You learned to walk. You learned to talk. And, as your score on the AP Biology exam will demonstrate, you learned to learn. One day, you may renew the cycle by helping to create a new belly button. Yours is the story of an animal — in the best sense of the word — and it is the focus of this chapter.

As you ponder the deep philosophical implications of your belly button, you'll do yourself a favor by keeping in mind a few overarching themes. These themes tie together the many details of animal bodies and behaviors into a meaningful whole. It's always easier to remember *what* when *what* is connected to *why*. Gas tanks, engines, wheels, and exhaust pipes all make much more sense when you consider that they serve particular functions within a larger system, and that the system itself functions as a transport device. The same principle applies to the charming, good-looking system sitting behind the steering wheel.

The living systems we call *animals* possess several levels of organization. The simplest level that can be called alive is the cell. Different types of cells organize themselves into groups with special functions; these specialized groups of cells are called tissues. Tissues, in turn, assemble into organs. Groups of organs operate together within organ systems. Organ systems are coordinated within an organism, a living unit that is greater than the sum of its parts. At each of these levels, structure correlates with function. For example, the cells, tissues, and organs of the circulatory system each have structures that enable them to perform specific tasks. These tasks individually support an overall function: distributing materials throughout the organism. This elegant connection between structure and function — across all levels of organization — is a beautiful result of evolution.

The Coming and Going of Energy

Energy is neither created nor destroyed. On the other hand, energy is continually transformed from one form to another. The same is true of matter. Transforming energy and matter into forms useful for surviving and reproducing is what living things do. On planet Earth, the important task of funneling energy from the environment in useful chemical forms has been taken on by a group of organisms called the autotrophs. Plants are well-known examples of autotrophs. All the other organisms on the planet fall into a group called the heterotrophs. Heterotrophs get their energy by feeding on the autotrophs or on each other. This autotroph/heterotroph system has been churning along pretty nicely for a few billion years.

As heterotrophs, all animals have to solve the same basic problems: How do I get the good stuff that contains energy? How do I use this energy? What do I do with the stuff I can't use? How do I keep myself running smoothly, so I can keep asking all these questions?

Hunting or gathering

Different animals have evolved different strategies for getting the good stuff that contains energy. Three major strategies have emerged. Herbivores acquire chemical energy by eating plants (gathering). Carnivores acquire chemical energy by eating animals (hunting). Omnivores see no reason to be so picky, and get their chemical energy by eating both plants and animals. For a time, herbivores, carnivores and omnivores succeed in meeting their energy needs by doing all this eating. As energy flows through them, they transform it in ways most beneficial to themselves. They keep eating for as long as they need energy. Eventually, they die, and no longer need to eat. At this point, they are kind enough to release whatever energy remains within them back to the environment.

Digesting

Getting chemical energy by eating is one thing. Being able to use that energy is another. In between these tasks lies the crucial process of digesting. For the most part, the matter eaten by animals must be broken down to release energy. Animal food comes in a wondrous variety of forms, but all these forms consist of one or another variety of molecule. During digestion, the different types of molecules within food are broken down into useful building blocks. The digestive system is a "disassembly line," un-building finished products into their parts, releasing energy in the process.

Using or storing energy

Having fed and digested, animals enter the assembly business. The energy and matter of digested food are channeled into thousands of different construction projects within animal cells. Compared to human attempts at construction, biological construction is marvelously efficient; energy and materials reliably flow to where they are needed, when they are needed. Leftovers are wisely stored for later use.

Excreting waste

Alas, in all construction there is waste. Not all food is entirely digested into useful packets of energy and material. Not all surpluses are stored. Some materials, frankly, aren't particularly useful to an animal, and find their proper place on a junk heap. Whatever the details, all these wastes must be eliminated. When animals dump their junk, we call it *excreting*. Of course, one animal's excretion may be another animal's filet mignon.

Staying normal: The importance of homeostasis

Eating, digesting, building, and excreting can get pretty complicated. Each of these internal processes entails many tasks, and the tasks can be tricky. What's more, these countless tricky tasks must all be coordinated. There's no way to pull it all off without carefully controlling the internal environment. Imagine each of the cells, tissues, organs, and organ systems that do all the work as a temperamental Goldilocks, unable to cope unless her porridge is "just right." Animals keep their many Goldilockses content through a process called homeostasis. *Homeostasis* means "steady state," and maintaining steady states can be a real challenge in the face of wildly changing external conditions. Animals live in scorching deserts, on frigid mountainsides, and in the murky waters of stagnant swamps. Sometimes food and water are plentiful; sometimes the cupboard is bare. Many animals inhabit several different kinds of environments and must adjust to them all. Homeostasis must be maintained across all the levels of an animal's organization. Such a coordinated effort requires endless sensing, communicating, and adjusting. Goldilocks is one finicky customer.

Balancing body temperature

One of the key challenges to homeostasis is maintaining an appropriate internal body temperature, also known as *thermoregulation*. Different animals have solved this problem in different ways, but some overall patterns have become evolutionarily popular. Moreover, the physical laws governing heat transfer limit the thermoregulatory toolbox. All heat transfer occurs in one of four ways: conduction, convection, radiation, and evaporation.

Conduction is the direct transfer of heat between objects in contact, such as between your skin and the water as you frolic in the ocean waves in Maui. *Convection* is the transfer of heat between an object and a fluid (liquid or gas) that circulates around it, such as from your skin to the gas molecules in a cool breeze that flows over the beach in Maui. Radiation is the transfer of energy to by electromagnetic waves, which results in the conversion of that energy to heat in an object that absorbs the waves. An example of this would be the heat transferred to your skin by the sun as you sit on the beach in Maui. *Evaporation* is the transfer of heat from an object as liquid upon the surface of that object evaporates. For example, if you hadn't prepared with this book, you might well lose heat by evaporation as you sweat profusely during the AP Biology exam, wishing that you were in Maui. Animals exchange heat with their environment using combinations of these four processes.

Ectothermic animals achieve appropriate body temperature mainly by absorbing heat from their surroundings. *Endothermic* animals adopt the opposite strategy; most of their body heat is generated by chemical reactions within their bodies. Regardless of whatever you may do in Maui, you are an endotherm.

Notice that skin features prominently in the process of thermoregulation. This makes sense, as skin makes up the outer surface of our bodies, directly contacting the environment with which we exchange heat. Skin is an important thermoregulatory organ whose major structures are shown in Figure 13-1. The outer layers of skin (*epidermis*) contain sweat pores, allowing passage of sweat produced within sweat glands in the middle layers of skin (*dermis*). Once secreted to the surface, sweat carries away heat by evaporation. Also within the dermis are many blood vessels. By dilating or constricting, these vessels allow greater or smaller volumes of blood close to the surface of the skin, where the heat carried by the blood can be released by conduction. Finally, the innermost layers of skin (*hypodermis*) contain fat cells that insulate the body, keeping endothermic heat inside.

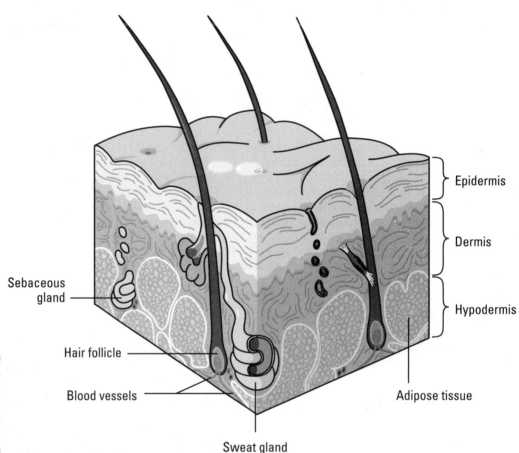

Figure 13-1:
The layers and structures of the skin.

Epidermis

Dermis

Hypodermis

Sebaceous gland

Hair follicle

Blood vessels

Adipose tissue

Sweat gland

Balancing water and solutes

Another challenge to homeostasis is maintaining the appropriate balance of water and solutes (dissolved particles, like salts) within your tissues, also known as *osmoregulation.* Water and solute concentrations are intimately connected due to the processes of diffusion and osmosis. If this idea sounds unfamiliar, spend a few moments with the lab on diffusion and osmosis in Chapter 4. Wherever solutes go, water tends to follow. A key organ system in osmoregulation is the excretory system, the centerpieces of which are the kidneys, extensively detailed in Figures 13-2 and 13-3. Kidneys help control the osmotic balance of the blood by controlling the concentrations of water and solutes within it. The blood, in turn, helps to control the osmotic balance of all the tissues through which it circulates. The watery, salty byproduct of the good work of the kidneys is urine, which passes from the kidneys, through ureters, to the bladder, and from there passes out of the body.

Kidneys are packed with nephrons, their functional units. The basic functions of the nephron are depicted in simple form in Figure 13-4. Nephrons filter the blood, separating water and small solutes from the larger blood components. This initial filtering occurs within a structure of the nephron called Bowman's capsule, in which the liquid portion of the blood is forced along with small solutes through the glomerulus. The filtrate (as in, the water and dissolved solutes) then proceed through a long and convoluted series of tubules — little tubes — on its way to the ureter. The long and winding tubules (about 50 miles worth per kidney!) have a large internal surface area, packed with several kinds of membrane protein channels. The tubules are closely intertwined with blood vessels, so that water and solutes can pass from the filtrate to the blood. Water, sugar, amino acids, vitamins, salts, and other materials are reabsorbed into the bloodstream as the filtrate moves through the tubules. Waste materials are transported into the filtrate. Excess water and solutes (urea, K^+, H^+) collect at the end of the tubules and are eventually excreted as urine, usually much to the relief of the animal.

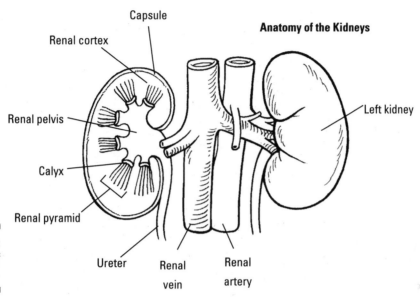

Figure 13-2: Structure of the kidneys.

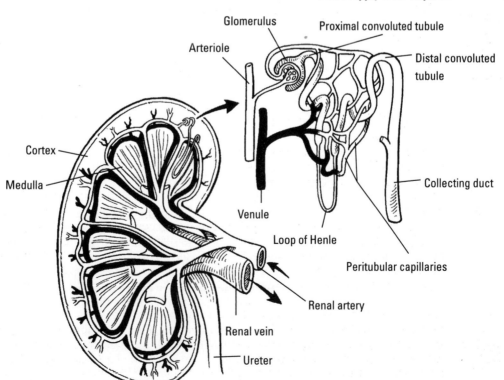

Figure 13-3: Structure of the kidneys' functional unit, the nephron.

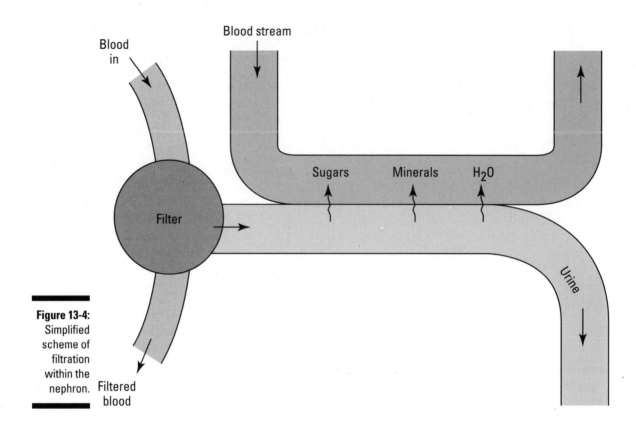

Figure 13-4:
Simplified
scheme of
filtration
within the
nephron.

Approaching by Systems

Animals are systems of systems (. . . of systems of systems . . .). One way to understand how the whole animal operates is to study it from the top down. Following this approach, this section surveys the organ systems common to the vast majority of animals, including and especially you. You've already been exposed to one organ system — the excretory system — in the discussion of homeostasis in the section earlier in this chapter, "Staying normal: The importance of homeostasis." In addition to simply making good sense, the "systems" approach will best prepare you for the exam. So, as a card-carrying heterotroph, pop some corn and ready yourself for a tour of the circulatory, nervous, musculoskeletal, digestive, endocrine, and immune systems.

Circulatory system

Compared to the cells with which they're built, most animals are very large. The molecules of gas, digested food, waste, and other materials that cells use to do their thing simply can't be transported throughout an entire animal body in the same way that they're moved through individual cells. To deal with this "internal transport" problem, animals have evolved circulatory systems. Circulatory systems help animals move materials *within* themselves, and they interface with other organ systems (like the digestive and respiratory systems) to help animals exchange materials with the environment *outside* themselves.

Two major kinds of circulatory system have evolved among animals: open and closed systems. Open circulatory systems (found mostly within insects and mollusks) transport a fluid called hemolymph. Hemolymph is a general-purpose body fluid, serving many functions, including those served by blood within other animals. The heart pumps the blood into a series of cavities called sinuses. Within the sinuses, hemolymph contacts the organs, directly exchanging materials with the cells. Circulating hemolymph returns to the heart through pores called ostia.

Other animals, including all vertebrates, have closed circulatory systems. In these systems, a heart — sometimes several hearts — pumps blood through an enclosed, branching network of vessels. The branches of this network divide and subdivide until the vessels are small and thin enough to allow direct exchange of materials between blood and the fluids surrounding cells (i.e., the "interstitial" fluids). Following exchange, the blood continues its circular trip through the vessels, which converge into larger and larger streams on their route back to the heart.

Circulatory system elements

The basic elements of a closed circulatory system, then, are:

✔ **Blood:** Blood bustles with cells, all suspended within a liquid called plasma. Blood cells come in two main types: red and white. Red blood cells, or erythrocytes, are the most common type. Erythrocytes are highly specialized structures, devoted to the task of carrying gases like oxygen (O_2) and carbon dioxide (CO_2) through the circulatory system. So focused are erythrocyte cells on this job that they entirely lack normal cellular amenities like nuclei and mitochondria. White blood cells, or leukocytes, form the other group of blood cells. Various kinds of leukocytes work together to help the animal body fight off infection. Large fragments of cells, called platelets, are also found within blood, and play an important role in blood clotting. All these cells and cell fragments swim about in the plasma, which accounts more than half of the total blood volume. Plasma is about 90 percent water, and contains dissolved salts, proteins, nutrients, wastes, and other materials. If you can dissolve it in water, plasma will transport it. Even if you can't dissolve it — like, say, cholesterol — you can probably attach it to a plasma protein, and plasma will still transport it.

✔ **Vessels:** In order to drive its flow through the closed network of vessels, blood needs a source of pressure. The heart fills this need. Different animals have different types and numbers of hearts, as well as different arrangements of blood vessels. Here, we unashamedly ignore all this lovely biological diversity, and focus on the human circulatory system. Fascinating as the two-chambered heart of a fish may be, you are unlikely to encounter it on the AP Biology exam.

✔ **Heart:** Human hearts are made of muscle. In particular, they are made of cardiac muscle, and are extensively wired with nerves that regulate beating, the rhythmic contraction of the heart muscle. The human heart contains four chambers: two atria and two ventricles, divided into left and right sides by a central septum. Large vessels through which blood exits the heart are called arteries, and large vessels through which blood enters the heart are called veins.

Capillaries

Once blood exits the heart, its path diverges from arteries into smaller arterioles, branching off into ever smaller vessels that ultimately arrive at capillaries, as shown in Figure 13-5. Capillaries are so small and thin that the blood within them can exchange materials with the interstitial fluid immediately outside them. Enabling this microscopic exchange is the central function of the circulatory system, and all the larger structures of the system are subservient to that cause.

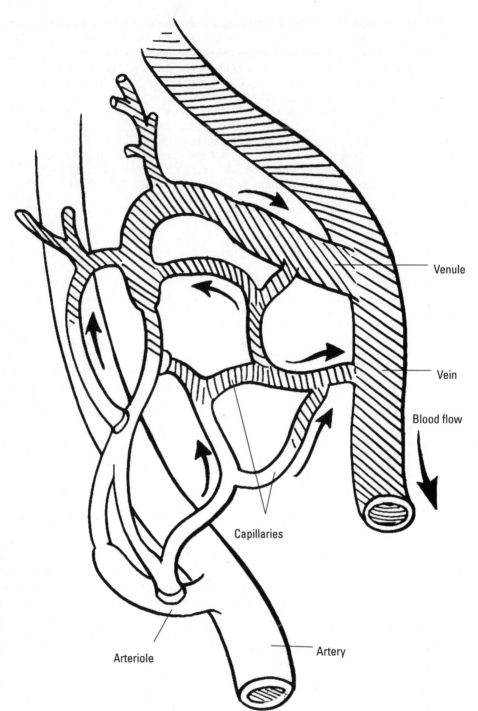

Figure 13-5:
Blood flow
through
arteries,
capillaries,
and veins.

Among the important materials exchanged across capillary walls are oxygen and carbon dioxide. Cells consume oxygen in order to burn sugar during cellular respiration. That same sugar-burning process gives off carbon dioxide. These two gases diffuse down concentration gradients across the capillary walls. Cells unload excess carbon dioxide into the circulating blood; the blood, in turn, unloads oxygen into the cells. Both gases are handled by a protein within erythrocytes called hemoglobin. Whether hemoglobin carries molecules of oxygen or carbon dioxide depends on the relative concentrations of the two dissolved gases.

In addition to oxygen, carbon dioxide and other gases, the materials swapped across capillaries include salts, water, and the molecular bits and pieces required to build carbohydrates, proteins, lipids, nucleic acids and other cellular building blocks.

Circulating blood moves through capillaries, and these capillaries merge into small vessels called venules (peek once more at Figure 13-5). Venules progressively join into veins, and veins terminate at the heart. Simple, right?

Double circulation

Well, almost. Blood must have a way to get rid of its cargo of carbon dioxide waste, and acquire a fresh cargo of oxygen for the next trip through the closed loop of the circulatory system. To solve this problem, many animals — including humans — have evolved a system of "double circulation," an overview of which is shown in Figure 13-6. In this system, the heart pumps blood not only to capillaries throughout the body and back (the "systemic" circuit), but also through a second loop into the lungs (the "pulmonary" circuit). Within the pulmonary circuit, the circulatory system interfaces with another organ system: the respiratory system.

The respiratory system is an organ system in its own right, but is so closely intertwined with the circulatory system (some people refer to the two together as the "circulorespiratory" system) that we'll treat the two systems together here. After returning to the heart from capillaries far and near, blood is pumped into the lungs. There, vessels branch into fine capillary networks that surround alveoli, tiny, gas-filled sacs within the lungs, shown in Figure 13-7. Humans fill their alveoli with oxygen-rich air by inhaling. Just as gases were swapped with the interstitial fluids surrounding cells, so oxygen and carbon dioxide now diffuse down concentration gradients across alveolar and capillary walls. Hemoglobin within the blood dumps its carbon dioxide and shoulders a new load of oxygen. Humans expel the carbon dioxide waste pooled within their alveoli by exhaling. Oxygen-loaded blood returns to the heart, ready now to be pumped out through the arteries.

I just called to say you're having a heart attack

Medicine and communications technology mingle in an exciting area called biotelemetry. Biotelemetry is the measurement and reporting of biological information from a remote location. As early as the 1950s, space programs in the U.S. and in the former Soviet Union were developing biotelemetry devices that could report the vital medical data of astronauts (like heart rate, blood pressure, and blood oxygen levels) in space to physicians sitting behind desks on Earth. As technology has advanced, these specialized applications have been spreading into uses beneficial to those of us who aren't actually in orbit.

Biotelemetry may become a common feature of artificial pacemakers implanted into human hearts and brains. Pacemakers are devices that control the timing of electrical impulses. The heart has natural pacemakers in clusters of nerve cells called the sinoatrial and atrioventricular nodes. Improperly functioning nodes can lead to serious heart malfunction and death. Artificial pacemakers have been used for decades to correct these kinds of problems, but as life-saving as these devices often are, they don't respond sensitively to changing conditions in a patient's heart. A similar class of devices, sometimes called "brain pacemakers," are being used to regulate electrical activity in the brain in order to treat symptoms of epilepsy, Parkinson's disease, depression, and even to help bring patients out of coma-like states. As with cardiac pacemakers, brain pacemakers must be made to respond more sensitively to changing conditions in patients' bodies. Biotelemetry may be a solution.

Sensors implanted in a patient's body can send wireless signals, like those used in cell phones, to provide constantly updated medical data. These signals can be sent over thousands of miles, if necessary, to help doctors keep track of potential problems. Current research aims to develop feedback systems that would allow a continuous stream of data from inside patients — wherever they are — to keep doctors and their slick software informed. In turn, doctors could use wireless technology to send instructions to the pacemakers within their patients, tailoring their output to meet the needs of the moment.

In addition to acting as a pump, the heart directs the flow of blood through the two loops of double circulation: the systemic and pulmonary circuits. The entrances, exits, and inner boulevards of the heart are shown in Figure 13-8. Blood emptied of oxygen and loaded with carbon dioxide enters the right atrium of the heart via the inferior and superior vena cava, veins that drain from the lower and upper body, respectively. A contraction forces this blood through the right atrioventricular valve into the right atrium, where another contraction forces the blood out of the heart and into the lungs via the pulmonary arteries. The pulmonary semilunar valve prevents backflow into the heart. After gas exchange in the lungs, oxygenated blood returns to the heart via the pulmonary veins, draining into the left atrium. A contraction forces the blood through the left atrioventricular valve into the highly muscular left ventricle. A powerful contraction of the left ventricle forces blood out through the aortic semilunar valve into the aorta, and from there into the branching network of arteries.

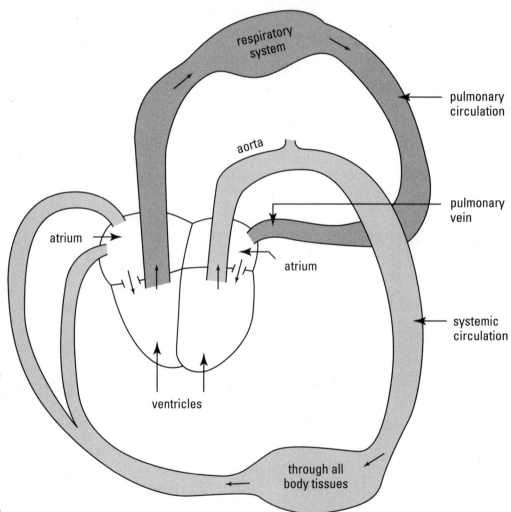

Figure 13-6:
Scheme
of double
circulation
through sys-
temic and
pulmonary
circuits.

Each of the four chambers of the heart must contract, and these contractions must be precisely timed, for at any given moment blood is returning to the heart or departing from it. The timing of cardiac contractions is controlled by bundles of nerves within the heart. Each heartbeat begins with an electrical signal generated by the sinoatrial node, or "pacemaker." This signal spreads through nerve fibers into both atria, which contract at the same time, each atrium forcing blood into the ventricle below it. The electrical signal delays for a fraction of a second at the atrioventricular node, then spreads through Purkinje fibers into the thickly muscular ventricles. The ventricles then contract, the right ventricle sending blood into the pulmonary circuit, the left ventricle sending blood into the systemic circuit.

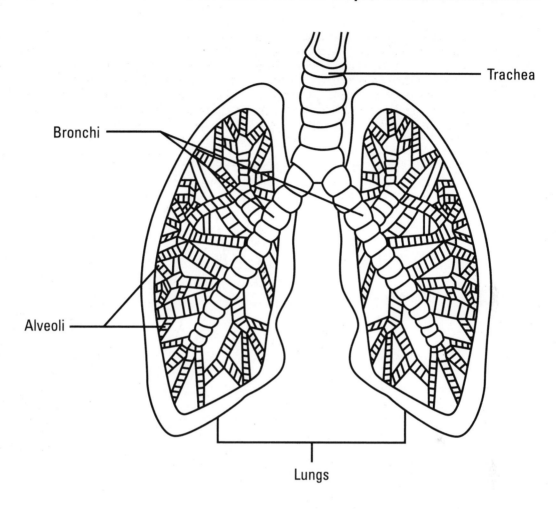

Trachea

Bronchi

Alveoli

Lungs

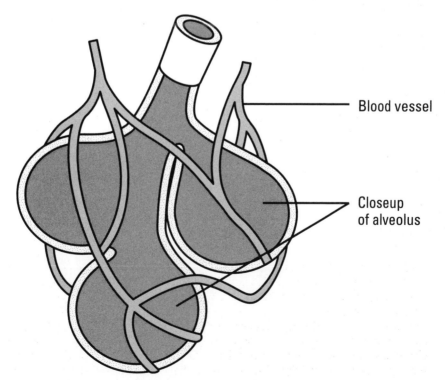

Blood vessel

Closeup
of alveolus

Figure 13-7:
Overview of
the human
lungs, and
the basic
structure of
alveoli.

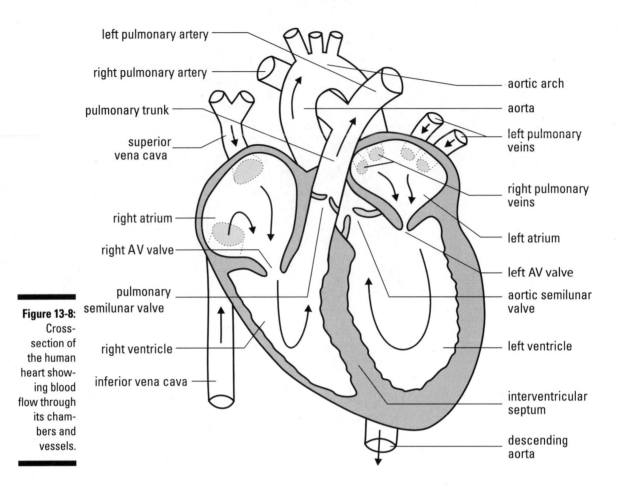

left pulmonary artery

right pulmonary artery

pulmonary trunk

superior
vena cava

right atrium

right AV valve

pulmonary
semilunar valve

right ventricle

inferior vena cava

aortic arch

aorta

left pulmonary
veins

right pulmonary
veins

left atrium

left AV valve

aortic semilunar
valve

left ventricle

interventricular
septum

descending
aorta

Figure 13-8:
Cross-
section of
the human
heart show-
ing blood
flow through
its cham-
bers and
vessels.

Nervous system

The nervous system is the organ system specializing in rapid communication throughout the body. Nerves conduct information in the form of electrical signals. These signals contain information about the state of affairs both within and outside of the animal. This sensory information is processed, also within nervous system structures, so that the animal can respond appropriately. Finally, command-and-control decisions about those responses are relayed through the nervous system. The basic unit of the nervous system through which all these signals move is the neuron, or nerve cell.

There are many variations on the neuron theme, but your basic neuron (shown in Figure 13-9) consists of dendrites, a cell body, an axon and a synaptic terminal. Axons are coated with a myelin sheath, periodically interrupted by nodes of Ranvier. The myelin sheath itself is maintained by Schwann cells. Neurons are supported by neuroglial cells. Signals are transmitted between neurons across a synapse, the space between the synaptic terminal of one neuron and the dendrites of the next.

Neurons fall into three major categories: sensory neurons, motor neurons, and interneurons. Sensory neurons (see Figure 13-10) transmit stimuli (information that eventually produces a response) from sensors that monitor the external and internal environment of the animal. Motor neurons convey impulses that produce responses within "effector" cells. Interneurons process sensory information and connect the sensory neurons to motor neurons. Together, the sensory and motor neurons comprise the peripheral nervous system (PNS). Nerve cells within the brain and spinal cord make up the central nervous system (CNS). Signals from the PNS to CNS are "afferent," while signals from the CNS to PNS are "efferent."

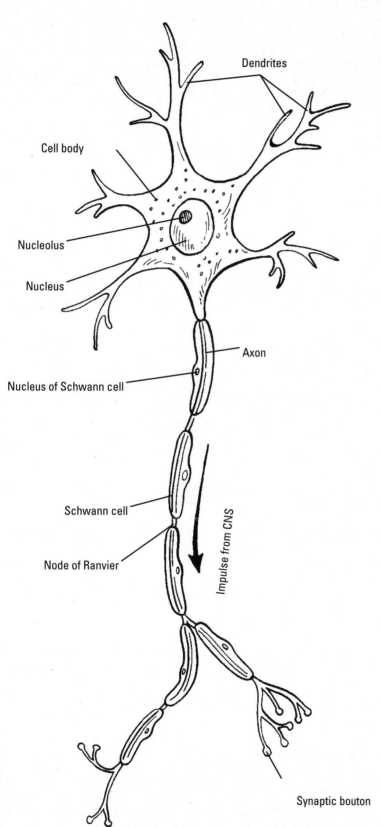

Dendrites

Cell body

Nucleolus

Nucleus

Axon

Nucleus of Schwann cell

Impulse from CNS

Schwann cell

Node of Ranvier

Synaptic bouton

Figure 13-9:
Structure of
motor
neurons.

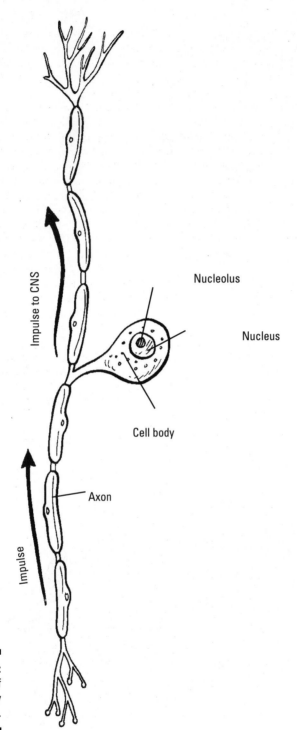

Figure 13-10:
Structure of
the sensory
neuron.

Central nervous system

To better share and coordinate information, nerve cell bodies sometimes cluster into functional groups. When these groups occur in the CNS, we call them nuclei (and when we do so, we are careful not to confuse them with atomic or cellular nuclei). When the clusters occur in the PNS, we call them ganglia.

The brain is a stunningly impressive feature of the CNS (shown in Figure 13-11), highly evolved for many different information-processing tasks. The brain sifts, sorts and integrates vast reams of sensory data in order to provide appropriate response impulses. Although a deep understanding of brain structure is unnecessary for purposes of murdering the AP Biology exam, a short primer on the topic would be prudent. The brain sits upon a brain stem that is connected directly to the spinal cord. The brain stem consists of the medulla oblongata, pons, and midbrain, and operates mostly to maintain basic animal functions, like breathing and sensing pain. At the posterior base of the brain is the cerebellum, which helps animals with things like posture and balance. At the center of the brain are the thalamus and hypothalamus. The thalamus sifts through reams of sensory data, helping to decide which bits are most important for further processing. The hypothalamus monitors details about the animal's internal environment and is also part of the endocrine system, an organ system responsible for controlling the body via chemical signals. The outermost layer of the brain, large and highly developed in humans, is the cerebellum. The cerebellum is divided into two halves called hemispheres, and is the brain structure associated with the sexier brain activities like thought, memory and perception.

Some signals never make it to the brain. When a sensory signal (like, that stovetop sure is hot) travels only to the spinal cord before being processed and bounced back to effector cells (such as, okay, I'll remove my hand), we call the process a reflex. Only later does the sensory data that stimulated the reflex make its way to the brain (such as, wow, my hand sure does hurt . . . good thing I removed it from that stovetop).

The Central Nervous System

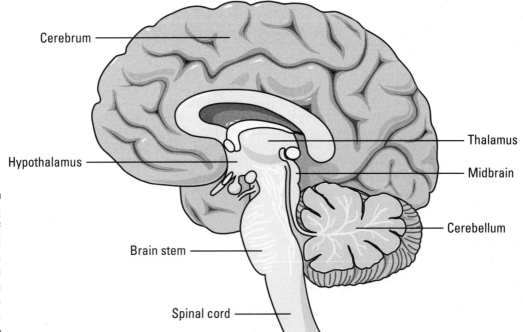

Figure 13-11: Sketch of the central nervous system focusing on structures of the brain.

Despite all this talk of electrical signals, rest assured that animal bodies are not packed with vast networks of copper wire. Biology's approach to sending electrical signals is more subtle, beautiful and, well, complicated. Before diving into the explanation, ask yourself how much you remember about active and passive transport across membranes. If the answer is "not so much," you may want to rekindle your friendship with Chapter 5.

Resting potential

When nerve cells aren't sending signals, they're busy maintaining something called a resting potential. A resting potential is a charge imbalance across the nerve cell membrane, as depicted in Figure 13-12. Typically, resting nerve cells keep their insides more negatively charged than the environment outside the cell (about −70 millivolts so, to be precise). In part, neurons do this trick by actively transporting positively charged sodium ions (Na^+) outside the cell. However, the membrane protein that pumps out the sodium ions simultaneously allows positively charged potassium ions (K^+) to enter the cell, thereby diminishing the charge imbalance. Some of the potassium ions, crowded inside the cell, diffuse down their concentration gradient and end up back outside the cell. This outward diffusion of K^+ helps create the inside-negative potential. The remainder of the resting potential is mostly accounted for by large amounts of negatively charged nucleic acids and proteins within the cell.

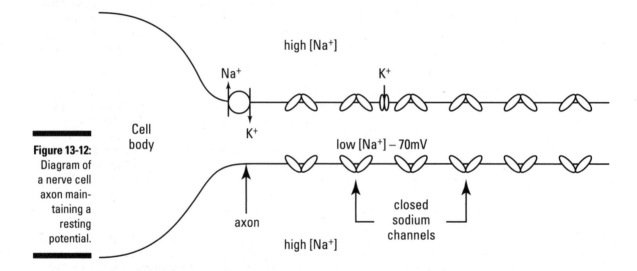

Figure 13-12: Diagram of a nerve cell axon maintaining a resting potential.

Given their choice, the excluded Na^+ ions would rush back into the cell, driven both by the charge imbalance and by the concentration gradient of sodium across the membrane. However, the membrane protein channels through which the sodium ions would happily rush are closed. The result is an electrochemical gradient — a difference of charge *and* concentration across the cell membrane. In this state, we say that the neuron is polarized. In short, a bunch of energy has been stored and awaits release.

Action potential

The stored energy of the resting potential is released by an action potential. An action potential can occur when an electrical stimulus opens voltage-gated ion channels in the membrane at the beginning of an axon. Once the channel gates are open, sodium ions at that spot rush back into the neuron, reducing some of the charge imbalance in their immediate neighborhood, as shown in Figure 13-13. In other words, that part of the axon starts to depolarize, with the membrane potential rising from −70 millivolts. Stronger stimuli depolarize the axon to greater extents, moving continuously through "graded" potentials. If the stimulus is strong enough, the amount of depolarization will cross a "threshold" potential (seen in Figure 13-13), usually around −50 millivolts. Passing a threshold potential causes nearby sodium channels to open, increasing the membrane potential further still. Stimuli that maintain the threshold potential long enough for the membrane to depolarize to about +35 millivolts trigger an all-or-nothing response called an action potential, shown in Figure 13-13. No matter what the strength of the stimulus, all action potentials are equivalent. "Stronger" signals are sent in the form of multiple action potentials, one after the other.

Once achieved, the series of events triggered by an action potential cannot be reversed. Voltage-gated sodium channels neighboring the depolarized area open, and the sodium channels at the original site soon close. With the gates open, this new area depolarizes, and the whole process repeats itself, spreading the depolarization along the length of the axon. This flow of charge along the axon is the electrical signal transmitted by the neuron. The myelin sheath, interrupted by nodes of Ranvier, speeds up transmission of the signal by restricting the points at which ions can rush across the membrane. In effect, the signal jumps from node to node.

In the immediate aftermath of the action potential, potassium ions rush outside the cell, driven out by the positive charge of the inrushing sodium ions. This process is called repolarization, and effectively reverses the distribution of ions maintained during the resting potential. You can imagine the electrical signal as a boat speeding down an axon river, leaving swirls of Na^+ and K^+ in its wake. In order to ready the neuron for another action potential, the sodium and potassium ions must be sent back to their proper resting potential places. This job is performed by a membrane protein called the Na^+/K^+ pump. Pumping can take a little time, during which the neuron is incapable of achieving another action potential. We call this stretch of time the *refractory period*.

Action potentials account for the transmission of signals along neurons, but not for the transmission of signals between neurons. To move from neuron to neuron, a signal must cross the synapse separating one neuron from the next. When an action potential reaches the end of an axon, called a synaptic terminal, it causes calcium channels to open, allowing calcium ions (Ca^{2+}) to rush into the terminal. There, awaiting this influx of calcium, are vesicles containing neurotransmitters.

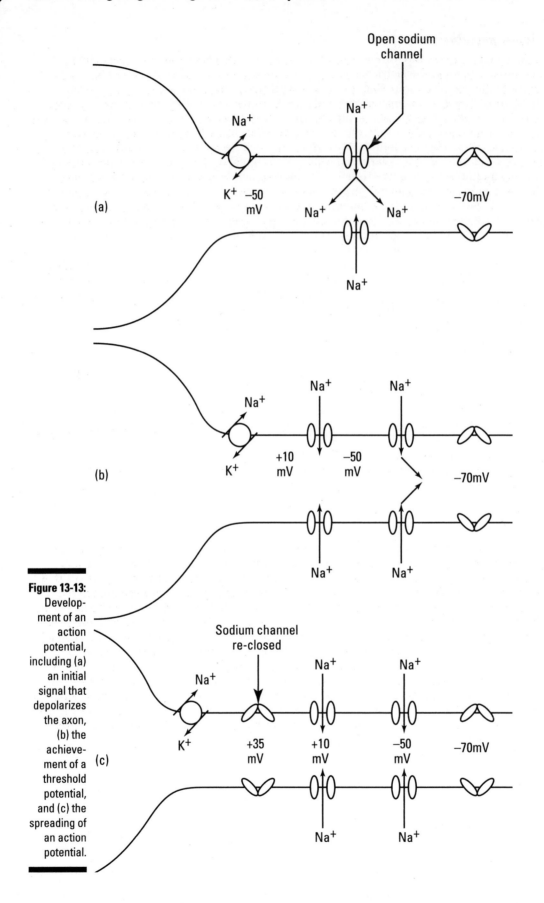

Figure 13-13:
Development of an action potential, including (a) an initial signal that depolarizes the axon, (b) the achievement of a threshold potential, and (c) the spreading of an action potential.

Neurotransmitters

Neurotransmitters are small molecules that serve as messengers between nerve cells. Inflowing calcium ions trigger neurotransmitter-containing vesicles to fuse with the membrane at the very end of the axon terminal (i.e., the presynaptic membrane). As depicted in Figure 13-14, the neurotransmitters are thereby released by exocytosis into the synaptic space, where they diffuse towards membrane surrounding a dendrite of a neighboring neuron (the postsynaptic membrane). Receptor proteins in the postsynaptic membrane recognize and bind to the neurotransmitters. The receptors are coupled to ion channels; when a neurotransmitter binds, the ion channel opens. Ions flow through the opened channels, altering the membrane potential of the postsynaptic neuron. Depending on the specific receptors bound by the neurotransmitters, the membrane potential may be altered so as to either stimulate or inhibit an action potential in the postsynaptic neuron. The same neurotransmitter can exert different effects on different neurons, depending on the receptor that binds it.

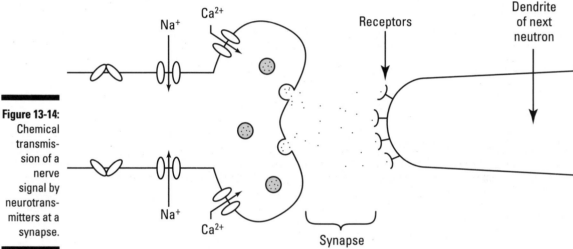

Figure 13-14: Chemical transmission of a nerve signal by neurotransmitters at a synapse.

What are the original stimuli that set the signals in motion? The answers are many and various. Different sensory structures respond to different physical stimuli. Typically, sensory organs contain specialized cells, and these cells contain specialized membrane proteins that convert a physical stimulus into a flow of ions across a membrane. Photoreceptors in the retina of the eye open ion channels upon absorbing light. Hair cells within the ear convert the mechanical vibrations of sound into ion currents. Sensory receptors in the skin contain ion channels that respond to heat or pressure. The senses of smell and taste rely on ion channels that open when receptor proteins bind to small molecules. Internally, there are gated ion channels that respond to a wide variety of chemical signals. The emergent theme is that all manner of physical stimuli are translated into the flow of ions across cell membranes — that is to say, they are translated into electrical signals. Electrical signals are transmitted along neurons by similar flows of ions. As signals move throughout the nervous system, they alternately assume electrical and chemical form as they move from neurons, through synapses, into other neurons.

Musculoskeletal System

Tuna swim. Cheetahs sprint. Geese fly. Humans occasionally have to reach for the remote control. In short, animals move. Movement involves the action of muscles on skeletal elements.

Scaffolding with skeletons

There are different types of skeleton among the animals. Some invertebrates employ *hydrostatic* skeletons, in which skeletal elements are created by filling cavities with fluid, making those cavities stiff with hydrostatic pressure. This type of skeleton is used by several kinds of worm, and by simpler animals living in watery environments. Other invertebrates, like crabs and insects, have an *exoskeleton,* or hard outer shell. Vertebrates like humans have an endoskeleton, in which hard scaffolding elements (bones) are encased within softer tissues like muscle and skin. All three types of skeleton give an animal shape, provide protection, and enable movement.

Endoskeletons are composed of bones that meet at joints. Some joints, such as occur between the plates of the skull, do not allow for movement. Most joints, however, allow for one of several kinds of movement. Ball-and-socket joints like the one in your shoulder allow the greatest degree of motion. Hinge joints like the knee allow back-and-forth movement in one plane — you know, like a door hinge. Pivot joints allow rotation around a central axis, as when you twist your forearm so that your palm faces up or down.

The bones within the human skeleton are composed of different kinds of tissue. The major mineral component that gives bones strength is calcium phosphate, $Ca_3(PO_4)_2$. Bones, made largely of cells, are alive, and so are equipped with both blood vessels and nerves. Bone interiors are filled with marrow, which contains fat cells and cells that are involved in making blood. Some parts of the inside of a bone may also contain spongy bone, a hard but porous network that provides lightweight strength. The hard, outer shells of bone (compact bone) are denser, and consist of functional units called osteons. Each osteon is built from a circular arrangement of bone cells, all surrounding a central Haversian canal. The canal contains blood vessels and nerves that serve the surrounding cells.

Joints are tied together for stability by ligaments, tough protein fibers. The contacting surfaces of a joint are covered with cartilage, a smooth and flexible material that prevents bone-to-bone friction and helps cushion impacts. Muscles that create motion around the joints are attached to bones by tendons, another kind of tough protein fiber.

Flexing your muscle

Vertebrates have three major kinds of muscle: skeletal, cardiac, and smooth. Skeletal muscles attach to bones and contract to create movement about skeletal joints. Skeletal muscles are composed of long fibers, with each fiber itself a bundle of long myofibrils. Skeletal muscles appear striated (striped) because of overlapping structures within the functional element of skeletal muscle, the sarcomere. Cardiac muscle is unique to the heart, and is similar to skeletal muscle in that it also contracts by means of sarcomeres, and is therefore striated. However, unlike the arrangement of long myofibrils within skeletal muscle, cardiac muscle fibers arrange themselves into branched, interconnecting bunches. Smooth muscle is not striated, nor is it as strong as skeletal or cardiac muscle. Smooth muscle contracts slowly, and is used for many kinds of involuntary contraction, such as are used to constrict blood vessels or create churning in the stomach.

The sarcomere is a clever bit of biology. Sarcomeres are the basic functional units (i.e., the individual structures that actually contract) within the myofibrils of skeletal and cardiac muscle. Myofibrils are built from two types of myofilament, thin filaments made of the protein actin, and thick filaments made of the protein myosin. The two kinds of myofilament overlap one another in a repeating pattern that produces the striated appearance of these muscles. Each repeating unit is a sarcomere, and a contraction consists of thin and thick filaments sliding over one another, as detailed in Figure 13-15.

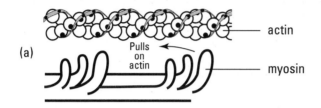

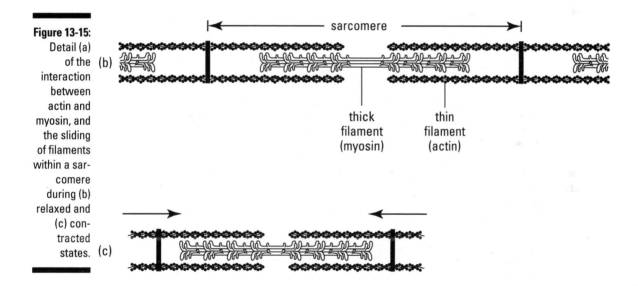

Figure 13-15: Detail (a) of the interaction between actin and myosin, and the sliding of filaments within a sarcomere during (b) relaxed and (c) contracted states.

A contraction is initiated by an electrical impulse from a motor neuron. The neuron sends its signal into a muscle fiber at a neuromuscular junction, releasing the neurotransmitter acetylcholine into the synapse between the nerve and muscle cells. When the postsynaptic terminal of the muscle cell binds acetylcholine, it creates an action potential in the muscle cell. Resting muscle cells store calcium ions (Ca^{2+}) within a specialized kind of endoplasmic reticulum (hello, Chapter 5) called the sarcoplasmic reticulum. The spreading action potential releases calcium from the sarcoplasmic reticulum into the cytoplasm of the muscle cell. Calcium binds to actin myofilaments in a way that causes them to bind to neighboring myosin myofilaments. This binding triggers myosin to burn ATP energy in order to power the sliding of one myofilament over another — this sliding, played out over the many sarcomeres of a myofibril, is the contraction.

Digestive system

The nice thing about trying to understand the digestive system is that it has a definite beginning (the mouth) and a definite end (the anus), and hopefully, never the twain shall meet. Digestion is what occurs between these two termini. A map of the winding highway between mouth and anus is shown in Figure 13-16. The tasks of the digestive system are to convert food into a form that can be absorbed by the body, to absorb whatever useful components are contained within the food, and to pass whatever remains as waste. In principle, it's pretty simple. However, there are many kinds of nutrients within foods, and each kind requires special handling. What is amazing about the digestive system is how systematic and efficient it is at doing its job. The following account of such systematic efficiency reflects the human digestive system, which is similar to other mammalian digestive systems.

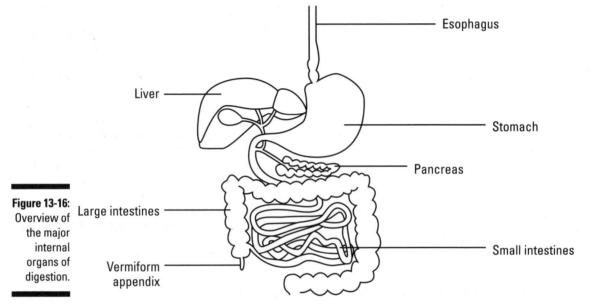

Figure 13-16:
Overview of
the major
internal
organs of
digestion.

Digestion begins in the mouth. As you chew a tasty mouthful of whatever it is that you find tasty, you are mechanically digesting — breaking down — the food. An enzyme within the saliva, salivary amylase, begins the process of chemical digestion by chemically breaking down sugars. Chewing forms the food into a ball, called a bolus. By swallowing, you push that ball into the esophagus, a muscular tube that guides the bolus into the stomach via a series of rhythmic contractions called peristalsis. Swallowing involves moving chewed food into the pharynx and over the epiglottis, a flap of tissue that covers the trachea during this maneuver. The epiglottis prevents you from unhelpfully forcing food down your trachea, into your lungs.

In the stomach, mechanical and chemical digestion continue. Mechanically, the stomach churns, breaking up the bolus, encouraging it to dissolve in gastric juice, a highly acidic fluid within the stomach that performs chemical digestion. Gastric juice contains high concentrations of hydrochloric acid. In addition to chemically breaking apart food substances, the acid helps to kill any potential pathogens contaminating the food. Gastric juice also contains pepsin, an enzyme that specializes in chemically digesting proteins. All the mechanical and chemical digestion in the stomach produces a soupy mixture called chyme.

Between the stomach and the small intestine sits the pyloric sphincter, a muscular ring that controls the passage of chyme from the stomach. Exiting the stomach through this sphincter, chyme finds itself in the duodenum, the initial stretch of small intestine (note that the small intestine is *long*, but *narrow*). In the duodenum, chyme is caught in a withering digestive crossfire. Digestive enzymes and chemicals converge from the pancreas, liver, gall bladder, and from the small intestine itself to chemically attack the chyme. Enzymes specializing in the breakdown of carbohydrates (pancreatic amylase), proteins (trypsin, chymotrypsin, peptidases), nucleic acids (nuclease), and fats (lipase) swarm through the increasingly digested food. Bile, a non-enzymatic chemical produced by the liver, helps to dissolve fats so that they can be more readily attacked by enzymes.

By the time the besieged chyme makes it out of the duodenum, it is almost entirely broken down into molecular bits and pieces that can be absorbed by cells. This absorption takes place in the remaining two stretches of small intestine, the jejunum and the ileum. The inner area of the small intestine (the lumen) is lined with countless projections called villi. The cells that line these villi themselves possess many membrane projections called microvilli. The result of these structures is to vastly increase the surface area in contact with digested food as it passes through the small intestine. Digested nutrients are absorbed into the cells of the villi by both active and passive transport. Each villus is served by a central network of blood vessels, so absorbed nutrients can be transported directly into the bloodstream for transport elsewhere in the body.

What began as a tasty mouthful is now a much-depleted mixture of water and materials that either remain undigested or were not selected for absorption. This mixture moves into the large intestine, whose primary task it is to reabsorb water. In addition to any water present in food, much water is added to the digesting mass of food as it moves through the digestive system. This precious water must be reclaimed; typically, up to 90 percent of it is.

As water is reabsorbed, the material passing through the large intestine becomes more solid. These solid wastes collect in the rectum, and are periodically excreted through the anus. So much for that tasty mouthful.

Endocrine system

Have you noticed how no one organ system operates independently of the others? As energy and material flow through animals, they are converted and reconverted into different forms, all according to the various needs of the animal. But what the animal needs is complicated. Cells, tissues, organs, and organ systems, operating at their own levels, all have various kinds of needs. For an animal to have much chance of surviving in the competitive tournament of life, materials and energy must flow to where they are needed, when they are needed. This lofty goal needs coordination, and coordination needs communication. The endocrine system is all about this kind of communication, ensuring that the systems and subsystems of the animal use materials and energy in the most appropriate ways.

The nervous system uses electrical signals to communicate messages that require fast delivery to very precise locations. The endocrine system sends its messages more slowly, as chemicals through the bloodstream and bodily fluids, causing longer-term changes in the activity of distributed groups of cells. The nervous and endocrine systems work as partners, each helping to regulate the other's activity as they guide the systems of the body toward appropriate responses.

The chemical signals sent by the endocrine system are called hormones. Hormones are secreted into bodily fluids by endocrine organs called glands, distributed throughout the body as shown in Figure 13-17. As hormones move through fluids, they are exposed to all sorts of cells, but only elicit a response from specific types of target cells. Different hormones target different groups of specialized cells.

Hormones tend to exert their effects on target cells in one of two ways:

- ✔ **The hormone may bind to a receptor on the outer surface of a target cell's plasma membrane.** Different receptors recognize different hormones. This binding event triggers a cascade of biochemical events within the target cell, increasing some activities and decreasing others. The peptide hormones operate in this manner.

- ✔ **A hormone may diffuse across the plasma membrane and bind to a specific receptor within a cell.** The hormone-receptor complex may then enter the nucleus of the cell and bind to DNA, directly altering the transcription of target genes to alter the activity of the target cell. The steroid hormones work in this way.

There are many endocrine glands in the human body, with partially overlapping areas of responsibility:

- ✔ Within the brain, the **pituitary gland** works with the **hypothalamus** to release hormones that regulate *other* endocrine glands, which helps to create a large-scale, coordinated response.

- ✔ The **thyroid and parathyroid glands,** located in the throat, work as an opposing pair to control the rate of metabolism, among other things.

- ✔ The **adrenal glands,** just above the kidneys, secrete hormones that produce the fight-or-flight response, in which the body suppresses other concerns to make materials and energy ready for quick action (such as fleeing from a tiger or, stupidly, standing your ground to face one in battle).

- ✔ The **pancreas** secretes an opposing pair of hormones, insulin and glucagon, that help the body to regulate the concentration of sugar in the blood.

- ✔ Hormones secreted by the **ovaries** (in females) and the **testes** (in males) promote the kinds of sexual developmental changes characteristic of each gender.

Hormones tend to act within interconnected pathways and in opposing pairs. Hormones within a pathway provide "feedback" to endocrine glands, helping to up- or down-regulate their secretion of more hormones. For example, when sensors in the bloodstream detect that blood calcium levels are high, they send signals to the thyroid gland. The thyroid secretes the hormone calcitonin, which goes on to interact with target cells in bone, in the intestines and in the kidneys, encouraging each of these target organs to take up or excrete calcium. The end effect is to decrease levels of calcium in the blood. If the calcium sensors detect low calcium levels, they stimulate the parathyroid glands to secrete parathyroid hormone. Parathyroid hormone interacts with the same targets as does calcitonin, but elicits opposite responses such that calcium levels in the blood increase. Thus, calcitonin and parathyroid hormone act as an opposing pair.

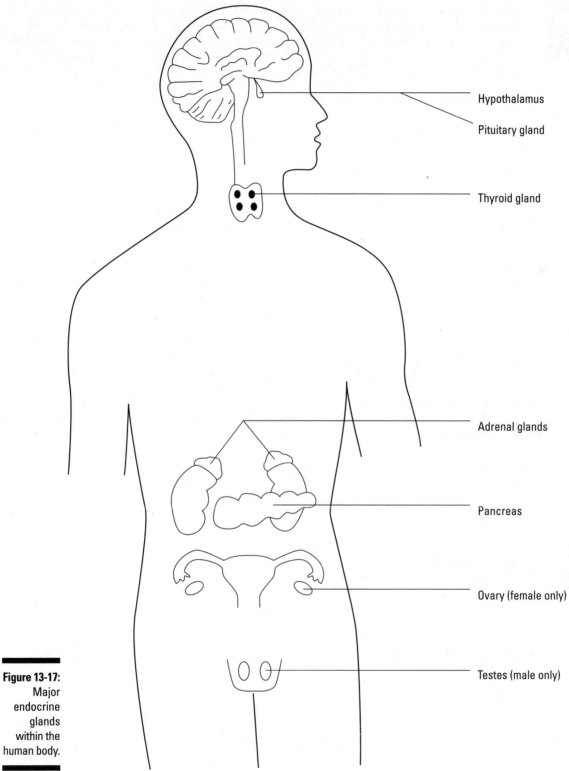

Hypothalamus

Pituitary gland

Thyroid gland

Adrenal glands

Pancreas

Ovary (female only)

Testes (male only)

Another example involving the thyroid gland demonstrates feedback. The hypothalamus secretes thyroid-releasing hormone (TRH), causing the anterior pituitary gland to secrete thyroid-stimulating hormone (TSH). TSH stimulates the thyroid to release thyroid hormones. In order to limit the release of thyroid hormones to a single, well-controlled pulse, both TSH and the thyroid hormones interact with the hypothalamus to diminish its secretion of TRH. These kinds of interactions are examples of negative feedback, a strategy widely employed by the endocrine system.

Immune system

With so many organs devoted to maintaining a biologically friendly internal environment, it's no surprise that other organisms seek to inhabit and exploit that environment. In particular, bacteria, viruses, fungi, and parasites continually attempt to set up shop within animal bodies. Although you can't exactly blame them, you don't have to let them have their way. Of course, many bacteria happily coexist with animals, thriving on skin and within digestive pathways. Some of these bacteria even provide useful services to the animal. But many other microorganisms pose a real and present danger to an animal, and must be dealt with harshly as invaders. Defense against biological invasion is the province of the immune system.

The immune system employs a three-pronged strategy in this ongoing battle:

- ✔ **The first line of defense is the skin.** Skin provides a physical barrier against entry into the vulnerable tissues of the body. In addition to simply blocking the way, the skin secretes oils, acidic sweat, and enzymes that make it difficult for microorganisms to pass through or to survive on its surface. Mucous membranes lining the entrances to the body (i.e., the orifices) serve a similar role. These initial defenses are nonspecific in that they defend generally against all forms of invader.

- ✔ **Threats that make it past the skin and mucous membranes have no reason to breathe easily, as they immediately encounter a second, nonspecific line of immune defense.** This second line of defense has three major components:

  - First, a class of white blood cells called **phagocytes** recognize and attack foreign particles, sometimes devouring them entirely. Although there are several kinds of phagocyte, all these kinds provide nonspecific immunity.

  - Second, cells damaged by invaders release chemical signals that produce **inflammation** at the damaged site. Inflammation involves an influx of blood and other fluids, and has several beneficial effects. More phagocytes are attracted to the inflamed area, concentrating their attack at the site of invasion. Materials involved in clotting and tissue repair begin their work, preventing further incursions and inhibiting the spread of invaders through the blood.

  - Third, entire families of **nonspecific antimicrobial proteins** are produced by animal bodies, and these proteins do things like tear apart bacterial cell walls or interfere with virus reproduction.

✔ **In addition to fighting a good battle in their own right, the nonspecific defenses buy valuable time for the body to mount a specific immune response, the third line of defense.** Unlike the non-specific defenses, specific immunity against particular invaders is not present before invasion; it must be acquired. The really interesting bit about the specific immune system is that it learns how best to attack particular invaders, attacks them, and then remembers the lesson in case the same type of enemy shows its ugly mug again. Specific immunity includes:

- **Humoral immunity,** which involves the production of antibodies (also called immunoglobulins), proteins that specifically recognize foreign "antigens" and recruit an immune response against them. Antigens are simply those substances which trigger a specific immune response, and are usually particular structural components of the invading particle. Humoral immunity is controlled by white blood cells called B lymphocytes. When a B lymphocyte recognizes an antigen, it sends signals that cause other B lymphocytes to proliferate (reproduce rapidly). The proliferating B lymphocytes fall into two categories: plasma cells, which generate antibodies against the recognized antigen, and memory cells, which allow an even faster immune response should that antigen pop up in the future. The growing supply of specific antibodies seek out and attach themselves to antigens, and act as red flags for other lymphocytes that move in to destroy the flagged invaders. When the body produces antigens in this way, it is called active immunity. If antigens are transferred into the body from elsewhere, as they are during a vaccination, it is called passive immunity.

- **Cell-mediated immunity,** which involves a class of white blood cells called T lymphocytes (or *T cells*). T lymphocytes act mostly to kill any of an animal's *own* cells that happen to be infected by a fungus or virus. During a specific immune response, T lymphocytes develop into subclasses of lymphocyte with particular responsibilities. Cytotoxic T cells directly attack invaders. Helper T cells send out chemical signals that set other lymphocytes in motion. Suppressor T cells keep the immune response in check by decreasing the activity of certain other lymphocytes; an excessive response can threaten an animal as much as the foreign invader. Finally, memory T cells (like memory B cells) hang out aver the battle is over, ready to help mount an even quicker defense if the same invader strikes twice.

Doing it Again: Reproduction

All those lovely organ systems took so long to evolve . . . it would be a shame to throw them away. To provide the countless generations over which animal bodies evolved, and to ensure that those bodies continue to evolve, one more organ system — *the* organ system, really — serves its all-important function: reproduction.

By an incredible stroke of luck for those studying for the AP Biology exam, all animals are *eukaryotes.* This means that all forms of animal reproduction follow the same basic rules, which makes them much easier to remember. Even better, if you've gotten to this point in the book by first passing through Chapters 7 and 11, you're ahead of the game. Chapter 7 covers meiosis, the eukaryotic form of cell division that produces sex cells. Chapter 11 covers plant reproduction which, while not as obviously exciting as animal reproduction, follows the same eukaryotic principles.

In case you defiantly skipped these previous chapters, here's a brief summary of the salient points: Animals reproduce sexually. This means that they produce new versions of themselves by combining genetic information from each of two representatives, a male and a female. This kind of genetic combination and recombination over successive generations is a delightfully effective way to create genetic diversity; diversity enhances the adaptability of the animal's genetic line over generations. To enable genetic recombination, the genetic material of an animal must cycle between haploid and diploid states. The haploid state contains only one complete version of the chromosomes, and is the state of gametes, sex cells like sperm and eggs. Gametes fuse to create diploid zygotes, which contain two complete versions of the chromosomes, one from each parent. Human body cells, for example, each contain a diploid set of 46 chromosomes; human sperm and egg cells, however, contain haploid sets of 23 chromosomes. Zygotes eventually develop into new animal individuals. The traits of the new animal depend in part on an interplay of the genetic information inherited from the parents. To reproduce, the new individual must divide its own diploid set of chromosome into haploid sets, producing gametes. And around we go.

This section explains how gametes are generated, how they fuse, and how the single diploid cell created by that fusion develops into a new animal. Chauvinistically, we'll describe the process as it occurs in human animals.

Getting ready: Gametogenesis

Gametogenesis, the formation of sex cells, comes in two varieties: generation of eggs and generation of sperm. With respect to the division of genetic material, the processes are essentially the same, each involving two rounds of meiotic division. Other aspects of the processes differ considerably. Egg production, or oogenesis, occurs within the ovaries. Sperm production, or spermatogenesis, occurs within the testes.

Here's how seriously biology takes reproduction: Oogenesis begins during the embryonic development of the female. That's right, female embryos start developing their eggs even before being born. Fetal cells called oogonia divide by mitosis, producing new cells called primary oocytes. After birth, the diploid primary oocytes grow larger within nourishing structures called follicles. The primary oocytes enter meiosis, but proceed only to prophase I (ahem, Chapter 7, anyone?). The oocytes remain in this state until the female reaches puberty, entering the cycle of menstruation. In this cycle, hormonal signals trigger the continuation of development of a single oocyte, once every 28 days (or so). Reanimated by this hormonal pulse, the primary oocyte completes meiosis I, but then stops once more. At this point, the egg is haploid, and is called a secondary oocyte. In humans, meiosis II does not occur until the egg connects with a sperm cell.

And what about those sperm? Perhaps predictably, males don't get around to their gametogenetic responsibilities until late in the game, during puberty. On the other hand, once males begin to produce sperm, it becomes a full-time job, continuing through all of adulthood. The process begins with spermatogonia cells, which divide repeatedly by mitosis into millions of primary spermatocytes. These diploid spermatocytes undergo a single round of meiosis as they develop into haploid secondary spermatocytes. The second meiotic division produces spermatids. Nourished by Sertoli cells, spermatids go on to develop into highly specialized sperm cells.

To the extent described so far, oogenesis and spermatogenesis are mostly similar, differing only in timing. There is a key difference in the meiotic cell divisions associated with the two processes, however. In spermatogenesis, each round of meiosis features equivalent divisions, so that a single spermatogonia produces four sperm cells. In oogenesis, the cell divisions are unequal, with each round producing one large oocyte, and a much smaller "polar body" that eventually fades away.

Creating an embryo

Each menstrual cycle includes an event called ovulation, in which a mature ovum (egg cell) is released from a follicle within an ovary, and enters a fallopian tube, a structure that connects the ovaries to the uterus, the organ within which an embryo will develop. Figure 13-18 diagrams these structures simply. During sexual intercourse, males deliver millions of sperm cells into the female reproductive tract, each one with long odds of advancing through the uterus, into the fallopian tube, and into contact with the waiting ovum. Having made contact, the sperm cell must make its way through the zona pellucida, a thick outer layer encapsulating the egg. Eventually, the sperm cell reaches and fuses with the membrane of the egg cell, triggering changes in this membrane that prevent further fertilizations — no other sperm need apply. Fusion of the two haploid gametes produces a diploid zygote, initiating the awe-inspiring process of embryonic development.

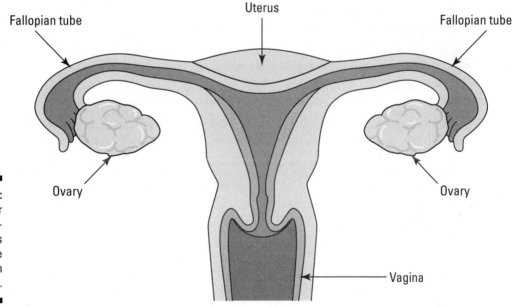

Figure 13-18:
Major reproductive organs of the human female.

Developing an embryo

Zygotes haven't much time to appreciate the glorious diploid novelty of their creation before they must get to work dividing into an embryo. The earliest stages of this process are shown in Figure 13-19. Embryonic development consists of a pre-programmed set of mitotic cell divisions called cleavages. While still in the fallopian tube, the zygote begins cleaving, subdividing into smaller and smaller cells without increasing in overall size. Within about three days, the embryo is a ball of about thirty-two cells called a morula, and has traveled from the fallopian tube into the uterus. The embryo continues cleaving, and after about four more days, has become a blastula (or *blastocyst* in humans), a ball of cells with a central depression. Several days later, the blastula implants into the inner lining of the uterus, from which it derives nutrients to support further development.

This further development begins with gastrulation, in which the hollow ball of the blastula folds in on itself to produce a cup-like structure called a gastrula. The gastrula now has a definable inner space, called the archenteron and an opening, called the blastopore. The cells of the gastrula occupy three increasingly distinct layers: an outer ectoderm, an inner endoderm, and a mesoderm layer in between these two. Development of the embryo proceeds from here by continuing divisions and specialization of cells (differentiation). Differentiation of cells involves a process called induction, in which "organizer" cells send signals to nearby cells, inducing them to express particular sets of genes that set them on a particular developmental path.

All the eventual tissues and organs of a fully developed fetus trace back to the original three layers of the gastrula:

- **Ectodermal cells** give rise to the epidermis, the linings of the nose and mouth, the lens of the eye, and the nervous system.

- **Endodermal cells** develop into the inner linings of the digestive and respiratory organs, and into parts of the liver, pancreas, and bladder.

- **Mesodermal cells** develop into the musculoskeletal, circulatory, and excretory systems, and into parts of the reproductive, digestive, and respiratory systems.

  Elegantly, all this diversity derives from simple distinctions of outside, inside, and middle within the gastrula.

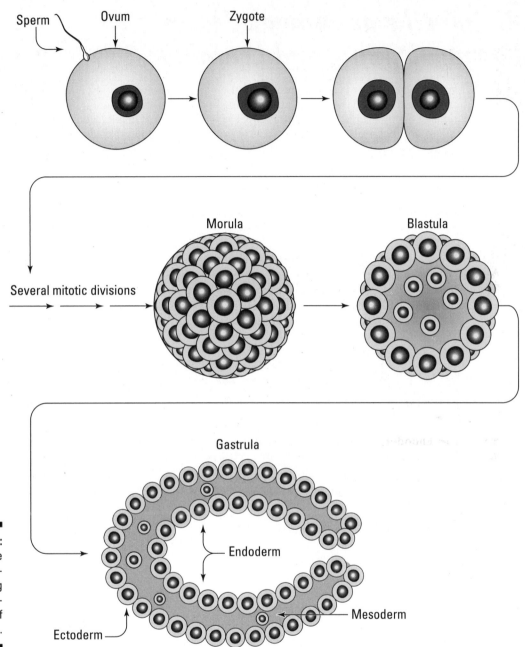

Figure 13-19:
Cleavage and gastrulation during early development of an embryo.

Acting Like an Animal: Moving, Communicating, and Learning

With all the detail involved in growing and operating an animal body, it seems somehow like the story could end there. But a functioning body is just the beginning. With systems upon systems of highly evolved organs attending to basic biological needs, animals can focus on bigger issues like moving from place to place, interacting with other animals, and benefiting from experience so as to do everything better. These sorts of things are collectively considered as *behavior*. Animal behavior is partly inherited, and therefore reflects countless generations of natural selection. But behavior is also induced by stimuli in an animal's environment. In short, behavior is the result of a grand dialog between genes and experience, and is immensely complicated. In this section, we distill the complexity of behavior into some of its major themes.

Three ways to move

If you think about it, "movement" covers a lot of ground. The function of any given movement isn't always immediately apparent. Reduced to their essentials, however, most animal movements seem to conform to the following three categories:

- **Kinesis** is movement in response to environmental stimuli that have no inherent direction, such as the weather. Animals alter their movements in order to dwell longer within desirable environments and speed their exit from undesirable environments. Confronted with icy rain and sleet, you might hasten your steps to move anywhere indoors. By contrast, faced with the balmy ocean breezes of Maui, you might while away the afternoon in a gently rocking hammock.

- **Movement by taxis** is hardwired within the animal, and occurs in response to stimuli that have direction. At a party, you might instinctively and unwittingly drift towards that lovely, enticingly scented someone on the other side of the room. Alternately, at the same party, you might instinctively and unwittingly drift away from an unlovely someone who seems to be emitting a foul odor.

- **Migration** usually involves longer term, long-distance movements that follow a cyclical pattern, often in accord with the seasons. Both geese and RV-driving retirees go south for the winter, and make their way back north come spring.

Four ways to communicate

Communication is simply the transmission of information from a sender to a receiver. The boundaries of communication extend far beyond smoke signals, email, and unsavory hand gestures. The following four modes of communication dominate animal behavior:

- **Chemical communication** employs chemical signals. Often, these chemicals are pheromones. Pheromones are chemicals that, once detected by an animal, cause some change in its bodily operation. Dogs secrete pheromones in their urine that signal to other dogs, "Hey, this fire hydrant is mine!" Ants secrete trails of pheromones that signal to other ants, "Hey, there's food this way!" Unappealing as the thought may be, pigs secrete pheromones that signal to other pigs, "Hey, I am soooo ready for love!" The extent to which humans employ pheromones is still a subject of some controversy.

- ✔ **Visual communication** involves signals that work by being seen. In addition to smoke signals, email, and unsavory hand gestures, visual communication includes things like the bared teeth of a wolf, the bright red feathers of a male cardinal, and a subtle smile or arched eyebrow from across the room at a party.

- ✔ **Auditory communication** involves signals that work by being heard. Examples include the use of echolocation by bats, the far-traveling songs of whales, and the frenzied honking of horns by frustrated taxi drivers across the globe.

- ✔ **Tactile communication** involves signals that work by being felt, such as Braille writing, the grooming habits of chimpanzees, and wrestling among tiger cubs. If tiger cubs were to groom chimpanzees while reading in Braille, that would also qualify, though no observations of this behavior have been made in the wild.

Seven ways to learn

We still have a lot to learn about learning. But we've learned a lot about it, too. Learning can occur in a wide variety of ways, some of them genetically pre-programmed, some imparted during impressionable early periods, and some involving more complicated, connecting-the-dots sorts of activities. The following categories are useful ways to classify the kinds of animal behavior we associate with learning:

- ✔ **Classical conditioning** occurs when animals forge some sort of connection—an *association* — between different stimuli. A famous example of classical conditioning is the Pavlovian response. A researcher named Pavlov conducted experiments in which dogs were exposed to a ringing bell immediately prior to being fed; soon, Pavlov observed that simply ringing the bell caused the dogs to salivate, anticipating the food they associated with the bell. Pulling the covers over one's head when the alarm clock sounds on a dreaded Monday morning is another example.

- ✔ **Operant conditioning** (also known as trial and error learning) occurs when an animal makes an association between its own behavior and another event. At the entrance to an unfamiliar building, you may once have tried to gain entry by pushing on a door handle. When that behavior resulted in your face crashing into that very door, you may subsequently have tried an alternate behavior: pulling on the door handle. If that new behavior succeeded in opening the door, you might have felt the thrill of a successful operant conditioning experience.

- ✔ **Observational learning** is learning that results from an animal's scrutiny of another's behavior. At the entrance to an unfamiliar building, you may once have observed an unlucky fellow human pushing on a door handle, then crashing into the door. You might then have suppressed your own impulse to push on that same door handle, using the benefit of observational learning to pull it open on the first try.

- ✔ **Habituation** is a form of learning that depends on *not* making associations between stimuli and responses. When you put on your shoes in the morning, you are initially quite aware of the sensation of them enclosing your feet. As the day wears on, the nerves within your feet constantly register the pressure of your shoes, but you soon lose all awareness of that stimulus. In another example, a dog may initially respond with great excitement to the stimulus of a thrown stick, fetching and returning that stick to the thrower. However, as each fetch-and-return response is followed by the same thrown-stick stimulus, the dog may gradually fail to respond, eventually gazing at the thrower as if to say, "yes . . . and?"

✔ **Insight learning** is mainly observed in humans and other primates. It involves understanding a goal and devising strategies that are likely to achieve that goal before ever making an attempt. Keenly aware of bananas placed above their reach, chimpanzees have been observed to stack boxes, constructing a makeshift staircase that leads to their banana goal. Humans display similar behaviors when seeking scientific knowledge, companionship, or out-of-reach bananas.

✔ **Imprinting** is an innate form of learning that must occur during a critical period in an animal's life, and has lasting effects. One amazing example of the power of imprinting involves an Italian hang-gliding enthusiast named d'Arrigo, and migratory birds born in captivity. Birds that typically migrate throughout the seasons often fail to develop normal migratory behavior if they are born in captivity (not in the wild). Under normal circumstances, these birds would receive early imprinting experiences from "mentor" birds that show them the migratory flight patterns. The hang-glider, d'Arrigo, took care to hatch some of these birds near his hang-glider wing, and in his presence. The birds quickly imprinted on d'Arrigo and his hang-glider, and he later acted as a mentor by carrying the hatchlings with him during glider flights, following the same flight patterns used by wild birds. The imprinting experiment worked, and the human-mentored birds successfully migrated when released into the wild.

✔ **Fixed-action patterns** are an inborn, instinctual type of learning. These fixed patterns produce behaviors which must run their course once they are initiated. Dramatic examples are found in the mating dances of many species of bird. Stimulated by the presence of a female, male birds commence a precisely choreographed dance, the movements of which are pre-programmed within the bird. Female birds judge these performances to help inform their selection of a mate.

Nine Ways to Behave

Sure, nine ways seem like a lot to commit to memory. Fortunately, these ways cluster around just a few general ideas. Some types of behavior have mostly to do with how closely related two animals are to each other. Other types of behavior are mostly about keeping other animals in their place and reminding them who's boss. Some behavior has simply to do with finding food. Here's how these behaviors relate to each other:

✔ Two types of feeding behavior are especially worth mentioning:

• **Foraging** refers to the set of strategies used by an animal to secure food. Some animals are specialists, zoning in on very specific food sources, such as seen with anteaters and ants. Other animals, like pigs, are generalists, feeding widely and variously.

• **Optimal foraging** emphasizes the idea that evolution conserves some foraging behaviors more than others. Conserved (i.e., naturally selected) behaviors are those which maximize the energy and nutrients gained from foraged food while minimizing the energy used and the risks taken to get that food. In short, optimal foraging is about cost-benefit analysis.

✔ Several types of behavior center on ideas of dominance and ownership. These behaviors include:

• **Agonistic behavior:** When two animals set their sights on the same chunk of meat, cozy little den, or nubile mate, they often engage in agonistic behaviors. These behaviors can involve intimidating displays of strength and aggressiveness, with one animal eventually signaling its submission. Although agonistic behaviors can lead to injury or death, they usually do not: They are displays, or rituals.

- **Dominance hierarchies:** Agonistic behaviors often crop up within another form of behavior called the dominance hierarchy. Through a sort of tournament of agonistic behaviors, groups of animals (i.e., a pack of wolves) establish who's in charge, who's next-in-charge, and so on, down to the lowest-ranking scrubs. Not everyone can be king or queen, but at least everyone knows their role, and that seems to be good for the pack as a whole.

- **Territoriality:** Territoriality is an especially prominent form of behavior that draws on themes of dominance and ownership. Animals often define areas that they consider their own, and defend the boundaries of that area against other animals. Guard dogs are familiar examples of the territory-minded creature. In terms of natural selection, territoriality is a good investment because it secures the things most critical to survival and reproduction: an area rich in food and a protected enclave for raising young.

Not all evolutionarily useful behaviors are (directly) about competing with other animals. Sometimes it is in an animal's long-term genetic interest to cooperate or even to sacrifice in the short term. Because these behaviors increase the odds of passing on an animal's genes, or at least a set of genes very similar to their own, we can expect that the behaviors will emerge over generations. The following are concepts that fall under this overall theme:

- **Altruism:** Altruism is behavior that assists another animal, even and especially at the expense of the original animal. Sharing food and fighting to protect the young are the most obvious examples of this kind of behavior, and they are frequent animal behaviors. Reciprocal altruism is a form of altruism that involves the expectation that a favor will be returned in due time. Among humans, defensive alliances like NATO are a large-scale example; I'll help you defend against your enemies because I expect that one day you may do the same for me. Reciprocal altruism is an unstable form of behavior because if the favor isn't returned, the animal that tends to sacrifice first may well not survive to pass its altruistic tendencies on to the next generation.

- **Inclusive fitness:** Inclusive fitness is the idea that behaviors leading to the survival and reproduction of a *related group* sometimes have more evolutionary staying power than behaviors which narrowly seek to promote survival of individuals. By putting your own life on the line for your cousins, you may increase the percent of your own genes represented in later generations; the gene pool of the family survives.

- **Coefficient of relatedness:** Closely tied to inclusive fitness is the *coefficient of relatedness*, a numerical measurement of how many genes two animals have in common. Your sister shares approximately fifty percent of your genes; your niece shares approximately twenty-five percent of your genes. On average, you're more likely to stick your neck out for your sister than for your niece. Although other factors enter into the calculus of deciding whether an animal risks itself for family, the fact remains that blood is thicker than water, for humans and for other animals.

Chapter 14

Answering Questions About Animals and Behavior

*T*his should be easy — all these questions are about you. Okay, maybe it won't be easy, but now that you're digesting the hearty meal that was Chapter 13, you may as well kick back and answer some questions about, well, *digestion* among other things. This chapter offers review and questions covering the material found in Chapter 13: Animals and Behavior. Multiple choice and free-essay response questions and answers are provided. In addition, an explanatory summary is given for a Lab on Physiology of the Circulatory System.

Pointers for Practice

The main points of Chapter 13 were the following:

✔ Though neither energy nor matter can be created or destroyed, living organisms continually transform both energy and matter into different forms that are useful for surviving and reproducing. Autotrophs funnel energy from the environment into chemical forms, and heterotrophs ingest this chemical energy by ingesting autotrophs or each other.

✔ Homeostasis is the critical task of maintaining a stable internal environment. The skin plays important roles in thermoregulation, the maintenance of appropriate internal temperature. The kidneys are central to osmoregulation, the maintenance of proper levels of solutes within body fluids. The endocrine system helps to regulate and coordinate the homeostatic systems within animal bodies.

✔ The circulatory system distributes materials throughout the body via a closed system of blood vessels. A heart serves as a pressure source to drive blood through these vessels. Blood contains erythrocytes (red blood cells) and leukocytes (white blood cells), platelets, and plasma, a fluid in which a wide variety of materials are dissolved. Erythrocytes are important for the exchange of oxygen and carbon dioxide with the environment. Leukocytes are important for fighting off infection. Platelets enable blood clotting in the event of injury. Plasma is the medium in which nutrients and chemical signals can be transported.

✔ In many animals, the circulatory and respiratory systems connect via a system of "double circulation," involving a pulmonary circuit and a systemic circuit. In this system, deoxygenated blood enters the heart, and is pumped directly to capillary beds that surround tiny air sacs within the lungs, called alveoli. Within alveoli, oxygen and carbon dioxide diffuse down concentration gradients such that blood unburdens itself of carbon dioxide and takes on fresh oxygen cargo. From the alveoli, blood returns to the heart, and from there is pumped to the rest of the body.

✔ The nervous system enables rapid communication and information processing within animal bodies. The neuron is the basic functional unit of the nervous system. Information is transmitted electrically along neurons by means of action potentials. Information is transmitted chemically between neurons by means of neurotransmitters. Sensory information travels along afferent nerves, from the peripheral nervous system (PNS) to the central nervous system (CNS, the brain and spinal cord). Motor information travels along efferent nerves, from the CNS to the PNS. Information processing occurs within clusters of nerve cells, called ganglia in the PNS, or nuclei in the CNS.

✔ The musculoskeletal system enables movement of skeletal elements about joints, driven by muscular contraction. Vertebrates have endoskeletons composed of bones. The functional unit of compact bone is the osteon, a circular arrangement of bone cells radiating from a central canal, through which pass nerves and blood vessels. Bones are secured to other bones at joints by ligaments. Bones are attached to muscles via tendons. Skeletal muscles contract in order to create motion about joints. The functional contracting unit of skeletal muscle is the sarcomere, an overlapping system of actin and myosin protein fibers. In addition to skeletal muscle, vertebrates possess cardiac muscle (within the heart, also employs sarcomeres) and smooth muscle (slowly contracting, does not have sarcomeres).

✔ The digestive system breaks down food by mechanical and chemical means, absorbs useful molecule-sized pieces of the digested food, absorbs water, and passes what remains as waste. Mechanical digestion occurs primarily by chewing and by the churning of the stomach. Chemical digestion occurs via enzymes, stomach acid and bile. A great deal of chemical digestion occurs in the duodenum, the initial stretch of small intestine just past the exit of the stomach. The remainder of the small intestine specializes in nutrient absorption at tiny folds called vili. The large intestine specializes in absorption of water.

✔ The endocrine system employs a system of glands that secrete chemical signals called hormones into body fluids. These signals travel through the fluids, eventually to elicit specific responses from target cells. As opposed to the nervous system, the endocrine system is used for slower, longer-term communication within animal bodies. Hormones help ensure that the body's organ systems work efficiently, directing resources to where they are needed when they are needed. Hormones often operate within feedback networks, wherein the presence of a hormone diminishes further secretion of that same hormone. Further, hormones often operate as opposing pairs, working together to produce a balanced, finely regulated response.

✔ The immune system guards against infection by foreign agents and fights off infections that do occur. Immunity includes both non-specific and specific measures. Non-specific immunity involves the skin, and certain cells and secreted substances within the body. Non-specific immunity itself prevents many infections, but also buys time for the onset of specific immunity — defenses targeted against specific invaders. Specific immunity includes humoral and cell-mediated immunity. Humoral immunity is organized around the production of antibodies, and is organized by B-lymphocytes. Cell-mediated immunity is carried out by T-lymphocytes. Both types of specific immunity feature the production of memory cells, lymphocytes that allow for a rapid, specific response to a second attack by the same invader.

✔ Gametogenesis includes the production of eggs, within the ovaries, and sperm, within the testes. Each process features two rounds of meiotic division to produce haploid gametes. Egg cells stall at prophase I until puberty, and do not undergo meiosis II until fertilization. Each meiotic division in egg cell production yields a large cell and a small polar body, which eventually fades away. In sperm production, early spermatogonia cells proliferate by mitosis before proceeding through meiosis; each meiotic division is equal during spermatogenesis.

✔ Fertilization produces a diploid zygote. A series of cleavages of this initial zygotic cell produce a hollow ball of undifferentiated cells called a blastula. The blastula folds in on itself to form a cup-shaped structure called the gastrula. From the three cell layers of the gastrula arise the three varieties of germ cell (endoderm, mesoderm, and ectoderm) that give rise to all the various specialized cell types in a vertebrate body. The ensuing process of cell differentiation and development features a phenomenon called induction, wherein organizer cells emit chemical messages that cause specific developmental events in neighboring cells.

✔ Among the various kingdoms of life, animals are pronounced in their capabilities of movement, communication, and learning. Animal movements may be directed (taxis), largely undirected (kinesis), or in response to environmental cycles (migration). Animal communications fall into four broad categories: chemical (e.g., taste, smell, pheromones), visual (e.g., seeing), auditory (e.g., hearing, echolocation), and tactile (e.g., touch). Animal learning is only partially understood, but involves some recurring themes: genetic effects, formative early experiences, making associations, and higher-level, imaginative activities.

Testing Your Knowledge

Directions: Choose the best possible answer, out of the five that are provided, for each question.

1. Thermoregulation involves all of the following processes EXCEPT:

    (A) Convection

    (B) Infusion

    (C) Radiation

    (D) Conduction

    (E) Evaporation

2. Deoxygenated blood flows through which of the following structures:

    (A) Aorta

    (B) Left ventricle

    (C) Pulmonary artery

    (D) Pulmonary vein

    (E) Left atrium

3. Which of the following statements are true?

    I. Neurons maintain an inside-negative resting potential

    II. Neurons transmit signals via propagating threshold potentials

    III. Stronger stimulation yields stronger nerve impulses

(A) I only

(B) II only

(C) III only

(D) I and II only

(E) II and III only

Questions 4 and 5 refer to the following list of options:

    I. Skeletal muscle

    II. Cardiac muscle

    III. Smooth muscle

4. Which of the above muscle types possess sarcomeres?

(A) I only

(B) II only

(C) III only

(D) I and II only

(E) II and III only

5. Which of the above muscle types is involuntary?

(A) I only

(B) II only

(C) III only

(D) I and II only

(E) II and III only

Questions 6–11 refer to the following answer choices. Answers may be used more than once.

(A) Stomach

(B) Small intestine

(C) Large intestine

(D) Pancreas

(E) Liver

6. Absorbs nutrients through villi

7. Absorbs significant amounts of water

8. Secretes pepsin

9. Secretes many digestive enzymes

10. Produces bile

11. Includes the duodenum

12 A bacterium swims up a gradient of dissolved sugar. This behavior best represents which of the following?

(A) Chemical communication

(B) Kinesis

(C) Operant conditioning

(D) Taxis

(E) Habituation

13. In humans, egg cells undergo meiosis II upon which of the following envents:

(A) Puberty

(B) Gastrulation

(C) Fertilization

(D) Folliculation

(E) Menstruation

Questions 14–18 refer to the following choices.

(A) Phagocyte

(B) Suppressor cell

(C) Plasma cell

(D) Memory cell

(E) Antigen

14. Facilitates a rapid response when the same invader infects again

15. A molecular piece, recognized by antibodies within the immune system

16. B-lymphocyte that generates antibodies

17. T-lymphocyte that moderates the cell-mediated immune response

18. Cell within the non-specific immune system that ingests foreign particles

19. The following graph depicts the amount of a certain antibody detected in the blood of a patient over a period of two months. Which immune system component is most directly responsible for the difference highlighted by the double-headed arrow?

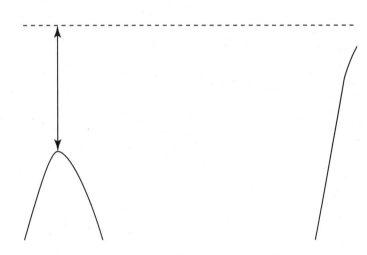

Figure 14-1:
Graph of antibody concentration versus time, reflecting data collected over two months from the blood of a single patient.

(A) Skin

(B) Helper T cells

(C) Phagocytes

(D) Memory B cells

(E) Memory T cells

Answering Free-Essay Response Questions

1. Whether at the level of molecules, cells or entire organisms, *recognition* is a key event in many biological processes. Describe the mechanism and role of recognition in each of the following scenarios: 1) an animal recognizes another of its own species, and 2) the kidney recognizes a signal from the thyroid.

Lab on Physiology of the Circulatory System

In the course of three exercises, this lab uses blood pressure and heart rate as windows onto the physiology of the circulatory system, and examines the response of that system to various stimuli, including posture, exercise, and temperature.

In the first exercise, students learn how to operate a sphygmomanometer, a device used to measure blood pressure. A sphygmomanometer consists essentially of an inflatable cuff, a pressure gauge, and a stethoscope (i.e., a listening device). The cuff is affixed around one's upper arm and inflated such that it restricts blood flow through the brachial artery of the arm. Restriction can be observed via the inability to detect heart sounds (i.e., sounds of Korotkoff) though the stethoscope. Pressure is then decreased very gradually while listening closely for the resumption of pulse sounds. Several different "phases" of sound are detected, the interpretation of which can be difficult. Ideally, the phases can be recognized and corre-lated with the cuff pressures at which they occurred. Based on these data, one assigns the systolic and diastolic pressures, the pressures within the artery during contraction and relaxation of the heart, respectively.

In the second exercise, students work in pairs, taking each other's blood pressure while reclining and standing, comparing results between trials in which, after standing, there is a time delay before taking measurements, and trials in which there is no delay. Pulse rates are also taken. In general, one expects the circulatory system to respond to standing (as opposed to reclining) by increasing output, delivering oxygen to muscles bearing the load of the standing person. In most people, standing therefore causes an increase in systolic pres-sure as the heart contracts more forcefully in order to send oxygen-laden blood to muscle tissues. Pulse rates typically increase as well, triggered by sensors in the body that detect the increase in blood pressure (i.e., the "barorecpetor reflex"). Finally, students subject them-selves to a few minutes of physical exercise, then take measurements. In general, the pat-terns observed when moving from reclined to standing positions are sharply pronounced after exercise.

In the third exercise, students observe the effect of changing temperature on the rate of heart-beats in the water flea, *Daphnia magna*. Since the water flea is ectothermic, its rate of metabo-lism depends directly on external temperature. The heart beats more or less rapidly, in concert with the metabolic rate. By inspecting a live water flea under a dissecting microscope, students can observe the beating heart of the flea, directly measuring changes in heart rate as the flea is immersed in media kept at different temperatures. The expected result is that heart rate increases linearly with increasing temperature. No such direct correlation between external temperature and heart rate is expected for endotherms, which homeostatically maintain a constant internal temperature.

Checking Your Work

Do yourself a favor. Don't leave this chapter behind you without first checking your answers. Animal physiology and behavior are a big chunk of the AP Biology exam. If you've got some mistakes in you, it's better to leave them here than take them with you into the exam.

1. Infusion has nothing whatever to do with heat transfer; all the other answers are modes of heat transfer. Answer B.

2. The answer is C. This is a tricky one, because in almost all cases, arteries carry oxygenated blood. What arteries really do is carry blood away from the heart. Recall that double circula-tion includes the pulmonary circuit, in which deoxygenated blood is sent to alveoli within lungs to rid itself of carbon dioxide and load up with oxygen. Thus, deoxygenated blood is sent from the heart to the lungs via the pulmonary arteries, returning to the heart as oxy-genated blood via the pulmonary veins.

3. The right choice is A. Neurons do maintain an inside-negative resting potential, which is a polarized state. If a neuron is sufficiently stimulated, it reaches threshold potential; if that threshold is maintained for long enough, it triggers a propagating action potential, which is the traveling impulse. Regardless of the strength of the stimulating impulses, all action potentials are equal.

4. D is the answer. Sarcomeres allow for rapid, forceful contractions, and are thus found in skeletal and cardiac muscle, but not smooth muscle.

5. The answer is E. Although skeletal muscle responds to voluntary motor impulses, cardiac and smooth muscle (found in the heart and in places like the lining of the stomach) are involuntary forms of muscle tissue, contracting without conscious control.

6. B is correct. After being well-digested on its trip through the mouth, stomach, and the initial stretch of small intestine, the duodenum, microscopic nutrients from food are absorbed at the extreme surface area created by villi and microvilli within the small intestine.

7. C is the right answer. Absorption of water is a major function of the large intestine.

8. The right answer is A. In addition to its mechanical churning and acidic gastric juice, the stomach aids in digestion by secreting pepsin, an enzyme that chemically breaks down protein.

9. D is correct. The pancreas secretes a powerful cocktail of enzymes that target all the major nutrient groups: proteins, carbohydrates, lipids, and nucleic acids.

10. E is right. The liver makes bile, a collection of fatty acids that solubilize fats to aid their digestion. Bile is stored and secreted by the gall bladder.

11. The answer is B. The small intestine includes the duodenum, jejunum, and ileum.

12. D is the answer. Since the bacterium is moving with respect to a stimulus that has a definite direction — the gradient of sugar — this kind of movement is taxis.

13. C is correct. Although egg cells progress from prophase I at the onset of menstruation during puberty, meiosis II does not occur until fertilization.

14. Hopefully you chose D. Memory cells (both B and T) maintain a molecular memory of an invader after a single infection. If the same invader shows up later, memory cells use that memory to speed a specific immune response.

15. E is right. Antigens are molecules or bits of molecules whose shape and other properties are recognized by elements of the immune system (e.g., antibodies); antigen recognition is key to determining self from non-self.

16. C is the answer. Plasma cells are the B lymphocytes that generate antibodies, crucial parts that underlie the specificity of the immune response.

17. The correct answer is B. Suppressor T cells moderate the specific immune response of other T cells, ensuring that the response isn't so severe that it kills the very animal being protected.

18. Choose A here. Phagocytes are cells of the non-specific response that engulf and break down bacteria, viruses, and other foreign particles.

19. Of the choices offered, D is best. The graph shows two pulses of antibody, the second larger than the first. Each pulse is preceded by a period of low-or-no antibody. During the low region prior to the first pulse, the patient must have been exposed to an antigen, presumably due to an infection. The patient's immune system produced a primary immune response, during which memory cells, including memory B lymphocytes, recorded a molecular memory of the infecting particle. Thus, when the patient was exposed to the invader a second time during the lull after the first pulse, the immune system was able to quickly generate an intense, specific response, as revealed by the high antibody count.

Here is a model answer to the free-essay response question:

Biological processes are regulated by countless events of recognition; the identities of specific organisms, cells, or molecules serve as stimuli for useful responses. Biological recognition can serve different roles and operate at very different levels, as exemplified by an animal recognizing another of its own species, or cells within the kidney recognizing a hormonal message from the thyroid.

Animals have a great interest in recognizing others of their species for purposes of mating, and of nurturing the offspring that result from successful mating. In one sense, intraspecies recognition is guaranteed at the molecular level, because attempts at mating between species fail to produce viable zygotes. This, in fact, is a precondition of taxonomically defining one species from another. On another level, animals find it useful to recognize others of their own species, because their conspecific cousins are typically less likely to pose a threat, and more likely to offer protection. Least specifically, groups of other animals like themselves may offer the simple protection of numbers. Most specifically, parental recognition of their offspring is required for animals to engage in the fiercely protective or seemingly altruistic behaviors observed among animals. This recognition can occur by visual, auditory, chemical, or tactile means. For example, birds and whales recognize the songs of their fellow birds or whales. Recognition of parents by offspring is often deeply instilled at the earliest ages, through imprinting.

Chemical recognition is key to the regulation of organs through the endocrine system. The endocrine system consists of a distributed collection of glands, each of which secretes chemical signals, called hormones, that regulate the activity of target cells, sometimes including the cells of other glands. In this way, animal bodies use chemical signals to facilitate communication between organs. Once a gland secretes a hormone into bodily fluids — often into the bloodstream — the message is widely distributed throughout the body, accessible at the level of capillaries to virtually all cell types of a body. Nevertheless, only certain target cells respond to the hormonal message; clearly, some process of recognition occurs. The process is one of molecular (and thereby cellular) recognition. Different types of hormone have different chemical structures, each of which has distinct physicochemical properties. These sets of properties act as unique signatures for the hormones. Different cell types within the body are equipped with different collections of receptor molecules. Each receptor molecule recognizes a specific kind of partner, each binding to the other; some receptors recognize hormones. Those cells with receptors complementary to a given hormone can respond to its message. For example, the thyroid gland secretes the hormone calcitonin in response to high levels of calcium in the blood. Once in the bloodstream, calcitonin is ignored by the majority of cells in the body, but is recognized by specific receptors in a few types of cell. In particular, cells within the tubules of nephrons in the kidney recognize calcitonin. The calcitonin-calcitonin receptor recognition at these cells leads to receptor binding. Binding in turn triggers biochemical events that result in decreased reabsorption of calcium as fluids pass through the nephron; excess calcium thus passes through the nephron into the ureter, eventually to be excreted.

Chapter 15

Taxonomy and Classification

*T*axonomy places all organisms on their proper perches in the great family tree of life. Taxonomy classifies animals into different categories and gives each type of animal a unique name — its scientific name. You may want to dismiss taxonomy as just too much bookkeeping. After all, what's the point of being so careful with names — why not just give animals the most colorful, poetic names possible? Well, that approach would result in one heck of a colorful, poetic mess.

Classifying organisms properly requires knowing a whole lot about their anatomy, physiology, and evolutionary history because we base the different categories of taxonomy on these very differences. As a result, each little name carries with it a massive cargo of information. In addition, having a single, systematic way of naming all creatures great and small prevents confusion because it means that everybody speaks the same language. With well over ten million species to consider, minimizing confusion is a high priority. In the end, taxonomy strives to make the best use of all that we know about biology and saves us from innumerable headaches.

Organizing Organisms

The taxonomic machine consumes knowledge about animal traits and evolutionary relationships (*phylogeny*), and sums it all up in a name. Because all life is part of one family tree, the most effective way to organize all that knowledge is in the form of a tree: a branched hierarchy. In the sections that follow, we get you thinking about that treelike organization of taxonomy as thick branches dividing and subdividing until they finally terminate at the leaves we call species.

From kingdoms to species

You could say that the biggest taxonomic category — the trunk of the family tree — is life, or *vita*, if you prefer Latin. But this is so obvious that we just assume it and move on. We give you the breakdown of the family tree in the following list, beginning with the largest category:

  ✔ Kingdom

  ✔ Phylum

  ✔ Class

- Order
- Family
- Genus
- Species

Individual organisms are typically referred to by their genus and species names only.

Real taxonomy begins with the five kingdoms (plus or minus). Every bacterium, amoeba, cactus, mushroom, and whale fits within one of the following kingdoms:

- Monera
- Protista
- Plantae
- Fungi
- Animalia

Now, a word to the wise. Over the past few decades, biologists have renewed debate about how best to organize the thickest branches of the taxonomic tree. Since the late 1960s, the dominating scheme has been the Five Kingdom system, and that is the system we describe here. A few alternative systems are used, however. Two related systems in particular, the Six Kingdom and Three Domain systems, have grown increasingly popular as our understanding of organisms at the molecular and genetic levels has grown. The Six Kingdom system simply divides Kingdom Monera into two kingdoms: Eubacteria and Archaebacteria. For the most part, The Three Domain system uses the Six Kingdom organization, and adds the level "Domain" above these kingdoms. All the kingdoms populated by eukaryotic organisms (plants, animals, fungi and protists) are contained within Domain Eukarya, and the Eubacteria and Archaebacteria kingdoms are promoted to Domains Bacteria and Archaea. Be aware of this ongoing debate because references to the Six Kingdom and Three Domain systems may show up on the exam.

To summarize, then, the taxonomic hierarchy from least to most specific is as follows: Kingdom, Phylum, Class, Order, Family, Genus, Species. Mnemonic devices abound for this sequence. Here are a few:

- Keep Pots Clean Or Family Gets Sick
- Kids Playing Chicken On Freeways Get Smashed
- Kurt Prefers Cheese Over Fried Green Spinach
- King Phillip Came Over For Good Sex

Take your pick. And remember that even though we may commonly refer to organisms by only their genus and species names, every wriggling bit of life has a complete set of seven names, as demonstrated in Table 15-1.

Table 15-1	The Seven Levels of Taxonomy Applied		
Level	*Venus Fly Trap*	*Komodo Dragon*	*Human*
Kingdom	Plantae	Animalia	Animalia
Phylum	Magnoliophyta	Chordata	Chordata

Level	Venus Fly Trap	Komodo Dragon	Human
Class	Magnoliopsida	Reptilia	Mammalia
Order	Caryophyllales	Squamata	Primates
Family	Droseraceae	Varanidae	Hominidae
Genus	*Dionaea*	*Varanus*	*Homo*
Species	*Dionaea muscipula*	*Varanus komodoensis*	*Homo sapiens*

You may have noticed from the table that species are given a two-part name, something like a first and last name. This convention is known as *binomial nomenclature.* Although mentioning "binomial nomenclature" is exactly the sort of thing that leaves you standing by yourself at parties, you need to understand it for the AP Biology exam. Names written in this system are always written in italics, and feature the genus name first, capitalized, and the species name second, in lowercase. Sometimes the genus name is abbreviated to its initial, as in *D. muscipula,* *V. komodoensis,* and *H. sapiens.*

Characteristics that count

The various taxonomic levels are anything but arbitrary. Generations of earnest scientists have toiled to find the most meaningful criteria with which to place organisms in family trees, or *phylogenies,* such as the simple one shown in Figure 15-1. Branches have been pruned and grafted, fused, and split in the light of new and better information. Systems are judged by the ability of their criteria to produce trees that most closely resemble evolutionary history. Good phylogenies have two major properties:

✔ **The position of a branch point on the tree should reflect how far back in time different groups diverged from a common ancestor.** Exactly how far back do I have to go before my pet lizard and I can call the *same* animal "grandma"?

✔ **The distance between branches at any one point in time should reflect just how far different groups have diverged.** Just how different *am* I from my pet lizard?

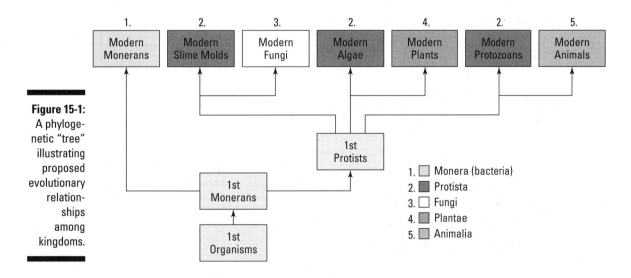

Figure 15-1: A phylogenetic "tree" illustrating proposed evolutionary relationships among kingdoms.

Endosymbiotic theory

Taxonomy and phylogeny ultimately boil down to questions of origins: who begat whom, and who originally begat the begetters, and so on. Some of the begetting is fairly straightforward, involving gradual adaptations to gradually changing conditions. Other times, dramatic changes in conditions seem to drive sudden and significant evolutionary change. And sometimes, a fortuitous event simply makes a big splash in the evolutionary pond. The origin of eukaryotes appears to have included a big splash in the form of *endosymbiosis,* a condition in which different organisms live together, one inside the other.

Key to the success of eukaryotic cells have been two powerful, mutually supportive organelles: the mitochondrion and the chloroplast. The mitochondrion consumes oxygen to efficiently extract energy from carbon sources like glucose, producing carbon dioxide and water in the process. The chloroplast consumes water and carbon dioxide as it captures energy from light and funnels it into the chemical energy of glucose, releasing oxygen in the process. Endosymbiotic theory proposes that these organelles were once prokaryotic cells, living inside larger host cells. The prokaryotes may initially have been parasites or even an intended meal for the larger cell, somehow escaping digestion.

Whatever the cause of their initial internment, these prokaryotes might soon have become willing prisoners to a grateful warden. The prisoner prokaryotes might have provided crucial nutrients (in the case of the primitive chloroplast) or helped to exploit oxygen for extracting energy (in the case of the primitive mitochondrion). The prokaryotes, in turn, would have received protection and a steady environment in which to live.

Multiple lines of evidence support the endosymbiotic theory. Endosymbiosis is observed elsewhere in biology. Mitochondria and chloroplasts have intriguing similarities in structure, reproduction, biochemistry, and genetic makeup to certain prokaryotes. The plain fact that mitochondria and chloroplasts have *any* genetic information of their own argues in favor of the theory. Because virtually all eukaryotes have some sort of mitochondria, while only photosynthetic eukaryotes have chloroplasts, it has been proposed that endosymbiosis occurred twice, in series. First, an aerobic (oxygen-using) heterotrophic prokaryote was taken in by a larger host cell. In time, the prokaryote co-evolved with the host, eventually becoming something like a mitochondrion. Next, a photosynthetic prokaryote was taken in by a mitochondrion-containing cell. This model of eukaryote origins is called *serial endosymbiosis.*

To which characteristics should you pay attention when deciding how similar or different two organisms really are? Which of these characteristics are the most important and revealing? These questions are more difficult than they sound. Older systems relied heavily on fossils and anatomical studies to reveal differences in *morphology,* the shapes or forms of structures in different organisms. For example, organisms can be classified based on whether or not they have a backbone, or whether they keep their DNA within a membrane-bound nucleus. Morphological characteristics remain important criteria in classifying different organisms. However, advances in molecular biology have revolutionized the field. By directly comparing the genetic composition and biochemistry of organisms, scientists have discovered similarities and differences that were previously hidden.

In hindsight, the huge impact of genetic data (the sequences of As, Gs, Ts, and Cs within an organism's chromosomes) on classification makes perfect sense. Only a fraction of genes contribute to morphological differences that can be observed in a fossil or an anatomical study. By examining genetic and biochemical information directly, we can feed much more data into our decisions. Furthermore, morphological differences that are large enough to observe can take a long time to evolve, limiting our ability to make decisions about the relatedness of creatures in recent evolutionary history. Genetic data are much more precise and are as clear as the difference between an A and a G.

Taxonomy is a big ship, and it takes a long time to turn. Much of the current system is based almost entirely on analysis of morphological data. In fairness, morphological data can be pretty subtle and revealing, including not only the structures of mature organisms, but also the structures they pass through during development, for example. Sometimes behavioral differences or geographic locations can inform decisions about classification, although these kinds of analyses are tricky because behavior and location can result from all sorts of factors other than evolutionary history. In the end, *all* observations (genetic, biochemical, morphological, geographic, and behavioral) should unite around a common understanding of the tree of life; the extent to which some observations disagree with others simply reveals how much we have yet to learn.

What's in a Name

Knowing an organism's taxonomic name is only profitable if you know the biological cargo carried by that name. Then, simply by knowing the name, you know a lot about the organism — who its cousins are, what kind of body type it has, whether or not it reproduces sexually, and so on. So, it's worthwhile to know some of the defining characteristics and major phyla of the Five Kingdoms: Monera, Protista, Plantae, Fungi, and Animalia. Also, it's testable.

Monera

By far, most of the species on the planet are subjects of kingdom Monera. Monera contains all the prokaryotic organisms, which are divided into two groups: eubacteria ("true" bacteria) and archaebacteria ("ancient" bacteria). These two groups are sufficiently different and important that they are increasingly considered as entirely different groups. Eubacteria and archaebacteria have some critical things in common, however: They are single-celled, lack membrane-bound organelles, and have cell walls.

Eubacteria

Eubacteria are nearly ubiquitous, thriving in all but the most extreme conditions. Though their microscopic scale may make them all seem pretty much the same, eubacteria are incredibly diverse, as they must be in order to flourish so widely. With so much diversity, it follows that there are many ways to classify the eubacteria. These ways include:

- Food and energy patterns
- Mode of movement
- Shape
- Cell wall properties

Both *autotrophic* (make their own food) and *heterotrophic* (feed to acquire energy) eubacteria exist. Among the autotrophs are those that synthesize food using light energy (*photoautotrophs*) and those that do so using chemical energy (*chemoautotrophs*) from inorganic compounds. Among the heterotrophs are eubacteria that can trap light energy but must feed to acquire carbon building blocks (*photoheterotrophs*) and other eubacteria that must feed to obtain both energy and carbon (*chemoheterotrophs*). Once they have acquired their food, eubacteria must be able to metabolize that food in order to use the energy within it. Some eubacteria must use oxygen to perform this task (*obligate aerobes*), and some must do their metabolism in the *absence of oxygen (obligate anaerobes).* Some eubacteria can go either way (*facultative anaerobes).*

Eubacteria are often *motile,* meaning that they can move themselves about, often in search of nutrient-rich environments. Different categories of eubacteria use different strategies for movement. Flagellar eubacteria employ whiplike flagella on their outer surfaces to power their travel. Some of these flagellated eubacteria move rather randomly, and others are capable of taxis, directed movement towards a stimulus. Spirochete eubacteria combine spinning filaments with a corkscrew shape to twist their way forward.

Differently shaped eubacteria clearly distinguishable underneath a microscope include:

- *cocci* (spherical)
- *bacilli* (rod-ike)
- *spirilla* (spiral-shaped)

Most eubacteria possess protective outer cell walls, built in part with a protein-sugar building block called peptidoglycan. Depending on the thickness of this layer and on other structural details, eubacteria respond differently to Gram staining, a tool used by microbiologists to identify types of bacteria within a sample. Bacteria with thinner peptidoglycan layers are identified as Gram-negative, and those with thicker peptidoglycan layers are pegged as Gram-positive.

Archaebacteria

Archaebacteria live in extreme conditions, often similar to the conditions thought to predominate during the early days of life on Earth. Accordingly, archaebacteria are believed to have deeply ancient evolutionary origins. Different groups of archaebacteria evolved to tolerate the harsh conditions of the younger Earth:

- **Methanogens:** The methanogens exploit high levels of methane gas in their use of energy.
- **Halophiles:** The extreme halophiles can and often prefer to live in very salty environments.
- **Thermophiles:** The extreme thermophiles evolved to tolerate hot environments. This last category of archaebacteria thrive today in places like hot springs and by hot-water vents on the ocean floor; in fact, the earliest living cells may have been extreme thermophiles that first took form at the bottom of the ocean.

Protista

Protists are an ancient group of eukaryotes. Many are single celled. Despite their seeming single-celled simplicity, the protists are more varied than are the subjects of all the other kingdoms. The far-ranging diversity of the protists makes them a taxonomic challenge. Some scientists have argued for splitting Kingdom Protista into as many as five separate protist kingdoms, based on genetic and biochemical evidence. "Give me a break," you mutter, "how different can one little protist really be from another?" Okay . . . you asked.

Protists can live freely as single cells or within large colonies of interdependent cells. They can be autotrophic or heterotrophic, and the heterotrophs can feed in weird ways. They can be quite similar to fungi — or not at all similar. They can reproduce sexually or asexually, and some can switch between these modes of reproduction. They may or may not be motile. Mercifully, one trait of the protists is uniformly true: They really dig water.

Despite the grumblings of taxonomists everywhere, the most widely used classification of protist groups refers to their food and energy patterns, and is one you should know about for the AP Biology exam. This scheme divides the protists into

- ✔ Animal-like (the protozoans)
- ✔ Plantlike (the algae)
- ✔ Funguslike (the slime molds and water molds)

These divisions of Kingdom Protista are not phyla, and they are not well-founded in evolutionary history. Nevertheless, they are deeply ingrained in the history of biology.

Protozoans are heterotrophic, consuming living cells or dead matter. Some important protist phyla (remember, kingdom, phylum, class, order, family, genus, species) are:

- ✔ **Apicomplexa:** Phylum Apicomplexa contains protist parasites such as plasmodium, the parasite responsible for the disease malaria.
- ✔ **Ciliophora:** Ciliophora contains organisms that use cilia, tiny vibrating hairs, to propel themselves through fluids.
- ✔ **Rhizopoda:** Rhizopoda includes the amoebas, protists that use pseudopods (seen in Figure 15-2), cellular extensions useful for movement and feeding.

amoeba

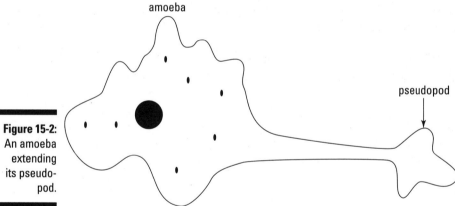

pseudopod

Figure 15-2:
An amoeba extending its pseudo-pod.

Algae are a group of protists that perform *photosynthesis,* the conversion of light energy into chemical energy. Algae swing this trick by using a collection of pigments (light-absorbing molecules) that are similar but not identical to those used in plants. All these photosynthesizing protists use the plant pigment chlorophyll a, for example, but also may use other pigments not found in plants. These pigments come in many colors, and the colors have been used to name different algal groups: green, golden, brown, and red algae. Green algae are believed to be the evolutionary precursors to plants. Golden algae live among groups of plankton, a ridiculously important food source in marine and freshwater ecosystems. Brown algae are all multicellular, and account for many varieties of seaweed. Red algae entirely lack the whip-like flagella common to many protists, and are often multicellular.

Other important groups of algae are

- ✔ **Diatoms** are an important component of plankton, the vital collection of tiny organisms that sustain life in oceans and lakes. Diatoms have unique, glass-like cell walls.

- ✔ **Dinoflagelletes,** named for their two flagella, are a major contributor to plankton.

- ✔ **Euglenophytes** (or *euglenoids*) typically thrive in freshwater environments. Euglenophytes can be autotrophic, heterotrophic, or a mixture of the two, depending on the availability of light and nutrients in their vicinity.

Funguslike protists include the slime molds and the water molds, and are important players in Biology because, like fungi, they decompose dead matter, returning precious resources to the environment. Also like fungi, some funguslike protists reproduce by means of spores. The resemblances between these protists and fungi may have resulted from *convergent evolution,* wherein organisms from different branches of the family tree evolved to become more and more like each other.

Plantae

The inhabitants of Kingdom Plantae would like you to revere them as unique in their status as multicellular, photosynthesizing eukaryotes. To their great consternation, their protist algae cousins keep reminding them that other kinds of organism do the multicellular, photosynthetic eukaryote thing too. To make matters worse, some types of algae are sometimes classified as plants. Try as they might, plants can't establish a unique identity solely on the basis of what they *are*, so they resort to stories about where they've *been*. Plants are distinct from multicellular algae in their connection to the land. While many algae still swim about in swarms of plankton, or sway as seaweed in watery depths, plants sink regal roots into soil. Even water-borne plants have family histories featuring long-term stints on land.

Still, plants owe a great debt to protists, because every last plant probably evolved from something that looked a lot like green algae. So, in plants we expect to find many of the core traits of green algae, along with extensive adaptations to life out of the water. This combination of traits was extensively described in Chapter 11. Here we provide a succinct summary, with an eye to classification.

First, understand that plants have broken the constraints of the normal taxonomic categories, like roots cracking through sidewalk. Kingdom Plantae isn't broken into phyla, but into divisions. Some of these divisions are all about algae: *chlorophyta* (green algae), *phaeophyta* (brown algae), and *rhodophyta* (red algae). Plants as we usually consider them probably evolved from chlorophytes and have since gone on to populate divisions of their own: *bryophyta* (mosses and liverworts) and *tracheophyta* (vascular plants). Tracheophytes contain important subdivisions, which in turn can be grouped based on whether the plants within them use seeds to reproduce. Subdivisions containing ferns, mosses and horsetails are grouped as the seedless vascular plants. Among the vascular plants that *do* have seeds, there are two important categories, the *gymnosperms* (cone-bearing plants) and the *angiosperms* (flowering plants). Unafraid of endless subdivision, the angiosperms have evolved further into monocotyledonous and dicotyledenous plants. For deeper detail on the delightful differences between gymnosperms and angiosperms, monocots and dicots, plant yourself back in Chapter 11.

Fungi

Fungi are the eukaryotic kings of decomposition. Fungi specialize in external digestion, a process whereby they secrete digestive enzymes into their environment, then absorb the nutritious bits and pieces. Although external digestion would be supremely gross were we humans to practice it, we should nevertheless be grateful that the fungi do their thing; the end result is that dead matter gets returned to the environment for all to use.

A signature feature of a fungus is the presence of *hyphae,* tiny threadlike structures made of chains of fungal cells, depicted in Figure 15-3. Hyphae can be loosely packed, as in the molds that form on bread and cheese. Alternately, hyphae can be densely packed, as in mushrooms. Hyphae form branching, interconnected masses called mycelia, which specialize in the secreting and absorbing business of external digestion.

In some ways, fungi might seem a bit like plants, but forget that notion. Some fungi team up with photosynthetic organisms like cyanobacteria or chlorophyte protists to form a symbiotic association called lichen, but these symbiotic teams are not plants. Many fungi reproduce sexually by means of haploid spore-producing structures called fruiting bodies, but these bodies are not fruits. Fungi may have polysaccharide cell walls, but these walls are made of chitin, not of the cellulose polysaccharide that builds plant cell walls.

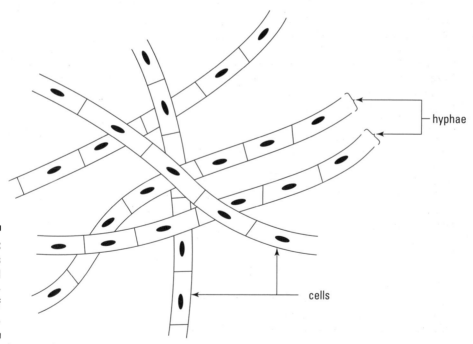

Figure 15-3:
Fungal cells assembled into a network of hyphae.

hyphae

cells

Though they might seem to be humble kings, many fungi are really rather famous, or at least infamous. Zygomycetes and ascomycetes include many of the hairy, unwelcome colonizations we find on our old or unrefrigerated food. Basidiomycetes include many of the mushrooms we enjoy as food. *Saccharomycetes* (budding yeasts) include species that we use to make food (bread).

Animalia

Trekking along the winding branches of classification can be tiring. Sure, the Monerans, Protists, Plants, and Fungi are colorful characters in the taxonomic Oz, but the day grows long. Welcome to Kingdom Animalia: There's no place like home!

Savor the familiar company of your multicellular, eukaryotic, heterotrophic friends. For 600 million years, we animals have shared close evolutionary bonds, doing the good work of evolving symmetrical bodies and sophisticated organ systems. Like other kingdoms, we've made some compromises over the thousands of millennia. We gave up the comforts of a cell wall, choosing to pack our many cells tightly together, interconnecting them with junctions so they could easily communicate and share. We invested heavily in sexual reproduction, and developed our embryos according to a common plan. We are a young and vibrant kingdom, honoring our eukaryotic traditions while embracing the diverse possibilities of specialization. The major results of our evolutionary exertions into multicellular specialization, sexuality, and sophistication are described in Chapter 13. Here, we summarize those results, emphasizing what sets us apart from the other kingdoms and what is diverse within our own.

After committing ourselves as a group to the multicellular way of life, we soon began branching out among the possibilities. An early branchpoint divided us between the *parazoans* (sponges), who demurred from specializing their cells into tissues, and the eumetazoans, who turned tissue-making into an art. Once the evolution of different tissues got off the ground, Kingdom Animalia could get serious about differentiating. Follow the description of this journey by referring to Figure 15-4 as you read.

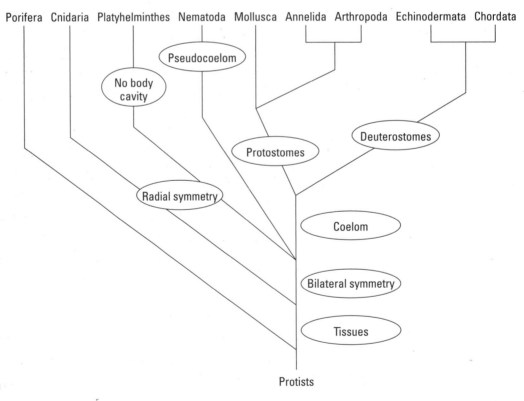

Figure 15-4:
Phylogenetic family tree of Kingdom Animalia, highlighting major evolutionary branchpoints.

Spinning their cells into useful tissues, eumetazoans branched into two groups with different philosophies on symmetry. One group, radiata, evolved bodies with radial symmetry, like a jellyfish — their tops are different from their bottoms, *or* their backs are different from their fronts, but they are otherwise symmetrical all the way around. The second group, bilateria, evolved different tops and bottoms *along with* different fronts and backs. The animals of bilateria are symmetrical about a single central axis; these animals need to know their heads from their behinds *and* their lefts from their rights. Eventually, evolution of sophisticated animal nervous systems would assist with the challenge of knowing one's behind from a hole in the ground.

Bilaterians parted ways over the issue of the coelom, a body cavity between the digestive tract and the body wall. Acoelomates went without such a cavity and also abstained from evolving a system of vessels to carry blood. Because a taste for specialization invites ever greater branching, the animals with a coelom divided over whether or not to enclose the coelom with a lining. The coelomates evolved such a lining of the gut; the pseudocoelomates did not. The final dramatic branching of the animals resulted from different approaches to embryonic development. The protostomes gave priority to the mouth, producing species that developed mouths from certain indentations in their early embryonic forms. The deuterostomes took these same indentations and developed them into anuses. Any ancient animals attempting to strike a compromise on this point appear not to have flourished.

A summary of the characteristics of important phyla within the animal kingdom is shown in Table 15-2.

Table 15-2	The Main Groups within the Kingdom Animalia		
Phylum	*Symmetry*	*Distinguishing Characteristics*	*Examples*
Porifera	None	No differentiated tissues	Sponges
Cnidaria	Radial	Stinging cells	Jellyfish, Hydra
Echinodermata	Radial	Endoskeleton, spines	Starfish, Sea urchin
Platyhelminthes	Bilateral	Act as parasites	Flatworms
Nematoda	Bilateral	Act as decomposers, parasites	Roundworms
Annelida	Bilateral	Act as decomposers, parasites	Segmented worms
Mollusca	Bilateral	Most have exoskeleton	Snails, Clams, Octopus
Arthropoda	Bilateral	Exoskeleton, jointed appendages	Insects, Spiders, Crustaceans
Chordata	Bilateral	Spinal chord, endoskeleton, advanced central nervous system	Fish, Reptiles, Birds, Mammals

Chapter 16

Answering Questions on Taxonomy and Classification

In This Chapter

▶ Picking up some pointers

▶ Testing out your knowledge

▶ Discovering answers and explanations

*N*ow that you've scaled the tree of life and surveyed its sweep as you sway in the canopy, it's time to put your lofty new perspective to use. This chapter tests your knowledge of the material covered in Chapter 15: Taxonomy and Classification. Multiple choice and free-essay response questions and answers are provided.

Pointers for Practice

The main points of this chapter are the following:

✔ Taxonomy places species into a hierarchy of categories. These categories sometimes change over time, as biologists gain a better understanding of the interrelatedness of different groups of organisms.

✔ Phylogeny is the science of placing species within an evolutionary family tree, showing which species gave rise to which other species. Cladistics is the science of developing tools to reveal evolutionary relatedness. Modern taxonomy aims to produce hierarchical categories that mirror the evolution of species. Today, genetic and biochemical data have great impact as they add to the store of knowledge gained from morphological, geographical, and behavioral data.

✔ Species are given unique taxonomic identities by placing them within a hierarchy of taxons, from least to most specific, of: kingdom, phylum, class, order, family, genus, species.

One helpful way to remember this sequence is the following sentence: King Phillip Comes Over For Good Sex (. . . or Spaghetti).

✔ Binomial nomenclature employs two-name identifiers for individual species. These names refer to the Genus and Species of the organism, are written in italics, capitalizing the first initial of the Genus, and placing the Species name entirely in lowercase. Sometimes, the Genus is abbreviated to its first initial. Thus, *Homo sapiens* becomes *H. sapiens*.

✔ The Five Kingdoms system divides life into kingdoms of Monera, Protista, Fungi, Plantae, and Animalia. The Six Kingdoms system splits Monera into kingdoms Eubacteria and Archaebacteria. The Three Domains system fits the Six Kingdoms under three Domains: Archaea, Bacteria, and Eukarya.

✔ Eubacteria and Archaebacteria are prokaryotes. Protists, Fungi, Plants, and Animals are eukaryotes. The evolution of eukaryotes seems to have involved a series of two endosymbiotic events, in which prokaryotes lived for a time within larger cells, eventually evolving within those cells into the mitochondrion and the chloroplast.

✔ Eubacteria can be autotrophic or heterotrophic, and thrive in widely diverse environments. Common schemes classify them by shape (cocci, bacilli, spirilli) or by Gram-stain (Gram-negative, Gram-positive).

✔ Archaebacteria have deeply ancient origins and thrive in extreme environments, such as in the presence of methane (methanogens), high salinity (extreme halophiles), or high temperatures (extreme thermophiles). The original cells may have been archaebacteria.

✔ Protists are single-celled and multicellular eukaryotes and are the most diverse kingdom. Some taxonomic systems split protists into several kingdoms in order to better reflect evolutionary lineages. A non-phylogenetic but common scheme divides the protists into animal-like (protozoans), plant-like (algae), and funguslike (absorptive) groups.

✔ Plants are multicellular, photosynthesizing eukaryotes, and probably evolved from green algae-like protists. The plant kingdom is not subdivided into phyla, but rather into divisions. Higher plants are divided into vascular (tracheophytes) and non-vascular (ferns, mosses, and horsetails) groups. Vascular plants are divided into seedless and seed-bearing varieties. Seed-bearing vascular plants include the gymnosperms (cone-bearing) and angiosperms (flowering). Angiosperms are either monocots or dicots.

✔ Fungi are eukaryotes that play an important biological role as decomposers. Fungi employ a tactic of external digestion in which they secrete digestive enzymes outside themselves, then absorb digested nutrients back into themselves. External digestion is facilitated by hyphae, branched networks of cells that assemble into masses called mycelia. Fungi include molds, mushrooms and yeasts, and are important components of plankton.

✔ Animals are multicellular, heterotrophic eukaryotes. Most animals have radial or bilateral symmetry. Bilateral animals are subdivided based on the presence or absence of a gut cavity, on whether or not that cavity is lined, and on differences in the embryological development of the mouth or anus.

Answering Multiple-Choice Questions

Directions: Each question is followed by five possible answers. Choose the best possible answer.

1. Which of the following organisms is most closely related to *Lynx rufus?*

    (A) *Felis catus*

    (B) *Canis rufus*

    (C) *Canis lupus*

    (D) *Lynx canadensis*

    (E) *Lutra lutra*

2. Which of the following taxons contains the others?

   (A) Species

   (B) Class

   (C) Order

   (D) Genus

   (E) Phylum

3. Which of the following observations support the endosymbiotic theory?

   I. Mitochondria and chloroplasts have their own genes

   II. Mitochondria and chloroplasts often exist by themselves

   III. Mitochondria and chloroplasts have membranes similar to those of prokaryotes

   (A) I only

   (B) II only

   (C) III only

   (D) I and III only

   (E) II and III only

4. All of the following are kingdoms EXCEPT

   (A) Chordata

   (B) Monera

   (C) Plantae

   (D) Fungi

   (E) Protista

   Use the following choices to answer questions 5–12. Each choice can be used once, more than once, or not at all.

   (A) Monera

   (B) Fungi

   (C) Plantae

   (D) Animalia

   (E) Protista

5. Includes organisms living symbiotically with algae in lichen

6. Includes prokaryotes that live in extreme conditions

7. Includes ants

8. Includes many bacteria that live in moderate conditions

9. Includes plant-like and animal-like organisms

10. Includes tracheophytes

11. Includes protozoans

12. Includes many land-based photosynthesizers

13. Which kingdom is the most diverse?

    (A) Protista

    (B) Animalia

    (C) Monera

    (D) Plantae

    (E) Fungi

Use Table 16-1 to answer questions 14–17:

Table 16-1	Diagnostic Testing		
Specimen Number	Photosynthetic Activity	Cell Wall Made with Carbohydrates	Membrane-bound Nucleus
1	+	+	+
2	–	+	+
3	+	+	–
4	–	–	+

Note: Diagnostic testing has ruled out the possibility of protist specimens.

    (A) Aminalia

    (B) Fungi

    (C) Plantae

    (D) Monera

    (E) Insufficient data

14. To what kingdom does specimen 1 belong?

15. To what kingdom does specimen 2 belong?

16. To what kingdom does specimen 3 belong?

17. To what kingdom does specimen 4 belong?

Answering Free-Essay Response Questions

Directions: Answer the following question in essay form, not in outline form, using complete sentences. Diagrams may be used to supplement answers, but diagrams alone are not adequate.

1. Compare and contrast the concepts of taxonomy, phylogeny, and cladistics. Explain the focus of each endeavor and how they interrelate to contribute towards an overall goal.

Checking Your Work

Revel in your correct answers. Unravel your incorrect answers. Be sure to understand all the answers you got wrong, because you'll have only one chance to get them right when you take the exam. For the moment, indulge in the luxury of being able to correct yourself.

Answers and explanations for the multiple choice questions are:

1. The correct answer is D because *Lynx canadensis* is of the same genus as *Lynx rufus*. Binomial nomenclature uses the genus name, followed by the species name. Organisms of the same genus are closely related. Answer B draws your attention because the species names are the same, but *Canis rufus* is of a different genus than *Lynx rufus*, so the two organisms are not as closely related as are *Lynx canadensis* and *Lynx rufus*.

2. Answer E is correct. Remember: <u>K</u>ing <u>P</u>hilip <u>C</u>omes <u>O</u>ver <u>F</u>or <u>G</u>ood <u>S</u>ex (...or <u>S</u>paghetti). The taxonomic levels in this sequence proceed from the broadest to the most specific, meaning that a kingdom contains all phyla and below, a phylum contains all classes and below, and so forth.

3. D is the right answer. Having their own genes and having membranes like those of prokaryotes suggest that chloroplasts and mitochondria 1) may well once have been independent organisms, and 2) may have descended from prokaryotes. Statement II is simply not true. Mitochondria and chloroplasts do not exist by themselves.

4. The right answer is A. The five kingdoms are Monera, Plantae, Animalia, Fungi, and Protista. Even in alternative taxonomic schemes, there is no kingdom of chordates. Chordata is actually a phylum within Kingdom Animalia.

5. The answer is B. Lichen — which are *not* plants — are symbiotic assemblies of fungi with cyanobacteria or algae.

6. A is correct. The prokaryotes tending to live in extreme conditions are known as archaebacteria. All archaebacteria and eubacteria inhabit Kingdom Monera.

7. If you chose D, be pleased with yourself. Some people may not think that insects are animals, but they are. Ants carry passports issued by Kingdom Animalia.

8. Bacteria that tend to live in moderate conditions are known as eubacteria, but all bacteria belong to a single kingdom — Monera, answer A.

9. Answer E takes it. Kingdom Protista is the most diverse kingdom, including some animal-like organisms, some plant-like organisms, and even some organisms that look and act like fungi.

10. The right answer is C. Tracheophytes are vascular plants, of both seed-bearing and seedless varieties.

11. E is correct. Protozoans are animal-like protists.

12. C is the right answer. Although there are photosynthetic prokaryotes and protists, the vast majority of land-based photosynthetic organisms are plants.

13. The most diverse kingdom is Protista, answer A. Kingdom Protista is so diverse, in fact, that it continues to confound taxonomists.

14. C is the answer. Only plants are photosynthetic AND have a carbohydrate-based cell wall AND have a nucleus.

15. B is the right answer. Although both fungi and animals lack photosynthetic activity and have nuclei, fungi have cell walls made of the carbohydrate chitin, whereas animal cells have no cell wall.

16. D is correct. Bacteria (within Monera) and plants both can or do have photosynthetic activity. Plants have cell walls made of the carbohydrate cellulose, and bacteria have cell walls that include much carbohydrate in the peptidoglycan layer. However, plants have nuclei, ruling them out. The prokaryotes of Monera lack nuclei.

17. Hopefully you chose A. Fungi and animals both satisfy the requirements of lacking photosynthesis and having nuclei, but fungi possess a carbohydrate-based cell wall, and animals have no cell walls.

Here is a model answer for the free-essay response question:

Taxonomy is the systematic endeavor to organize different species within hierarchical taxons, such that each species has a unique identity and name within the system. The hierarchy of taxons proceeds from least to most specific in the sequence, Kingdom, Phylum, Class, Order, Family, Genus, Species. Once assigned a unique taxonomic sequence, an organism can be universally referred to in the system of binomial nomenclature, giving the Genus and Species assignments only, as in *Homo sapiens*.

One function of taxonomy is to streamline scientific communication, avoiding confusion between the millions of species. Another function of taxonomy is to enable scientists to understand as much as possible about the biology of an organism simply from its taxonomic identity. In order for this second function to occur most effectively, the hierarchical taxons must correlate with the most significant biological criteria; when this is the case, similarities and differences between organisms can be predicted and explained by their proximity in the hierarchical tree.

Traditional criteria for taxonomic classification were developed from a study of morphological, developmental, geographical and behavioral differences. This approach was significantly but not completely successful; many classifications suggested similarities and differences between species that did not exist, and failed to reveal similarities and differences that did exist.

Phylogeny is the science of placing species as accurately as possible within an evolutionary family tree. Phylogenetic trees are similar in structure to taxonomic hierarchies, but the criterion for placement within a phylogenetic tree is specifically evolutionary relatedness. Experience has shown that evolutionary relatedness is the most meaningful correlate of biological similarity, and is therefore the best criterion for taxonomic classification. Phylogeny has taken great strides as a result of the explosion of genetic and biochemical data available for a multitude of organisms, since these "molecular" data reveal more subtle distinctions than are typically obtained from more traditional kinds of data. Still, molecular data are not a complete solution, are not universally available, and must always be considered in the light of other data. Ideally, all observations of species should fit into a coherent whole.

Cladistics is the science concerned with finding those kinds of data and tools that best reveal meaningful descriptions of similarity and difference between species, especially with regards to evolutionary relatedness. Cladistics serves as a sort of bridge between taxonomy and the world of biological observations, filtering more relevant data from less relevant data, and prompting changes in taxonomic classifications and schemes when it is clear that they reveal far less than they could.

Taxonomy and phylogeny are thus overlapping efforts with related but distinct goals, each aided by cladistic techniques, as summarized by the figure below.

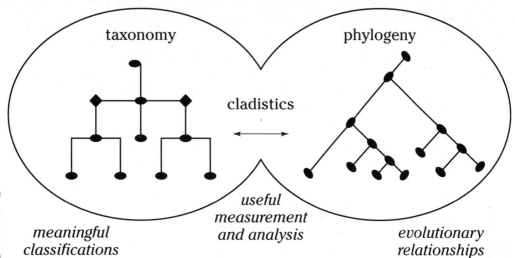

Chapter 17

Getting Along in the World: Ecology

. . . .

In This Chapter

▶ Touring the biosphere, biome by biome

▶ Confronting the ecological costs of human success

▶ Following the flow of energy through trophic levels

▶ Living and dying with population dynamics

▶ Working and playing with others within ecosystems

. . . .

*W*e're all in this together. Understand that, and you're more than halfway towards understanding this chapter, which focuses on ecology. Ecology examines the relationships of organisms with each other and with their physical environment. These relationships interconnect, forming large ecological networks. Different types of environment support different networks, but some ecological relationships are found just about anywhere you find life. Highly successful organisms, like humans, can sometimes disrupt the very networks that support them and their ecological neighbors. Ecology interests itself in everything from global climate patterns down to individual organisms; in practice, ecology can get pretty complicated. Fortunately for you, the principles which underlie it are not.

Homing in on Biomes

Because ecology examines the interactions of organisms with each other and with their environment, ecology must pay attention to both *biotic* and *abiotic* (living and nonliving) factors.

The simplest biotic factor is an individual organism. Individuals are members of populations, groups of the same species living in the same area. Populations of different species within an area form communities. Communities can be defined within small areas, or they may be defined as occupying great swaths of the globe.

The major abiotic factors are temperature, water, sunlight, and wind. Together with things like soil composition and the occasional tsunami, wildfire, or other catastrophe, these abiotic factors go a long way towards determining what types of organisms live where they do, when they do, and how they do. Temperature, water, sunlight, and wind are the primary components of climate, the weather characteristic of a particular region.

The interplay of biotic and abiotic factors across the globe produces large ecosystems, discernible across wide geographic areas; these large ecosystems are called biomes. Collectively, all the ecosystems of the earth constitute the biosphere, which is as majestic as it sounds: all life on earth, from the skies to the ocean depths. Ecology is a grand endeavor.

Using Climates to Carve Out Different Biomes

Any serious traversal of the world would likely encounter more than eight climates. In fact, finding uncontroversial distinctions between climates is not easy, and systems for doing so are typically the subject of debate. In the sections that follow, we describe the factors that govern the climates as well as how climates shape different biomes.

Climate governors

Temperature, water, sunlight, and wind interact with each other and with geography (for example, mountains, valleys) to produce areas of different climate across the globe. Within global climactic regions, different localities may experience large changes in climate depending on the specifics of their location and on the changing seasons. Climactic differences translate into ecological differences, even on very small scales.

Temperature, water, sunlight, and wind are the major factors that govern the climate in any particular area, and an area's climate is a major contributor to its biome. The following list describes these major factors as well as how these factors can affect species:

- ✔ **Temperature helps shape the biology of an area because cells can only do what they need to do within a limited range of temperatures.** Frozen cells, for example, don't usually fare too well when thawed. Although some types of organism have evolved remarkable adaptations to extreme heat or cold, these adaptations are expensive in terms of energy and resources; most life flourishes under more temperate conditions.

- ✔ **Life needs water (on earth, anyway).** For land-borne organisms, gaining access to water is an absolute prerequisite for living. For water-borne species, maintaining an appropriate balance of water and internal solutes is a constant requirement. Furthermore, water flows, and can carry things like heat and nutrients with it.

- ✔ **Sunlight powers biology.** Photosynthesizers like plants or algae use sunlight directly, and the rest of us use it indirectly. All sorts of evolutionary adaptations among photosynthesizers function to increase access to light. As the earth orbits the sun while spinning on its tilted axis, the sunlight conditions change across the globe; these periodic changes in sunlight are the cue for many seasonal changes among plants and animals.

- ✔ **Wind interacts with both temperature and moisture to make areas more or less hospitable to organisms.** Wind carries with it varying degrees of heat and moisture; this means that wind inevitably causes some areas to be warmer and some cooler, some drier and some wetter. Like water, wind can also erode and transport suspended particles, helping to reshape the physical environment.

Most biomes fall into one of two categories: aquatic (water) and terrestrial (land). Naturally, a few biomes exist at the interface of water and land, and blur this neat distinction — it can't always be nice and neat can it?

Aquatic biomes

Aquatic biomes divide themselves among marine and freshwater varieties, which differ significantly in the salt concentrations of their waters, with marine biomes possessing roughly three times more dissolved salt. Both types of aquatic biome vary with depth, in a pattern called vertical stratification. Deep bodies of water have an upper layer called the photic zone, through which enough sunlight passes to support photosynthesis. Below the photic zone lies the aphotic zone, a dark region. Not only light but temperature differs across the layers of deep water. Typically, upper layers are warmer and lowers layers cooler, with a steep temperature gradient, called a thermocline, separating warm and cold regions. The bottom layer or "floor" of an aquatic biome is called the benthic zone, and is typically dark and cold. However, life may still occur in the benthic zone, feeding on detritus, nutritious bits that fall to the benthic floor from higher layers.

Major freshwater biomes include:

- ✔ **Lakes and ponds are the freshwater biomes characterized by still or standing water.** Shallow regions nearer to shore nicely support aquatic plants, and are called the littoral zone. The photic zone of a lake, where photosynthetic organisms may thrive, is called the limnetic zone. The dark, aphotic zone of a lake — which may be absent in a pond — is called the profundal zone. In general, deeper lakes are less capable of supporting abundant life than shallower lakes, because a smaller fraction of their waters occurs within the well-lit littoral and limnetic zones.

- ✔ **Rivers and streams are freshwater biomes that feature water flowing in one direction.** The beginning, or source, of a river or stream is characteristically narrow, with clear water. Flowing water gradually erodes the channels that contain it, so rivers and streams tend to grow turbid (i.e., less clear) as they flow over distance, picking up soil and other particles as they flow. Smaller flows converge as tributaries to larger flows, so that rivers and streams tend to grow larger as they travel from their source. By the time they empty into the ocean, at their mouth, rivers are typically quite wide, often depositing their accumulated load of sediment in a triangular area called a delta. Because rivers and streams accumulate from waters that drain from such a broad expanse of land, they are particularly susceptible to pollution.

- ✔ **Wetlands and estuaries are aquatic biomes found at interfaces.** Wetlands, often found at the boundaries of larger bodies of water, may be covered in water only periodically, or may be covered with a shallow layer of water year-round. Wetlands may form within shallow basins, along the banks of rivers, or along coastal areas. Wetlands are notable for the variety of aquatic plants that they support, which in turn help to support vast numbers of species. Wetlands are quiet overachievers, rich in biodiversity. Estuaries are biomes found at the freshwater-saltwater interface where rivers or streams empty into the ocean. Water salinity varies within estuaries, and estuarial waters are often well-supplied with nutrients carried by the turbid waters of the rivers that feed them. Like wetlands, estuaries are biologically diverse biomes.

Marine biomes correlate largely with different zones defined by depth and by proximity to shore, as shown in Figure 17-1. Marine waters close to shore lie within the intertidal zone. Water slightly further from shore, still not of great depth, lies within the neritic zone. Most of the oceans consist of deeper waters, collectively called the oceanic pelagic zone. The *benthic* (floor) region of the oceans is sometimes called the abyssal zone, and supports highly adapted forms of life.

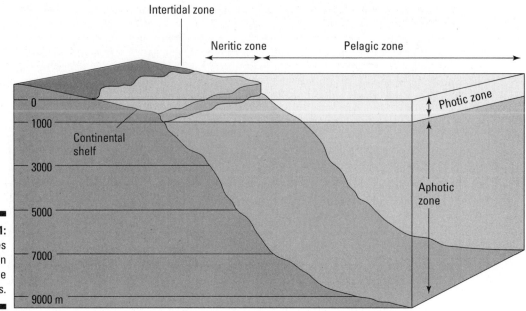

Figure 17-1: Zones within marine biomes.

Marine biomes include:

- **Intertidal zones support unique communities adapted to the ebbs and flows of the tide.** Intertidal organisms benefit from the twice-daily deposition of nutrients by the incoming tides, but must find ways to anchor and protect themselves from the buffeting of waves.

- **Neritic zones are home to prolific biomes called coral reefs.** Coral reefs enjoy a steady supply of nutrients from currents and, because they lie within the photic zone, from photosynthetic organisms of their own. Reef ecosystems are founded on the extensive exoskeletal structures made by coral, which provide habitat for an embarrassment of biological riches. Despite their diversity, coral reefs seem to be fragile biomes, and the impact of human activities on the long-term survival of coral reefs is hotly discussed.

- **The oceanic pelagic biome is geographically the largest on the planet.** The waters of this biome are circulated by currents, but are also separated into distinct layers due to differences in light, temperature, and salinity. Within the photic region, photosynthetic plankton abound, serving as the foundation upon which this biome is built. Plankton feed other inhabitants of the photic zone, but also feed species in the aphotic zone when they die and drift towards the ocean floor. Across depths, many varieties of fish, squid, turtle and marine mammal feed either directly on plankton or indirectly, by feeding on each other.

- **Abyssal communities, living in the deepest, darkest regions of the ocean, depend on droppings from above, the nutrient-rich detritus that descends from the upper photic layer.** Organisms inhabiting the abyss are adapted to a cold, dark, high-pressure environment, one in which meals are hard to find. An interesting exception to this condition is found in communities that surround volcanic hydrothermal vents on the ocean floor; there, chemosynthetic microorganisms employ ancient biochemistry to eke out a living at the scalding, sulfurous fringes of the vents. These hardy bacteria support exotic, newly discovered communities.

Terrestrial biomes

Once ancient life found its way onto land several billion years ago, it got serious about setting up shop. The quarter of the earth's surface that isn't under water supports a diverse array of biomes, whose distinctions arise largely from differences in climate and physical geography. Different biomes support different types and amounts of plant life, leading in turn to other differences. Like aquatic biomes, terrestrial biomes may possess distinct vertical layers defined by access to sunlight.

Terrestrial biomes tend to be distributed along latitudes, reflecting the fact that different climates are found at different latitudes. The terrestrial biomes include:

- **Tropical forest:** Tropical forests cluster in a band around the equator, extending north to the Tropic of Cancer, and south to the Tropic of Capricorn. Tropical forests have very distinct vertical layers whose characteristics emerge from differing access to sunlight. The canopy, the topmost layer, consists of the spreading branches and leaves of the tallest trees; the canopy absorbs the vast majority of light, and restricts air circulation in the lower layers. The understory, a middle layer, is composed of trees and vines found directly underneath the canopy. These plants grow opportunistically, seizing on any light that seeps through cracks in the canopy. The ground, the lowermost layer, contains a rich bed of decaying organic matter. This decay is critical to the survival of the forest, and is helped along by "decomposers" like bacteria, fungi, earthworms, and termites. Tropical forests also display a broad array of epiphytes, plants that live on other plants instead of rooted in the ground; moss and orchids are examples of epiphytes. Tropical forests receive varying degrees of precipitation, with lower altitude forests receiving less rain, and higher altitude "rainforests" receiving large amounts of rain.

- **Temperate deciduous forest:** These forests occur in moderate climates found primarily in the middle latitudes, north and south of the tropics. These climates include enough precipitation to support the growth of large trees, and tend to feature warm summers and cold winters. During the winters, the deciduous trees cannot maintain photosynthesis in cold conditions and lose a great deal of water; as a result, they lose their leaves. During these seasonal cold periods, many of the animal inhabitants of these biomes either go into hibernation or migrate to warmer regions for the winter. Although temperate deciduous forests are vertically stratified, they are less clearly divided into vertical layers than tropical forests; the canopies of temperate deciduous forests are less dense, admitting more light to the layers below.

- **Coniferous forest:** Like temperate deciduous forests, coniferous forests possess vertical layers. Unlike temperate deciduous forests, the trees that populate a coniferous forest tend to be of only one or a few species (though those species may differ between forests). Coniferous trees are either male or female, and reproduce by means of pollen- or egg-containing cones. Coniferous forests occur in temperate regions, like temperate deciduous forests, but also extend further towards the poles, into colder climates. "Taiga" refers to a vast biome that includes the cold, northern coniferous forests, ones that are blanketed with snow for much of the year. Coniferous trees possess many adaptations to cold weather, and do not typically lose their foliage in the winter as do deciduous trees. Climates supporting coniferous forests tend to receive a significant fraction of precipitation in the form of snow, but since these climates are warmer for a portion of each year, the snow eventually melts into liquid water that is available to the trees and to other vegetation.

- **Temperate grassland:** In addition to the presence of grasses, grasslands are defined by the significant absence of trees or large shrubs. Many factors can help to prevent trees from succeeding in grasslands, to include periodic droughts, fires and the grazing of animals. Although these biomes tend to be quite fertile, and thus of agricultural interest, they have relatively little in the way of biodiversity.

- **Savanna:** Similar in many ways to grasslands, savanna is found in more tropical areas and includes scattered trees. Savanna is especially prominent on the continent of Africa. Rainy seasons alternate with periods of drought. As a result of this climactic pattern, the savanna supports many grazing animals with vegetation that grows during the rainy season, but those same animals must migrate in order to access water and food during the dry season. Predators follow the migrating herds. During the dry season, fires play an important role in reshaping the physical environment.

- **Tundra:** Especially prominent in the arctic, tundra is characterized by extreme cold and fierce winds, which combine to ensure that very little water is available for use by vegetation. Consequently, plant life is severely restricted. A defining feature of tundra is permafrost, a permanently frozen layer of soil just beneath the topsoil. This frozen layer prevents the passage of large roots required of large trees, which are therefore not present on the tundra.

- **Desert:** The defining abiotic factor of the desert biome is aridity, the absence of moisture. Deserts may be hot, cold, or alternate between temperature extremes, but they are dry in either case. Desert-inhabiting plants and animals have evolved adaptations to maximize their ability to extract and conserve water from their arid environment.

Impacting Survival

Despite our short tenure on the planet (less than a million years), we modern *Homo sapiens* have definitely left our mark. The human population has risen at a staggering rate since about the mid-17th century. And since the industrial revolution, this exploding human population has increasingly impacted the distribution of matter and energy within the biosphere. Unchecked, this trend could spell our undoing. Understanding the impact of our own activity on ecosystems requires the science of ecology. Similarly, we need sophisticated ecological insight into our activities if we are to make informed decisions, weighing the benefits of human endeavors against the risks that go with them. As a science, ecology is not about promoting a particular point of view, but rather about understanding the world as we observe it.

Major ecological issues impacted by human activity include habitat loss, disruption of chemical cycles, buildup of toxins, and alteration of the makeup of the atmosphere. Among other things, all these results of human activity threaten to drastically reduce the store of biodiversity on the planet, which makes the world's ecosystems more fragile, less able to adapt to further environmental change.

As humans increase their numbers, they build. They farm. They mine. They cut. The spread of these human activities necessarily infringes on habitats previously used by other species. Millions of other species. Moreover, species are not distributed evenly across the world's ecosystems, but cluster much more densely in some systems than in others; damaging a relatively small percentage of habitats can result in the loss or reduction of a disproportionately large number of species. For example, coral reefs are a marine ecosystem that occupy but a fraction of a percent of the ocean floor, but provide habitat and resources for about a third of marine fishes. Current studies suggest that human development has damaged the vast majority of known reefs, causing the complete destruction of many. As with any complex ecological issue, the evidence isn't ironclad, but clearly indicates that we'd be wise to more closely consider the ecological impact of our developments.

Terrestrial ecosystems are similarly threatened by loss of habitat. Human developments like roads slice habitats into increasingly smaller fragments, severely disrupting ecosystems. The impact of human development is magnified in the case of migratory species, as they cross multiple habitats and participate in multiple ecosystems. Concerns like these have prompted research into the concept of sustainable development, an area in which we incorporate current ecological science into the costs-versus-benefits analysis of decisions we make about development. The goal of sustainable development is to acknowledge the practical needs of continued human development while striving to ensure the long-term survival of the interconnected ecosystems that support all life on the planet.

The basic chemical components of life naturally move through various states within cycles that have evolved over billions of years. Nitrogen (see Figure 17-2), oxygen, carbon (see Figure 17-3), phosphorous, and sulfur all participate in ecological cycles, and human activity measurably impacts all these cycles. The unintended consequences can wreak substantial ecological havoc. For example, the burning of fossil fuels dumps sulfur dioxide and nitrogen dioxide into the atmosphere. In the atmosphere, these gases dissolve in water vapor, eventually to return to earth in the toxic form of acid rain. Excess nitrogen compounds that run off from synthetic fertilizers accumulate in aquatic ecosystems and can lead to the massive overgrowth of algae, resulting in the depletion of oxygen from those environments and the death of aquatic species.

Toxic byproducts of human manufacturing, construction and other activities have a troubling tendency to accumulate in the physical environment. Water and wind, constantly circulating throughout the environment, carry toxins with them, helping the toxins to accumulate. For example, pesticides widely applied to agricultural crops are washed by rain into the soil, from which they run off into streams and rivers, eventually to be deposited in the oceans, each tributary river and stream adding its own toxic load. Along the way, the toxins become incorporated into food chains, concentrating further still at successively higher levels of those chains. What may have been a perfectly safe level of pesticide when applied to a crop can become dangerous when concentrated through natural, inevitable ecological processes.

Human impact on the composition of the atmosphere is a *politically* controversial issue. Though not at all settled, the *scientific* discussion of this issue is less controversial. There is great consensus, for example, that chlorofluorocarbons (CFCs) used in manufacturing and in consumer products end up in the atmosphere, where they deplete a protective sheet called the ozone layer. As CFCs break down, chlorine compounds from them engage in a chain reaction that results in the chemical conversion of ozone, O_3, to molecular oxygen, O_2. Although atmospheric ozone levels grow and shrink with the seasons, it is clear that recent decreases in ozone exceed these seasonal fluctuations, and correlate with human development. As ozone levels decrease, more damaging ultraviolet radiation gains passage through the atmosphere to impact the ecosystems below.

The most currently discussed area of human impact on atmospheric composition deals with greenhouse gases. Just as the transparent panes of glass in a greenhouse allow the passage of light into the interior, but trap the resulting heat within, certain gases in the atmosphere allow sunlight to reach the earth, but trap the heat that emanates upwards from the surface. Human industry and automobile exhausts dump many gases into the atmosphere, including large quantities of carbon dioxide. Carbon dioxide and other exhaust gases exert a greenhouse effect. The predicted result of continued increases in greenhouse gas levels is an averaged global warming, with chaotic effects on countless local climates, melting of polar ice caps, rising of sea levels, and rogue's gallery of other ecological ugliness. Steadily accumulating evidence suggests that human activities have already contributed significantly to changes in global climate, with measurable ecological effects. The precise extent of the human impact in this area is contested, but the presence of such an impact is not seriously in doubt. Unfortunately, the issue is both highly complex and dramatically important. This is clearly an area where sound and sober ecological science should temper high-stakes discussions about how best to balance pressing human desires with long-term survivability.

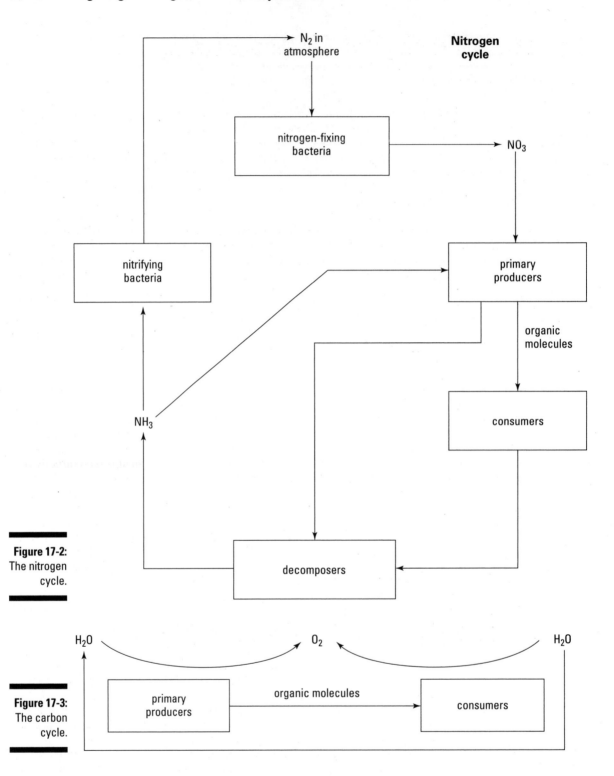

Figure 17-2:
The nitrogen cycle.

Figure 17-3:
The carbon cycle.

Earning a Trophy for Understanding Trophic Levels

Living things need a continual input of energy. Virtually all of this energy originates in sunlight, and flows through different levels as organisms do what they need to do to keep going (photosynthesize or eat). These levels are called trophic levels. The simplest kind of relationship between organisms at different trophic levels is the food chain, a linear sequence of organisms, each feeding on the previous one:

Grass→Mouse→Snake→Hawk

Food chains don't exist in isolation, however, because each organism can simultaneously belong to several different food chains. Food chains therefore interconnect, forming larger food webs. Within a food web, there are many possible paths as one ascends the trophic levels. The transfer of energy between trophic levels is not very efficient, with the majority of energy being lost as heat from one level to the next. At the same time, the energy that does get transferred to higher levels tends to be stored more densely than in lower levels. In other words, you have to consume a much greater mass of grass than you have to consume of cow in order to get the same amount of energy. A whole lot of grass goes into every bit of beef.

Producing, or being, food

Organisms that produce their own food (typically, from sunlight) are called autotrophs. In the jargon of ecology, autotrophs are known as primary producers. Primary producers include plants, photosynthetic protists, cyanobacteria, and chemosynthetic bacteria. These kinds of organisms serve as the energy foundation of ecosystems; many organisms feed directly on the primary producers, harvesting some of their stored energy and concentrating it within their own bodies. Wipe out the primary producers and you'll wipe out an ecosystem.

Each day, the energy equivalent of dozens of atomic bombs streams to the Earth from the sun. Most of this energy is lost as heat. A small percentage of this energy is captured by various photosynthetic organisms, and stored usefully as chemical energy. As small a yield as this may seem, it is enough to account for nearly two hundred billion tons of organic material generated by primary producers each year.

Consuming, or Eating Produced Energy

The primary producers, or autotrophs, support the energy needs of consumers, or heterotrophs. Heterotrophs are ecologically classified as either primary consumers, secondary consumers, tertiary consumers, or detritivores. All these types of consumers may also be classified as herbivores, omnivores, or carnivores. Herbivores eat only plants, omnivores eat both plants and animals, and carnivores only eat animals. Primary consumers eat autotrophs, and therefore are herbivores. Secondary consumers eat primary consumers and are thus carnivores. Tertiary consumers eat the secondary consumers, and also are carnivores. Of course secondary or tertiary consumers may also eat autotrophs, in which case they would be omnivores. Detritivores are an interesting class of organisms that only eat dead and decaying matter.

Primary producers and the various levels of consumers occupy distinct trophic levels within an energy pyramid. Since so much energy is lost between trophic levels, most organisms within an ecosystem are necessarily producers. These producers can support a smaller but still sizable number of primary consumers. The numbers of secondary and tertiary consumers grow progressively smaller, as shown in Figure 17-4.

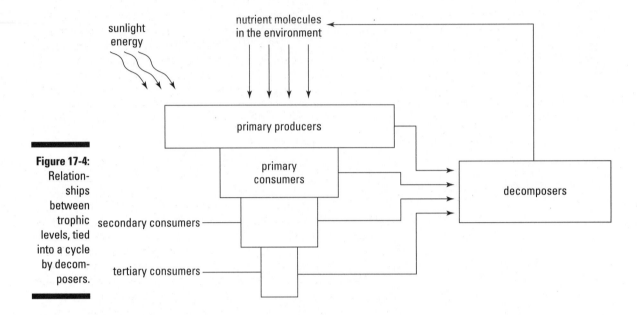

Figure 17-4: Relationships between trophic levels, tied into a cycle by decomposers.

Taking care of leftovers

Detritivores, who get their energy by consuming dead plants and animals (detritus), are also called decomposers. Decomposers include bacteria, fungi, and even some animals, such as vultures and jackals. Although all organisms provide some amount of decomposition (for example, by getting rid of wastes), decomposers make a profitable lifestyle out of it. By accelerating decomposition, detritivores help to recycle matter through the ecosystem, making raw materials available for use once more by primary producers. In this way, the decomposers link the trophic levels into a sustainable cycle.

Being Part of the Team

We really are all in this together. Ecosystems arise from this togetherness as organisms live and die, competing and cooperating for resources in the same area. Over time, the countless moving parts (organisms) within these systems fall into relatively stable patterns, with each organism unwittingly playing a role as the whole ecosystem chugs along. These stable arrangements suffer disturbances, and can fall entirely apart if disturbed too greatly. However, lesser disturbances simply cause the ecosystem to make some shuffling rearrangements, eventually to fall into another stable pattern, called an *equilibrium*.

Filling to capacity

Changes in the populations of organisms within an ecosystem disturb equilibria, and these kinds of changes and their effects have been extensively studied within a field called population dynamics. Some of the basic principles of population dynamics are described here.

Populations of species live within habitats. The maximum population that can be sustained by a particular habitat is called the carrying capacity. Each species has its own associated carrying capacity but, like most things within ecosystems, these separate carrying capacities are interconnected. For example, a cave that can sustain a large population of insects can consequently sustain a large population of bats. As insect populations grow, so might bat populations. Given unlimited resources, the maximum growth rate a species can attain is called its biotic potential. The ideal conditions necessary to reach a biotic potential are never actually realized, but the concept is useful as a measurement of the intrinsic ability of populations to grow.

Two types of factors limit the ability of a population to approach its biotic potential: density-independent factors and density-dependent factors. Density-independent factors exist regardless of the density of the population — the number of a given species within a given space. Density-independent factors include natural disturbances such tornados, earthquakes and floods. Earthquakes do their rumbly thing, completely oblivious of the populations there to sense the rumbling. By contrast, density-dependent factors exert their effects to a greater or lesser degree, depending on population density. Some examples of density-dependent factors include disease and food availability. The cold and the flu run more rampantly through crowded urban environments than they do across equally-sized populations distributed over a greater area. Whatever the specifics, any type of factor limits population growth either by increasing death rates or decreasing birth rates. Or both. Within defined ecosystems, populations can also change due to immigration or emigration into or out of the boundaries of the system.

Populations that experience little pressure from either density-dependent or density-independent factors undergo exponential or "J" growth, in reference to the J-shaped curve of a population-versus-time graph. Exponential growth cannot be sustained indefinitely in any real environment, so populations eventually reach their characteristic carrying capacity. As they do so, the steep slope of the J-curve levels off, producing an S-shaped curve. Once this leveling has occurred (see Figure 17-5), the population tends to fluctuate slightly above and below the carrying capacity for as long as the ecosystem remains generally in equilibrium. The magnitude of these fluctuations depends on the reproductive strategy of a species. Species that produce few offspring (but nurture those few offspring extensively) tend to fluctuate closely about their carrying capacity; we call these types K-selected species. Other species aggressively reproduce, creating as many offspring as possible and leaving those offspring to their own devices. These types of species may fluctuate wildly above and below their carrying capacity; we call these types R-selected species. The "K" and "R" in these terms refer to the variables K and R in an equation used to model S-shaped population growth, shown in Figure 17-6. In this model, K stands for the carrying capacity and R stands for the rate of population growth (the difference between birth and death rates). K-selected species tend to specialize at making the most efficient use of their environment, whatever its carrying capacity. R-selected species attempt to thrive by the brute force of aggressive reproduction.

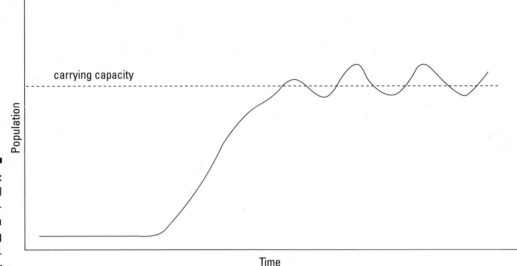

Figure 17-5:
Exponential growth limited by a carrying capacity.

Figure 17-6:
A model for S-shaped population growth over time. ΔN is the change in the number of a species, Δt is the change in time, N is the number at the initial time, R is the rate of growth and K is the carrying capacity.

$$\frac{\Delta N}{\Delta t} = R \cdot N\left(\frac{K - N}{K}\right)$$

Establishing a lasting equilibrium involves a process called ecological succession, in which the mixtures of species within an ecosystem change, and carrying capacities are in flux. The interdependent changes of succession — the maturing of an ecosystem — reflect the fact that populations live together as communities, sharing habitat. Eventually, succession leads to an equilibrium state called a climax community.

The first plants and animals that colonize a new habitat are called pioneer species. Most pioneer species are plants and microorganisms, because consumers can't sustain themselves in the absence of producers. Additionally, these trailblazing organisms are typically opportunistic and able to endure harsh conditions. Pioneer species promote primary succession, in which a largely lifeless habitat progressively gains the ability to sustain larger populations and larger numbers of species. Key to primary succession is the breakdown of inorganic matter (for example, rocks) into smaller and smaller pieces consistent with the development of soil. Lichens and mosses are often central players in this process. As soil develops and is enriched with decaying organic matter, new species move into the habitat, either cohabiting with the pioneer species or, more often, largely out-competing them. Primary succession is a slow process and can take thousands of years. Today, we can observe primary succession on volcanic islands, and on land exposed by retreating glaciers.

Secondary succession occurs in the aftermath of a catastrophic event, such as a fire, flood, forest-clearing, or overgrazing. In such cases, habitats may be severely damaged and populations wiped out, but the soil remains intact. The habitat may return to something resembling its original state, but often matures into something quite distinct from the original habitat. Secondary succession is driven by species that can readily use the nutrients available from the intact soil, in an otherwise barren area.

Finding your niche

A niche is often loosely described as the "role" an organism plays within its ecosystem, but this definition carries the misleading connotation that organisms do what they do with the express purpose of supporting the ecosystem. More accurately, a niche is the sum of all the biotic (living) and abiotic (nonliving) resources that an organism uses. Emerging from this definition are the details of how an organism survives, and how it reproduces.

Through many generations of evolution within an ecosystem, most species acquire a unique niche, because this arrangement reduces competition, enabling better survival and reproduction. Organisms have unique structures tailored to their niche. Hummingbirds, for example, possess long beaks that grant them access to energy-rich nectar, an abiotic resource produced by flowers, which are biotic resources. Flowers, in turn, grow by using water, carbon dioxide, and minerals (all abiotic resources), and reproduce by means of pollinating hummingbirds, which are biotic resources.

Living together and liking it — or not

Organisms share habitats. Like students sharing the habitat of high school, different organisms come to different arrangements with their neighbors; with some they cooperate, with others they compete, and others still they may hunt as prey (we don't recommend doing this at your high school, though). Three major types of relationship crop up within ecosystems: symbiosis, competition, and predation.

Symbiosis is a close and enduring relationship between organisms of different species. Symbiotic relationships can take the form of mutualism, commensalism or parasitism. In mutualism, both species benefit. In the subtropics, for example, ants protect acacia trees from other insects, and in turn benefit from acacia nectar. In commensalism, one species benefits while the other receives neither benefit nor harm. Clownfish, for example, can swim unharmed among the poisonous tentacles of the sea anemone; the clownfish is protected by the anemone, and the anemone is neither helped nor harmed by this arrangement. In parasitism, one species benefits while the other is harmed. For example, ticks draw nourishment from the blood of a host, essentially stealing the host's nutrients and energy.

Competition is a relationship that harms both species. Competition occurs over scarce resources, and typically grows more intense with greater scarcity. Organisms of the same species may compete as well as organisms of different species.

Finally, predation is a relationship in which one organism hunts another. For one of the organisms, the relationship ends in death; for the other, it ends in a meal.

Chapter 18

Answering Questions About Ecology

● ●

In This Chapter

▶ Putting pointers to memory

▶ Testing your knowledge

▶ Trying out some labs

▶ Checking your work

● ●

*T*he central lesson of ecology may well be that we're all in this together, but that doesn't mean that we're all holding hands with the authors of the AP Biology exam, singing *Kumbaya*. They'll throw some curveballs at you. Use this chapter to help bat a few back. Here you'll find review and questions covering the material found in Chapter 17: Getting Along in the World: Ecology. Multiple choice and free-essay response questions and answers are provided. Also, an explanatory summary is given for a Lab on Dissolved Oxygen and Aquatic Primary Productivity.

Pointers for Practice

The main points of Chapter 17 are the following:

✔ Ecology examines the interactions of organisms with each other and with their physical environment. Ecological interactions occur among both biotic (living) and abiotic (nonliving) factors.

✔ The major abiotic factors are temperature, water, sunlight, and wind. Together with geography, these factors largely define climate.

✔ The ecosystems of the world fall into broad categories called biomes. Biomes may be aquatic or terrestrial, and may also occur at land-water interfaces. Aquatic biomes are divided into freshwater (lake/pond, river/stream, wetland, estuary) and marine (intertidal, neritic, oceanic pelagic, abyssal) varieties. Terrestrial biomes distribute roughly according to latitude and include tropical forest, temperate deciduous forest, coniferous forest (including taiga), temperate grassland, savanna, tundra and desert.

✔ Both aquatic and terrestrial biomes may possess vertical stratification, or differences in structure that result from differing access to light. In aquatic biomes, the major vertical zones are the photic and aphotic zones, where light penetrates or fails to penetrate, respectively. Photosynthetic primary producers of aquatic ecosystems are restricted to the photic zone. In terrestrial biomes like forests, taller plants tend to spread their leaves widely overhead, forming a light-absorbing umbrella called a canopy. This arrangement may severely restrict the penetration of light to lower levels, which limits the kinds of organisms that can thrive there. In tropical forests, strong vertical stratification produces three major layers: the canopy, the understory, and the ground layers.

✔ As a natural consequence of the success of the human species, human population has increased tremendously in the last few centuries. Combined with the intensive use of fossil fuels beginning with the industrial revolution, this trend has ensured that humans exert a major impact on world ecosystems. This impact threatens our own sustained survival if left unchecked. Major areas of human impact include habitat loss, disruption of chemical cycles (e.g., nitrogen, carbon, sulfur, phosphorous), buildup of toxins, and alteration of the atmosphere (e.g., ozone layer depletion, greenhouse gas emission). These impacts have the effects of reducing biodiversity and potentially altering climate, among other things.

✔ Energy enters ecosystems in the form of sunlight, captured by photosynthetic primary producers. This energy is transferred and transformed within ecosystems via trophic relationships, like food chains and food webs. A food chain is a linear sequence of organisms, each one serving as food to the next. Interconnected food chains make up food webs.

✔ Primary producers (i.e., autotrophs) form the foundation of a food web, the first trophic level. Successive levels are populated by consumers (herbivores, carnivores, and omnivores) who feed on producers, on other consumers or on both. Detritivores (i.e., decomposers) help break down dead organic material, recycling its chemical components within an ecosystem. Because the transfer of energy between trophic levels is highly inefficient, most biological matter (i.e., biomass) within an ecosystem is necessarily devoted to primary producers. Producers support a smaller amount of biomass in the form of primary consumers, which in turn supports an even smaller biomass of secondary consumers, and so on.

✔ The maximum population of a given species that can be sustained within a given habitat is called a carrying capacity. The maximum growth rate a species can attain, given unlimited resources, is called biotic potential. Density-dependent and density-independent factors limit growth rates, keeping them below biotic potential. Growth that isn't severely limited by these factors is exponential, creating a J-shaped curve on a plot of population versus time. As population approaches carrying capacity, growth levels off, producing an overall S-shaped curve.

✔ Once at carrying capacity, population fluctuates above and below capacity, typically in one of two characteristic ways. K-selected species fluctuate closely about the carrying capacity, while R-selected organisms fluctuate wildly above and below carrying capacity, with fluctuations averaging out over time.

✔ Ecosystems undergo processes of maturation called succession. Primary succession involves the initial development of a barren environment into an ecosystem that has attained equilibrium. Primary succession requires the early involvement of soil-developing pioneer species. Secondary succession is a kind of re-equilibration that occurs in the wake of a violent environmental event, one that leaves only the soil intact.

✔ A niche is the sum of all biotic and abiotic resources used by a species within their ecosystem. Niches arise naturally as the arrangements which make most efficient use of available resources.

✔ Organisms interact within ecosystems in several different ways, to include symbiosis, competition and predation. Within the mode of symbiosis, there are three major subcategories: mutualism (both species benefit), commensalism (one species benefits, the other is not impacted), and parasitism (one species benefits, the other is harmed). In competition, both species are harmed, usually one more so than the other. In predation, one species dies and the other feeds.

Answering Multiple-Choice Questions

Directions: Choose the best possible answer, out of the five that are provided, for each question.

1. Aphotic zones prominently feature all of the following *except:*

    (A) Darkness

    (B) Nutrient-rich detritus

    (C) Squid

    (D) Primary producers

    (E) Complex food webs

2. Which of the following factors is *not* a major determinant of climate?

    (A) Temperature

    (B) Soil

    (C) Water

    (D) Sunlight

    (E) Wind

3. Which of the following statements are true?

    I. Energy transmission between trophic levels is efficient

    II. All primary producers are plants

    III. Detritivores support primary producers

    (A) I only

    (B) II only

    (C) III only

    (D) I and II only

    (E) II and III only

Questions 4–8 refer to the following answer choices. Answers may be used more than once.

    (A) Carrying capacity

    (B) Biotic potential

    (C) Density-dependent factor

    (D) Density-independent factor

    (E) Equilibrium

4. Disease

5. Intrinsic growth rate

6. No net change

7. Rainfall

8. Sustainable population

9. Which of the following types of inter-species interaction can involve at least one organism being harmed?

   I. Predation

   II. Competition

   III. Symbiosis

   (A) I only

   (B) II only

   (C) III only

   (D) I and II only

   (E) I, II and III

10. A biodiversity index is a measure of the number of different species within an area and the degree to which those species are interspersed. Higher numbers of different species and greater intermixing of those species within an area lead to higher indices of biodiversity. A three square-acre area was defined from global positioning coordinates, and the biodiversity index of that area was measured every five years, four separate times over a 15-year period, with the following results:

Year 0:	Index = 289
Year 5:	Index = 324
Year 10:	Index = 13
Year 15:	Index = 102

    Which of the following best accounts for the observed changes in biodiversity?

    (A) Primary succession

    (B) A high percentage of K-selected species

    (C) A low percentage of R-selected species

    (D) Secondary succession

    (E) Sustained growth near biotic potentials

Answering Free-Essay Response Questions

1. Explain the following ecological phenomena, giving an example of each: succession, limiting factors, and carrying capacity.

Lab on Dissolved Oxygen and Aquatic Primary Productivity

This lab consists of two major sections, each devoted to an important experimental measure of the conditions within aquatic ecosystems. The first section concerns the level of oxygen dissolved within the waters of an aquatic ecosystem, revealing how these levels can vary as a function of temperature. The second section focuses on primary productivity, the rate at which carbon-containing (i.e., organic) compounds are made by primary producers within an aquatic ecosystem, revealing how such productivity can vary as a function of the amount of light available.

Oxygen (O_2) availability is a more critical limiting factor in most aquatic ecosystems than it is in most terrestrial ecosystems due to the limited solubility of oxygen in water. At relevant temperatures, the amount of oxygen free for use by organisms is about twenty to forty times smaller in aquatic environments, because only a limited amount of oxygen can dissolve in water. Moreover, whatever oxygen does dissolve in a given body of water circulates through that water much more slowly than does oxygen within the atmosphere. Thus, different regions of a given aquatic environment can have significantly different levels of dissolved oxygen. Since many aquatic species rely heavily on oxygen for their metabolism, dissolved oxygen levels can often limit the growth of aquatic species. Many different factors contribute to observed levels of dissolved oxygen (DO), including water salinity, water temperature, oxygen levels in the atmosphere over the water, and the extent of photosynthesis by primary producers within the water.

To determine the effect of temperature on DO, students use provided kits to directly measure DO in water samples that have been equilibrated at three different temperatures (e.g., 5, 20, and 30 degrees Celsius). Depending on the kit used, DO may be measured in any of several units: parts per million (ppm), milligrams oxygen per liter water (mg/L), or milliliters oxygen per liter water (mL/L). These units can be interconverted by using the following equations:

ppm oxygen = mg/L = (mL/L)/0.698

Measured DO levels can be related to the ability of primary producers to fix carbon within organic compounds as follows:

(mL/L) $\times$ 0.536 = mg carbon incorporated / L

The expected results of this lab are that warmer temperatures result in lower levels of DO. This result may be counter-intuitive at first, because warmer temperatures typically result in higher solubility of solids in water; the reverse is true for solubility of gases.

The second section of this lab employs water samples that contain suspended primary producers, such as algae. Since these producers can engage in the light-dependent process of photosynthesis, the primary productivity is measured indirectly from measurements of DO, by relating DO levels to the basic chemical equation of photosynthesis:

$6\ CO_2 + 6\ H_2O \rightarrow C_6H_{12}O_6 + 6\ O_2$

From the above equation, it is clear that the molar amount of carbon dioxide fixed in organic form as glucose varies one-to-one with the amount of oxygen produced in the process. Converting from molar units to more convenient volume and mass units, the same equation suggests that for every mL of oxygen produced, 0.536 mg of carbon are fixed into organic form. Thus, samples with greater primary productivity display a greater rate of increase in DO.

Students fill six identical tubes with identical volumes of water-algae mixtures. The ability of light to enter these tubes is controlled by wrapping the tubes with varying layers of screening material. More wrapped layers of screen result in decreasing amounts of penetrating light. Students measure the initial DO of the water prior to incubating within the various tubes. Then, students incubate the tubes overnight, under a light source. The tubes include two controls: a "light," unscreened tube and a "dark," completely screened tube. The four remaining tubes possess different amounts of screening, and admit amounts of light intermediate between the light and dark controls. After twenty-four hours incubation under a floodlight, DO levels are measured for each of the six samples.

The difference between initial DO and the final DO of the dark control tube is defined as the intrinsic respiration rate of the system.

From the initial DO and final DO measurements of the sample tubes, students calculate the gross productivity and net productivity of the samples. Gross productivity is defined as the difference between the final DO of a given sample and the final DO of the dark control tube (i.e., final sample DO - final dark DO). Net productivity is defined as the difference between final DO of a given sample and the initial DO (i.e., final sample DO - initial DO). The results are plotted as productivity (gross or net) versus light intensity.

The key relationship is net productivity versus light, as this relationship best reflects the effect of varying light levels on the ability of primary producers to fix carbon via photosynthesis. The expected results of the lab are that the darkest bottles exhibit the lowest net productivity, with increasing productivity observed at increasing levels of admitted light. These results help explain vertical stratification within aquatic ecosystems; in particular, they reveal why one expects very different ecosystems to arise in photic versus aphotic zones.

Checking Your Work

As you dove into the practice questions, you may have felt yourself descending darkly into aphotic confusion, or you may have floated buoyantly in the photic zones of ecological knowledge. The AP Biology exam is a sink or swim sort of thing, so be sure to "get photic" before the exam: Check your work.

1. Aphotic zones are the deeper, darker regions of lakes and marine environments, where little or no light penetrates. Thus, they simply cannot support many primary producers, most of which are photosynthetic. The answer is D.

2. The answer is B. Although soil composition is an important abiotic factor of ecosystems, it is not a major determinant of climate; if anything, climate helps to determine soil composition. By contrast, temperature, sunlight, wind, and water all contribute significantly to climate.

3. C is correct. Detritivores help to decompose materials, making their chemical components available for use once more by primary producers. Energy flow between trophic levels is notoriously inefficient, which leads to the pyramid-shaped relationship between trophic levels, with most biomass devoted to producers, and decreasing levels of biomass attributed to increasing levels of consumers. Finally, while most primary producers are photosynthetic, not all photosynthesizers are plants (e.g., cyanobacteria), and not all primary producers use light (e.g., chemoautotrophs).

4. C is the answer. Disease limits the reproductive success of a species, and occurs more frequently in denser populations.

5. The answer is B. The biotic potential is the growth rate of a species when it has all required resources and isn't limited by density-dependent or density-independent factors. Biotic potential is therefore a good measurement of the intrinsic growth rate of a species, unmasked by other factors.

6. E is right. Although equilibrium can be a dynamic state, with significant change in several directions, the basic condition of equilibrium is the absence of overall, "net" change. As equilibrium, changes in one direction (e.g., births) are offset by changes in the opposite direction (e.g., deaths).

7. D is correct. The rain falls as it will, regardless of the population density within an ecosystem. Of course, in extreme cases, this explanation breaks down; climate-impacting human activities could conceivably alter the extent of rainfall. Still, for the most part weather is considered a density-independent factor.

8. A is the way to go here. A carrying capacity is a limit to the population a species can sustain within a given habitat. Populations can exceed carrying capacity for a time, but eventually correct themselves to lower levels. Over the long run, fluctuations about the carrying capacity even out.

9. E is right. That species may be harmed during predation or competition is fairly obvious. It's easier to forget, however, that symbiosis includes the mode of parasitism, in which one species benefits while the other is harmed.

10. The answer is D, secondary succession. High levels of biodiversity followed by a sharp decrease, and then a rebound, are consistent with secondary succession. Imagine, for example, that a fire sweeps through a forested area; most species might be wiped out, but the intact soil of the burned out area would support the beginnings of repopulation. Primary succession is about maturing to a point of equilibrium, which is not observed in the data. High numbers of K-selected species and low numbers of R-selected species are each consistent with small fluctuations about stable population levels, the opposite of what is seen in the data. Sustained growth near biotic potentials suggests rapid, continuous growth, which is also not shown in the data.

Here is a model answer to the free-essay response question:

Succession refers to the maturing process of an ecosystem, and occurs in two major forms: primary and secondary. Both forms involve changes in physical environments and species populations, until such changes level off at equilibrium. In primary succession a lifeless environment is remade into one that supports greater biological abundance and diversity. This remodeling is initiated by pioneer species, opportunistic and resilient organisms that tend to break down inorganic matter into soil. For example, lichen may take hold on a rocky surface, helping to degrade the rock into smaller, rougher pieces suitable for the growth of moss. Together, lichen and moss may further develop the new soil such that it can support small leafy plants. After further breakdown of rocky particles and the continued contributions of decaying plant life, enough topsoil may develop to support shrubs, which eventually engender the growth of trees. After a time, the trees, shrubs, and ground-dwelling plant populations may equilibrate into a climax community (e.g., a forest), in which the mix of species and their populations no longer undergo sustained change. Secondary succession refers to the re-equilibration of an ecosystem after it has been devastated by some extreme event like a fire or tornado, killing the majority of species but leaving good soil intact. Communities arising from such "wiped-clean" environments can also attain a climax equilibrium, but the precise character of that equilibrium state may differ considerably from that of the primary succession. Forests re-grown in the wake of clear-cut logging exemplify secondary succession.

Limiting factors are those phenomena which prevent populations from growing at their biotic potential, or the maximum growth rate possible with unlimited resources. Limiting factors may be either biotic or abiotic, operate by modifying birth and death rates, and come in two major varieties: density-dependent and density-independent. Density-dependent growth factors exert themselves to a greater or lesser degree depending on how many organisms of a given species inhabit a given area. Density-independent growth factors exert themselves regardless of the population density of a species. Examples of density-dependent factors are disease, predation, and competition for food and shelter. Examples of density-independent factors are climate and geography. Most density-dependent factors are biotic, while most density-independent factors are abiotic.

Carrying capacity is an upper limit to the population of a species that an environment can sustain. Different environments possess different carrying capacities for the same species. Real-life populations tend to fluctuate in a dynamic equilibrium about a carrying capacity, with various factors causing corrections to populations that deviate too far above or below the capacity. A classic example of this behavior involves predator-prey relationships; as predators begin to over-hunt their prey, prey populations fall. This decrease in prey leads to increased competition between predators for food, decreasing predator populations. As predator populations decline, prey populations rebound, which in turn supports a greater number of predators, starting the cycle anew.

Part IV
Inheriting and Evolving

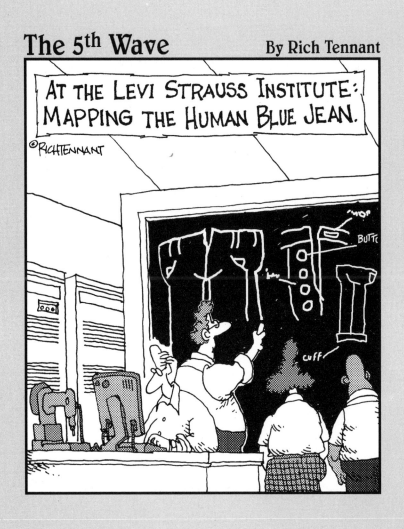

The 5th Wave   By Rich Tennant

AT THE LEVI STRAUSS INSTITUTE: MAPPING THE HUMAN BLUE JEAN.

In this part . . .

*I*n the big picture, it's meaningless to think about life without thinking about the passing of generations. Generations are a minimum requirement of evolution, and if Life ever got a tattoo, it would read "I ♥ Evolution." In this part, we speak of heredity, the story of life's endless string of love stories.

We begin by looking at heredity from the outside in, examining the rules we can use to connect outward appearances to the genes that produce them. Next, we examine the inner molecular workings of heredity and the ways we have learned to toy with them. Finally, we step back to survey the machinations of evolution over time — both shorter times and longer times. We describe the journey from a lifeless planet to our present planetary zoo and summarize the kinds of evidence that support our evolutionary story. Of that story, we conclude, two things are certain: Evolution needs selection, and selection needs variation.

Chapter 19

Heredity: Looking Like Your Parents

. . . .

In This Chapter

▶ Counting peas for cues to genetics: the unlikely story of Gregor Mendel

▶ Using Punnett squares to model Mendelian inheritance

▶ Coming to terms with non-Mendelian inheritance

▶ Puttering through pedigrees and probability

▶ Seeing the chromosome for the genes

. . . .

Genetics tells stories. Generations are dramatic chapters of these stories, each a wildly unique combination of genes. As with all good drama, genetic events are both improbable and inevitable, individual and universal. Each of us is the unique result of precisely the same process of heredity. This chapter is about that process, and about how our understanding of it arose from the curious impulse of an Austrian monk, crouched over a pea plant.

Mendel's Meddling Pays Off

Our curious, meddling Monk was Gregor Mendel. In addition to doing monk-y things, Mendel was also a high school natural sciences teacher. Ambling through the monastery gardens in the middle 1800s, Mendel grew curious about how plant traits (i.e., tall or short) get handed down from plant parents to plant offspring. At the time, the dominating theory of inheritance, in plants and in people, was "blending." In blending, it was thought, parental traits completely intermixed within offspring, creating new, intermediate traits. Mendel nursed a suspicion that the blending theory might be incorrect. Systematically, Mendel conducted a study of heredity in pea plants, meticulously controlling which plants mated with which others, and making careful records about the collections of traits in offspring pea plants. The upshot of Mendel's unlikely study was to disprove blending. Good old Gregor even published a paper on his findings, humbly documenting the evidence that blending is wrong. Predictably, no one took notice. Only decades later, with Mendel resting six feet below his plants, did the peas hit the fan.

Key to understanding Mendel's results is the concept of the gene, an indivisible unit of heredity that determines a specific trait. In pure Mendelian inheritance, genes do not blend, but are either passed on or fail to pass on entirely. The rules by which these indivisible, non-blending genes express themselves as traits were a major focus of Mendel's work, and understanding those means understanding a handful of terms:

- ✔ **Allele:** One of two or more alternate forms of a gene. Many alleles for a given gene can exist, but sexually reproducing organisms — like peas and people — carry only two, one from each parent.

- ✔ **Dominant allele:** An allele that is expressed as a trait regardless of the presence of a different allele. Dominant alleles are typically represented by an italicized capital letter, like *T,* for tall.

- ✔ **Recessive allele:** An allele that is expressed as a trait only in the absence of a dominant allele. Recessive alleles are typically represented by a lower-case letter, like *t,* for short.

- ✔ **Homozygous dominant:** An organism is homozygous for a gene when it carries two identical alleles, one from each parent. If those identical alleles are of the dominant allele (as in, *TT*), then the organism is homozygous dominant, and expresses the dominant trait.

- ✔ **Homozygous recessive:** A homozygous recessive organism carries two alleles for the recessive form of a trait (as in, *tt*), and expresses the recessive trait. In fact, recessive traits are only expressed in a homozygous recessive organism because the presence of a dominant allele would mask the recessive trait.

- ✔ **Heterozygous:** A heterozygous organism carries two different alleles for a given trait (as in, *Tt*), one from each parent. In pure Mendelian inheritance, this means that one allele is dominant and the other is recessive, such that the organism will express the dominant trait (as in, tall).

Recall that the prefix "homo-" means "same" and the prefix "hetero-" means different, and you'll remember the meaning of homozygous and heterozygous.

Finally, you may have noticed by now that there are several different combinations of inherited alleles that can result in the same trait being expressed; three pea plants, *TT, tT,* and *Tt,* for example, are all tall. This situation means that we have to be careful to distinguish between the genetic makeup of and organism and the traits it expresses:

- ✔ **Genotype:** The genes carried by an organism, and specifically which alleles of those genes.

- ✔ **Phenotype:** The observed traits of on organism, which arise from the interaction of genes and environment.

Continuing to meddle

All of Mendel's observations were useful only because he so carefully controlled which pea plants bred with which others. Mendel maintained "true-breeding" or "purebred" lines of plants, meaning that those plants were homozygous for a particular trait of interest, say height or pea color. Because these plants were homozygous, the possible combinations of alleles in offspring plants could be determined, which meant that Mendel could compare the phenotypes of offspring plants with their expected genotypes.

The most informative experiments were those in which Mendel cross-bred pea plants of different pure-bred varieties. These "crosses" resulted in "hybrids," plants that were guaranteed to be heterozygous for a particular allele — at least in the first generation. Mendel discovered that traits would sometimes skip generations, so that it became very important to keep track of how many generations had passed since the original cross between purebred plants. The sequence of generations is represented by the sequence $P, F_1, F_2 \ldots F_n$.

Here, *P* stands for *parental,* the original pair of mating organisms. Subsequent generations are labeled *F* for *filial,* with a number subscript denoting how many generations they are removed from *P.*

In Mendel's early work, he crossed pure-breeding pea plants to create plants that he knew to be heterozygous for a particular trait, like height. We can visualize all the possible outcomes of a mating event by using a Punnett square, as shown in Figure 19-1 below for the mating of a pure-breeding tall plant with a pure-breeding short plant:

Figure 19-1:
A Punnett square, showing a cross between homozygous dominant and homozygous recessive parents (*TT* x *tt*).

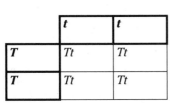

In the Punnett square above, the two alleles of each parent are shown in bold, one parent to a side. The possible outcomes of mating between those parents are shown in the remainder of the squares, each containing two alleles, one from each parent. Performing this kind of cross between, say, pure-breeding tall and pure-breeding short plants, Mendel observed that the offspring (in other words, the F_1 generation) were all tall. This observation clearly contradicted the theory of blending, and is summarized in the *Law of Dominance:* when two varieties breed, each homozygous for a different allele, all offspring will express the trait of only one of the parents. The expressed trait corresponds to the dominant allele, and the unexpressed trait corresponds to the recessive allele.

Equipped with heterozygous plants, Mendel was able to perform crosses between heterozygous partners. When this experiment is done with respect to a single trait, it is called a *monohybrid cross,* and is depicted in the Punnett square in Figure 19-2.

Figure 19-2:
Punnett square depicting a monohybrid cross (as in, F_1 x F_1).

	T	**t**
T	*TT*	*Tt*
t	*Tt*	*tt*

Notice the difference from the *P* x *P* cross shown in Figure 19-1: the offspring are predicted to be of three different genotypes: *TT, Tt* and *tt,* in a ratio of 1:2:1. Due to the dominance of the tall allele, these three genotypes correspond to two different phenotypes, tall and short, in a ratio of 3:1.

A similar experiment, mating plants that are hybrid for two traits, say height and pea smoothness, is called a *dihybrid cross*, and is summarized in the Punnett square in Figure 19-3 (*S* = smooth allele, *s* = wrinkled allele).

	TS	*tS*	*Ts*	*ts*
T S	*TTSS*	*TtSS*	*TTSs*	*TtSs*
tS	*TtSS*	*ttSS*	*TtSs*	*ttSs*
Ts	*TTSs*	*TtSs*	*TTss*	*Ttss*
ts	*TtSs*	*ttSs*	*Ttss*	*ttss*

Figure 19-3: Punnett square depicting a dihybrid cross.

The results of a dihybrid cross are slightly more complicated than those of a monohybrid cross, but are equally predictable. Nine genotypes are expected, (*TTSS, TtSS, TTSs, TtSs, ttSS, ttSs, TTss, Ttss,* and *ttss*), corresponding to four phenotypes in a 9:3:3:1 ratio.

Phenotypic ratios of 3:1 for a monohybrid cross and 9:3:3:1 for a dihybrid cross are hallmarks of Mendelian inheritance.

Sticking with our experiments on tall/short and smooth/wrinkled pea plants, these ratios make the following predictions: in a monohybrid cross, the ratio predicts that three-quarters of offspring will be tall, and one-quarter will be short. In a dihybrid cross, nine-sixteenths will be tall and smooth, three-sixteenths tall and wrinkled, three-sixteenths short and smooth, and one-sixteenth short and wrinkled. The more offspring that are produced, the closer the actual numbers approach the ones predicted from Mendel's model of inheritance.

Much has been learned about genetics since Mendel's pea-planting days, but the major results of his work endure in the form of two laws:

✔ *Law of Segregation:* Each sexually reproducing organism carries two alleles (as in, alternative versions of each gene), one from each parent. These alleles are separated during gamete formation (as in, sperm or egg production).

✔ *Law of Independent Assortment:* The inheritance pattern of one trait does not affect the inheritance pattern of other traits. In other words, the separation of one set of alleles during gamete formation occurs independently of the separation of others.

Though Gregor Mendel had no conception of DNA or chromosomes, these two Laws correspond to processes of chromosome segregation during meiosis. Because traits are encoded by genes that physically occur on chromosomes, some genes are "linked", in the sense that they occur on the same chromosome. These instances of linkage, which result in non-Mendelian inheritance, are discussed next.

Breaking Mendel's law: Linked genes

Mendel's Laws of Segregation and Independent Assortment ceases to apply when genes are *linked*. Linked genes are those that occur on the same chromosome. Genes that are on the same chromosome tend to be inherited together, because chromosomes are passed on as units. But there's an added wrinkle: during prophase I (as in, prophase, the first round of meiosis) homologous chromosomes align into tetrads and recombine during the process of "crossing over." If all this talk of tetrads and crossing over sounds like gibberish, you'll feel more at home after a brief review of Chapter 7.

Recall that each chromosome is made up of sister chromatids. Within each chromatid, genes are arranged one after the other in a linear sequence. When homologous chromosomes (one from each parent) align during prophase I, corresponding chunks of homologous chromatids may swap between chromosomes, mixing up the sets of alleles originally inherited from either parent. The further apart two genes sit on a chromatid, the more likely it is that crossing over will occur at some point between them; in other words, the further apart two genes are on a chromatid, the more likely they are to be "unlinked" through crossing over.

So, by keeping track of how frequently linked genes are inherited together, you can actually calculate how far apart they are on a chromatid. This kind of calculation is called *gene mapping*, and the maps you can calculate showing the proximity of genes to one another are called *linkage maps*. Genes sitting next to one another will almost always be inherited together, and will display inheritance patterns least like those predicted from Mendel's Laws, because the genes don't assort independently. Gene's sitting at opposite ends of a chromatid are still linked, but will display inheritance patterns closer to those predicted by Mendel's Laws, because those genes will more frequently become unlinked due to crossing over. One *map unit* corresponds to a one percent frequency of crossing over between the two genes.

Several other kinds of things, *not related* to gene linkage, result in non-Mendelian behavior, such as:

- **Incomplete dominance:** Sometimes the relationship between dominant and recessive alleles isn't an all-or-nothing sort of situation. One allele may be only partially dominant over the other, allowing the partially recessive allele to be expressed to some extent in a heterozygote. This situation is called incomplete dominance, and results in a phenotype intermediate between that of either allele. For example, if a homozygous red-flowered snap dragon (*RR*) is crossed with a homozygous white-flowered snap dragon (*R'R'*) the resulting offspring will be pink-flowered snap dragons (*RR'*). Notice the difference in notation from before: instead of the lower-case "*r*" that would be used for a completely recessive allele, *R'* is used. *R* is incompletely dominant over *R'*.

- **Codominance:** Sometimes in a heterozygote, the two different alleles can be simultaneously expressed to the full extent. This situation is called *codominance*. An example of codominance is found in the alleles that determine blood type. Heterozygous persons who possess both *A* and *B* alleles express A- and B-type blood antigens equally, and are therefore blood type AB.

- **Epistasis:** Some genes are expressed to a greater or lesser extent due not to dominance or recessiveness, but to the presence or absence of entirely different genes. *Epistasis* is when the expression of a gene (the phenotype) depends on the presence or absence of another gene. Epistasis is seen in albinism. One gene codes for the production of pigment and another gene codes for the precise color of pigment. If the gene that promotes pigment production is absent or inactive, then no pigment of any color is made, leading to the "albino" phenotype.

- **Multiple alleles:** A given gene may exist in more than two alternate forms (alleles). Although a given individual will possess only up to two different alleles, those two may be drawn from a much larger pool of responsibilities.

- **Polygenic inheritance:** Some traits are controlled by many different genes, as in the case of skin color in humans. These genes may be linked or unlinked. Polygenic inheritance differs from multiple alleles in that the former results from the combined expression of several different genes, whereas multiple alleles refer to several different versions of the *same gene*.

- **Pleiotropy:** When more than one phenotype is controlled by a single gene, that gene is said to be *pleiotropic*. In cats, for example, the genetic makeup that results in white fur color can also lead to deafness.

Pedigrees and probabilities

Geneticists use *pedigrees* to study inheritance patterns through many generations. A pedigree is a graphic representation of inheritance. Think of a pedigree as a type of family tree that shows who has been affected by a certain trait. In a pedigree, a square represents a male, a circle represents a female, and a shaded square or circle shows an individual that is affected by the trait of interest. If a square or circle is not shaded this shows that the individual is not affected by the trait. Males and females connected by a horizontal line are mates that have produced offspring. Those offspring are depicted below their parents within the pedigree, connected to them by a vertical line. Pedigrees are useful tools for determining the specific genotypes that produce specific phenotypes.

To extract the genetic information from a pedigree, it helps to think in terms of probability. You've thought in terms of probability earlier in the chapter, during the discussion of Mendelian inheritance patterns. By using Punnett squares, you can calculate the probability of any given offspring genotype resulting from a "cross" or mating between parents of any given genotype. From the probabilities of the offspring genotypes, you can calculate the probabilities of offspring phenotypes. All this analysis is useful for pedigree analysis, because the majority of human genes are inherited in a Mendelian manner. By inspecting the inheritance of a trait across the generations of a pedigree, you can discover whether that trait follows the pattern predicted for a dominant allele, a recessive allele, or some other pattern.

Calculating probability is pretty simple. The probability of something impossible is zero (0). The probability of something certain is one (1). The probability of either of two equally likely events is one out of two (0.5). The probability of any of six equally likely events is one out of six (0.167), and so on. Now, here's the rub: the probability of any *series* of independent events occurring *together* equals the *product* of their individual probabilities. So, the likelihood of flipping a coin heads *and also* rolling a five on a single die equals (0.5)(0.167) = 0.083, or 8.3%. Probabilities add over repeated attempts. In other words, if you perform ten repetitions of the coin-flip-die-roll experiment, there is an 83% chance ($10 \times 0.083 = 0.83$) that you'll achieve the heads-plus-five combination one time.

Knowing Something about Chromosomes

On the molecular scale, chromosomes are huge structures, and can engage in all sorts of complicated behaviors. Because each chromosome contains so many genes, imagine the difference in phenotype that might result from swapping out entire chromosomes. Actually, you don't have to imagine — in humans, the difference between having an X chromosome versus a Y chromosome is precisely the difference between being female and being male.

The importance of X

Diploid human cells contain 46 chromosomes, 23 from each parent. One chromosome of each set of 23 is a sex chromosome, of either the X or Y variety. Females have two X chromosomes, and males have an X and a Y chromosome. All the other, non-sex chromosomes are called autosomes. *Sex-linked genes* are those found on the X chromosome. The piddling Y chromosome has relatively few genes, as reflected by its smaller size. Countless opportunities for gender-based genetic jokes emerge from this fact.

Common diseases caused by chromosome disorders

You can't just mess up a chromosome without some consequences. Most chromosome aberrations lead to cell death, but some types of faulty chromosomes lead to notable "chromosome disorders." Here are a few of them.

Aneuploidy is the condition of having the wrong number of chromosomes. Aneuploidy results from *nondisjunction* — the improper segregation of chromosomes during meiosis. Nondisjunction leads to gametes with too many or too few chromosomes, and some such gametes can be successfully fertilized, leading to viable offspring with the incorrect chromosome number. Down's syndrome occurs in individuals with three copies of chromosome 21 (i.e., trisomy 21). Trisomy 13 is associated with Patau syndrome and trisomy 18 is associated with Edwards syndrome, both serious disorders that typically result in death within a year of birth.

Aneuploidy can also take place with the sex chromosomes. There is some evidence that males who receive an extra Y chromosome, and are thus XYY, are more prone to violent behavior. Males with Klinefelter syndrome have an extra X chromosome (XXY), and display many typically female phenotypes. Females who lack a second X chromosome (i.e., are XO) are sterile, and have a disorder called Turner's syndrome.

Disorders also arise from having chromosomes with pieces missing (*deletions*), or with pieces relocated from one chromosome to another (*translocations*). *Inversion* is a form of chromosomal defect in which a piece of chromosome breaks off, flips around, and then reattaches in the opposite direction. *Duplication* is a defect in which chromosomal segments occur repeatedly, one copy after another. Depending on the size and location of the deletion, translocation, inversion, or duplication, more or less serious disorders may emerge.

Other kinds of chromosomal weirdness include *ring chromosomes* (in which the tips of a chromosome have been deleted, and the ends fused into a circle), and *marker chromosomes*, small pieces of unidentified chromosome floating about, potentially causing genetic trouble.

Sex-linked disorders

In females, corresponding alleles on each of the homologous X chromosomes often undergo the usual kinds of dominant/recessive interactions already discussed. In males, however, alleles on the single X chromosome will be expressed even if they are recessive, since no dominant allele can be present to mask them. This arrangement accounts for the phenomenon of a trait skipping a generation, showing up in a male even though that same trait was absent in the male's mother; the mother was a "carrier" for the recessive trait. Sons cannot receive X-linked traits from their fathers because a son can only result from the combination of a maternally inherited X chromosome with a paternally inherited Y-chromosome.

Sex-linked disorders, then, are a problem particularly for males. For example, hemophilia is a genetic disorder that impairs the ability for blood to clot, meaning that even minor cuts can result in large amounts of bleeding. Hemophilia occurs far more frequently in males because it is a sex-linked, recessive trait. Other examples of sex-linked disorders include color blindness and muscular dystrophy.

Inactivating X

Female mammals inherit two X chromosomes, but one of these X chromosomes becomes almost completely inactivated during embryonic development. The inactivated X chromosome condenses into a compact object known as a Barr body. Only a few of the genes of the Barr body remain active. In any given cell, either of the two X chromosomes may become inactivated. Depending on differences in the alleles contained within each X chromosome, X inactivation may lead to different phenotypes between different cells of the female.

Chapter 20

Answering Questions About Heredity

In This Chapter

▶ Getting in some pointers for practice

▶ Seeing what you know

▶ Checking out your work

*W*hen it comes to your own heredity, you pretty much have to take what's given to you. The AP Biology test is much the same way, with a key exception: you can *prepare* for the test. Wouldn't it have been nice to have been able to prepare for life? Don't squander the opportunity. Here you'll find review and questions covering the material found in Chapter 19: Heredity: Looking Like Your Parents. Multiple choice and free-essay response questions and answers are provided.

Pointers for Practice

The main points of Chapter 19 were the following:

✔ A genotype is the genetic makeup of an organism, while a phenotype is the physical trait within an organism. Phenotypes arise from genotypes interacting with other factors.

✔ Alleles are different versions of a gene. In pure Mendelian inheritance, an allele may be dominant or recessive. A dominant allele is one that is expressed as a trait if it is present. A recessive allele is one that is expressed as a trait only in the absence of a corresponding dominant allele. The presence of dominant and recessive alleles corresponds to Mendel's Law of Dominance, and contradicts the old theory of "blending."

✔ Law of Segregation: Each sexually reproducing organism carries two alleles, one from each parent. These alleles are separated during gamete formation (i.e., sperm or egg production).

✔ Law of Independent Assortment: The inheritance pattern of one trait does not affect the inheritance pattern of other traits. In other words, the separation of one set of alleles during gamete formation occurs independently of the separation of others.

✔ An organism with two different alleles for a given trait is said to be heterozygous (e.g., *Tt*). An organism with two identical alleles for a given trait is said to be homozygous for that trait. These individuals may be either homozygous dominant (having two dominant alleles, *TT*) or homozygous recessive (having two recessive alleles, *tt*). When homozygous dominant individuals mate with homozygous recessive individuals, all offspring will be heterozygous for the given trait, and these heterozygous offspring are called hybrids.

- ✔ In a monohybrid cross, two individuals heterozygous for a given trait mate. This mating produces offspring with a 1:2:1 likelihood of having any of three genotypes, *TT:Tt:tt*. Because of the Law of Dominance, this distribution of genotypes corresponds with a 3:1 likelihood of dominant:recessive phenotypes. In a dihybrid cross, individuals mate who are heterozygous for two given traits. The offspring of dihybrid crosses have a 9:3:3:1 likelihood of exhibiting any of the four possible phenotypic combinations.

- ✔ Genes located on the same chromosome do not assort independently because they are physically linked. These genes may become unlinked during the "crossing over" event of meiosis. The further apart two genes lie along the linear sequence of a chromosome, the more likely they are to become unlinked. By carefully observing the degree to which genes are inherited together, one can create "linkage maps," depicting the relative position of genes along a chromosome.

- ✔ In practice, there are many deviations from pure Mendelian inheritance:

    - In codominance, multiple dominant alleles can be expressed as full-fledged traits simultaneously.

    - In incomplete dominance, an incompletely dominant allele may combine with an incompletely recessive allele to give the appearance of a "blended" trait, though this *apparent* blending actually emerges from the combined activity of two discrete alleles.

    - In epistasis, the expression of one gene depends on the presence or absence of another gene.

    - Complex traits often arise from the combined activity of multiple (i.e., more than two) alleles for a given gene, or from multiple genes, as in polygenic inheritance.

    - In pleiotropy, one gene contributes to the expression of multiple different traits.

- ✔ Pedigrees are graphical tools used to analyze family trees in order to determine the genotypes that gave rise to observed phenotypes within the family. In a pedigree, males are represented as squares, and females as circles. Generations are represented as vertical layers, with older generations towards the top. Mating between individuals is represented by a horizontal line, and offspring that result from a mating are connected by vertical lines. Individuals who express a given phenotype are completely filled in, while individuals who are merely carriers for a trait (if known) are half-filled in.

When inspecting pedigrees, always look for an individual expressing a recessive trait, because that individual's genotype is known: homozygous recessive (unless the trait is sex-linked recessive, in which case mothers will pass the trait on to sons).

- ✔ The probability of an impossible event is zero. The probability of a certain event is 1. Intermediate probabilities are represented as fractions between zero and 1. The probability of a given event occurring after repeated attempts is the sum of the probabilities for each attempt. The probability of any given series of independent events is the product of the individual probabilities.

- ✔ Human females possess two X chromosomes, and human males possess one X- and one Y-chromosome. Children always inherit an X-chromosome from the mother, but may inherit either an X- or a Y-chromosome from their father, who determines the sex of the child. Sex-linked genes are those found on the X-chromosome. Males are particularly susceptible to X-linked genetic disorders because any disorder-associated, recessive allele inherited from the mother cannot be masked by a normal, dominant allele on a second X-chromosome.

- ✔ Most serious chromosomal defects result in an inviable zygote. However, some chromosomal disorders are expressed in living organisms. Aneuploidy is the possession of an incorrect number of chromosomes. Deletions involve the absence of a piece of a chromosome, and insertions involve the presence of extra pieces within a chromosome. Translocations — the combination of a deletion and an insertion — involve the breaking off of a piece from one chromosome, and the addition of that same piece to another chromosome.

Answering Multiple-Choice Questions

Directions: Choose the best possible answer, out of the five that are provided, for each question.

1. Five thousand pea plants grow as offspring from a series of identical dihybrid crosses. Which of the following most likely represent the data from an examination of all five thousand specimens, observing them for smooth/wrinkled peas (smooth is dominant) and for yellow/green peas (yellow is dominant)? The four phenotypes are listed in order in each case: smooth/yellow, smooth/green, wrinkled/yellow, wrinkled/green.

   (A) 878, 2904, 886, 332

   (B) 329, 2807, 928, 936

   (C) 334, 937, 941, 2788

   (D) 2798, 943, 935, 324

   (E) 2411, 861, 866, 862

2. Assume that in a certain plant, height is determined by a single gene. The dominant allele for this gene, *T*, corresponds to the tall phenotype. The recessive allele, *t*, corresponds to the short phenotype. Which of the following is true of a tall plant?

   I. Must possess *TT* or *Tt* genotype

   II. Can determine its genotype by crossing it with a short plant

   III. Can determine its genotype by crossing it with another tall plant

   (A) I only

   (B) II only

   (C) III only

   (D) I and II only

   (E) II and III only

Questions 3–7 refer to the following answer choices. Answers may be used more than once.

   (A) Codominance

   (B) Incomplete dominance

   (C) Pleiotropy

   (D) Polygenic inheritance

   (E) Epistasis

3. Metabolic rate, which emerges from the interconnected activities of hundreds of gene products

4. Blood type, which is determined by the presence or absence of blood antigen proteins A and B, which may be expressed simultaneously

5. A man possesses a gene for baldness, whose expression precludes the expression of a gene he also possesses for red hair color

6. Mutations in a single gene, coding for protein *TBX5*, result in multiple defects of the heart and limbs in a disorder called Holt-Oram syndrome

7. Sickle cell disease, in which homozygous dominant individuals are normal, heterozygous individuals have a mild form of the disease, and homozygous dominant individuals have a severe form of the disease

8. Which of the following types of trait is most likely represented by the pedigree shown in Figure 20-1?

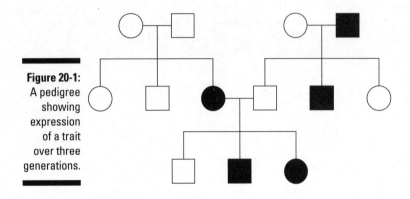

Figure 20-1:
A pedigree showing expression of a trait over three generations.

(A) Sex-linked dominant

(B) Sex-linked recessive

(C) Autosomal dominant

(D) Autosomal recessive

(E) Inconsistent with any of the above

Answering Free-Essay Response Questions

1. Explain Mendel's Laws of Segregation and Independent Assortment, and describe how each corresponds to precise events within meiosis.

Checking Your Work

Set against the practice questions, would you say that your mastery of heredity is dominant or recessive (. . . or incompletely dominant)? Find out. Check your work:

1. The answer is D. The expected outcome for a dihybrid cross (see Figure 20-2) is a phenotypic ratio of 9:3:3:1, dominant/dominant, dominant/recessive, recessive/dominant, recessive/recessive. Applied to a basis set of five thousand plants, this predicts the following: 2812 smooth/yellow, 938 smooth/green, 938 wrinkled/yellow, 312 wrinkled/green. In any actual dataset, one expects some variation from the predicted values. Within reasonable error, answer D most closely mirrors the expected result.

Figure 20-2:
Punnett
square
depicting a
dihybrid
cross,
where alle-
les *Y* and *y*
correspond
to yellow
and green
peas, and
alleles *S* and
s corre-
spond to
smooth and
wrinkled
peas,
respectively.

	YS	**yS**	**Ys**	**ys**
YS	YYSS	YySS	YYSs	YySs
yS	YySS	yySS	YySs	yySs
Ys	YYSs	YySs	YYss	Yyss

Genotypes with dominant/dominant phenotypes: *YYSS*, 2 x *YySS*, 2 x *YYSs*, 4 x *YySs*.

Genotypes with dominant/recessive phenotypes: *YYss*, 2 x *Yyss*.

Genotypes with recessive/dominant phenotypes: *yySS*, 2 x *yySs*.

Genotypes with recessive/recessive phenotypes: *yyss*.

2. D is the answer. An organism expressing the dominant phenotype must possess at least one dominant allele, and may possess two dominant alleles (i.e., is either heterozygous or homozygous dominant).

To discern between the two possible genotypes, one performs a test cross, mating the organism with a partner that is homozygous recessive. Measurably different pheno-typic ratios are expected from the two possible outcomes. To convince yourself of the usefulness of a test cross, diagram the Punnett squares for each of the two cases, as shown in Figure 20-3. In the first case (Figure 20-3), a test cross with a homozygous dominant individual produces entirely heterozygous offspring, and therefore offspring that all possess the dominant phenotype. In the second case (Figure 20-4), a test cross with a heterozygous individual produces offspring that have equal likelihood of possessing the dominant or the recessive phenotype.

✔ **Case 1:** Test cross with homozygous dominant individual

✔ **Case 2:** Test cross with heterozygous individual

Figure 20-3:
Punnett
squares
depicting
test-crosses
with
homozygous
dominant.

	t	**t**
T	Tt	Tt
T	Tt	Tt

Figure 20-4:
Punnett squares depicting test-crosses with heterozygous individuals.

	t	*t*
T	*Tt*	*Tt*
t	*tt*	*tt*

3. D, again, is correct. Because metabolic rate is a trait that emerges from the combined activity of many genes, it is a good example of polygenic inheritance.

4. A is right. If a person possesses alleles for both the A- and B-antigens, both antigen proteins will be expressed on the surface of blood cells. Such a scenario represents codominance.

5. The answer is E. Because the expression of the gene for hair color depends on the expression of the gene for baldness, the baldness gene is epistatic to the hair color gene.

6. C is the answer. Because the gene for the *TBX5* protein determines multiple, distinct traits, that gene is pleiotropic.

7. B is correct. The sickle cell disease trait is a good example of incomplete dominance because heterozygotes exhibit a phenotype that is intermediate between either homozygous dominant or homozygous recessive individuals.

8. D is the best answer. First, orient yourself to the pedigree. Three generations are shown, corresponding to each of the three vertical layers. The first, oldest generation is shown in the top layer, in which two matings are indicated by horizontal lines connecting male and female individuals. Each mating produced three offspring, as indicated by the vertical lines connecting to the second generation in the middle layer. Siblings from each mating are connected. A female sibling from one group mated with a male sibling from another group, as indicated by the horizontal connector in the middle layer. This second-generation mating resulted in three offspring, as shown by the vertical line descending to the three siblings in the lowest layer. Next, as always with pedigrees, look for the recessive trait, because the genotype is known (homozygous recessive). Although the trait (indicated by shaded squares and circles) was present in one parent in two of the three matings, it was absent in both parents of one of the matings (the top-left mating). Therefore, each parent in that mating must have been heterozygous; in the case of the daughter affected with the trait, each parent must have passed on the recessive allele. Futhermore, the male in the second-generation mating must have been heterozygous, such that he could pass on the recessive allele to two of his three children. Since the second-generation mating produced both a male and a female child with the trait, the trait cannot be sex-linked recessive, and is therefore autosomal recessive.

Here is a model answer to the free-essay response question:

Mendel asserted that physical traits were determined by specific heritable factors, and that these factors occurred in pairs: one factor for each trait is inherited from each parent. According to Mendel, there existed but two different versions of each factor (i.e., different alleles), a dominant version and a recessive version. Any given individual must possess either two dominant alleles (homozygous dominant), two recessive alleles (homozygous recessive), or one allele of each type (heterozygous). Inheritance of even one dominant allele would ensure expression of the dominant version of the trait. Only in an individual possessing two recessive alleles would the recessive form of the trait be expressed.

Mendel's first Law, the Law of Segregation, states that the two alleles that an individual possesses for each trait are segregated during gamete formation. In other words, during the process of making sex cells, each sex cell receives only one allele of the paired set. This allele eventually meets up with a corresponding partner during fertilization.

Mendel's second Law, the Law of Independent Assortment, states that alleles for each trait segregate independently of all the others. In other words, whether a given sex cell receives the allele for smooth or wrinkled peas has no bearing on whether it will receive the allele for green or yellow peas.

Each of the two Laws corresponds to a discrete physical event in meiosis, the process of cell division that is central to the formation of sex cells. Alleles for traits are stored within a linear sequence of DNA, and a great many alleles may be packaged into a single chromosome. Maternal and paternal alleles are stored within distinct maternal and paternal versions of each chromosome. During meiosis, each gamete receives only one set of chromosomes, not the double set present in the body cells of an organism. This reduction in chromosome number is necessary, because fertilization involves combining the chromosomes from one gamete with those of a second gamete; in order for the total chromosome number to be constant from one generation to the next, each gamete must possess only one set of chromosomes. This important condition is achieved during meiosis, which consists of two analogous rounds of division. In the first division, meiosis I, maternal and paternal versions of chromosomes are segregated into different cells, as an original cell divides into two. In the second division, meiosis II, the sister chromatids of individual chromosomes are segregated into different cells as two cells divide into four. The meiotic events corresponding to Mendels Laws occur during meiosis I.

Meiosis I consists of four phases: prophase I, metaphase I, anaphase I, and telophase I. During prophase I, homologous chromosomes (maternal and paternal) pair, with two sister chromatids from each of two chromosomes aligning into a "tetrad". In this state, corresponding alleles may swap between the homologous chromosomes. This swapping occurs during a process called crossing over. Crossing over helps to promote the independent assortment of alleles, even when those alleles are physically linked by inclusion on the same chromosome. During metaphase I, all the pairs of homologous chromosomes line up, two by two, along the centerline of the cell. At this stage, whether the maternal or paternal chromosome of each pair lines up on one side or the other of the centerline is entirely random, and this randomness is critical: during the subsequent phases of meiosis I, the maternal and paternal chromosomes are irrevocably segregated into different cells, and eventually into different gametes. The complete physical separation of these chromosomes (with their myriad alleles) corresponds to the Law of Segregation. The randomness of the alignment at centerline during metaphase I (as well as the process of crossing over during prophase I) corresponds to the Law of Independent Assortment.

Chapter 21

Genetics: Getting Down to DNA Level

• •

In This Chapter

▶ Uncovering the universal molecular basis of heredity

▶ Musing on mutations and their useful functions

▶ Inspecting the genetics of viruses and bacteria

▶ Sifting through the toolbox of genetic engineering

• •

*I*n the final analysis, nineteenth-century Austrian monks and their pea plants will get you only so far. If you really want to know about the nitty-gritty basis for genetics, you've got to get microscopic. You've got to talk about DNA and its molecular friends. After you examine heredity at that level, you see that we humans are not only very like pea plants, but we are like every other living thing as well.

Looking at the Genetic Machinery

It's true: Chapter 3 was a long way back. The thought of cracking open those old biochemical chestnuts is probably unappealing. And maybe you remember genetic information flow well enough that you needn't review? Just in case, it wouldn't hurt to bookmark Chapter 3 as you wade through the present section. Here's a friendly little recapitulation of the really important bits:

Genetic information is stored within the polymeric molecule, DNA, encoded in a linear sequence of nucleotide bases: A, G, C, and T. Information lies within different sequences of these bases, just as words are encoded by sequences of letters within an alphabet. In Chapter 19, genes were considered simply as discrete heritable units that confer certain traits. In this chapter, a gene is considered as a sequence of DNA that acts as the blueprint for an RNA. The RNA may in turn act as the blueprint for a protein.

The double-helical structure of DNA is key to its function. The structure is built from two strands that run in opposite directions, intertwining with one another along their length. Each strand has its own sequence of bases. The sequence of one strand can be determined from the sequence of its partner because the bases of one strand partner with their opposing partners according to well defined pairing rules: A pairs with T, G pairs with C.

The major use of genetic information is to provide the blueprint for building proteins, the workhorse molecules of the cell. These blueprints are written in the DNA in the form of genes. At the simplest level, you can think of each gene as a linear sequence of DNA bases that codes for the linear sequence of amino acids in a protein. There are variations on this basic theme, as you'll soon see.

The information in the DNA sequence of a gene flows through two major processes on the way to becoming incarnated as protein: transcription and translation. In transcription, the information in the DNA sequence is rewritten in the form of RNA, a polynucleotide that is very similar to DNA, encoding information in a series of four nucleotide bases: A, U, G, and C. RNA and DNA are sufficiently similar in structure that they can base-pair into a hybrid double helix, A pairing with U, G pairing with C. The chemical mechanism of transcription relies on this RNA-DNA pairing to ensure that information is reliably copied from DNA to the RNA working copy, called a transcript.

Before proceeding to translation, RNA transcripts undergo various kinds of processing, particularly within eukaryotic cells. Within eukaryotes, transcripts receive protective caps on one end, and protective polyadenosine tails on the other end. In addition, transcripts are spliced, joining certain regions, called exons, and cutting out other regions, called introns. These various processes serve the functions of quality control and editing: before the cell commits itself to building a protein, it wants to be sure that the building plans are complete and correct. Processed transcripts are crowned with the title "messenger RNA" (mRNA) and sent forth from the nucleus.

mRNAs enter the final phase of genetic information flow, translation, in which the cell builds a protein by using the information encoded within an mRNA. Ribosomes are the elegant molecular machines that build proteins. Ribsomes do their construction with the necessary assistance of transfer RNAs (tRNAs), a fleet of related RNA molecules that do most of the actual translation. Each tRNA carries with it a particular amino acid, the type of molecular building block from which proteins are constructed. tRNAs carrying different amino acid cargoes are further distinguished by differences in structure, particularly by differences in their "anticodon" regions. Anticodons are three-base RNA sequences that match up with three-base sequences on an mRNA, called codons. For the most part, the matching process relies on regular RNA base-pairing rules: A pairs with U, G pairs with C. Important exceptions to these rules are discussed in the next section.

As an mRNA blueprint feeds through the active site of a ribosome, tRNAs enter the site as well. tRNAs that make proper anticodon-codon matches are recognized by the ribosome, which then attaches the amino acid carried by the tRNA to an elongating chain of amino acids, called a polypeptide. Ultimately, then, genes code for polypeptides. When the ribosome recognizes a stop signal on the mRNA, the polypeptide is released. Polypeptides may undergo further processing, but one way or another they end up as intricately structured molecular wonders called proteins.

Using the Genetic Code

The crux of translation, then, is the process by which tRNAs and the ribosome decipher the genetic code. Be you a bacterium or a beleaguered high school student, the basic process is the same. To which party this comparison is most gratifying depends on your point of view.

Figure 21-1 is the key used by cells to crack the genetic code.

Each box represents a unique mRNA codon, the three-base sequence that gives instruction to the ribosome (and the attendant tRNAs). Because you are clever, you will immediately have noticed that several codons may each correspond to the same amino acid. This situation is called "degeneracy" and its importance is described below. What's more, some codons code for no amino acid at all, but for some other instruction to the ribosome. Note that for any given mRNA sequence, there are three possible "reading frames," three different ways in which to divide the linear sequence into three-base codons.

First Letter ↓	Second Letter				Third Letter ↓
	U	C	A	G	
U	phenylalanine	serine	tyrosine	cysteine	U
	phenylalanine	serine	tyrosine	cysteine	C
	leucine	serine	STOP	STOP	A
	leucine	serine	STOP	tryptophan	G
C	leucine	proline	histidine	arginine	U
	leucine	proline	histidine	arginine	C
	leucine	proline	glutamine	arginine	A
	leucine	proline	glutamine	arginine	G
A	isoleucine	threonine	asparagine	serine	U
	isoleucine	threonine	asparagine	serine	C
	isoleucine	threonine	lysine	arginine	A
	methionine & START	threonine	lysine	arginine	G
G	valine	alanine	aspartate	glycine	U
	valine	alanine	aspartate	glycine	C
	valine	alanine	glutamate	glycine	A
	valine	alanine	glutamate	glycine	G

Figure 21-1: The genetic code.

The degeneracy (i.e., redundancy) in the genetic code is not random. For example, different codons that correspond to the same amino acid often differ only in the third base of the codon. This arrangement is echoed in the fact that some tRNAs can recognize different codons, each of which specifies the same amino acid. In a sense, there is some "give" in the third base of a codon; the loose codon-anticodon pairing at the third position is called "wobble." One function of wobble is to provide a buffer against harmful mutations. Because of wobble, at least some mutations in a DNA sequence will have no effect on the polypeptide product of translation.

The genetic code is almost completely universal; it is used by all known living organisms with only minor variations. This suggests that the code evolved very early in the history of life. Furthermore, the universality of the code means that genes from one species can be transferred into another species, where they may be used to make protein. Genes that have been cut-and-pasted between species are called transgenes.

Expressing genes

"Gene expression" can refer to any or all of a number of processes that occur between gene and protein. The extent to which a particular gene is expressed can be affected by regulating transcription, processing, mRNA export from the nucleus, mRNA binding to the ribosome, mRNA degradation, and translation. Often, many of these processes are regulated for the same gene.

Why does it all have to be so complicated? Having more ways to influence gene expression allows cells to respond appropriately to changes in their environment. For example, if a cell wants to make a long-term, extreme increase in the expression of one gene, that cell might increase the gene's transcription (as discussed in the next section). For another gene, the cell might achieve a rapid, temporary tuning by regulating translation.

Changing Genes When They Don't Fit Quite Right

Genes aren't written in stone; they're written in DNA. They can be rewritten. Moreover, any given gene, as written, can be expressed to a greater or lesser extent, depending on its usefulness at the moment.

Over many, many generations, ancestral lines of cells "re-write" their DNA through the process of natural selection; individual variations in genes are either passed on or not depending on their usefulness to the organisms in which they occur. Over time, more useful genes retain shelf space in the genetic library, while less useful genes find themselves in the evolutionary wastebasket. Less dramatically (but more frequently), a gene may survive, but only by enduring gradual change via mutation.

Gradual change over deep evolutionary time does precious little for a given cell at a given moment. For that moment, the genes are as they are — but there's nothing to prevent a cell from changing the expression of the gene. Some of the best-studied strategies cells use to alter gene expression are enhancing, repressing, and inducing.

Mutating for a reason — or not

Understand this: mutations do not occur for a reason. They simply occur. Whether those mutations are retained has to do with whether they help or hurt an organism in its struggle to survive and reproduce.

Different kinds of mutations have different kinds of consequences. First, it matters in which type of cell the mutation occurs: mutations in somatic (body) cells may affect the individual cell, but have no chance of being passed on in the ancestral line. By contrast, mutations in gametes (sex cells) are the real fodder for evolution, because they may be inherited. Whether they occur in somatic cells or in gametes, most mutations fall into the categories of substitution, insertion or deletion.

A substitution is the swapping of one nucleotide base for another. Although substitutions may originally occur in only one strand of DNA, the process of DNA replication tends to incorporate a corresponding mutation in the base-paired opposing strand of the double helix. A substitution may have no effect on the protein product of a gene, if the new codon is one that happens to code for the same amino acid; here is where the degeneracy of the genetic code buffers against mutations. When mutations are buffered in this way, they are called *silent mutations*. Alternately, a substitution may result in a codon that corresponds to a different amino acid, and these kinds of substitutions are called *missense mutations*. The severity of the missense mutation depends entirely on the role of the mutated amino acid within the protein product, and on how similar the new amino acid is to the original. Finally, and most dramatically, substitutions may convert a codon from one of the codes for an amino acid into one that codes for the STOP instruction (UAA, UGA, or UAG). Such a mutation results in the translation of a shorter, prematurely terminated protein product, and is called a *nonsense mutation*.

Insertions and deletions involve the addition or removal, respectively, of nucleotide bases with respect to the original DNA sequence. These kinds of mutations are almost always harmful because they alter the reading frame of the gene, so that every codon following the insertion or deletion is effectively changed. This kind of mutation is called a *frameshift mutation*. When the number of inserted or deleted bases is a multiple of three, however, no frameshift results, and the ultimate effect on the protein product is much less severe.

Many mutations are harmful, killing or crippling the mutated cell. Others are essentially neutral, and a very small fraction of mutations yield some sort of benefit. The more beneficial the mutation, the more likely it is to be passed on to subsequent generations — provided, of course, that the mutation originally occurred within a gamete.

Enhancing, repressing, inducing

The molecular toolbox used by cells to regulate gene expression is large, varied, and the subject of intense study. There are a few well-studied types of transcriptional regulation, however, with which you'll want to be most familiar for the AP Biology exam: enhancing, repressing, silencing, and inducing.

Eukaryotic genes often make use of DNA sequences called enhancers. These are stretches of DNA that lie well "upstream" of the region of the gene that codes for protein, preceding as well as the promoter region to which RNA polymerase binds. Special proteins called transcription factors bind to specific sequences within the enhancers. Although enhancers may occur thousands of bases before the promoter for a gene, the DNA appears to bend into a loop such that the enhancer region lies close in three-dimensional space to the promoter region. When this happens, the transcription factors may assist RNA polymerase in binding to the promoter and initiating transcription of the gene. Transcription factors that enhance transcription in this way are called activators.

Other upstream regions of eukaryotic genes appear to play a role opposite to that played by enhancers. Silencers are sequences to which transcription factors may bind to decrease transcription of a gene. Silencers are less common than enhancers. Eukaryotic cells have developed other means to decrease transcription of specific genes. For example, genes can be buried within inaccessible regions of chromosomes, so that activators or RNA polymerase cannot bind.

Because they are so easy to study, prokaryotes have been extensively probed for clues about how transcription is regulated. In prokaryotes, two key strategies are repressing and inducing. These strategies are similar in many ways to silencing and enhancing in eukaryotes.

In prokaryotes, genes that have related functions are often grouped together within clusters called operons. These genes tend to be transcribed in an all-or-none manner, as they are all served by a single promoter that precedes the first gene in the operon. Repressing and inducing both rely on regulating the access of RNA polymerase to this promoter.

Upstream from the operon's promoter lies a regulatory gene; this regulatory gene codes for a repressor protein specific to that operon. In their active form, repressor proteins bind promoters, preventing RNA polymerase from binding in order to transcribe the operon. Sometimes, repressor proteins remain inactive until they are bound by a small molecule called a co-repressor. Co-repressors can act as feedback inhibitors. For example, in the bacterium *Eschericia coli*, genes related to production of the amino acid tryptophan are clustered within the *trp* operon; when high levels of tryptophan are present in the cell, tryptophan acts as a co-repressor, binding to and activating a repressor protein that shuts down transcription of the *trp* operon as seen in Figure 21-2.

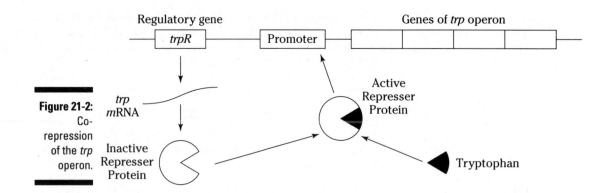

Figure 21-2:
Co-
repression
of the *trp*
operon.

Alternately, a repressor protein may be converted from active to inactive form when bound to a small molecule called an inducer. In another example from *Eschericia coli*, the sugar allolactose binds to a repressor protein, deactivating it to allow transcription of the *lac* operon, which encodes proteins involved in lactose metabolism. Thus, allolactose induces transcription of the *lac* operon.

Replicating Viruses and Bacteria

Before any pea plants or people were around to flaunt their fancy eukaryotic genetics, there were bacteria. Billions of years of bacteria. There continue to be bacteria, as there will most likely be bacteria well after the evolutionary sun has set on people and pea plants. Out of respect, then, take a moment to consider the time-honored means by which bacteria replicate, passing on their genes to the next generation.

Bacterial genomes (the collection of bacterial genes) occur within large circles of double-stranded DNA. Each bacterial chromosome contains a unique sequence called the origin of replication. At the origin, the enzymes involved in DNA replication commence to copying the bacterial genome, extending from the origin in both directions at the same time. Eventually (often within a few minutes), the bacterial genome is copied, and the new copy is gifted to a daughter cell as the bacterium divides into two identical cells. This division is called binary fission. Because bacteria divide so frequently, they rapidly progress through generations. As a result, bacteria have many chances to experience mutations, and to test the effects of those mutations; in other words, bacteria can evolve quickly.

In addition to the occurrence of random mutations, bacteria may create new genetic variations through recombination, the joining of genetic material from two bacteria into one. The major varieties of bacterial recombination are transformation, transduction, and conjugation. Transformation involves a bacterial cell taking in DNA from the external environment. Transduction involves the transfer of genes to a bacterial cell by phages, viruses that specifically infect bacteria. Conjugation is the transfer of genetic material from one bacterium directly to another across a bridge called a pilus.

Though they aren't technically alive, viruses nevertheless replicate, and can evolve. Viruses are basically groups of genes surrounded by a protein shell. Virus genomes may be composed of DNA or RNA, and may contain only a single strand or may be double stranded. Whatever the case, the nucleic acid genome is packed within a protein shell called a capsid, and the capsid may itself be surrounded by a membrane layer. These shell components protect the genome, and include structures that help the virus to infect specific cell types. Typical virus replication schemes involve the virus transducing (e.g., injecting or endocytosing) its genome into a host cell. Once inside, the viral genome hijacks the host cell's own materials and machinery to make copies of itself — new viral genomes and new viral capsid components. Once made, the virus parts self-assemble into new viruses, which may burst out of the infected cell to pursue infectious careers of their own. Like bacteria, viruses can reproduce rapidly, giving themselves ample opportunities for evolution.

Taking a look back at retroviruses and prions

Retroviruses and prions are two infectious agents with deviously interesting ways of replicating themselves. A retrovirus possesses an RNA genome, which it packs inside a capsid like any other virus. The retroviral cleverness really begins after the virus has infected a cell, transducing the viral genome into the cell. There, the virus employs its own special version of the enzyme reverse transcriptase, a protein that creates DNA strands based on RNA templates (essentially the opposite of what occurs during transcription). The retroviral reverse transcriptase makes a DNA version of the viral genome. Once made, this reverse-transcribed DNA genome integrates into the genome of the infected cell! That's right: the retrovirus melds its genome with that of its unwitting host. The virus may lie dormant in this state (i.e., as a "provirus") for a long time, replicating along with the cell. When the conditions are suitable, however, the virus may transcribe itself back into RNA form, and use protein-coding sequences within this transcript to make viral proteins. Once synthesized, these viral proteins assemble with the newly-transcribed, RNA version of the viral genome, resulting in new viral particles. It may be many generations before a retrovirus comes out of its hiding place.

Prions were discovered relatively recently, and represented something quite unexpected: infectious particles that can replicate without involving DNA or RNA. The same prion protein can exist in different forms, with different shapes and properties. The normal form of prion protein can convert over time into an infectious, toxic form. When the toxic form of a prion protein comes in contact with the normal form, it catalyzes conversion of the normal protein into a toxic protein. Large numbers of proteins in the toxic form aggregate into large, sheet-like assemblies called amyloid. Amyloid has been implicated in several prion-related diseases like bovine spongiform encephalopathy (i.e., mad cow disease) and Alzheimer's syndrome.

Of plasmids and phages

In addition to the large, double-stranded DNA circles that form bacterial genomes, bacteria make use of smaller DNA circles called plasmids. Plasmids contain smaller numbers of genes and have their own origins of replication. Bacteria can take in plasmids through transformation, transduction, and conjugation. Within bacteria, plasmids are often copied by a process called rolling circle replication. In this process, the plasmid is replicated, starting from an origin, and multiple copies are churned out one after another in a long, connected chain. In this chain, each connected sequence of plasmid DNA is called a "concatemer." Enzymes snip concatemers apart, then join the free ends together to form new circular plasmids. Plasmids often contain related clusters of genes that work together to give bacteria particular functions, such as resistance to antibiotics.

Phages are viruses that specialize in the infection of bacteria. They operate in the same way as already described for viruses. A phage particle, consisting of the phage genome encapsulated within a protein shell, lands on the outer surface of a bacterial cell membrane. Special protein parts attached to the capsid allow the phage to secure itself firmly to the membrane, then drive a hollow spike through the membrane into the bacterial cell's interior. The phage injects its genome through the spike, into the cell. From there, the phage genome can hijack the bacterial cell. Within infected bacteria, phages tend to take part in one of two kinds of life cycle: lytic and lysogenic. In the lytic cycle, the phage genome immediately recruits bacterial machinery to start producing many copies of phage genes and phage proteins. These raw materials assemble into new phage particles, eventually exploding the infected cell, spilling all the new phage to the outside where they may go on to infect new cells. Alternately, phages may enter the lysogenic cycle. In this cycle, the phage genome incorporates itself into the bacterial genome, similar to what was described in the life cycle of retroviruses. Incorporated prophage DNA may be silent for many generations, quietly replicating along with the bacterial DNA. When conditions are right, the prophage DNA can go active, producing new phage particles in the same way as done in the lytic cycle. Phages know when to hold 'em, fold 'em, walk away, or run.

Engineering Genes

Ever since scientists sniffed out the rules by which genes code for proteins, molecular biologists have devoted themselves to cutting, pasting, editing, monitoring, and generally giving genes a thoroughly hard time. The techniques by which all this gene-foolery is conducted are many, and any attempt to do them justice here is doomed from the start. However, below you'll find an exam-friendly list of some important molecular techniques, along with the basic principles of their operation.

Gel electrophoresis

Gel electrophoresis is a very common technique used by molecular biologists to separate mixtures of biomolecules like DNA, RNA, and proteins. Usually, this method uses a slab of gelatinous material composed of agarose or polyacrylamide. At the microscopic level, the gel is like an interwoven network of fibers. A sample mixture is gently introduced into one end of the gel, and the entire gel is placed in an electric field, so that negatively charged molecules move towards one end of the gel, and positively charged molecules migrate towards the other end. Different molecules move at different rates. After a time, the different types of molecule within the sample mixture are separated, and can be identified, quantified, or recovered in purified form.

All other things being equal, smaller molecules migrate faster through the gel than do larger molecules. However, differences in shape or the density of charge between molecules can cause deviations from that guideline.

Polymerase chain reaction

The polymerase chain reaction (PCR) is used to make many, many copies of a nucleic acid sequence that is initially present in very small numbers within a sample. PCR is widely used in medical diagnosis, DNA sequencing, forensics, and for countless other applications in labs across the world. The fundamental elements of your basic PCR experiment are: a DNA sample, DNA polymerase enzyme, single-stranded DNA molecules called "primers," and an excess of individual DNA nucleotides (A, G, C, and T). The primers have sequences that are complementary to sequences that flank the portion of DNA that you want to copy. The DNA polymerase used in PCR is a special version that can withstand very high (boiling) temperatures. The mixture of these components is cycled repeatedly through a series of three temperatures, as shown in Figure 21-3. During the first stage, the sample is heated to a very high temperature, near boiling, in order to "denature" or break apart double helices into their component single strands. During the second stage, the sample is cooled to a low temperature to allow "annealing" between the single strands and complementary primers that serve as the anchors for new DNA synthesis. During the third and final stage of each cycle, the sample-primer complexes are heated to a medium temperature to allow DNA polymerase to extend the primers into full-length complementary strands. Each three-stage cycle roughly doubles the number of copies of the DNA segment of interest that were present in the previous cycle. So, in a matter of hours, you can exponentially increase the concentration of a DNA target sequence from only a few copies to millions of copies. That's handy . . . Nobel Prize–winning handy.

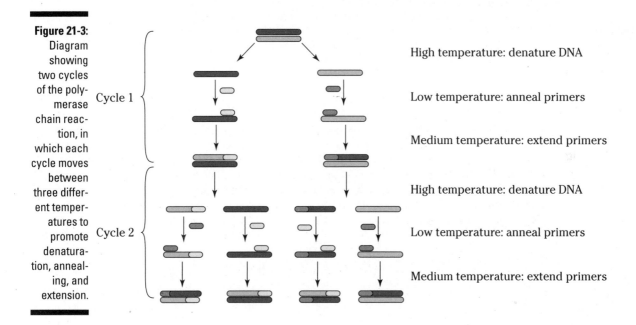

Figure 21-3: Diagram showing two cycles of the polymerase chain reaction, in which each cycle moves between three different temperatures to promote denaturation, annealing, and extension.

High temperature: denature DNA

Low temperature: anneal primers

Medium temperature: extend primers

High temperature: denature DNA

Low temperature: anneal primers

Medium temperature: extend primers

Cycle 1

Cycle 2

Microarray technology

An array is simply a group of different things arranged in an orderly manner. A microarray is a very small array — small in size, not in number of elements. Having endured several paragraphs about gene expression earlier in this chapter, can you think of anything that biologists might want to put into an array? Hint: genes. Although there are several kinds of microarray at use in biological research, the most common is the DNA microarray, and the most common use of DNA microarrays is to measure differences in gene expression between cell types (e.g., between healthy cells and cancer cells).

In a typical DNA microarray, DNA sequences corresponding to thousands of different genes are "spotted" onto a small chip. Each spot is only a fraction of a millimeter across, and contains many identical copies of a sequence corresponding to one unique gene. Importantly, the DNA within the spots (the "probe" DNA) is single-stranded; this means that the DNA will bind tightly and selectively to strands with the complementary sequence. These single-stranded DNAs are chemically attached to the chip, so that different sequences stick within their own spots. The microarray of probe DNAs is the critical tool used to analyze gene expression in different cell types.

Samples of different cell types are chemically treated to extract all the mRNAs present within them. The collection of mRNAs extracted from a cell at a given time serves as a kind of record of gene expression, indicating which genes are "turned on" and which genes are "turned off." Different cell types differ in gene expression patterns, often in interesting ways. Complementary DNA (cDNA) copies are made of the extracted mRNAs. These cDNAs are single-stranded, and are labeled with fluorescent tags. Different fluorescent colors are used for cDNA from different cell types. The cDNAs corresponding to individual cell types are the "targets" for the microarray "probe" sequences.

Finally, the fluorescently labeled targets are "hybridized" with the microarray probes. As the cDNA mixture flows across the microarray, complementary target, and probe sequences stick to each other due to base-pairing (A with T, G with C). After target-probe hybridization, the microarray is scanned to determine which microarray spots are occupied by fluorescently-tagged cDNA targets. Because each spot corresponds to a different gene, and because cDNAs from different cell types are tagged with different colors, you can determine which genes are expressed more or less between cell types.

Cloning

Relax — we aren't talking about human cloning here. We're not even talking about the cloning of sheep or mice. What we're talking about here is molecular cloning, the replication of biological molecules of interest (usually DNA sequences). One major use of molecular cloning is to amplify genes of interest so that researchers can study them in detail or make large quantities of the protein or RNA encoded by the gene. Although it is possible to use PCR to amplify DNA sequences, it is often more convenient to harness the DNA-replicating power of bacteria to make vary large quantities of a specific DNA sequence, and that is the approach most commonly used in molecular cloning. There are many varieties of molecular cloning, but the most common ones use bacteria, plasmids, the double-stranded DNA of interest, and a special class of DNA-cutting proteins called restriction enzymes.

Restriction enzymes recognize specific double-stranded DNA sequences (usually 6-8 bases in length), and cuts the DNA at these specific sites. Different varieties of restriction enzyme snip at different sequences. When restriction enzymes do their snipping, many of them leave single-stranded "overhangs," with one strand of the DNA double-helix slightly longer than the other at the snipped end. Because of these overhangs, any two pieces of DNA snipped by the same variety of enzyme are usually quite easy to knit back together.

Plasmids, you may recall, are circular bits of DNA that often contain clusters of related genes and are replicated within bacteria, doubling in number each time bacteria divide by binary fission. See where this is going? By snipping a DNA of interest and a plasmid with the same set of restriction enzymes, a molecular biologist can then insert the interesting DNA into the plasmid, and knit the whole assembly back together into something that looks a whole lot like the original plasmid, with the interesting sequence added in. This plasmid "construct" is then transformed into bacteria; the bacteria are persuaded (chemically or otherwise) to take the construct inside themselves. The bacteria may make several copies of the plasmid within themselves. Even better, the molecular biologist can grow up trillions of these transformed bacteria simply by feeding them and keeping them happy enough to divide. In the end, the bacteria are harvested and exploded, and hugely amplified numbers of plasmid construct are purified, each construct containing the DNA sequence of interest. All now rejoice. Except for the exploded bacteria.

The promise of gene therapy

Gene therapy is a tantalizing biomedical idea that has encountered some serious bumps on the road to becoming a practical reality in the clinic. Still, the basic biological concepts behind gene therapy are important, and its future may yet be bright. Some of the nastiest and most tragic human diseases result from defects in single genes. Cystic fibrosis, for example, is caused by a mutant form of the cystic fibrosis transmembrane conductance regulator (CFTR) gene. The gene codes for a protein that regulates the flow of certain ions across cell membranes. The mutant form of the gene causes serious abnormalities in the lungs and digestive system, and people born with mutant CFTR genes often die in their 20s and 30s, painfully. How wonderful would it be to be able to introduce normal CFTR genes into the cells of cystic fibrosis patients? This is the sort of goal that drives gene therapy research.

The basic idea is to grow up large quantities of the normal form of a gene (think: molecular cloning), and then insert the normal genes into the cells of a patient, persuading the patient's cells to accept the new genetic material as their own (think: transduction, etc.). The major challenges are in getting enough of the right genetic material into the right cells, getting those cells to accept the addition, and avoiding unintended side-effects along the way. Many current approaches to gene therapy use viruses to deliver the normal version of a gene into human cells carrying the abnormal version. This approach makes use of the fact that viruses are experts at delivering genes into cells, and integrating those genes into host chromosomes. In essence, the idea is to "infect" the patient into wellness. An obvious challenge is that the viruses best adapted to infecting humans are generally those that pose us the greatest health risks, so these viruses must be modified in clever ways to harness their infectious power while diminishing their ability to cause harm. Viruses aren't the only "vectors" under study as ways to introduce normal genes into human cells; there are several non-viral approaches as well, but these suffer from their own limitations. With enough biological insight, the early promise of gene therapy may yet be amplified into powerful, highly specific treatments.

Chapter 22

Answering Questions on Genetics

· ·

In This Chapter

▶ Remembering pointers

▶ Testing your knowledge

▶ Digging into labs

▶ Seeing how you did

· ·

*T*his chapter provides review and practice questions for the material found in Chapter 21: Genetics: Getting Down to DNA Level. Multiple choice and free-essay response questions and answers are provided. Also included is a summary of a Lab on the Genetics of Organisms. You've come so far . . . now extract the critical bits of Chapter 21 and get them into your DNA.

Pointers for Practice

The main points of Chapter 21 were the following:

✔ Genetic information flows through the following path: DNA → RNA → protein. Transcription rewrites the information found in genes, and translation deciphers the information by using the genetic code.

✔ The genetic code maps the relationships between three-base triplets within mRNAs and amino acids or START/STOP instructions used during translation. Transfer RNAs are the molecules primarily responsible for deciphering the genetic code at the ribosome.

✔ The genetic code is essentially universal, meaning that all known life on earth uses a nearly identical code to read the information within genes, in order to make proteins. The codons corresponding to the twenty common amino acids are basically the same in bacteria and blue whales. This deep similarity implies that all life is evolutionarily related.

✔ Gene expression refers to the collection of processes used by cells to turn genes on and off, and to dial in different levels of gene activity (i.e., how much is made of the gene's protein product). Gene expression is critical because cells need to be able to turn genes on and off in order to respond to changing conditions. Moreover, what makes different cells different (e.g., white blood cell versus a neuron) is the expression of different genes and the expression of the same genes at different levels.

✔ Prokaryotes control gene expression (among other ways) by using induction and repression. Both induction and repression function in the context of an operon, a cluster of genes whose transcription is controlled by a single promoter. Upstream of this promoter lies the gene for a regulatory protein; this protein binds specifically to the promoter for that operon, repressing its transcription by blocking the binding of RNA polymerase. In co-repression, a co-repressor molecule binds to the regulatory protein, activating it, so that the protein binds the promoter. In induction, an inducer molecule binds to the regulatory protein, inactivating it, so that the protein does not bind the promoter. Co-repressor and inducer molecules are often metabolites within biochemical pathways related to the genes within the operon.

✔ Eukaryotes control gene expression (among other ways) by using enhancing and silencing. Both enhancing and silencing employ DNA sequences far upstream (e.g., thousands of DNA bases away) of the promoter for a gene. Regulatory proteins called transcription factors bind to these upstream sequences. Because the DNA between the enhancer/silencer and the promoter forms a loop, the transcription factors are brought close to the promoter. Transcription factors associated with enhancers assist RNA polymerase in beginning transcription of the gene. Transcription factors associated with silencers prevent RNA polymerase from beginning transcription of the gene. Enhancers are much more common than silencers. Eukaryotes seem to use other means to decrease transcription, such as by burying genes within inaccessible regions of a chromosome.

✔ Bacteria replicate by binary fission, in which one bacterium divides into two, each with an identical copy of the bacterial genome. Bacterial genomes must be copied prior to fission. Bacterial chromosomes are large circular loops of double-stranded DNA. One sequence within this loop is called the origin of replication, and it is the site where replication enzymes begin to copy the chromosomal DNA, moving out in both directions from the origin, eventually to meet again when replication is complete.

✔ Plasmids are small circular loops of double-stranded DNA that tend to contain groups of functionally related genes. Bacteria use plasmids as modular additions to their genomes. Plasmids contain their own origins of replication, and replicate alongside bacterial chromosomes in a process called rolling circle replication. In this process, multiple, connected copies of the plasmid (i.e., concatemers) are made, then split apart into individual copies that close into individual plasmid circles. Plasmids can be transferred between bacteria by transformation (uptake of DNA from outside the cell), transduction (injection of DNA into the cell) and conjugation (transfer of DNA between cells across a pilus).

✔ Viruses replicate only by hijacking enzymes and other materials within cells that the viruses infect. Viruses may have genomes of either DNA or RNA, and these nucleic acids may be either single- or double-stranded. Viral genomes are packed within hollow protein shells called capsids. Viruses infect cells by attaching to the outer cell surface, and injecting or endocytosing the viral genome into the cell interior. There, viral genomes make use of the cell's own resources to make many copies of themselves, eventually to burst out of the cell and infect other cells.

✔ Retroviruses are viruses with RNA genomes. Once the retroviral genome enters an infected cell, a retroviral enzyme called reverse transcriptase makes a DNA copy of the retroviral genome. This DNA copy integrates with the host cell's own genome. From its hiding place within the host genome, retrovirus genes are transcribed in order to make new retroviral genomes and proteins, which assemble into new retrovirus particles that can exit the infected cell to infect other cells. HIV, the infectious agent associated with AIDS, is a retrovirus that infects cells of the immune system.

✔ Phages are viruses that specifically infect bacteria. Once phage genomes enter a bacterial cell, they may enter either lytic or lysogenic cycles. In the lytic cycle, phage genomes recruit bacterial resources to make new phage particles that eventually burst from the bacterial cell to infect other bacteria. In the lysogenic cycle, phage genomes integrate with the bacterial chromosome, becoming prophages that replicate with the chromosome and are passed on during binary fission, sometimes for many generations. At suitable times, the prophage may become active, transcribing new copies of phage genomes and proteins that assemble into new phage particles, as in the lytic cycle.

✔ Prions are infectious protein particles. Prions are notable because they can replicate directly as proteins, without making use of genetic information encoded within nucleic acids. Prion proteins exist in normal and toxic forms, which differ in shape but not in their primary structure (i.e., amino acid sequence). When toxic forms of prion protein contact normal versions, they may convert the normal proteins into the toxic form. Aggregates of toxic prions associate into large, sheet-like structures called amyloid. Amyloid is associated with diseases like mad cow disease and Alzheimer's syndrome.

✔ Genetic engineering uses the techniques of molecular biology to alter genes from naturally occurring organisms into new, "recombinant" forms. These alterations may involve editing of a DNA sequence or introducing genetic material from one organism into another organism of a different species. Genes transferred between species in this way are called transgenes. Restriction enzymes are important tools in genetic engineering. These enzymes recognize short double-stranded DNA sequences and cut DNA at sites containing those sequences. Different restriction enzymes cut at different sequences. Many restriction enzymes cut double-stranded DNA in such a way that they leave single-stranded overhangs. These overhangs create "sticky ends" that allow DNAs cut by the same enzymes to be joined together. Thus, by cutting two separate DNAs with the same set of restriction enzymes, the resulting fragments can be recombined to form new DNA sequences in a cut-and-paste manner.

✔ Recombinant plasmids can be formed by using restriction enzymes to cut-and-paste a DNA sequence of interest into a plasmid. Recombinant plasmids can be introduced into bacteria, replicated within those bacteria, and exponentially replicated as the bacteria divide. This process is called molecular cloning.

✔ Gel electrophoresis is a technique used to separate mixtures of biomolecules (e.g. nucleic acids and proteins) into their components. The mixture is introduced into a porous gel, usually made of agarose or polyacrylamide. The gel is placed into an electric field. Under the influence of this field, charged molecules migrate to one end or the other of the gel, positively charged molecules towards the negative pole, and negatively charged particles to the positive pole. Smaller molecules, which can pass more easily through the pores of the gel, tend to move more rapidly through the gel. Thus, molecules within a mixture are separated based on charge and size.

✔ The polymerase chain reaction (PCR) is a technique used to create millions of copies of a nucleic acid sequence that is initially present in much lower numbers within a sample. PCR uses single-stranded DNA primers that bind to complementary sequences flanking the sequence of interest. In addition, PCR employs a heat-stable DNA polymerase enzyme and an excess of nucleotides. Through multiple cycles of heating and cooling, primers bind to regions flanking a target, and DNA polymerase associates with the primer-target complex and copies the target sequence. Each cycle doubles the concentration of target sequence so that its total concentration increases exponentially through the cycles.

✔ Microarrays are tools used to assess the concentrations of different biomolecules within samples. DNA microarrays can be used to measure gene expression by measuring the relative amounts of different mRNAs in extracts from cells. DNA copies of the mRNAs extracted from cells (i.e., cDNAs) are labeled, often with fluorescent tags. These tagged cDNAs are hybridized with DNA microarrays. The DNA microarray consists of many tiny spots, each spot containing DNA sequences genes, one gene per spot. During hybridization, cDNAs bind to spots containing sequence from their gene of origin. The hybridized chips are scanned to visualize the fluorescence of bound cDNAs. By comparing the fluorescent brightness of different spots, researchers can assess which genes are turned on and which are turned off within the original cells.

Answering Multiple-Choice Questions

Directions: Choose the best possible answer, out of the five that are provided, for each question.

1. Gene expression may typically refer to which of the following processes?

    I. DNA replication

    II. Transcription

    III. Translation

    (A) I only

    (B) II only

    (C) III only

    (D) I and II only

    (E) II and III only

2. Which of the following types of mutation may result in a truncated (i.e., shortened) polypeptide?

    I. Missense mutation

    II. Nonsense mutation

    III. Silent mutation

    (A) I only

    (B) II only

    (C) III only

    (D) I and II only

    (E) II and III only

Questions 3-7 refer to the following answer choices. Answers may be used more than once.

    (A) enhancer

    (B) operon

    (C) inducer

    (D) repressor

    (E) co-repressor

3. Molecule that binds to a regulatory protein, inactivating it, to promote transcription

4. Occurs in eukaryotes, promotes transcription

5. Protein that binds to a promoter, thereby inhibiting transcription

6. Molecule that binds to a regulatory protein, activating it, to inhibit transcription

7. Group of genes organized into a transcriptional unit under the control of a single promoter

8. A patient suffers from an infection. A doctor cultures a blood sample from the patient to determine the nature of the infection. From the blood sample, the doctor is able to identify that a single species is responsible for causing the infection, and is able to develop an experimental treatment. The doctor administers the experimental treatment to the patient, and successfully controls the infection. Then, the doctor takes a second blood sample from the patient. Analysis of the second blood sample reveals large numbers of dead bacteria as well as large numbers of virus particles. The doctor smiles, and nods her head knowingly. What was the most likely active component of the treatment?

   (A) Small-molecule antibiotic

   (B) Small-molecule antiviral

   (C) Protein-based antibiotic

   (D) Protein-based antiviral

   (E) Phage

9. A researcher infects a culture of *Eschericia coli* with a bacteriophage that enters the lysogenic cycle promptly after infection. Subsequently, the researcher heats the infected bacterial culture to a very high temperature, effectively killing the bacteria and destroying any virus particles that remain in the culture. Then, the researcher adds a sample of the heat-killed solution to another, healthy culture of *Eschericia coli*. Two days after making this addition, the researcher isolates bacteria from the culture and discovers that they contain DNA sequences corresponding to the prophage state of the bacteriophage used to infect the original culture. In order, which two processes most likely account for this observation?

   (A) Conjugation, transformation

   (B) Conjugation, transduction

   (C) Transduction, conjugation

   (D) Transduction, transformation

   (E) Transformation, transduction

Answering Free-Essay Response Questions

1. Referring to the molecular structures involved, explain how a mutation can lead to a change in phenotype.

Lab on the Genetics of Organisms

This is a four-week lab that uses the common laboratory organism *Drospohila melanogaster*, the fruit fly, as a vehicle to test hypotheses about genetic inheritance. The fruit fly is chosen for this study for the same reasons that is has been the subject of genetic study for decades; it is easily handled, has many easily observed genetic traits, and reproduces quickly. Over the course of the lab, three generations of fruit flies are observed: the parental generation and two subsequent, "filial" generations (i.e., P, F_1 and F_2). By observing the relative numbers of normal and mutant variations of traits across these generations, you can test hypotheses about the mode of inheritance of those traits. Specifically, you gather data that support either monohybrid, dihybrid, or sex-linked inheritance. Each of these inheritance patterns has a distinct signature that can be predicted by using Punnett squares to calculate the ratio of offspring that should possess a trait based on the predicted genotype of the parents. If these references to inheritance and Punnett squares seem unfamiliar, you'll improve your life considerably by reviewing Chapter 19 before reading further.

Fruit flies pass through life cycles that have several well-defined stages. After adults mate (i.e., perform a cross), females lay small eggs. In this lab, the females deposit their eggs onto a nutritious culture medium stored within a vial. After a day or so, the eggs hatch into larvae. Over several days, larvae grow and molt, eventually becoming pupae. In this lab, pupae are recognized by their tendency to emerge from the culture medium, crawling up the sides of the vial. After several more days, pupae mature into adults, now capable of mating. Males and females are easily distinguished from each other because of differences in size, coloring, and other body features.

The kinds of traits typically observed in this lab are eye color and the morphology (i.e., shape and appearance) of eyes, wings, and legs. The fruit fly traits studied are present in well-defined normal and mutant varieties. Normal traits are also called "wild-type."

At the beginning of the experiment, students receive a vial containing male-female pairs of adult flies. At this point, the flies have already mated (i.e., have performed a P X P cross), and the eggs (i.e., the F_1 generation) may have progressed into larvae. Students collect the parental flies and inspect each under a dissecting microscope, recording for each the sex and the presence of normal versus mutant phenotype. Based on these results, students label the vial to identify the type of cross that produced the F1 generation. For example, a label might read "small wing female X normal wing male." After examination, the parents are kept separate from the F_1 generation to prevent confusion and mating between generations.

By the second week, the F_1 generation is mature enough that they can be examined for phenotypes. Students inspect all the F_1 flies, recording sex and phenotype for each. Then, 5 or 6 male-female pairs from the F_1 generation are placed in a fresh vial in order to mate, performing an F_1 X F_1 cross. At the beginning of the third week, students remove the adult F_1 flies from the vial, and allow another week for the F_2 generation to mature. At the beginning of the fourth week, students collect and examine the F_2 generation, recording sex and phenotype as done for the previous generations.

Because the data from this lab involve repeated measurements over hundreds of flies, statistical analysis is a key feature. Prior to analyzing the collected data, students make a "null" hypothesis about whether the trait they've been examining (e.g., eye color, wing size, etc.) is passed down as a monohybrid (single-gene), dihybrid (two-gene), or sex-linked (on the X chromosome) trait. In general, the more flies from which data are collected, the more reliable will be the comparison of the data with the student's hypothesis about which mode of inheritance is at play.

Based on their hypotheses, students construct Punnett squares portraying the inheritance of alleles for the traits during the P X P and F_1 X F_1 crosses. Based on these Punnett squares, students make predictions about the ratio of genotypes and phenotypes for the studied trait in the F_1 and F_2 generations. To remind yourself how to make this kind of prediction from a Punnett square, revisit Chapter 19. By comparing the actual data to the predictions of the null hypothesis, students determine whether the trait was passed down in the mode they predicted.

To most reliably compare the data to the prediction, students use a statistical tool called the chi-square, χ^2:

$$\chi^2 = \Sigma \, (o - e)^2 \div e$$

where o = an observed number, e = an expected number, and Σ = the sum over all observations. Students calculate a chi-square value for each of their predictions, and compare that value to a distribution of critical values for chi-squares (see Table 22-1).

Table 22-1	Chi-Square Values		
Probability, p	***Degrees of freedom, df***		
	1	2	3
0.05	3.84	5.99	7.82
0.01	6.64	9.21	11.3
0.001	10.8	13.8	16.3

Students compare their calculated chi-square against the set of critical values listed for the appropriate number of degrees of freedom. In this experiment, the degrees of freedom equal the number of possible phenotypes minus one. At a given level of probability, if the calculated chi-square is greater than or equal to the critical value, then the null hypothesis is rejected. For example, if there are three possible phenotypes, the degrees of freedom are two; if the calculated chi-square is 7.83, then the null hypothesis is rejected at p = 0.05, but is accepted at p = 0.01. Because the conventional cutoff for accepting hypotheses is p = 0.05, the null hypothesis (i.e., the student's guess about the mode of inheritance) would be rejected in this case. The fact that the hypothesis is rejected at p = 0.05 means that only 5% of the time would the observed data be consistent with the hypothesis; 95% of the time the observed data would be inconsistent with the hypothesis.

Checking Your Work

Experience the thrill that comes with being right. Check your work. If the results aren't so thrilling, then be sure to brush up on your weak areas, so you can experience the thrill on test day.

1. The answer is E. Although DNA replication copies the genes so that they may be passed on to the next generation, gene expression refers to those processes that determine which of the genes are selected for transcription into mRNAs and translation into proteins.

2. D is the answer. Truncated polypeptides result from mutations that convert a codon from one that codes for an amino acid into one that codes for the STOP signal. Missense mutations can have this effect, and nonsense mutations quite often have this effect. Silent mutations alter codons in such a way that there is no change to the amino acid sequence of the polypeptide.

3. C is correct. Inducers, well, induce. Because repressor proteins always inhibit transcription by binding to promoters, inducers promote transcription by preventing repressor proteins from doing their thing.

4. A is right. Enhancers are DNA sequences that occur far upstream of a promoter and bind transcription factors. The DNA that separates an enhancer from its corresponding promoter loops out, bringing the enhancer close to the promoter. In this arrangement, the bound transcription factors assist RNA polymerase in the act of starting transcription.

5. The answer is D. Repressors, well, repress. Repressor proteins bind to promoters, and thereby block RNA polymerase from initiating transcription.

6. E is the answer. Like inducers, co-repressors bind to repressor (regulatory) proteins. However, co-repressors bind to proteins that are inactive when the co-repressor is absent. When the co-repressor binds, the repressor protein is able to bind to a promoter to inhibit transcription.

7. B is correct. Operons occur in prokaryotes. A single promoter heads up an operon, and drives transcription of one long transcript that contains codes for several genes.

8. E is the best answer. Since the infection was caused by a single species, we can infer that the infectious agents originally within the patient were either bacteria or viruses, but not both. Thus, administering small molecule or protein-based medicines might have controlled an infection, but would not have led to the results obtained from analysis of the second blood sample. Administering a phage treatment, however, might explain those results. Since phages are viruses that specifically infect bacteria, a phage treatment could result in an wide-spread infection of the very bacteria that infected the patient, thereby killing the infectious bacteria. The patient's infection would be controlled, and the second blood sample would contain both killed bacteria and particles of the phage virus that killed them.

9. The answer is D. The infection of the bacterial culture by the bacteriophage involved _transduction_, the transfer of genetic information by using viruses. Because the virus was one that went directly into the lysogenic cycle, the viral genetic material became incorporated into the bacterial genome. This culture was then heated, killing the bacteria and inactivating any virus, so that any subsequent conjugation or transduction would be prevented. However, bacterial DNA containing the prophage insertion was still intact, and was transferred to the second culture of bacteria. Because some bacteria isolated from the second culture con-tained DNA sequence corresponding to the prophage, these bacteria must have taken up the DNA from their external environment, in the process called _transformation_.

Here is a model answer to the free-essay response question:

Mutations are changes in the DNA sequence within which genes are written. Genetic informa-tion originates in ordered sequences of adenine (A), thymine (T), guanine (G) and cytosine (C) base monomers within the linear DNA polymer. This information flows through the process of transcription into another polymer, messenger RNA (mRNA), and from there into still another polymer, a polypeptide. Polypeptides are the polymers that form proteins, the biochemical workhorses of cells. Because proteins perform most of the critical tasks of cells, and because they comprise much of a cell's structure, changes to proteins can result in changes in cell function. Changes in cell function can give rise to changes in phenotype.

DNA exists as a two-stranded double helix with a spiral staircase structure. The outer back-bone of this structure consists of an alternating chain of phosphates and deoxyribose sugars. Connected to each sugar is one of the nitrogenous bases, A, T, G, or C. Each phosphate-sugar-base unit is a nucleotide, a monomer link in the DNA chain. On the inside of the double helix, complementary bases associate in base pairs, following the pairing rules, A with T, G with C. During transcription, the double helix is unzipped to allow access to RNA polymerase, an enzyme that synthesizes a complementary RNA copy of the information on one DNA strand. The RNA molecule is very similar to DNA, except that RNA sugars are ribose, and the base uracil (U) is used instead of thymine (T). Transcription occurs within the nucleus.

After transcription, RNA transcripts are processed and exported from the nucleus as mRNAs. Each mRNA contains information corresponding to a gene, which is used to synthesize a polypeptide gene product during the process of translation. Translation occurs on the ribo-some, the molecular machine responsible for making proteins. A ribosome binds to an mRNA and scans it until finding a three-base sequence, AUG, that signifies the starting site for protein synthesis. From this point on, the RNA bases are organized into three-base triplets, or codons, within a single reading frame. Each three-base codon specifies the identity of a single amino acid, and the sequence of codons specifies the sequence of amino acids in a polypeptide.

The molecules responsible for decoding the mRNA are the transfer RNAs (tRNAs). Each tRNA has a three-base anticodon that complements a particular mRNA codon. In addition, each tRNA is bound to a particular amino acid. As the ribosome scans along an mRNA, tRNAs enter the ribosome-mRNA complex. When a correct codon-anticodon pairing is made, the ribosome catalyzes peptidyltransfer, the transfer of an amino acid from the matched tRNA to an elongating chain of amino acids. Eventually, the ribosome reaches a codon on the mRNA that signifies the end of synthesis, and the newly synthesized polypeptide is realeased. Poly-peptides fold into the functional structures called proteins.

Because of the process of genetic information flow described above, mutations in DNA can result in changes in phenotype. A single base change (e.g., A to G) results in a corresponding change within an mRNA (e.g., U to C) during the process of transcription. The change in the mRNA propagates to protein during the process of translation; an altered mRNA codon may pair with a different tRNA, one that bears a different amino acid. The polypeptide product of translation will therefore have a different sequence of amino acids, and this change may well alter the function of the protein, and thus the cell, and ultimately the phenotype.

Chapter 23

Evolving: Past, Present, and Future

· ·

In This Chapter

▶ Peering into the past to get a picture of how we got here

▶ Hefting the evidence for our evolutionary past

▶ Seeing patterns in the big evolutionary picture

· ·

*T*he more things change, the more they stay the same. Sure, the ancient earth may once have harbored nothing but lifeless chemicals, and sure, those chemicals may have arranged themselves into something resembling a simple cell. Yes, ancient cells may have given rise to more and more complex versions of themselves, eventually organizing into elaborate multicellular organisms. So, fine, over billions of years, a sterile planet may have transformed itself into one bustling with numberless hordes of diverse life. But all this diversity finds unity in a single idea: evolution.

How Life Got Here

Once you have living organisms reproducing and evolving, a whole lot of possibilities open up. But this begs the question, how did life originate in the first place? Of course, there are different schools of thought on this topic, but since you're preparing for the AP Biology exam, lets agree to focus on scientific explanations. Among scientists, there are also variations in thought, but there is also strong consensus on one point: The first living things probably arose spontaneously from nonliving things, in a natural process.

Without even setting foot into biology, it is fair to say that nonliving, chemical processes can evolve; groups of chemicals can undergo series of reactions that result in more and more complex chemicals that have greater variety of function. This process of chemical evolution most certainly occurred on the early Earth. Notable experiments probing the chemistry that may have happened on the Earth as it was about four billion years ago suggest that many of the basic chemical building blocks used by cells (precursors to amino acids and nucleotides, for example) would have been available as a result of natural chemical processes.

The next step is one that currently induces many scientists to hunch their backs in labs, attempting to deduce how a collection of organic molecules became ordered into living cells. Again, there is a diversity of scientific opinion about just how this happened, but the prevailing view sounds something like this: The collection of organic molecules included ones that strongly resemble the monomer precursors of biological polymers like RNA, DNA, and proteins. Experiments suggest that these monomers chemically linked together into polymers, the earliest of which probably resembled RNA, but possibly including others resembling peptides or proteins. The fact that RNAs can sometimes act as enzymes considerably strengthens this argument, because early RNA-like polymers could have been both catalysts and repositories of genetic information, two key elements necessary for cells.

Groups of polymers may have aggregated within droplets, enclosed by membranes. Recall that the basic structure of a cell membrane is that of a simple lipid bilayer. Phospholipids (or any other lipid with distinct hydrophobic and hydrophilic parts) tend to spontaneously form enclosed membranes when they are suspended in water. Once you have nucleic acid-like organic polymers enclosed within membranes, you've got a powerful recipe for the emergence of life. Within distinct droplets, mutations to the organic polymers can accumulate, yielding molecules with different properties.

Each droplet serves as a tiny little lab. Successful experiments, like the ability to catalyze replication of nucleic acids, are conserved within the droplets. Membranes can occasionally split and fuse, as a spontaneous chemical event, and these activities lay the foundation for cell division and recombination. Replicating, occasionally-mutating organic molecules within enclosed membranes seem to have all the ingredients necessary for the evolution of metabolism and heredity. In others words, these ordered collections of molecules have the fundamental properties of cells. And we're off!

The earliest life seems to have arisen around 3.5 billion years ago, a scant few hundred million years after the Earth's crust ceased to be molten. Not bad. These pioneering life forms most likely resembled simple prokaryotes. From the beginning, biology has largely been the story of bacteria, and some scientists contend that it still is mostly the story of bacteria.

For about 2 billion years, prokaryote or prokaryote-like microorganisms were the only game in town. There is debate about exactly when bacteria and archaea split into separate evolutionary lines, with different arguments asserting dates as early as 3 billion years ago to as recently as 2 billion years ago. In the middle of this range, about 2.5 billion years ago, there is evidence that significant amounts of oxygen began to accumulate in the atmosphere, most likely as a result of the photosynthetic activity of certain bacteria. This event was important because it set the stage for the development of oxygen-based metabolism. In a sense, your lungs were a birthday present sent to you from your cyanobacterial grandfathers a few billion years ago. That was thoughtful.

About 2 billion years ago the first eukaryotic upstarts took to the stage, having probably evolved recently from groups of prokaryotes that had learned to work and play together (i.e., to live symbiotically). For about a billion years, the eukaryotes kept it simple, living as single-celled organisms. But a little fewer than a billion years ago, a group of single-celled eukaryotes called the protists began to take seriously the idea of living together in closely interdependent communities. These communities become so cooperative and interwoven that it is more useful to think of them as single, multicellular organisms. From these early multicellular protists, all plants, animals, and fungi evolved.

The journey from the first cell to our current biological cornucopia is the story of evolution. Scientists debate the episodes of that story, and how best to understand them. One of the running debates, for well over a century, has been about whether there is a distinction between macroevolution and microevolution, and if so, how to define that difference. The debate continues. Since the advent of molecular biology, with its insight into the molecular details of mutation, there has been a surge of thought that there is no fundamental distinction: evolution is evolution. But it's important to understand what is usually meant by macroevolution and microevolution, if only to better follow the debate.

The big picture: Macroevolution

Macroevolution, as it is usually described, is concerned with evolution on the grand scale, with the branching out of new species and larger groups, like families and phyla. The question is whether there are distinct events and phenomena that control evolution on this scale. The big idea behind macroevolution is that of common descent, the proposition that all life descends from a single ancestor.

Some of the questions addressed by evolutionary biologists concerned with macroevolution are as follows:

- ✔ Does evolution always occur gradually, or are there periods of intense evolutionary change, alternating with periods of relative stability? The former hypothesis is called gradualism, and the latter is called punctuated equilibrium.

- ✔ What were the causes and the evolutionary effects of the mass extinctions that are evident in the history of life from the fossil record?

- ✔ What is the relationship between evolution and biodiversity; how does each affect the other over long periods of evolutionary time?

Clearly, these are interrelated types of questions. Macroevolutionists ask big picture questions that cover a lot of ground, seeking big picture answers that address a lot of issues. In any event, the concerns of macroevolution typically don't descend to levels below that of whole species.

The details: Microevolution

Microevolution is concerned with changes on the small scale, to include changes in the frequency of individual alleles within species and populations. The pioneering inheritance studies of our favorite Austrian monk, Gregor Mendel, were microevolutionary in scope.

Microevolution focuses on smaller groups of organisms living within well-defined habitats, and attempts to correlate changes in the habitat with changes in the genetic makeup of the organisms living within it. The sources of microevolutionary change include:

- ✔ **Mutation:** Random alterations to the DNA sequences that make up genes and which are passed from one generation to the next.

- ✔ **Natural selection:** The process by which traits that are favorable in a given environment become more common in subsequent generations, and traits that are less favorable become less common.

- ✔ **Gene flow:** The movement of alleles between different populations of organisms. Immigration and emigration are major sources of gene flow.

- ✔ **Genetic drift:** Changes in the frequency of alleles within a population due to neither natural selection nor gene flow, but from random events.

- ✔ **Nonrandom mating:** A condition which can alter the frequency of alleles within a population due to the fact that mates select their partners based on specific criteria, such as strength or aggressiveness.

Are we evolving? Using the Hardy-Weinberg equilibrium

One concern of population geneticists is to predict the likelihood of a phenotype, like a disease, from the distribution of genotypes within a population. Conversely, these geneticists try to predict the distribution of genotypes from the frequency of phenotypes. The primary tool used in these efforts is statistics. All the number-crunching occurs under an umbrella of an assumption called the Hardy-Weinberg principle, which is as follows: the frequency of alleles and genotypes within a population remains constant. In other words, the population is at genetic equilibrium, often called a Hardy-Weinberg equilibrium. This model describes a population that is a closed system, and one that does not evolve. It therefore is most appropriate for studies over small time scales. But used appropriately the model can be a powerful predictive tool. What's more, *deviations* from Hardy-Weinberg behavior can be important clues that something is happening that violates the assumptions of the model — something, sometimes, like evolution.

The simplest case we can subject to Hardy-Weinberg analysis is that of a single gene, one which occurs in two different alleles, a dominant (G) and a recessive (g). Let's say that the frequency of allele G equals p, and the frequency of allele g equals q:

frequency G = p

frequency g = q

Because all of the occurrences of the gene in a population must be of one allele or the other, p plus q equals the total. If we define the total as 1, then:

$$p + q = 1$$

Therefore, if we know that 75% of the alleles are G, p = 0.75, and we can calculate that 25% of the alleles must be g, because q = 0.25. Moreover, we can calculate the probability of any given genotype. Why? Well, because 1 x 1 = 1. That means:

$$(p + q) \times (p + q) = p^2 + 2pq + q^2 = 1$$

Homozygous dominant individuals have a p^2 probability, heterozygotes have a 2pq probability, and homozygous recessive individuals have a q^2 probability. So, given our earlier scenario in which 75% of all alleles are G, we can calculate the probability of any individual being heterozygous:

$$2pq = (2) \times (0.75) \times (1 - 0.75) = 0.375 \text{ or } 37.5\%$$

If all this reminds you of Punnett squares and Mendelian inheritance, that's because the Hardy-Weinberg model is basically a Punnett square applied to an entire population. Good catch.

Population genetics is a branch of microevolution that attempts to explain and predict changes in allele frequencies by using these statistical models. These models often make the simplifying assumptions about things like gene flow, genetic drift, and nonrandom mating. The only source of change in the frequency of alleles is assumed to be natural selection, and all members of a given species are assumed to be equally likely mating partners. Of course, reality always falls short of these assumptions, but the results of population genetics can nevertheless provide useful insights into evolution on the small scale, over shorter periods of time (i.e., not on the geological time scale).

How We Know It's So

Telling impressive-sounding stories about how we all got here over billions of years is one thing. Providing evidence is another. Fortunately, the story of evolution is not only supported by evidence, it actually emerged from having to explain evidence. There are many varieties of evidence that support evolution, but the two major categories are fossils and molecules.

Fossil records

A fossil is any preserved remain or trace of an organism. Although many of us picture dinosaur skeletons when we hear the word, fossils include the remains of other animals, the remains of plants, and even the remains of microorganisms. A preserved footprint is a fossil, believe it or not. The complete collection of fossils available for study is the fossil record. The scientists who study the fossil record are paleontologists.

Although there are many ways in which a fossil can form, the most important source of fossils is sedimentary rock. Sedimentary rock is formed from the repeated deposition of sand and silt into layers, as typically occurs in areas where water covers or moves over land. When organisms die, they may settle or be washed into areas of sediment deposition. With the passage of time, the sediments continue to settle, newer layers on top of older layers, at varying rates depending on climates, sea level, and other factors. These layers compress and solidify into rock, trapping the remains of organisms within them.

Depending on the environment of a particular fossil, the remains may be preserved to a greater or lesser extent. Predictably, the harder portions of organisms, like bone and shell, are best preserved. Nevertheless, in rare circumstances, even traces of softer organic materials are evident, such as in fossils of ancient leaves.

The convenient thing about sedimentary fossils is that it is easy to figure out which fossils are older than which other fossils: older fossils occur in lower layers and newer fossils occur in higher layers. Once formed into rock, sedimentary layers are still easily discerned. This technique is called relative dating. Relative dating is extremely useful for determining who is older than whom, but less useful for determining how old anyone is in particular.

A complementary technique is radiometric dating, which is also known as absolute dating. Radiometric dating makes use of the fact that radioactive isotopes decay into other elements over very precise periods of time. The half-life of an isotope is the amount of time it takes for one half of a sample of that isotope to decay. Half-lives are the Swiss quartz watches of nature. By measuring the ratios of different isotopes within a sample, scientists can estimate the age of that sample. Although the measurement may be more or less precise, it is an absolute measurement, an actual age.

Living proof: DNA evidence in plants and animals

The fossil record isn't the only record. There's one inside every cell. DNA sequences are a mother lode of information about the evolutionary past. The use of DNA sequences to determine evolutionary relatedness was discussed in Chapter 15: Taxonomy and Classification, but the basic idea is as follows. Any two organisms are related by a last common ancestor. Closely related organisms have recent last common ancestors, while more distantly related organisms have more ancient last common ancestors. The more time that has passed since the last common ancestor, the more mutations will have accumulated in the DNA of the related organisms. Therefore, by comparing the DNA sequences of organisms — in very careful ways, with lots of cross-checking — we can build family trees showing who descended from whom.

Within genomes, the DNA sequences that code for ribosomal RNA (rRNA, the biopolymers that make up most of the structure of ribosomes) are singled out for study because they mutate more slowly than do other sequences. The reason for this slow rate of mutation is that ribosomes are so central and critical to the business of cells that most mutations are simply not tolerated. The slow mutation of rRNA sequences makes them ideal for measuring evolutionary relatedness across very long timescales.

In addition to the DNA within nuclear genomes, eukaryotes have another source of DNA: mitochondria. Mitochondrial DNA is especially valuable in demonstrating ancestral lineages because it is passed down solely by females. In addition, mitochondrial DNA tends to mutate much more rapidly than nuclear DNA, so it can be used to reveal evolutionary divergence on shorter timescales.

New genomes are being sequenced regularly, thanks to dramatic improvements in sequencing technology. The sun has risen on the era of molecular paleontology.

Continuing to Grow and Change

So it seems from the evidence that life has been brewing for billions of years, undergoing fathomless rounds of evolution. Environments change, and the cast of biological characters changes in response. Have any patterns emerged in all that evolutionary time? Well, sure. Here are a few of the big ones.

Patterns of evolution

One useful way to discern patterns in evolution is to focus on a particular trait. Then, at different timepoints, take snapshots of the distribution of variations in that trait within a population. When the data are viewed in this way, several evolutionary trends can become apparent: directional selection, stabilizing selection, and disruptive selection.

✔ **Directional selection:** Natural selection that favors an extreme form of a trait. Over generations, the selected trait becomes more pronounced, as shown in Figure 23-1. Alternately, directional selection is understood as the increase in frequency of a selected allele. An example of directional selection is found in the lineage of horses. Fossil evidence clearly shows that over time, horses have steadily evolved larger bodies and longer legs. Presumably, these traits were favorably selected on the open grassland environments within which the horse evolved.

Figure 23-1:
Directional
selection, in
which an
extreme
form of a
trait is
favored.

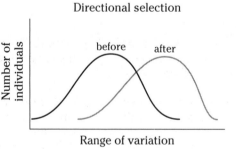

Directional selection

before   after

Number of individuals

Range of variation

✔ **Stabilizing selection:** Natural selection that disfavors extreme forms of a trait, instead favoring the intermediate form. Over generations, the intermediate form becomes more represented within the population, as shown in Figure 23-2. Casual observers might mistake stabilizing selection with the absence of selection, but Figure 23-2 makes clear that evolution is occurring, because the frequency of the trait changes within the population over generations. Stabilizing selection, though it may be subtle, is probably the most common mode of selection. The shark is a rich example of stabilizing selection, as most of its traits have persisted for millions of years.

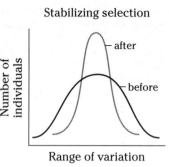

Figure 23-2:
Stabilizing selection, in which an intermediate form of a trait is favored.

✔ **Disruptive selection:** Natural selection that favors either extreme form of a trait over the intermediate form. Over generations, the extreme forms become more represented and the intermediate form less so, as shown in Figure 23-3. Darwin observed evidence for disruptive selection during his trip to the Galapagos. On the islands there, he observed two varieties of finch, close enough to have probably descended from a recent common ancestor, but with distinct differences in beak size; one variety had quite large beaks and the other had quite small beaks. Darwin correlated this observation with another: on these islands, the seeds on which the finches fed seemed to occur in either large or small varieties, such that only large or small, but not medium-sized beaks would be useful. Although disruptive selection seems to be rare, it is of great interest because it is one way that new species might evolve.

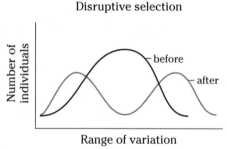

Figure 23-3:
Disruptive selection, in which either extreme form of a trait is favored.

Groups of species undergo these various kinds of selection and, over time, may engage in several patterns of evolution. In particular, different species can undergo convergent evolution, divergent evolution, parallel evolution, and coevolution.

✔ **Convergent evolution** is the process in which species that are not closely related to each other independently evolve similar kinds of traits. For example, dragonflies, hawks and bats all have wings. None of these organisms owes its wings to genes inherited from any of the others. Each kind of wing evolved independently, suggesting that the trait of flight is a useful one for the purpose of survival and reproduction. These independently evolved wings are called *analogous structures*.

✔ **Divergent evolution** is the process in which a trait held by a common ancestor evolves into different variations over time. A common example of divergent evolution is the vertebrate limb. Whale flippers, frog forelimbs, and your own arms most likely evolved from the front flippers of an ancient jawless fish. Because they share a common evolutionary origin, these are examples of *homologous structures*.

An important consequence of divergent evolution is *speciation*, the divergence of one species into two or more descendant species. There are four major ways speciation can occur:

- *Allopatric speciation* occurs when a population becomes separated into two entirely isolated subpopulations. Once the separation occurs, natural selection and genetic drift operate on each subpopulation independently, producing different evolutionary outcomes. This is the most common form of speciation.

- *Peripatric speciation* is somewhat similar to allopatric speciation, but specifically occurs when a very small subpopulation becomes isolated from a much larger majority. Because the isolated subpopulation is so small, divergence can happen relatively rapidly due to the *founder effect*, in which small populations are more sensitive to genetic drift and natural selection acts on a small gene pool.

- *Parapatric speciation* occurs when a small subpopulation remains within the habitat of an original population, but enters a different niche. Effects other than physical separation prevent interbreeding between the two separated populations. Because one of the genetically isolated populations is so small, however, the *founder effect* can still play a role in speciation.

- *Sympatric speciation*, the rarest and most controversial form of speciation, occurs with no form of isolation (physical or otherwise) between two populations.

✔ **Parallel evolution** is sometimes difficult to distinguish from convergent evolution. Parallel evolution occurs when different species start with similar ancestral origins, then evolve similar traits over time. This kind of thing happens because the two different species, though they don't necessarily share a common ancestor, experience similar kinds of environmental pressures, and survive only by undergoing similar adaptations. A classic example of parallel evolution is found among plants, in which several similar but distinct forms of leaf evolved in parallel and are evident today.

✔ **Coevolution** occurs when two (or more) closely interacting species exert selective pressures on each other, so that they evolve together in a kind of conversation of adaptations. Examples of coevolution are common among predator-prey and host-parasite pairs. More picturesque examples of coevolution occur among hummingbirds and the flowers from which they seek nectar and unwittingly pollinate.

Drifting, selecting, and adapting

In order for natural selection to be really effective, it must possess one key raw material: genetic variation. Without variation, there are no new genetic choices from which to select, like being presented a dessert cart carrying a single lonely slice of cake.

Within a particular environment, genetic drift, gene flow, nonrandom mating, and mutation are all potential sources of genetic change in a population, as described in the section on microevolution. However, on their own, these processes cannot produce adaptation. The agents of genetic change (drift, flow, etc.) may produce individuals well-suited to a particular environment, but increasing the frequency of that favorable trait in a lasting way requires natural selection. In fact, the whole concept of adaptation is empty without the concept of natural selection: an adaptation is a useful trait that has been favored by natural selection.

Once you have genetic variation and natural selection, expect adaptation. But don't expect perfection. Natural selection may be the most powerful phenomenon the world has ever seen, but it has its limitations:

First, in any given organism, natural selection typically acts by modifying pre-existing traits and structures. If a radically new environment renders an old structure entirely obsolete, natural selection may not be able to perform the required renovation. Instead, species better suited to the new environment will increase the frequency of their genes.

Second, natural selection can only make do with the genetic variation with which it has been provided. If you hand the cook a scrawny chicken, don't expect lobster for dinner.

Finally, even as natural selection promotes adaptation by increasing the frequency of favorable traits, genetic drift undoes that work by introducing wrinkles into the very things that selection has smoothed. Sigh.

Chapter 24

Answering Questions on Evolution

In This Chapter

▶ Getting some pointers
▶ Practicing with some questions
▶ Working on labs
▶ Checking your work

This chapter provides review and practice questions for the material found in Chapter 23: Evolving: Past, Present and Future. Multiple choice and free-essay response questions and answers are provided. Also included is a summary of a Lab on Population Genetics and Evolution. From the very first chapters up to Chapter 23, your understanding of biology has evolved — now complete the journey by answering just a few questions more.

Pointers for Practice

The main points of Chapter 23 were the following:

✔ **Life on Earth has evolved over approximately 3.5 billion years, first appearing only a few hundred million years after the surface of the earth cooled enough to become solid.**

✔ **Prior to the beginnings of biological evolution, there occurred a period of chemical evolution.** During this period, natural chemical and physical processes created a stockpile of organic molecules that served as precursors for the first organic polymers. These polymers had the essential properties of the biopolymers that are critical to all cells: nucleic acids and proteins. Collections of ancient polymers probably became encapsulated within membranes that served the basic functions of cell membranes. Once organic polymers arose that were capable of catalysis and replication, and were isolated within membranes, the stage was set for the development of metabolism and heredity, the essential functions of cells.

✔ **Macroevolution is the branch of evolutionary science that focuses evolution at the levels of species and higher.**

✔ **Microevolution is the branch of evolutionary science that focuses on changes in the frequency of alleles and genotypes within species and populations.**

✔ **Whether macroevolution and microevolution are truly distinct, or whether macro-evolution is simply the result of microevolution over long periods of time is debated.**

✔ **Microevolution occurs as the result of five processes: genetic drift, gene flow, mutation, nonrandom mating and natural selection.** The first four factors serve as engines of genetic variation. Natural selection sifts through the variants, determining which variations increase in frequency and which decrease in subsequent generations. Adaptation results from the action of natural selection on genetic variation.

✔ **Population genetics uses statistics to model genetic variation within well-defined populations.** A major tool of population genetics is the Hardy-Weinberg analysis. The Hardy-Weinberg model assumes that a population is at genetic equilibrium, meaning that the total collection of alleles in a population remains constant. Thus, for any gene that occurs in two alleles, one dominant and one recessive, the probability of observing one of those two alleles is unity, so $p + q = 1$. Populations at genetic equilibrium do not evolve because there is no source of genetic variation. The results of the Hardy-Weinberg analysis are useful, among other things, for highlighting deviations from the assumption of genetic equilibrium.

✔ **Fossils are any preserved remains or traces of a living organism.** The largest and most informative group of fossils occur within sedimentary rock. Because the layers of sedimentary rock correspond to the passage of time, the relative ages of fossils within sedimentary rocks can be determined. This is called relative dating.

✔ **Naturally occurring isotopes provide a complementary way to date fossils.** Because different isotopes decay with different, well-defined half-lives, the ratio of certain isotopes measured within fossils and rocks can give an absolute (i.e., not relative) measure of the age of those samples.

✔ **With the explosion of genetic sequence data now becoming available, comparison of DNA sequences between organisms (both currently living and dead but well-preserved) is a major source of evolutionary information.** Because genetic variations accumulate over time, organisms with more closely related DNA sequences tend to share a more recent last common ancestor.

✔ **Directional selection** favors a single extreme form of a trait. **Stabilizing selection** favors an intermediate form of a trait. **Disruptive (or diversifying) selection** favors either extreme form of a trait. Stabilizing selection is probably the most common mode of evolution. Disruptive selection is probably the least common mode, but is important because it may be a source of new species.

✔ Convergent evolution is the evolution of similar traits starting from distinct evolutionary origins. Convergent evolution produces analogous structures. Divergent evolution is the evolution of variant traits starting from a common evolutionary origin. Divergent evolution produces homologous structures. Parallel evolution is the evolution of similar traits starting from similar but distinct evolutionary origins. Coevolution is mutual evolution of traits in species that exert selective pressures on one another.

✔ Allopatric speciation occurs between large populations separated by a geographic barrier. Peripatric speciation occurs between a large population and a physically isolated small population. Parapatric speciation occurs between a large population and a smaller one within the same habitat, but in different niches. Sympatric speciation occurs between populations that occupy both the same habitat and niche.

✔ **Natural selection can never produce organisms that are perfectly suited to their environment, for several reasons.** Natural selection modifies structures that already exist, it can only act on the genetic variation that is provided to it, and the work of natural selection is constantly undone by genetic drift.

Answering Multiple Choice Questions

Directions: Choose the best possible answer, out of the five that are provided, for each question.

1. For approximately how long were prokaryotes the only form of life on the planet?

    (A) A few hundred million years

    (B) 3.5 billion years

    (C) 2.5 billion years

    (D) 1.5 billion years

    (E) There are no reliable estimates

2. Which of the following are typical subjects examined in the field of microevolution?

    I. the effect of immigration on allele frequencies

    II. the role of mate selection on genetic variation

    III. the rate at which new species appear

    (A) I only

    (B) II only

    (C) III only

    (D) I and II only

    (E) II and III only

    Questions 3-7 refer to the following answer choices. Answers may be used more than once.

    (A) Absolute dating

    (B) Relative dating

    (C) Mitochondrial DNA

    (D) Ribosomal RNA genes

    (E) Sedimentary rock

3. Used to determine which fossils are older than others

4. Provides sequence data useful for determining evolutionary change over relatively long periods of time

5. Used to estimate the actual age of fossils

6. Provides sequence data useful for determining evolutionary change over relatively short periods of time

7. Substrate for the raw materials of relative dating

8. Approximately 0.04% of the Caucasian population of the United States suffers from the genetic disorder, cystic fibrosis. Individuals who carry two copies of the recessive mutant allele exhibit the disease. Estimate the percentage of non-affected carriers within that population.

    (A) 16%

    (B) 1.96%

    (C) 3.92%

    (D) 0.0004%

    (E) Not enough information is provided

9. A chain of volcanic islands sits about 2,500 miles from the nearest continent. Nearly half a million years ago, a bird migrating from the continent unknowingly carried with it larvae from a certain species of insect common on that continent. The migrating bird took a brief layover on one of these islands, during which the larvae become dislodged and were left behind. Subsequently, the larvae developed. Today, the chain of islands displays an impressive variety of insects related to but distinct from each other, and from the original variety of insect on the continent. This anecdote best exemplify which of the following?

(A) Allopatric speciation

(B) Parapatric speciation

(C) Peripatric speciation

(D) Sympatric speciation

(E) Synpatric speciation

Answering Free-Essay Response Questions

1. Explain what is meant by genetic equilibrium, and under what conditions equilibrium is attained. Using the Hardy-Weinberg model, calculate the frequencies of alleles and genotypes in a population of butterflies that are either brown or white, given the following information: out of a total of 75,000 butterflies, 28,000 are white. The brown allele (B) is dominant and the white allele (b) is recessive. If some mutation were to cause the homozygous recessive genotype to become lethal, how would the calculated frequencies change?

Lab on Population Genetics and Evolution

In this lab, students use the Hardy-Weinberg model to calculate allele and genotype frequencies, and through a series of case studies, discover how deviations from Hardy-Weinberg behavior can be caused by interesting evolutionary activity.

Prior to beginning the experiments, it is critical to understand the basic tenets of the Hardy-Weinberg model:

✔ Evolution is seen as a change in the frequency of alleles within a population.

✔ In the simplest case, any given gene occurs in one of two alleles, a dominant allele, A, or a recessive allele, a. The frequency of allele A = p, and the frequency of allele a = q. Because all instances of the gene must be either A or a, p + q = 1.

✔ Because $1 \times 1 = 1$, $(p + q) \times (p + q) = 1 = p^2 + 2pq + q^2$. The term p^2 corresponds to the frequency of homozygous dominant genotypes. The term $2pq$ corresponds to the frequency of heterozygous genotypes. Term q^2 corresponds to the frequency of homozygous recessive genotypes.

✔ For the statistical model to hold true, five conditions must be in effect:

• The population must be large. This minimizes the random effects of genetic drift.

• Mating must be random. This rules out non-statistical effects on allele frequency due to preference in breeding partners with particular traits.

- Alleles do not mutate. Obviously, changing the alleles changes the frequency of alleles within the population, and this is forbidden in the model.

- Immigration and emigration do not occur. This rules out changes in allele frequency due to gene flow.

- Natural selection does not occur. By definition, natural selection means changing the frequency of alleles within a population, and therefore must be excluded from the model.

With these basics understood, students progress to the first part of the lab, in which they estimate the frequency of certain alleles within their classroom population. The trait determined by these alleles is the ability or inability to taste the chemical phenylthiocarbamide, PTC. Individuals who possess a dominant allele, A, will experience a bitter taste when placing a PTC-dipped test paper on their tongue. Individuals who lack the dominant allele (i.e., who are homozygous recessive, aa) will taste nothing. Everyone in the class tests themselves for PTC-tasting ability, and the results are recorded.

The frequency of tasters is calculated by dividing the number of tasters by the total number of people in the class. The frequency of nontasters is calculated by dividing the number of nontasters by the total number of people in the class. The two frequencies sum to 1.

Because tasters are either homozygous dominant or heterozygous, and because nontasters are homozygous recessive, their frequencies are expressed as:

$$\text{frequency of tasters} = p^2 + 2pq$$

$$\text{frequency of nontasters} = q^2$$

By using these equations, p and q are easily calculated. Once calculations are made for the classroom dataset, students compare the classroom results to those observed for the population of North America (55 percent tasters, 45 percent nontasters). Typically, the two sets of results differ significantly; the intent is to demonstrate the importance of a large population size to the Hardy-Weinberg model.

Students next embark on a series of three short case studies to demonstrate the potential biological significance of deviations from the assumptions of the Hardy-Weinberg model. Case I attempts to simulate five rounds of random mating between members of the classroom. At the beginning of the mating, each class member is heterozygous, and therefore holds four cards, two with the dominant allele (A) and two with the recessive allele (a). These four alleles represent the four gametes produced at the end of meiosis.

Students are to randomly select breeding partners, with no preference regarding gender, appearance, odor or membership on any of the school's various athletic teams. Once partners have been selected, mating is performed by exchanging cards. Each person shuffles their four gamete-cards and selects one card to contribute to a given fertilization. Each round of mating consists of two such fertilizations, with cards reshuffled in between the two. The results of each fertilization are recorded.

Prior to the next round of mating, students assume the genetic identity of the offspring they produced in the previous round, each student from a mating pair taking on the genetic identity of one of the two offspring. New cards are doled out to accurately reflect the mixture of alleles that would result from meiosis. The whole random-selection, two-offspring process repeats. After five rounds, all the class data are pooled, and everyone calculates the frequency of A and a alleles present after the fifth round, simply by adding up the number of each allele, and dividing by the total number of alleles. These results are compared to the predicted results of the Hardy-Weinberg model. Because each class member started as a heterozygote, and because the model assumes that allele frequencies do not change, the Hardy-Weinberg prediction is that, after five rounds, the frequencies of alleles A and a are each 0.5.

Typically, the classroom results differ significantly from the prediction. Again, this demonstrates the importance of a much larger population for the model to really apply. In addition, the social realities of a high school classroom dictate that very few of the matings will actually be anything like random.

In Case II, students perform the same exercise as done in Case I, but with an added twist. Any time offspring are produced with the homozygous recessive genotype, aa, those offspring are considered inviable (i.e., do not survive), and fertilization must be repeated until two viable offspring are created. This situation mimics that of sickle-cell anemia, a genetically determined condition in which homozygous recessive individuals usually die before reaching reproductive age.

After five rounds of mating, selecting each time against the homozygous recessive genotype, allele frequencies are once again calculated. The expected result is that the frequency of the alleles significantly change from their starting points, at 0.5 apiece. These changes in frequency deviate from the predictions of the Hardy-Weinberg model; the reason for the deviation is that natural selection occurred, favoring the A allele relative to the a allele.

At the same time, the results of Case II suggest that it is highly unlikely for any unfavorable recessive allele to be completely banished from a large population; the allele would be able to "hide" within heterozygotes.

Case III further investigates a scenario related to sickle-cell anemia. Data from actual human populations reveal that, in some areas, the frequency of the recessive, anemia-related allele is much higher than is predicted from its lethal homozygous recessive phenotype. The reason for this deviation seems to be that heterozygous individuals are mildly resistant to a dangerous form of malaria that is prevalent in those areas. Thus, although natural selection disfavors the homozygous recessive genotype, it selects in favor of the heterozygous genotype, elevating the frequency of the recessive allele. This phenomenon is called the heterozygote advantage.

Students model the heterozygote advantage by performing more rounds of mating, following the rules of Case II, with a twist: any time offspring are created with the homozygous dominant (AA) genotype, a coin is flipped. Heads indicates that the offspring dies (e.g., succumbs to malaria because it lacks the heterozygote advantage), while tails indicates that the offspring survives. Students are encouraged to perform as many rounds of mating as possible, because the heterozygote advantage is a subtle one, any may require many generations to exhibit a measurable effect.

Checking Your Work

Think of this part as a form of natural selection. Each of the answers you gave to the practice questions is sort of like one of your offspring. Not all of them will necessarily survive. But that's okay. As painful as it might be to watch your incorrect answers die, their deaths prevent the further spread of erroneous knowledge within your brain. That's just learning, red in tooth and claw.

Answers and Brief Explanations
for the Review Questions

1. The answer is D. The best consensus estimates are that prokaryotes arose around 3.5 billion years ago, and that eukaryotes evolved into being about 2 billion years ago.

2. D is the answer. The rate at which new species are created, whether gradually or during occasional periods of intense evolution, is a classic subject of macroevolution.

3. B is correct. Relative dating is a technique used on groups of fossils found in sedimentary rock. Fossilized organisms are assumed to have died during the approximate time that sediments within the rock were originally deposited. Therefore, older fossils occur in lower layers.

4. D is right. The function of ribosomal RNAs is so critical to the survival of cells that the DNA sequences encoding them are severely constrained from evolving, and do so only very slowly.

5. The answer is A. Absolute dating, most commonly in the form of radiometric dating, attempts to measure the actual age of fossils. Absolute dating complements relative dating.

6. C is the answer. Mitochondria have their own DNA, consistent with the proposal that mitochondria originate from a free-living bacterium that was engulfed by another cell, after which the two endosymbiotically co-evolved. Mitochondrial DNA is subject to fewer evolutionary constraints than nuclear DNA, and so evolves more rapidly.

7. E is correct. The layering within sedimentary rock is the key feature that allows paleontologists to distinguish the passage of time.

8. C is the answer. Cystic fibrosis is a recessive condition, so individuals with the disease are homozygous recessive. Because these individuals represent 0.04% of the population, their frequency is 0.0004. The frequency of the recessive phenotype corresponds to q^2, so $q = (0.0004)^{1/2} = 0.02$. Moreover, $p + q = 1$, so $p = 0.98$. Carriers are heterozygotes, whose frequency is $2pq = (2)(0.98)(0.02) = 0.0392$, or 3.92%.

9. (C) The anecdote describes peripatric speciation because the small group of insects carried as larvae to the chain of volcanic islands represent a small subpopulation that becomes geographically isolated from a larger population. These few larvae evolved as an isolated colony, and would have been subject to the founder effect due to the smallness of their population.

Here is a model answer to the free-essay response question:

Genetic equilibrium, the basic assumption of the Hardy-Weinberg model of population genetics, is the condition in which the total frequency of alleles within a given population is constant over generations. For example, if a gene may present in either a dominant or recessive allelic form (i.e., B or b), then the percents of alleles B and b add up to 100%. Put another way,

> frequency of B = p
>
> frequency of b = q
>
> p + q = 1

where p and q represent allele frequencies expressed as numbers between 0 and 1. If the assumption of genetic equilibrium holds true, then no matter how many generations pass, the following is true:

$$p^2 + 2pq + q^2 = 1$$

This final relation is extremely useful because it allows one to calculate the frequency of each allele and genotype within a population, given only the frequencies of observed phenotypes. Specifically,

frequency dominant phenotype = $p^2 + 2pq$

frequency recessive phenotype = q^2

Actual populations never hold to the ideal of genetic equilibrium, because agents of genetic variation and natural selection are at work. Although this at first appears to be a limitation on the Hardy-Weinberg model, it is actually a strength; deviations from the model signify the presence of these agents, which is biologically interesting.

The factors that disrupt genetic equilibrium are genetic drift, gene flow, nonrandom mating, and natural selection. Genetic drift refers to the disruption of equilibrium by random effects, and is especially pronounced in small populations, where there is less likelihood that simultaneous drifting events will cancel out. Gene flow refers to the gain or loss of alleles from a population due to immigration or emigration. Nonrandom mating refers to changes in allele frequency that arise when individuals select mating partners based on observed favorable traits, corresponding to particular alleles. Mutation refers to the direct alteration of allele frequency due to chemical processes that alter the DNA sequence of the alleles themselves. Natural selection is the process by which favorable alleles are amplified in successive generations and unfavorable alleles are diminished.

In the given scenario, the total population of butterflies is 75,000, and those displaying the recessive white phenotype total 28,000. These data can be used to calculate the frequencies of the dominant and recessive phenotypes (FDP and FRP, respectively) as follows:

Brown (dominant phenotype) butterflies = 75,000 – 28,000 = 47,000

FDP = 47,000 / 75,000 = 0.63

FRP = 28,000 / 75,000 = 0.37

The calculated FDP and FRP allow calculation of allele frequencies:

FRP = 0.37 = q^2; therefore q = 0.61

p + q = 1; therefore p = 1 – q = 0.39

As a check, one can independently re-calculate the FDP, using p and q:

FDP = $p^2 + 2pq = (0.39)^2 + (2)(0.39)(0.61) = 0.63$

With the p and q calculated, calculating the individual genotype frequencies is straightforward:

frequency of BB = $p^2 = 0.15$

frequency of Bb = 2pq = 0.48

frequency of bb = $q^2 = 0.37$

As a check, it is important to note that the sum of the genotype frequencies is 1.

If some mutation were to cause the homozygous recessive genotype (bb) to become lethal, genetic equilibrium would be disrupted. As the population reestablished equilibrium, natural selection would diminish the frequency of the recessive allele (b), because off-spring with this genotype would not reproduce, Correspondingly, the frequency of the dominant allele (B) would increase. Because the recessive phenotype has become lethal, white butterflies would fall out of the population. However, the frequency of the recessive allele would not fall entirely to zero, because recessive alleles would persist within heterozygotes.

Part V

Putting It All into Practice, or, Practicing What Has Been Preached

The 5th Wave   By Rich Tennant

"Did any of you fall for that trap in question 7?"

In this part . . .

You've had your fill of big ideas and little details. You're bursting with biology, anxious to use your knowledge of the inner workings of life for something useful, like slaughtering the AP Biology exam. To this end, we offer two full-length practice tests, complete with answers and explanations. Sharpen your teeth on these tests, and use them to fine-tune the last stages of your exam preparation.

Chapter 25

Test 1

....

In This Chapter

▶ One hundred challenging multiple-choice questions

▶ Free-response questions complete with grading outline

....

*T*ake the following test under timed conditions to simulate the actual AP Biology exam. Then, check your work by using the answers and explanations provided in Chapter 26.

1 Ⓐ Ⓑ Ⓒ Ⓓ	41 Ⓐ Ⓑ Ⓒ Ⓓ	81 Ⓐ Ⓑ Ⓒ Ⓓ
2 Ⓐ Ⓑ Ⓒ Ⓓ	42 Ⓐ Ⓑ Ⓒ Ⓓ	82 Ⓐ Ⓑ Ⓒ Ⓓ
3 Ⓐ Ⓑ Ⓒ Ⓓ	43 Ⓐ Ⓑ Ⓒ Ⓓ	83 Ⓐ Ⓑ Ⓒ Ⓓ
4 Ⓐ Ⓑ Ⓒ Ⓓ	44 Ⓐ Ⓑ Ⓒ Ⓓ	84 Ⓐ Ⓑ Ⓒ Ⓓ
5 Ⓐ Ⓑ Ⓒ Ⓓ	45 Ⓐ Ⓑ Ⓒ Ⓓ	85 Ⓐ Ⓑ Ⓒ Ⓓ
6 Ⓐ Ⓑ Ⓒ Ⓓ	46 Ⓐ Ⓑ Ⓒ Ⓓ	86 Ⓐ Ⓑ Ⓒ Ⓓ
7 Ⓐ Ⓑ Ⓒ Ⓓ	47 Ⓐ Ⓑ Ⓒ Ⓓ	87 Ⓐ Ⓑ Ⓒ Ⓓ
8 Ⓐ Ⓑ Ⓒ Ⓓ	48 Ⓐ Ⓑ Ⓒ Ⓓ	88 Ⓐ Ⓑ Ⓒ Ⓓ
9 Ⓐ Ⓑ Ⓒ Ⓓ	49 Ⓐ Ⓑ Ⓒ Ⓓ	89 Ⓐ Ⓑ Ⓒ Ⓓ
10 Ⓐ Ⓑ Ⓒ Ⓓ	50 Ⓐ Ⓑ Ⓒ Ⓓ	90 Ⓐ Ⓑ Ⓒ Ⓓ
11 Ⓐ Ⓑ Ⓒ Ⓓ	51 Ⓐ Ⓑ Ⓒ Ⓓ	91 Ⓐ Ⓑ Ⓒ Ⓓ
12 Ⓐ Ⓑ Ⓒ Ⓓ	52 Ⓐ Ⓑ Ⓒ Ⓓ	92 Ⓐ Ⓑ Ⓒ Ⓓ
13 Ⓐ Ⓑ Ⓒ Ⓓ	53 Ⓐ Ⓑ Ⓒ Ⓓ	93 Ⓐ Ⓑ Ⓒ Ⓓ
14 Ⓐ Ⓑ Ⓒ Ⓓ	54 Ⓐ Ⓑ Ⓒ Ⓓ	94 Ⓐ Ⓑ Ⓒ Ⓓ
15 Ⓐ Ⓑ Ⓒ Ⓓ	55 Ⓐ Ⓑ Ⓒ Ⓓ	95 Ⓐ Ⓑ Ⓒ Ⓓ
16 Ⓐ Ⓑ Ⓒ Ⓓ	56 Ⓐ Ⓑ Ⓒ Ⓓ	96 Ⓐ Ⓑ Ⓒ Ⓓ
17 Ⓐ Ⓑ Ⓒ Ⓓ	57 Ⓐ Ⓑ Ⓒ Ⓓ	97 Ⓐ Ⓑ Ⓒ Ⓓ
18 Ⓐ Ⓑ Ⓒ Ⓓ	58 Ⓐ Ⓑ Ⓒ Ⓓ	98 Ⓐ Ⓑ Ⓒ Ⓓ
19 Ⓐ Ⓑ Ⓒ Ⓓ	59 Ⓐ Ⓑ Ⓒ Ⓓ	99 Ⓐ Ⓑ Ⓒ Ⓓ
20 Ⓐ Ⓑ Ⓒ Ⓓ	60 Ⓐ Ⓑ Ⓒ Ⓓ	100 Ⓐ Ⓑ Ⓒ Ⓓ
21 Ⓐ Ⓑ Ⓒ Ⓓ	61 Ⓐ Ⓑ Ⓒ Ⓓ	
22 Ⓐ Ⓑ Ⓒ Ⓓ	62 Ⓐ Ⓑ Ⓒ Ⓓ	
23 Ⓐ Ⓑ Ⓒ Ⓓ	63 Ⓐ Ⓑ Ⓒ Ⓓ	
24 Ⓐ Ⓑ Ⓒ Ⓓ	64 Ⓐ Ⓑ Ⓒ Ⓓ	
25 Ⓐ Ⓑ Ⓒ Ⓓ	65 Ⓐ Ⓑ Ⓒ Ⓓ	
26 Ⓐ Ⓑ Ⓒ Ⓓ	66 Ⓐ Ⓑ Ⓒ Ⓓ	
27 Ⓐ Ⓑ Ⓒ Ⓓ	67 Ⓐ Ⓑ Ⓒ Ⓓ	
28 Ⓐ Ⓑ Ⓒ Ⓓ	68 Ⓐ Ⓑ Ⓒ Ⓓ	
29 Ⓐ Ⓑ Ⓒ Ⓓ	69 Ⓐ Ⓑ Ⓒ Ⓓ	
30 Ⓐ Ⓑ Ⓒ Ⓓ	70 Ⓐ Ⓑ Ⓒ Ⓓ	
31 Ⓐ Ⓑ Ⓒ Ⓓ	71 Ⓐ Ⓑ Ⓒ Ⓓ	
32 Ⓐ Ⓑ Ⓒ Ⓓ	72 Ⓐ Ⓑ Ⓒ Ⓓ	
33 Ⓐ Ⓑ Ⓒ Ⓓ	73 Ⓐ Ⓑ Ⓒ Ⓓ	
34 Ⓐ Ⓑ Ⓒ Ⓓ	74 Ⓐ Ⓑ Ⓒ Ⓓ	
35 Ⓐ Ⓑ Ⓒ Ⓓ	75 Ⓐ Ⓑ Ⓒ Ⓓ	
36 Ⓐ Ⓑ Ⓒ Ⓓ	76 Ⓐ Ⓑ Ⓒ Ⓓ	
37 Ⓐ Ⓑ Ⓒ Ⓓ	77 Ⓐ Ⓑ Ⓒ Ⓓ	
38 Ⓐ Ⓑ Ⓒ Ⓓ	78 Ⓐ Ⓑ Ⓒ Ⓓ	
39 Ⓐ Ⓑ Ⓒ Ⓓ	79 Ⓐ Ⓑ Ⓒ Ⓓ	
40 Ⓐ Ⓑ Ⓒ Ⓓ	80 Ⓐ Ⓑ Ⓒ Ⓓ	

Multiple-Choice Questions

Time: 80 minutes

Directions: Choose the best answer from the choices provided for each question.

1. The oxygen released by plants and other autotrophs during photosynthesis derives from which of the following sources?

    (A) H_2O_2

    (B) H_2O

    (C) OH^-

    (D) CO_2

    (E) CO

2. Both prokaryotic and eukaryotic cells possess which of the following:

    (A) Cell wall and spliceosomes

    (B) DNA and ribosomes

    (C) Plasma membrane and mitochondria

    (D) Flagella and Golgi apparatus

    (E) Endoplasmic reticulum and chloroplasts

3. Which of the following are most closely related to humans?

    (A) Enterobacteria

    (B) Cyanobacteria

    (C) Benthic archaea

    (D) Viroids

    (E) Amoeba

4. The evolution of eukaryotes was most directly enabled by which of the following?

    (A) Diversification within the prokaryotes

    (B) Chemical evolution of organic polymers

    (C) Evolutionary split between prokaryotes and archaea

    (D) Prokaryotic autotrophs increasing atmospheric oxygen

    (E) Decrease of the Earth's surface temperature

5. Which of the following types of organisms likely spends the smallest portion of its life cycle in the diploid state?

    (A) Gymnosperms

    (B) Mammals

    (C) Reptiles

    (D) Fungi

    (E) Angiosperms

6. Which of the following infectious agents contains no genetic information?

    (A) Retrovirus

    (B) Staphylococcus

    (C) Prion

    (D) Phage

    (E) Pneumococcus

7. The major functions of a sperm cell are to transport themselves and the genetic cargo they carry within them. Which are the cell structures most likely to be found in sperm?

    (A) Mitochondria, nucleus, flagellum

    (B) Chloroplast, nucleus, flagellum

    (C) Mitochondria, nucleus, cilia

    (D) Mitochondria, nucleus, ribosomes

    (E) Mitochondria, vacuole, flagellum

8. Of the following materials, which do NOT pass through the tubules of the nephron?

    (A) Water

    (B) Glucose

    (C) Urea

    (D) Proteins

    (E) Sodium

Go on to next page

9. Which of the following organisms contributes most to the foundation of its trophic system?

   (A) Jellyfish

   (B) Blue whale

   (C) Plankton

   (D) Squid

   (E) Lobster

10. A somatic cell within a certain eukaryote contains 12 chromosomes. The cell is within interphase. Another cell within the same organism has just completed meiosis I. How many chromosomes and chromatids are within each meiotically divided cell?

    (A) 12, 24

    (B) 6, 12

    (C) 6, 6

    (D) 12, 12

    (E) 24, 24

11. Ectrodactyly is a rare genetic disorder associated with a clawlike deformation of the hands. If a male and female each exhibiting the ectrodactylic phenotype produce a child with normal hands, the genotypes of the mother, father, and child must be:

    (A) AA, AA, aa

    (B) Aa, Aa, aa

    (C) Aa, Aa, AA

    (D) aa, aA, aa

    (E) aa, AA, Aa

12. A bacterial cell swimming towards dissolved nutrients is an example of:

    (A) Migration

    (B) Kinesis

    (C) Nutritropism

    (D) Aversion

    (E) Taxis

13. Which of the following statements is true about ribonucleic acid?

    I.   RNA carries genetic information

    II. RNA can serve structural and catalytic roles

    III. All replicating organisms contain RNA

    (A) I only

    (B) II only

    (C) III only

    (D) I and II only

    (E) I, II, and III

14. Sensors in the circulatory system of a dog detect a drop in blood pH. Which of the following organ systems increases its activity in response?

    (A) Respiratory system

    (B) Nervous system

    (C) Endocrine system

    (D) Digestive system

    (E) Circulatory system

15. A toxin that cleaves certain lipids enters a eukaryotic cell. Which of the following organelles is least likely to be directly impacted by the toxin?

    (A) Nucleus

    (B) Endoplasmic reticulum

    (C) Ribosome

    (D) Golgi apparatus

    (E) Lysosome

16. All of the following processes generate a net gain of ATP EXCEPT:

    (A) Respiratory pathways of the cytoplasm

    (B) Respiratory pathways of the mitochondria

    (C) Oxidative phosphorylation

    (D) Glycolysis

    (E) Calvin cycle

Go on to next page

17. A pedestrian steps off a corner and suddenly notices a speeding bus approaching him. Which of the following responses would most likely occur within the pedestrian's digestive system?

    (A) Increased secretion of bile

    (B) Increased hydrolytic activity within the duodenum

    (C) Decreased secretion of glucagon

    (D) Increased hydrolysis of glycogen

    (E) Increased secretion of insulin

18. In a taiga biome, which of the following types of organism would most likely be a primary producer?

    (A) Red algae

    (B) Green algae

    (C) Gymnosperm

    (D) Diatom

    (E) Leafy shrub

19. Some archaea are known as extremophiles for their ability to survive in environments of extreme:

    I. temperature

    II. Salinity

    III. CH_4 concentration

    (A) I only

    (B) II only

    (C) III only

    (D) I and II only

    (E) I, II, and III

20. Which of the following structures or processes is least involved with thermoregulation?

    (A) Blood vessel dilation

    (B) Blood vessel contraction

    (C) Secretions from glands in the skin

    (D) Esophageal peristalsis

    (E) Respiratory rate

21. Given the recombination frequencies listed in the table below, what are the relative positions of the four genes?

Genes	Map Units
A and B	5
B and C	9
B and D	16
A and D	11
A and C	14

    (A) ABCD

    (B) ACBD

    (C) BCAD

    (D) BCDA

    (E) DABC

22. During infection of a cell, a retroviral reverse transcriptase makes an error. Which of the following biopolymers is incorrectly synthesized?

    (A) mRNA

    (B) viral DNA

    (C) host DNA

    (D) mtDNA

    (E) rRNA

23. Each of the following processes requires ATP hydrolysis EXCEPT:

    (A) Facilitated diffusion of urea

    (B) Antibiotic export through bacterial efflux pumps

    (C) Sarcomere contraction

    (D) Flagellar movement

    (E) Translation of polypeptides

Go on to next page

24. A child undergoes infection by the same bacterial strain twice in the same year. The second time the child gets infected, the symptoms are far less severe and persist for a shorter time. Which cells are most responsible for the diminished effects of the second infection?

    (A) Plasma cells

    (B) Erythrocytes

    (C) Cytotoxic T cells

    (D) Helper T cells

    (E) Memory cells

25. Viruses and bacteria may both have each of the following structures EXCEPT:

    (A) Proteins

    (B) RNA

    (C) DNA

    (D) Membrane

    (E) Peptidoglycan

26. pH measurements are made on two solutions. The first solution is at pH 7.5 and the second is at pH 9.5. What is the concentration of H⁺ in the first solution relative to the second solution?

    (A) Twice as concentrated

    (B) Twice as diluted

    (C) One hundred times more concentrated

    (D) One hundred times more dilute

    (E) Two hundred times more concentrated

27. Which of the following statements are true of pulmonary arteries?

    I.   Carry oxygenated blood

    II. Carry blood to the lungs

    III. Are part of the systemic circuit

    (A) I only

    (B) II only

    (C) III only

    (D) I and II only

    (E) II and III only

28. An organism exhibits a dominant phenotype. How can you determine its genotype?

    (A) Cross it with organisms that also have the dominant phenotype

    (B) Cross it with heterozygous organisms

    (C) Cross it with organisms of intermediate phenotype

    (D) Cross it with homozygous recessive organisms

    (E) Cross it with homozygous dominant organisms

29. Which of the following types of molecule necessarily contains nitrogen?

    I.   Lipids

    II. amino acids

    III. nucleotides

    (A) I only

    (B) II only

    (C) III only

    (D) I and II only

    (E) II and III only

30. A eukaryotic cell incurs a mutation. The mutation impairs a gene that codes for a protein that facilitates vesicle fusion. Which of the following processes could be most directly affected by the mutation?

    (A) Translation at the rough endoplasmic reticulum

    (B) Nuclear export of mRNAs

    (C) Secretion of peptide hormones

    (D) Respiratory chemiosmosis

    (E) Transcription of genes involved with lipid synthesis

31. A pack of hyenas follow a pride of lions. After lions feast on their kills and depart, the hyenas move in to feed on whatever remains. The relationship between the hyenas and the lions is best described as:

    (A) Predation

    (B) Commensalism

    (C) Parasitism

    (D) Mutualism

    (E) Competition

Go on to next page

32. Characteristic properties of this taxon include hyphae and long periods in haploid state.

    (A) Protists

    (B) Monera

    (C) Plants

    (D) Archaea

    (E) Fungi

33. Neurotransmitter release is most directly triggered by:

    (A) Sodium influx

    (B) Sodium efflux

    (C) Calcium influx

    (D) Calcium efflux

    (E) Potassium influx

34. Respectively, veins and arteries typically have the following characteristics:

    (A) Thick walls, valves

    (B) Thin walls, valves

    (C) Valves, thin walls

    (D) Valves, thick walls

    (E) Thick walls, thin walls

35. The substances responsible for digestion of fats include:

    I.   Lipase

    II. Chymotrypsin

    III. Bile

    (A) I only

    (B) II only

    (C) III only

    (D) I and II only

    (E) I and III only

36. The following tissues possess sarcomeres:

    I.   Skeletal muscle

    II. Smooth muscle

    III. Cardiac muscle

    (A) I only

    (B) II only

    (C) III only

    (D) I and III only

    (E) II and III only

37. In humans, fertilization occurs within the:

    (A) Vas deferens

    (B) Fallopian tube

    (C) Uterus

    (D) Ovarian follicle

    (E) Endometrium

38. The replication of a certain organism involves the synthesis of concatemers. Among the following choices, the organism is most likely:

    (A) *Eschericia coli*

    (B) Feline immunodeficiency virus

    (C) *Saccharomyces cerevisiae*

    (D) *Canis lupus*

    (E) *Drosophila*

39. A child possesses 47 chromosomes within each somatic cell. What is the best description for this child's condition?

    (A) Polyploidy

    (B) Triploidy

    (C) Trisomy

    (D) Monosomy

    (E) Euploidy

40. The key attribute conferred by the structure of root hairs and microvili is:

    (A) Selective permeability

    (B) Defense against infectious attack

    (C) Environmental monitoring

    (D) Absorptive surface area

    (E) Osmoregulation

Go on to next page

41. Which pieces of evidence support the endosymbiotic theory of eukaryotic evolution?

    I.   Mitochondria replicate by division

    II. Chloroplasts possess DNA distinct from nuclear DNA

    III. Mitochondrial inner membranes resemble those of prokaryotes

    (A) I only

    (B) II only

    (C) III only

    (D) I and III only

    (E) I, II, and III

42. Codon bias is a tendency for different organisms to employ some synonymous codons more than others within genes. Extreme codon bias would be most apparent in which of the following?

    (A) The amino acid composition of proteins

    (B) The proportions of A, G, C, and T nucleotides

    (C) The representation of different tRNAs

    (D) Transcriptional regulation

    (E) Post-transcriptional regulation

43. What is the most likely evolutionary advantage of sexual reproduction?

    (A) Sexual reproduction is more efficient than asexual reproduction

    (B) Sexual reproduction minimizes adverse mutations

    (C) Sexual reproduction is associated with faster replication

    (D) Sexual reproduction leads to significant genetic recombination

    (E) Sexual reproduction is associated with more numerous offspring

44. Which group is thought to most closely resemble the first living cells?

    (A) Cyanobacteria

    (B) Archaebacteria

    (C) Eubacteria

    (D) Proteobacteria

    (E) Protists

45. Under low-oxygen conditions, yeast generate ATP by doing which of the following?

    (A) Reductive phosphorylation

    (B) Glycolysis

    (C) Gluconeogenesis

    (D) Chemiosmosis

    (E) They do not generate ATP in these conditions

46. Which of the following is a likely effect of sympathetic nervous activity?

    (A) Increased digestion

    (B) Decreased blood pressure

    (C) Decreased bladder constriction

    (D) Decreased pulse

    (E) Contraction of vessels

47. The light-independent reactions of photosynthesis:

    I.   Do not occur in the presence of light

    II. Reduce carbon dioxide

    III. Consume ATP

    (A) I only

    (B) II only

    (C) III only

    (D) II and III only

    (E) I, II, and III

48. Logistic or S-shaped population growth is primarily enforced by:

    (A) Growth rate

    (B) Density-dependent factors

    (C) Density-independent factors

    (D) Predation

    (E) Carrying capacity

Go on to next page

49. Action potentials:

    I.   Occur when membrane potentials are inside-positive

    II. Have strength that depends on the stimulus strength

    III. Are propagating, local depolarizations

    (A) I only

    (B) II only

    (C) III only

    (D) I and II only

    (E) I and III only

50. Which of the following are the most chemically similar?

    (A) Cellulose and glycogen

    (B) Hemoglobin and tRNA

    (C) Lipid bilayers and steroids

    (D) Peptidoglycan and chitin

    (E) Water and ethanol

51. The following processes employ DNA-RNA hybrids:

    I.   DNA replication

    II. Transcription

    III. Translation

    (A) I only

    (B) II only

    (C) III only

    (D) I and II only

    (E) II and III only

52. Which of the following is unnecessary for adaptation?

    (A) Replication

    (B) Selection

    (C) Time

    (D) Competition

    (E) Variation

53. Which of the following structures is most closely associated with the hypothalamus?

    (A) Pons

    (B) Pituitary gland

    (C) Cerebellum

    (D) Cerebrum

    (E) Pineal gland

54. In which structure of the eye are photons used to activate ion channels?

    (A) Cornea

    (B) Lens

    (C) Sclera

    (D) Optic nerve

    (E) Retina

55. All of the following phenomena are consistent with Mendelian inheritance except?

    (A) Independent assortment of chromosomes during meiosis

    (B) Masking of one allele by another allele

    (C) AB blood types

    (D) Phenotypes with more than one possible genotype

    (E) Offspring with phenotypes not present in their parents

56. An operon codes for a group of proteins that work together to synthesize a nucleotide precursor. A regulatory protein associated with the operon binds that precursor. The nucleotide precursor probably acts as:

    (A) An enzyme inhibitor

    (B) An inducer

    (C) A co-repressor

    (D) A repressor

    (E) A silencer

57. What is the source of the electrons that become energized within the photosystems of chlorophyll?

    (A) Carbon dioxide

    (B) NADPH

    (C) Oxygen

    (D) Water

    (E) $FADH_2$

Go on to next page

58. All of the following types of organism possess both male and female reproductive parts within the same structure EXCEPT:

    (A) Cherry trees

    (B) Orchids

    (C) Monocots

    (D) Dicots

    (E) Spruce trees

59. From earliest to latest, which best describes the progression of developmental structures?

    (A) Blastula, gastrula, zygote

    (B) Gastrula, blastula, zygote

    (C) Gastrula, zygote, blastula

    (D) Zygote, gastrula, blastula

    (E) Zygote, blastula, gastrula

60. Among five human populations, with all else being equal, the population that will grow most rapidly in the next few decades is the one with the greatest proportion of people in which age group?

    (A) 10–20 years

    (B) 20–30 years

    (C) 30–40 years

    (D) 40–50 years

    (E) 50–60 years

Questions 61–64

    (A) Primary structure

    (B) Secondary structure

    (C) Hydrophilic effect

    (D) Quaternary structure

    (E) Hydrophobic effect

61. Major difference between the structures of hemoglobin and myoglobin

62. Regularly repeating structural elements

63. Results in uneven distributions of polar and nonpolar amino acids to the interior and exterior of protein structures

64. Directly determined by genetic information

Questions 65–69

    (A) Monocots

    (B) Dicots

    (C) Angiosperms

    (D) Gymnosperms

    (E) Bryophytes

65. Pollen must travel between male and female cones

66. Lack vasculature

67. Have branching roots and leaves with parallel veins

68. Have taproots and leaves with branching veins

69. Ova and pollen reside within the same structure

Questions 70–74

    (A) Activation energy

    (B) Competitive inhibitor

    (C) Noncompetitive inhibitor

    (D) Catalyst

    (E) Free energy change

70. Can be overcome with sufficiently high substrate concentration

71. Lowers the energy of a transition state

72. Binds to an enzyme in a location other than the active site

73. Determines the rate of reaction

74. Determines the spontaneity of reaction

Go on to next page

Questions 75–79

Refer to the following phylogeny to answer questions 75–79.

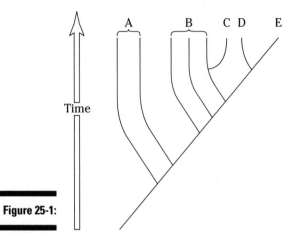

Time

Figure 25-1:

Choose the letter of the phylogenetic branch that best matches the group listed in each question.

75. Animals

76. Protists

77. Plants

78. Prokaryotes

79. Fungi

Go on to next page

Questions 80–83

The bar graph below represents the relative abundance of five species within the same community. Refer to this graph to answer questions 80–83.

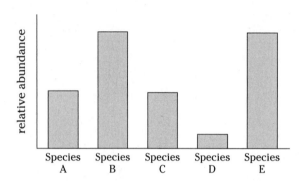

Figure 25-2:

80. The graph suggests that species C is probably a:

(A) Detritivore

(B) Primary producer

(C) Primary consumer

(D) Secondary consumer

(E) Predator

81. Supposing the species in the graph inhabit a marine community, species D would most likely be:

(A) Green algae

(B) Shrimp

(C) Herring

(D) Shark

(E) Baleen whale

82. If the population of species D diminished, which species are most likely to increase in population?

(A) A and B

(B) A and C

(C) B and C

(D) B and E

(E) C and E

83. Which of the following is the most likely food chain that includes these species?

(A) E → B → D

(B) B → A → D

(C) D→ C → B

(D) D →E → A

(E) A → E → D

Go on to next page

Questions 84–85

The curves within the diagram below depict the dependence of oxygen solubility in water on temperature and on salinity (i.e., concentration of dissolved salt). Use the diagram to answer questions 84–85.

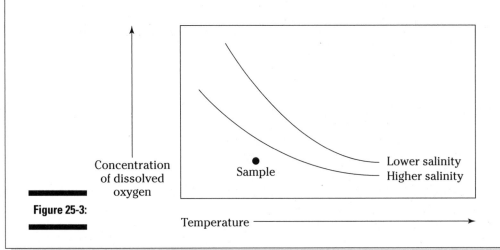

Figure 25-3:

84. Under what conditions is oxygen most soluble in water?

   (A) High temperature, high salinity

   (B) High temperature, low salinity

   (C) Low temperature, high salinity

   (D) Low temperature, low salinity

   (E) Moderate temperature, moderate salinity

85. In a certain deep lake, the water temperature decreases with increasing depth. A sample of water is collected from a depth near the bottom of the lake; the temperature at that depth is measured, and the concentration of dissolved oxygen in the sample is measured. The results of the sample analysis are shown in the figure. What is the most likely explanation for the measured concentration of dissolved oxygen?

   (A) The deeper waters of the lake are very saline

   (B) An abundance of respiring organisms in the deep water consume much of the oxygen

   (C) Mineral matter on the lake's bottom constantly oxidizes, sequestering the free oxygen from the water

   (D) High water pressure in the deep water limits oxygen solubility

   (E) Light doesn't penetrate into the deep water, so photosynthetic organisms don't produce oxygen

Go on to next page

Questions 86–89

The figure below depicts interactions between two water molecules, a sodium cation and a molecule of ammonia. Refer to the figure and to the five choices to answer questions 86–89.

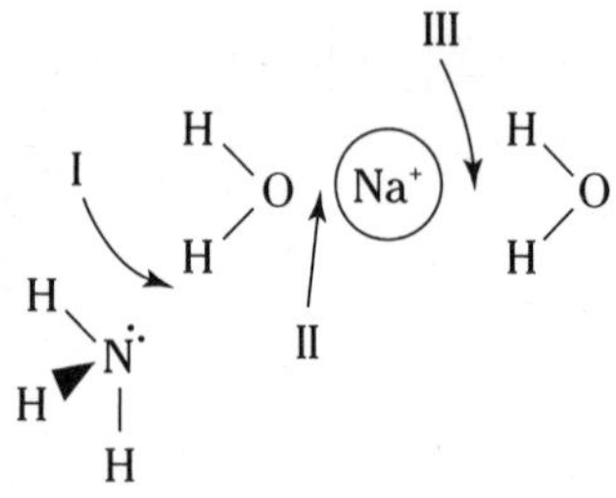

Figure 25-4:

(A) Interaction I only

(B) Interaction II only

(C) Interaction III only

(D) Interactions I and II

(E) Interactions II and III

86. Which interaction(s) are ion-dipole interactions

87. Which interaction(s) are hydrogen bonding interactions

88. Which interaction(s) are attractive?

89. Which interaction(s) are repulsive?

Go on to next page

Questions 90–94

Refer to the figure below and to the provided choices to answer questions 90–94.

Regulatory gene

Figure 25-5:

(A) Regulatory gene

(B) Operon

(C) Repressor

(D) Co-repressor

(E) Inducer

90. The entire transcriptional unit in the figure

91. Structure II, which competes with RNA polymerase

92. Structure III, if that molecule inactivates structure II

93. Structure III, if that molecule activates structure II

94. Sequence I, if that sequence expresses structure II

Go on to next page

Questions 95–97

The figure below depicts various mechanisms by which hormones can exert their effects. Use the figure to answer questions 95–97.

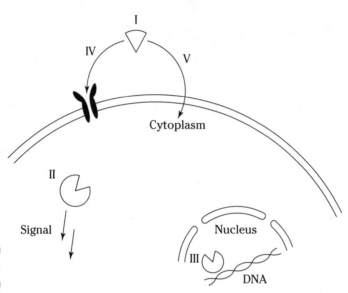

Figure 25-6:

95. If hormone I is a steroid, it most likely:

    (A) Enters the cell by path IV, binds to receptor II

    (B) Enters the cell by path V, binds to receptor II

    (C) Enters the cell by path IV, binds to receptor III

    (D) Enters the cell by path V, binds to receptor III

    (E) Does not enter the cell

96. If hormone I is a peptide, it most likely:

    (A) Enters the cell by path IV, binds to receptor II

    (B) Enters the cell by path V, binds to receptor II

    (C) Enters the cell by path IV, binds to receptor III

    (D) Enters the cell by path V, binds to receptor III

    (E) Does not enter the cell

97. The usual chemical properties of the classes of hormone that enter the cell by paths IV and V, respectively, are:

    (A) Polar, nonpolar

    (B) Nonpolar, polar

    (C) Polar, polar

    (D) Nonpolar, nonpolar

    (E) None of the above

Questions 98–100

Choose from the following to answer questions 98–100.

    (A) Operant conditioning

    (B) Classical conditioning

    (C) Habituation

    (D) Imprinting

    (E) Fixed action pattern

98. The loss of an association

99. Trial and error learning

100. Irreversible learning during a critical period

Go on to next page

Four Free-Response Questions with Grading Outline

Time: 10 minutes to read the questions, 90 minutes to answer

Directions: Answer the following free-response questions, addressing each part. You may include diagrams to support your answers, but each answer should be in essay form.

1. Water has unique physical and chemical properties that have enabled it to serve critical functions in biology. Identify four such properties and, a) explain their physical basis, and b) describe their importance to biology.

2. Describe the cellular and molecular structures and events that result in the contraction of striated muscle. Include an explanation of the event that triggers contraction.

3. Describe the structure of a plasma membrane and describe the role of the membrane in cellular homeostasis as well as in oxidative phosphorylation.

4. Previously, diabetics treated themselves with insulin that was laboriously purified from pigs. Today, most diabetics inject themselves with "recombinant" human insulin that has been purified from bacterial culture. Describe a way to engineer bacteria to produce human insulin, make detailed reference to at least three major molecular biological techniques.

Grading Outline for Question 1 (*10 points*):

✓ **Identify unique properties of water (*2 points*):** highly polar, hydrogen bonding ability, adhesive and cohesive properties, surface tension, large heat capacity, self-ionization, solid form less dense than liquid

✓ **Explain water behavior in terms of fundamental properties (*4 points*):** polarity contributes to all the others, high charge separation between oxygen atom and two hydrogen atoms produces a permanent dipole, dipole leads to solvent properties and self-ionization, hydrogen bonding leads to adhesive and cohesive properties, surface tension, heat capacity, and idealized ice crystal

✓ **Give examples of each property functioning in biology (*4 points*):** adhesion and cohesion produce transpiration, heat capacity allows bodies of water to serve a climate-moderating heat sinks, water-filled bodies maintain internal temperature, evaporative cooling effect of sweat, ice floats over liquid water, pH buffers work in water

Grading Outline for Question 2 (*15 points*):

✓ **Impulse transmission at neuromuscular junction (*5 points*):** action potential from motor neuron induces calcium influx at presynaptic terminal, calcium triggers acetylcholine release into synapse via exocytotic vesicles, acetylcholine activates receptors at postsynaptic terminal, binding triggers depolarization

✓ **Contraction of muscle fiber (*10 points*):**

- Sufficient depolarization opens voltage-gated ion channels, triggers an action potential, action potential propagates along muscle fiber membrane, its spread facilitated by transverse tubules, calcium flows in from reservoir in sarcoplasmic reticulum

- Calcium binds troponin, calcium-bound troponin displaces tropomyosin, tropomyosin displacement exposes actin, myosin headgroups attach to actin, ATP hydrolyzed to drive power stroke of myosin, new ATP needs to bind to release complex, sliding actin and myosin filaments intercalated within each sarcomere

Grading Outline for Question 3 (*12 points*):

- ✔ **Plasma membrane structure (*4 points*):** phospholipid bilayer, polar headgroups exposed to solvent, lipids tailgroups sequestered in bilayer interior, proteins within membrane act as sensors and as transport channels (active transport, facilitated diffusion), sterols maintain membrane fluidity, fluid mosaic model

- ✔ **Role of plasma membrane in cellular homeostasis (*4 points*):** selectively permeable barrier, wastes diffuse out down gradient, nutrients selectively allowed to enter or are imported, transport through selective protein channels or via endocytosis/exocytosis

- ✔ **Role of plasma membrane in oxidative phosphorylation (*4 points*):** provides the membrane that enables chemiosmosis, electrons descending the electron transport chain release energy that is used to pump hydrogen ions into mitochondrial intermembrane space, against both charge and concentration gradients, reservoir of hydrogen ions is released through ATP synthase to make ATP

Grading Outline for Question 4 (*12 points*):

- ✔ **Isolate target gene (*4 points*):** use polymerase chain reaction to amplify gene directly from human DNA or assemble gene from synthetic DNA fragments, fuse gene with highly active bacterial promoter sequence

- ✔ **Generate recombinant plasmid (*4 points*):** digest plasmid DNA and amplified insulin gene DNA with same set of two different restriction ezymes, restriction enzymes recognize 6–8 basepair palindromic sequences and cut, leaving complementary overhangs, assemble and ligate (with ligase) recombinant plasmid with insulin gene insert

- ✔ **Transform bacteria and harvest insulin (*4 points*):** Transform bacteria by using chemical or physical means to promote uptake of external DNA, grow up recombinant bacteria in selective media for homogenous cultures, induce expression of insulin, either harvest and purify bacteria or add tag to insulin gene that promotes secretion of peptide

Chapter 26

Answers to Test 1

. . . .

In This Chapter

▶ Answer key to Test 1

▶ Explanations of the answers

. . . .

Well, you've laid it all on the line. Here's where the line lays it all on you. See on which side of the line your answers fall. If they fall hard on the wrong side, just pick them up, dust them off, and give them a shot with Test 2.

1. B. During the light-dependent reactions, water is split and molecular oxygen is released.

2. B. Bacteria need genes and proteins too.

3. E. Amoeba are single-celled eukaryotes.

4. D. The increase in atmospheric oxygen drove the evolution of aerobic respiration and enabled the elaborate eukaryotic way of life.

5. D. Fungi use both sexual and asexual modes of reproduction, involving long-lived haploid states.

6. C. Prions are entirely protein and propagate through contact with other proteins.

7. A. Sperm need energy, genes, and a means of locomotion.

8. D. Proteins are too large to pass through the glomerulus.

9. C. Plankton are primary producers.

10. B. After meiosis I, homologous chromosomes are separated, but each still has two sister chromatids.

11. B. If both parents had the phenotype and produced an unaffected child, the disorder can't be recessive; it must be dominant, with each heterozygous parent giving a normal, recessive allele to the child.

12. E. Taxis is directed movement toward or away from a stimulus.

13. D. mRNAs carry genetic information, tRNAs (and others) are structural, rRNA, spliceosomal RNAs (and others) are catalytic, but viruses are replicating organisms that may possess only DNA.

14. A. Low blood pH signifies excess carbon dioxide in the form of carbonic acid, and triggers increased respiratory rate.

15. C. All the listed organelles except ribosomes contain significant membrane components.

16. E. The Calvin cycle expends ATP to fix carbon dioxide in the form of sugar.

17. D. Emergencies activate the sympathetic nervous system, which makes quick energy readily available.

18. C. Gymnosperms like pine trees are the only listed primary producers that thrive in taiga.

19. E. Archaea are resourceful and tough.

20. D. Esophageal peristalsis simply moves chewed food down to the stomach.

21. E. Recombination frequency during crossing over increases with the distance between genes. Map units are a measure of recombination frequency that is directly proportional to distance.

22. B. Reverse transcriptase makes a DNA copy of the retroviral RNA genome.

23. A. Facilitated diffusion is still diffusion, and therefore is a form of passive transport.

24. E. Memory cells retain a molecular memory of an invader; this memory facilitates a rapid, specific immune response in the event of a second infection.

25. E. Viruses have lots of variations, but peptidoglycan occurs only in bacterial cell walls.

26. C. $pH = -\log [H^+]$. Lower pH means more hydrogen ion, and pH is on a log scale, so two units means 10^2.

27. B. Pulmonary arteries are part of the pulmonary circuit, carrying deoxygenated blood from the heart to the lungs.

28. D. A Mendelian test cross is a cross with a homozygous recessive individual. The phenotypic ratios of the offspring can be diagnosed for the unknown genotype of the parent.

29. E. Amino acids have amino groups and nucleotides have nitrogenous bases.

30. C. Secretion occurs via exocytosis of vesicles containing the secreted molecule. Exocytosis relies on membrane-membrane fusion.

31. B. In commensalism, one party benefits while the other neither gains nor loses.

32. E. Hyphae and haploid states are hallmarks of fungi.

33. C. Calcium cation influx triggers fusion of neurotransmitter-containing vesicles with the pre-synaptic membrane.

34. D. Veins have valves to prevent backflow in low pressure conditions. Arteries have muscular, thick walls to control flow in high pressure conditions.

35. E. Bile dissolves fats and lipase hydrolyzes fats. Chymotrypsin hydrolyzes proteins.

36. D. Skeletal and cardiac muscle are striated because they contain sarcomeres, which are absent in smooth muscle.

37. B. Sperm must make a long journey to the Fallopian tube in order to find an egg.

38. A. Bacteria (e.g., *E. coli*) often replicate plasmids along with their major chromosome. Plasmid replication occurs via a rolling circle mechanism that involves synthesis of connected plasmid repeats called concatemers.

39. C. Trisomy is three copies of a chromosome. Triploidy is three copies of all the chromosomes.

40. D. In biology, branches and folds are almost always about increasing surface area.

41. E. Each piece of evidence paints a picture of an organelle formerly known as an organism.

42. C. In order to accommodate the biased use of codons, the organism requires a biased set of anticodons.

43. D. The crossing over and independent assortment of chromosomes during meiosis are key sources of genetic recombination; recombination provides variation that allows species to adapt to their environment over generations.

44. B. Archaea and eubacteria are the best approximations we have today of those ancient cells, and the extremities and peculiarities of archaea make them the better bet.

45. B. Under low oxygen conditions, yeast engage in fermentation (i.e., anaerobic respiration), which functions to ensure that at least the meager ATP profits of glycolysis can still be had.

46. C. The sympathetic nervous system produces the fight-or-flight response, which is occasionally accompanied by the pee-your-pants response.

47. D. The light-independent reactions simply don't require light; they can still operate in the presence of light.

48. E. Logistic growth curves are the result of exponential growth limited by a carrying capacity.

49. E. Action potentials are an all-or-nothing response; once triggered, their strength is independent of the strength of the stimulus.

50. A. Cellulose and glycogen are both polymers of glucose.

51. D. Transcription exploits RNA-DNA basepairing to make RNA transcripts from genes. DNA replication begins with an RNA primer. Translation does not directly involve DNA.

52. D. Competition is only one source of selection pressure.

53. B. The hypothalamus and the pituitary work closely together to coordinate diverse body functions.

54. E. The retina contains the eye's photoreceptors, which convert optical information into nerve impulses that can be interpreted in the brain.

55. C. The AB blood type is an example of codominance, a non-Mendelian phenomenon.

56. C. The nucleotide precursor acts as a feedback inhibitor, preventing an excess of itself.

57. D. At the beginning of the light-dependent reactions, water is split to provide the electrons that will be energized by incoming light and sent down the electron transport chain.

58. E. Spruce trees are conifers, gymnosperms in which each cone-bearing tree is either male or female. All the others are angiosperms, flowering plants whose flowers contain both male and female reproductive structures.

59. E. Zygotes blast gas.

60. A. Pyramid-shaped populations, with the greatest proportion of young people, are the ones that will grow the fastest.

61. D. Myoglobin acts as a monomeric protein; hemoglobin acts as a tetramer.

62. B. α-helices and β-sheets are regular, repeating structural elements stabilized by backbone-backbone interactions.

63. E. The hydrophobic effect drives protein tertiary folding, tending to sequester hydrophobic parts to the inside of a folded protein structure.

64. A. DNA codes for RNA. RNA codes for the amino acid sequence of a protein.

65. D. Cone-bearing gymnosperm plants are either male or female.

66. E. Bryophytes were early-evolving plants that lack xylem and phloem.

67. A. Monocots branch below ground and play it straight above ground.

68. B. Dicots do the opposite of monocots.

69. C. Angiosperms produce flowers, which have both egg-bearing ovaries and pollen-bearing anthers.

70. B. Competitive inhibitors bind at the active site of an enzyme, competing with substrate.

71. D. Catalysts accelerate reactions by decreasing the activation energy of a reaction; this can be done by lowering the transition state energy, increasing the ground state energy of the reactant, or both.

72. C. Noncompetitve inhibitors don't compete with substrate for the enzyme's active site, so their effects can't be overcome by adding more substrate.

73. A. The activation energy is the difference between the transition state energy and the ground state energy of the reactant, and determines the rate (i.e., the kinetics) of the reaction.

74. E. The difference in free energy between the product and the reactant of a reaction determines the extent to which the reaction will happen on its own (i.e., the equilibrium).

75. E. Animals are the most recent kingdom to grace the planet.

76. B. Protists are a diverse (i.e., multi-branched) kingdom, and the evolutionary forebears of plants.

77. C. Plants evolved relatively recently from protists.

78. A. Prokaryotes go way back.

79. D. Fungi and animals share a more recent common ancestor than do plants and animals.

80. C. With its second-tier abundance, species C is probably an organism that eats primary producers, and is therefore a primary consumer.

81. D. Because it is the least abundant, species D is probably high up the food chain, and may be a predator, like a shark.

82. B. Since the predators prey on those in the trophic level below them, species A and C would experience a population rebound if their tormenting hunter were to disappear.

83. B. Food chains tend to progress from the most abundant species to the least abundant species.

84. D. Higher temperatures cause dissolved gases to bubble out of solution, and dissolved solids compete with gases for water molecules. So, the less heat and the less salt, the more dissolved oxygen.

85. E. The sample contained less dissolved oxygen than was possible at its temperature and salinity. The most likely reason is that the sample originated from the aphotic zone, where photosynthetic organisms don't continually release oxygen into their aqueous environment.

86. E. The sodium cation interacts with the opposing dipoles of two different water molecules.

87. A. The lone pair of ammonia hydrogen bonds with an adjacent water.

88. D. Hydrogen bonding is attractive. Plus, the water molecule whose partial negative pole faces the sodium cation interacts with that ion favorably.

89. C. The water molecule whose partial positive pole faces the positively charged sodium ion interacts with the ion unfavorably.

90. B. Operons are multi-gene transcriptional units preceded by a single promoter.

91. C. Repressor proteins are the products of regulatory genes, and these proteins inhibit promoter binding by RNA polymerase.

92. E. By inactivating the repressor, the molecule induces transcription of the operon.

93. D. When it binds and activates the repressor protein, the molecule cooperates with the repressor in the act of inhibiting transcription of the operon.

94. A. Regulatory genes frequently reside upstream of the operon they regulate.

95. D. Steroid hormones are nonpolar, so can diffuse through plasma membranes. Once inside the cell, they tend to regulate transcription by binding transcriptional regulators in a complex within the nucleus.

96. A. Peptide hormones tend to be polar, so they must enter the cell with the help of membrane associated receptors. From that point, peptide hormones often act by binding regulatory proteins in a complex within the cytoplasm.

97. A. The different physicochemical properties of these types of hormones determine the pathway by which they can enter the cell.

98. C. Doing something out of habit means that the thing has lost its stimulatory impact, so you no longer form associations with it.

99. A. Trial and error learning is a form of operant conditioning. Did you guess right? If not, keep guessing . . . you see?

100. D. Imprinting happens young and it happens deeply. If only you'd started studying for this exam at birth.

Chapter 27

Test 2

*T*ake the following test under timed conditions to simulate the actual AP Biology exam. Then, check your work by using the answers and explanations provided in Chapter 28.

1 ⒶⒷⒸⒹ	41 ⒶⒷⒸⒹ	81 ⒶⒷⒸⒹ
2 ⒶⒷⒸⒹ	42 ⒶⒷⒸⒹ	82 ⒶⒷⒸⒹ
3 ⒶⒷⒸⒹ	43 ⒶⒷⒸⒹ	83 ⒶⒷⒸⒹ
4 ⒶⒷⒸⒹ	44 ⒶⒷⒸⒹ	84 ⒶⒷⒸⒹ
5 ⒶⒷⒸⒹ	45 ⒶⒷⒸⒹ	85 ⒶⒷⒸⒹ
6 ⒶⒷⒸⒹ	46 ⒶⒷⒸⒹ	86 ⒶⒷⒸⒹ
7 ⒶⒷⒸⒹ	47 ⒶⒷⒸⒹ	87 ⒶⒷⒸⒹ
8 ⒶⒷⒸⒹ	48 ⒶⒷⒸⒹ	88 ⒶⒷⒸⒹ
9 ⒶⒷⒸⒹ	49 ⒶⒷⒸⒹ	89 ⒶⒷⒸⒹ
10 ⒶⒷⒸⒹ	50 ⒶⒷⒸⒹ	90 ⒶⒷⒸⒹ
11 ⒶⒷⒸⒹ	51 ⒶⒷⒸⒹ	91 ⒶⒷⒸⒹ
12 ⒶⒷⒸⒹ	52 ⒶⒷⒸⒹ	92 ⒶⒷⒸⒹ
13 ⒶⒷⒸⒹ	53 ⒶⒷⒸⒹ	93 ⒶⒷⒸⒹ
14 ⒶⒷⒸⒹ	54 ⒶⒷⒸⒹ	94 ⒶⒷⒸⒹ
15 ⒶⒷⒸⒹ	55 ⒶⒷⒸⒹ	95 ⒶⒷⒸⒹ
16 ⒶⒷⒸⒹ	56 ⒶⒷⒸⒹ	96 ⒶⒷⒸⒹ
17 ⒶⒷⒸⒹ	57 ⒶⒷⒸⒹ	97 ⒶⒷⒸⒹ
18 ⒶⒷⒸⒹ	58 ⒶⒷⒸⒹ	98 ⒶⒷⒸⒹ
19 ⒶⒷⒸⒹ	59 ⒶⒷⒸⒹ	99 ⒶⒷⒸⒹ
20 ⒶⒷⒸⒹ	60 ⒶⒷⒸⒹ	100 ⒶⒷⒸⒹ
21 ⒶⒷⒸⒹ	61 ⒶⒷⒸⒹ	
22 ⒶⒷⒸⒹ	62 ⒶⒷⒸⒹ	
23 ⒶⒷⒸⒹ	63 ⒶⒷⒸⒹ	
24 ⒶⒷⒸⒹ	64 ⒶⒷⒸⒹ	
25 ⒶⒷⒸⒹ	65 ⒶⒷⒸⒹ	
26 ⒶⒷⒸⒹ	66 ⒶⒷⒸⒹ	
27 ⒶⒷⒸⒹ	67 ⒶⒷⒸⒹ	
28 ⒶⒷⒸⒹ	68 ⒶⒷⒸⒹ	
29 ⒶⒷⒸⒹ	69 ⒶⒷⒸⒹ	
30 ⒶⒷⒸⒹ	70 ⒶⒷⒸⒹ	
31 ⒶⒷⒸⒹ	71 ⒶⒷⒸⒹ	
32 ⒶⒷⒸⒹ	72 ⒶⒷⒸⒹ	
33 ⒶⒷⒸⒹ	73 ⒶⒷⒸⒹ	
34 ⒶⒷⒸⒹ	74 ⒶⒷⒸⒹ	
35 ⒶⒷⒸⒹ	75 ⒶⒷⒸⒹ	
36 ⒶⒷⒸⒹ	76 ⒶⒷⒸⒹ	
37 ⒶⒷⒸⒹ	77 ⒶⒷⒸⒹ	
38 ⒶⒷⒸⒹ	78 ⒶⒷⒸⒹ	
39 ⒶⒷⒸⒹ	79 ⒶⒷⒸⒹ	
40 ⒶⒷⒸⒹ	80 ⒶⒷⒸⒹ	

Multiple-Choice Questions

Time: 80 minutes

Directions: Choose the best answer from the choices provided for each question.

1. Which of the following groups exhibits radial symmetry?

    (A) Frogs

    (B) Sharks

    (C) Flatworms

    (D) Rotifers

    (E) Jellyfish

2. Which of the following is most involved in cell division?

    (A) Fibroblasts

    (B) Protein kinases

    (C) Ethylene

    (D) Abscisic acid

    (E) Amylase

3. The digestive tract of koalas contains an enlarged cecum where bacteria ferment masticated eucalyptus leaves. The koala benefits because it cannot otherwise digest the leaves. The bacteria benefit because they acquire nourishment from the leaves that the koala eats. This relationship is an example of:

    (A) Predation

    (B) Commensalism

    (C) Parasitism

    (D) Mutualism

    (E) Competition

4. All of the following are NOT the primary cargo within phloem EXCEPT:

    (A) Sugars

    (B) Phosphates

    (C) Ammonia

    (D) Nitrates

    (E) Chitin

5. The preponderance of evidence suggests that which kingdom is the oldest?

    (A) Animalia

    (B) Plantae

    (C) Monera

    (D) Fungi

    (E) Protista

6. A tRNA anticodon has the sequence 3'-UAC-5'. Which genetic instruction corresponds to this anitcodon?

    (A) Tyrosine

    (B) Histidine

    (C) Valine

    (D) Start

    (E) Stop

7. The main function of arteries is to:

    (A) Carry all blood

    (B) Carry blood to the heart

    (C) Carry blood away from the heart

    (D) Carry oxygenated blood

    (E) Carry deoxygenated blood

8. All of the following are functions of the stomach EXCEPT?

    (A) Mechanical digestion

    (B) Chemical digestion

    (C) Absorption of water

    (D) Mixing

    (E) Storage

Go on to next page

9. Which trophic level would contain the least biomass?

(A) Autotrophs

(B) Primary consumers

(C) Secondary consumers

(D) Herbivores

(E) Plants

10. If a cell produces a lot of protein, which of the following organelles would be especially numerous?

(A) Nucleus

(B) Mitochondria

(C) Microfilaments

(D) Lysosomes

(E) Ribosomes

11. A brown cow mates with a white cow. The resulting offspring has brown and white coloration. This is an example of:

(A) Complete dominance

(B) Codominance

(C) Incomplete dominance

(D) Partial dominance

(E) Genetic mutation

12. Depolarization occurs within an axon when:

(A) Sodium ions rush into the cell

(B) Potassium ions rush into the cell

(C) The sodium potassium pump moves various ions

(D) Calcium ions rush into the cell

(E) Neurotransmitters are released

13. Interphase includes all of the following EXCEPT:

(A) Production of proteins

(B) DNA synthesis

(C) Growth

(D) Cytokinesis

(E) Production of organelles

14. The wings of a bird are analogous to which of the following?

(A) Lobster claws

(B) Whale flippers

(C) Butterfly wings

(D) Human arms

(E) Frog forelimbs

15. Cytokinesis differs between plants and animals differs in that plants:

(A) Form a ring of microfilaments inside the plasma membrane between the two newly formed cells

(B) Form a cleavage furrow

(C) Possess identical sister chromatids

(D) Form a cell plate

(E) Use myosin to contract microfilaments

16. Which of the following is produced by the Krebs cycle?

(A) NADPH

(B) Pyruvate

(C) $1/2\ O_2$

(D) CO_2

(E) NAD^+

17. Transpiration occurs in 200-meter tall redwood trees primarily because:

(A) Root pressure pushes the water up

(B) Evaporation of water through the stomata pulls water up

(C) Gravity creates pressure within xylem

(D) Photosynthesis in the leaves requires water

(E) Water naturally moves from roots to leaves

Go on to next page

18. On an island, the size of a population of birds has remained constant for the past 200 years. What is the probable average number of offspring produced by each successfully breeding pair?

    (A) 0

    (B) 1

    (C) 2

    (D) 3

    (E) 4

19. Humans are evolutionarily closest to:

    (A) Tarsiers

    (B) Orangutans

    (C) Lemurs

    (D) Gorillas

    (E) Chimpanzees

20. Which of the following two organ systems are least functionally interconnected?

    (A) The respiratory and skeletal systems

    (B) The skeletal and muscular systems

    (C) The respiratory and circulatory systems

    (D) The digestive and excretory systems

    (E) The nervous and endocrine systems

21. Green flowers are dominant to yellow flowers in pea plants. Two heterozygous green pea plants are crossed and 1,000 offspring are produced. About how many of the offspring are expected to be yellow?

    (A) 0

    (B) 250

    (C) 500

    (D) 750

    (E) 1000

22. Which of the following techniques are used to amplify DNA sequences?

    I. Polymerase chain reaction

    II. Transformation of recombinant plasmids

    III. Site-directed mutagenesis

    (A) I only

    (B) II only

    (C) III only

    (D) I and II only

    (E) I, II, and III

23. All of the following are types of carbohydrate *except:*

    (A) Starch

    (B) Cellulose

    (C) Glucose

    (D) Glycogen

    (E) Insulin

24. Oxygenated blood is channeled through which of the following structures?

    (A) Right ventricle

    (B) Inferior vena cava

    (C) Pulmonary arteries

    (D) Pulmonary veins

    (E) Tricuspid valve

25. All of the following occur frequently in plasma membranes *except:*

    (A) Phospholipids

    (B) Sphingolipids

    (C) Ergosterol

    (D) Cholesterol

    (E) Soluble proteins

26. The common amino acids number:

    (A) 19

    (B) 20

    (C) 21

    (D) 22

    (E) 23

Go on to next page

27. What is the purpose of interferon in the immune system?

    (A) Attack abnormal body cells

    (B) Engulf invading organisms

    (C) Stimulate neighboring cells to produce proteins to aid in defense against viruses

    (D) Attract phagocytes to foreign cells

    (E) Increase blood supply to damaged areas

28. What is the correct sequence of bonds on the spectrum of electron-sharing, from most shared to least?

    (A) Covalent, ionic, hydrogen

    (B) Covalent, hydrogen, ionic

    (C) Hydrogen, ionic, covalent

    (D) Hydrogen, covalent, ionic

    (E) Ionic, hydrogen, covalent

29. What will happen to a cell placed into a hypertonic solution?

    (A) It will expand

    (B) It will contract

    (C) Nothing

    (D) It will lyse

    (E) It will take in water

30. Which organelle is much more numerous in muscle cells than in fat cells?

    (A) Mitochondrion

    (B) Lysosome

    (C) Nucleus

    (D) Golgi apparatus

    (E) Ribosome

31. Which of the following is a density-dependent factor?

    (A) Tornadoes

    (B) Earthquakes

    (C) Hurricanes

    (D) Disease

    (E) Rain

32. Which of the following best summarizes how modern scientists view evolution?

    (A) Genotypes compete against each other and the superior takes control

    (B) An accumulated effect of gene flow, genetic drift, and mutations

    (C) Acquired characteristics are selected

    (D) The change of organisms over time

    (E) The survival and reproduction of phenotypes that produce fertile offspring

33. All of the following function directly in homeostasis *except:*

    (A) Large intestine

    (B) Nephron

    (C) Plasma membrane

    (D) Blood

    (E) Microtubules

34. Which of the following sequences does not occur in the circulatory system of the human body?

    (A) Descending aorta-arteries-arterioles

    (B) Pulmonary arteries-lungs-pulmonary veins

    (C) Veins-venules-capillaries

    (D) Superior vena cava-right atrium-right ventricle

    (E) Left atrium-left ventricle-aorta

35. Which of the following muscle types is involuntary and contains sarcomeres?

    (A) Smooth

    (B) Slow-twitch skeletal

    (C) Fast-twitch skeletal

    (D) Vascular

    (E) Cardiac

Go on to next page

36. All of the following are true of human gametogenesis EXCEPT:

    (A) Oogonia divide by mitosis to produce primary oocytes

    (B) Primary oocytes proceed to prophase I and then halt until puberty

    (C) Secondary oocytes and polar bodies formed at the end of meiosis I are equal daughter cells

    (D) Polar bodies disintegrate

    (E) An egg is formed at the end of meiosis I

37. Skeletal muscle contraction in mammals can best be summarized by which of the following statements?

    (A) Calcium ions rush into nerve cells, resulting in muscle contraction

    (B) Myosin acts to pull actin filaments towards the center of the sarcomere

    (C) Sodium and potassium ions diffuse across the plasma membrane of muscle cells, causing contraction

    (D) Microfilaments and microtubules relax, shortening the sarcomere

    (E) Cytokines bind to muscle cells, triggering a contraction

38. Which of the following statements is true about viral DNA and RNA?

    (A) Both function as genomes

    (B) Both are composed of deoxyribose sugars

    (C) Both are composed of ribose sugars

    (D) Both are uniformly double stranded

    (E) Both are uniformly single stranded

39. In which of the following does one gene control the expression of another, independently inherited gene?

    (A) Pleiotropy

    (B) Epistasis

    (C) Multifactorial inheritance

    (D) Codominance

    (E) Incomplete penetrance

40. Phototropism is achieved by the action of which of the following?

    (A) Gibberellins

    (B) Cytokinins

    (C) Ethylene

    (D) Auxin

    (E) Abscisic Acid

41. A forest fire destroys a large swath of forest habitat, effectively isolating a small population of red-nosed rabbits within an area that escaped destruction. The remaining population will be especially prone to:

    (A) Gene flow

    (B) Natural selection

    (C) Genetic drift

    (D) Stabilizing selection

    (E) Directional selection

42. Which of the following chemical moieties is not found in DNA?

    (A) Phosphate groups

    (B) Deoxyribose sugar

    (C) Nitrogenous bases

    (D) Purines

    (E) Amide bonds

43. All of the following are functions of the excretory system *except*:

    (A) Storing urine

    (B) Filtering wastes from the blood

    (C) Modifying the contents of blood

    (D) Modifying blood pressure

    (E) Controlling the exocrine glands

44. Which of the following kingdoms is the most diverse?

    (A) Animalia

    (B) Plantae

    (C) Fungi

    (D) Monera

    (E) Protista

Go on to next page ⟶

45. Which of the following is incorrectly ordered, from simple to complex?

    (A) Tissues-organ systems-organism

    (B) Cells-tissues-organs

    (C) Organism-community-population

    (D) Organism-population-ecosystem

    (E) Population-ecosystem-biosphere

46. Which structure specializes in gas exchange?

    (A) Alveoli

    (B) Bronchi

    (C) Trachea

    (D) Bronchioles

    (E) Epiglottis

47. What results from the influx into the matrix of hydrogen ions stored in the mitochondrial intermembrane space?

    (A) The mitochrondria swells

    (B) ADP is phosphorylated

    (C) Water is split

    (D) pH of the matrix increases

    (E) ATP is hydrolyzed

48. Which of the following are found in a tundra ecosystem?

    I.   Biotic factors

    II. Abiotic factors

    III. Permafrost

    (A) I only

    (B) II only

    (C) III only

    (D) I and III

    (E) I, II, and III

49. Which of the following types of hormone least directly impacts the activities of the ovaries and uterus?

    (A) Gonadotropin releasing hormone

    (B) Follicle stimulating hormone

    (C) Androgens

    (D) Progesterone

    (E) Luteinizing hormone

50. Which of the following can digest cellulose?

    I.   Humans

    II. Cows

    III. Fungi

    (A) I only

    (B) II only

    (C) III only

    (D) I and II only

    (E) II and III only

51. Which of the following modifications is specifically recognized by the ribosome prior to translation ?

    (A) 5' cap

    (B) Polyadenosine tail

    (C) Methylated bases

    (D) Exon splice sites

    (E) Promoter

52. The appendix of humans and the hip bones of whales are said to be:

    (A) Vestigial structures

    (B) Homologous structures

    (C) Analogous structures

    (D) Ancestral structures

    (E) Embryonic structures

53. All of the following events occur during embryonic development *except:*

    (A) Cleavage

    (B) Morula is formed

    (C) Blastula is formed

    (D) The follicle develops

    (E) Gastrulation

54. Photosynthesis mainly occurs in which structure?

    (A) Epidermis

    (B) Palisade mesophyll

    (C) Spongy mesophyll

    (D) Guard cells

    (E) Vascular bundles

Go on to next page

55. A cell contains three pairs of homologous chromosomes: X_1/X_2, Y_1/Y_2, and Z_1/Z_2. Which gamete could result from these homologous chromosomes?

    (A) X_2, X_1, Z_1

    (B) Y_1, Z_1, Z_1

    (C) X_2, Y_2, Y_1

    (D) Y_1, Y_2, Z_2

    (E) X_2, Y_2, Z_2

56. Which of the following occurs only outside mitochondria?

    (A) Krebs cycle

    (B) Electron transport chain

    (C) Oxidative phosphorylation

    (D) Formation of a proton gradient

    (E) Glycolysis

57. All of the following are products of the light-dependent reactions of photosynthesis *except:*

    (A) ATP

    (B) Glucose

    (C) NADPH

    (D) O_2

    (E) H^+

58. If a goose sees an egg outside of its nest it will roll the egg back into the nest, even if the egg is not one of its own. The goose will do the same with any object that looks like an egg. If the egg-like object is removed, the goose will persist in its rolling behavior. What type of behavior is this?

    (A) Imprinting

    (B) Instinct

    (C) Fixed action pattern

    (D) Associative learning

    (E) Trial and error learning

59. When both tall and short people decrease in frequency within a population, while those of medium height increase in frequency, which of the following is most clearly at work?

    (A) Sexual selection

    (B) Directional selection

    (C) Stabilizing selection

    (D) Sympatric selection

    (E) Disruptive selection

60. Which biome has the most biodiversity?

    (A) Tundra

    (B) Grasslands

    (C) Tropical rainforest

    (D) Taiga

    (E) Desert

Go on to next page

Questions 61–64

Questions 61–64 refer to Figure 27-1, which shows various trophic levels.

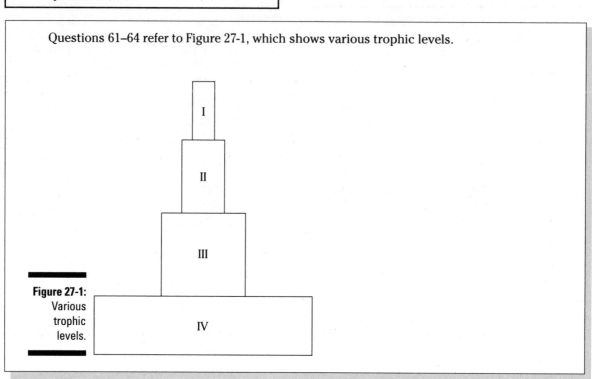

Figure 27-1:
Various
trophic
levels.

61. Trophic level I refers to:

(A) Primary producers

(B) Primary consumers

(C) Tertiary producers

(D) Tertiary consumers

(E) Quaternary consumers

62. Trophic level II refers to:

(A) Primary producers

(B) Detritivores

(C) Secondary consumers

(D) Tertiary producers

(E) Predators

63. Trophic level III refers to:

(A) Carnivores

(B) Primary consumers

(C) Secondary consumers

(D) Tertiary consumers

(E) Decomposers

64. Trophic level IV refers to:

(A) Primary producers

(B) Primary herbivores

(C) Primary omnivores

(D) Plants

(E) Decomposers

Go on to next page

Questions 65–67

Questions 65–67 refer to the Figure 27-2. The shaded boxes and circles indicate a disease phenotype.

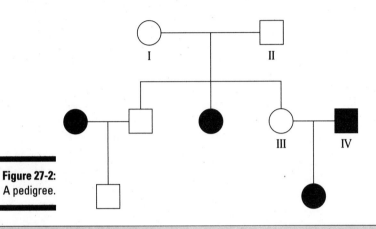

Figure 27-2:
A pedigree.

65. What is the probability that future offspring of III and IV will have the disease?

(A) 0%

(B) 25%

(C) 50%

(D) 75%

(E) 100%

66. The disease in the pedigree is inherited as:

(A) An autosomal dominant trait

(B) An autosomal recessive trait

(C) An X-linked dominant trait

(D) An X-linked recessive trait

(E) A Y-linked trait

67. For the disease-associated allele, individuals I and II are:

(A) Homozygous recessive

(B) Homozygous dominant

(C) Heterozygous

(D) Codominant

(E) Epistatic

Go on to next page

Questions 68–71

Answer questions 68–71 by choosing from the following:

(A) Grassland

(B) Desert

(C) Tundra

(D) Tropical rainforest

(E) Deciduous forest

68. Characterized by trees that lose their leaves during winter

69. Driest of the biomes

70. Characterized by low-lying shrubbery, the absence of trees, and year-round cold climate

71. Very vertically stratified

Questions 72–75

Answer questions 72–75 by choosing the substance secreted by each structure.

(A) Salivary amylase

(B) Gastric Juice

(C) Bile

(D) Chymotrypsin

(E) Aminopeptidase

72. The liver

73. The mouth

74. The pancreas

75. The stomach

76. What type of evolution is particularly evident between predator and prey?

(A) Divergent evolution

(B) Convergent evolution

(C) Parallel evolution

(D) Co-evolution

(E) Macroevolution

77. In a certain species of flower, purple leaves are dominant to orange leaves and straight leaves are dominant to jagged leaves. If two plants heterozygous in both characteristics are crossed, what is the expected phenotypic ratio of the offspring?

(A) 5:5:3:2

(B) 7:4:2:1

(C) 4:4:4:3

(D) 10:2:2:1

(E) 9:3:3:1

78. Prokayotes lack which of the following?

I.   Nucleus

II. Ribosomes

III. Membrane-bound organelles

(A) I only

(B) II only

(C) III only

(D) I and II only

(E) I and III only

Go on to next page

Questions 79–80

Answer questions 79–80 by referring to Figure 27-3. The lanes correspond to fragments generated from samples taken from five victims who were brutally burned in a fire, and to samples taken from a set of parents.

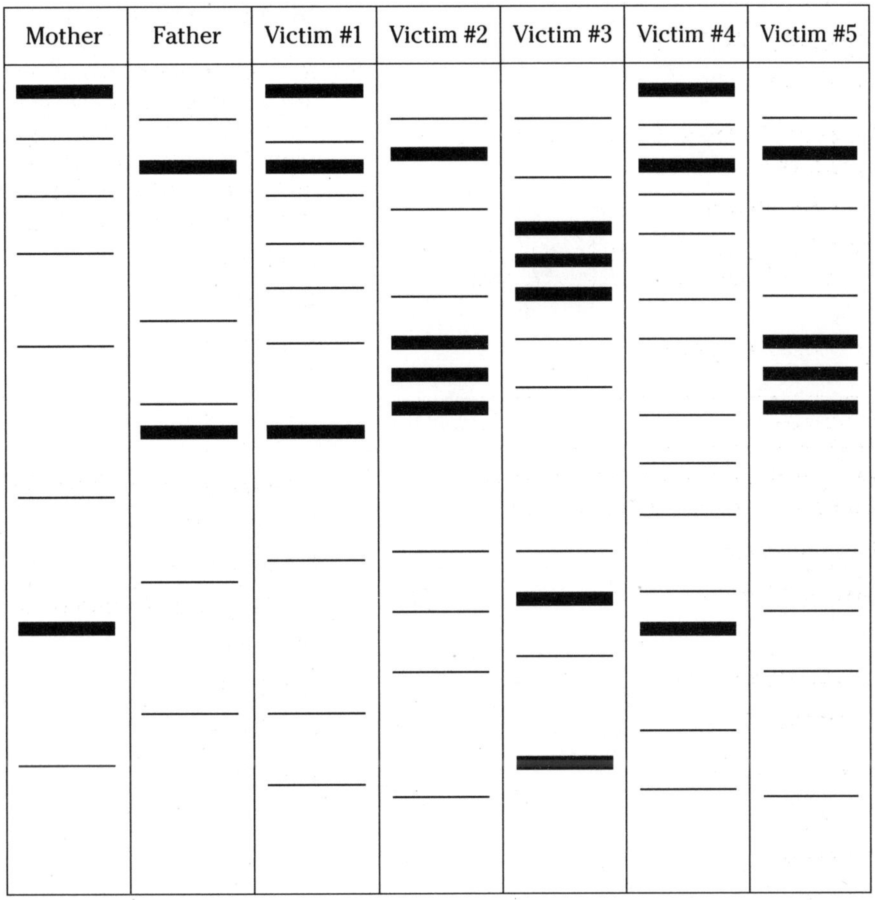

Figure 27-3: A restriction fragment length polymorphism analysis.

79. Which victim is the son of the parents whose fragments are shown?

   (A) Victim 1
   (B) Victim 2
   (C) Victim 3
   (D) Victim 4
   (E) Victim 5

80. Which two victims are twins?

   (A) Victims 1 and 2
   (B) Victims 3 and 4
   (C) Victims 4 and 5
   (D) Victims 1 and 5
   (E) Victims 2 and 5

Go on to next page

Questions 81–82

Refer to Figure 27-4 to answer questions 81–82.

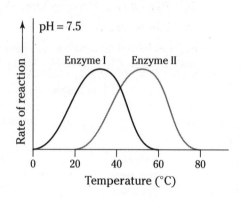

Figure 27-4:
Plots of temperature- and pH-dependent enzyme activity.

81. Which temperature would yield the optimal combined activity of enzymes I and II?

(A) 30 °C

(B) 40 °C

(C) 50 °C

(D) 60 °C

(E) 70 °C

82. Which enzyme is most likely to operate in the stomach?

(A) I

(B) II

(C) Either I or II

(D) III

(E) IV

Go on to next page

Questions 83–87

To answer questions 83–87, choose the item that best fits then given description.

(A) Erythrocytes

(B) White blood cells

(C) Platelets

(D) Plasma

(E) Lymph

83. Liquid portion of blood that carries many dissolved substances

84. Defend against foreign particles

85. Filters through capillaries

86. Cells that lack nuclei

87. Cell fragments

Questions 88–89

To answer questions 88–89, refer to Figure 27-5.

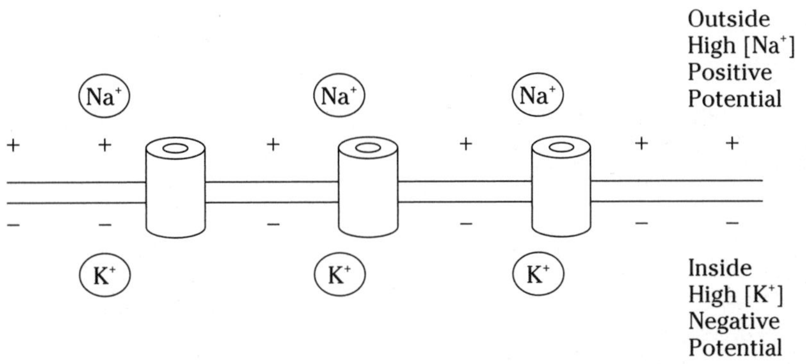

Outside
High [Na^+]
Positive
Potential

Figure 27-5: A longitudinal cross section of an axon.

Inside
High [K^+]
Negative
Potential

88. The figure shows a neuron in what state?

(A) Resting

(B) Immediately prior to depolarization

(C) Refractory period

(D) Immediately after repolarization by the sodium-potassium pump

(E) Recovery

89. What is the exchange ratio of sodium to potassium ions catalyzed by the sodium-potassium pump?

(A) One sodium ion for every potassium ion

(B) Two sodium ions for every two potassium ions

(C) Three sodium ions for every three potassium ions

(D) Three sodium ions for every two potassium ions

(E) Two sodium ions for every three potassium ions

Go on to next page

Question 90 refers to Figure 27-6.

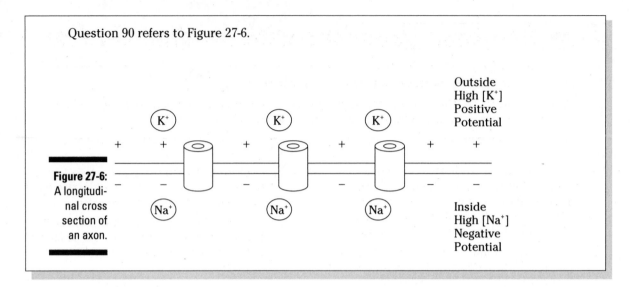

Figure 27-6: A longitudinal cross section of an axon.

90. The figure shows a neuron in what state?

(A) Resting

(B) Immediately prior to depolarization

(C) Refractory period

(D) Immediately after repolarization by the sodium-potassium pump

(E) Recovery

Questions 91–95

To answer questions 91–95, choose the plant group that best fits the given description.

(A) Charophytes

(B) Bryophytes

(C) Seedless vascular

(D) Gymnosperms

(E) Angiosperms

91. Leaves are adapted to cold, dry conditions

92. Ancestors of terrestrial plants

93. First plants to have a sporophyte-dominated life cycle

94. Form seeds inside of an ovary

95. First terrestrial plants

Questions 96–100

To answer questions 96–100, choose the molecular structure that best fits the given description.

(A) Helicase

(B) Ligase

(C) Primase

(D) Okazaki fragment

(E) DNA polymerase

96. Enables DNA replication via short RNA-DNA hybrids

97. Unwinds DNA

98. Elongates DNA strand

99. Joins discontinuous fragments

100. Defining feature of lagging strand synthesis

Go on to next page

Free-Response Questions with Grading Outline

Time: 10 minutes to read the questions, 90 minutes to answer

Directions: Answer the following free-response questions, addressing each part. You may include diagrams to support your answers, but each answer should be in essay form.

1. Compare and contrast the replication cycles of phages and retroviruses. Use the themes of that analysis to explain why viruses are both promising tools for gene therapy and also carcinogenic threats.

2. Describe the human circulatory and respiratory systems, emphasizing their interconnectivity and the action of sensors and effectors in maintaining homeostasis within those systems.

3. Explain why hormonal regulation is important specifically in plants. Identify two plant hormones and describe their effects.

4. What are the properties of living things? List and describe them, using one example each of a living and a nonliving thing for illustration.

Grading Outline for Question 1 (*12 points*):

✔ **Compare and contrast phage and retrovirus life cycles (*6 points*):** Phages and retroviruses have same general architecture, with genetic information in the form of nucleic acids packaged within protein capsid shells. Phages have DNA genomes, but retroviruses have RNA genomes. In addition to protein capsids, retroviruses may have outer membrane envelopes. Phages exclusively infect bacteria, but retroviruses infect eukaryotes. Both infect by gaining entry into host cells. Phages inject genomes into bacterial cells through tailspikes that puncture bacterial membranes. Retroviruses may use membrane envelopes to enter host cells via receptor-mediated endocytosis. Once inside, phages may enter lytic cycle, rapidly hijacking host cell materials to synthesize and assemble new phage particles, lysing host cell to release them. Alternately, phages may enter lysogenic cycle, integrating viral DNA with host genome, residing dormantly as prophage, replicating with host cell until re-emerging into lytic cycle. Retroviruses use viral reverse transcriptase to make DNA version of viral genome, then integrate with host genome, replicate with it, until re-emerging to actively build new retrovirus particles that exocytose.

✔ **Promise of viruses for gene therapy (*3 points*):** Retroviruses may be engineered as vectors for therapeutic genes that integrate with host cell genomes, interrupting adverse genes, or supplementing/repairing defective versions of needed genes.

✔ **Carcinogenic threat of viruses (*3 points*):** Carcinogenesis is the generation of cancerous growth. Cancer arises from unregulated cell growth. Integration of viral DNA into host genome can interrupt host genes normally used to regulate cell growth, causing carcinogenic dysregulation.

Go on to next page

Grading Outline for Question 2 (*14 points*):

✔ **Description of circulatory and respiratory systems (*8 points*):**

- Circulatory system enables flow of blood through vessels that perfuse tissues. Blood carries nutrients, wastes, respiratory gases (oxygen and carbon dioxide), chemical signals, nutrients, osmolytes, cells of immunity, and heat. Circulatory system has pulmonary and systemic circuits. Heart provides pressure source to force flow through arteries, carrying blood away from heart, to lungs or to rest of body tissues. Arteries branch into arterioles, then capillaries. Fluid moves out of capillaries due to hydrostatic pressure, returns due to osmotic pressure. Arteries are thick-walled and muscular. Lymphatic fluid filters out. Blood returns to heart via capillaries, then venules, then veins. Veins are thin walled and use valves to prevent backflow. Venous flow is driven by biomechanical pressure. Lymph returns.

- Respiratory system takes in oxygen and releases carbon dioxide, enabling continued cellular respiration. Intercostal muscles, rib case, and diaphragm mechanically drive inspiration and expiration via negative pressure and compression. Air enters at nares and mouth, passes through pharynx and larynx into trachea, bronchi, bronchioles and into alveoli where gas exchange occurs by passive diffusion across alveolar and capillary walls.

✔ **Interconnectivity and homeostasis (*6 points*):** Alveoli are the major interface of the systems, with a huge interfacial surface area achieved by branching. Respiratory rate is modulated by pH of blood. Excess carbon dioxide forms carbonic acid within blood, lowering pH. Low pH is detected by sensors, which stimulate increased respiration to clear carbon dioxide. Extremely low oxygen levels can also be detected and increase respiratory rate. Blood pH and relative concentrations of blood oxygen and carbon dioxide modulate the activity of hemoglobin, the protein in erythrocytes that shuttles respiratory gases between body tissues and alveoli.

Grading Outline for Question 3 (*10 points*):

✔ **Importance of hormonal regulation in plants (*4 points*):** Hormones are regulatory chemical signals that enable a coordinated response to the environment. Plant cells secrete many different hormones, and are equipped with hormone receptors that are tied to signal transduction and integration pathways. Because they are rooted in place, plants must be very responsive to their local environment. Hormones control plant growth, development, flow of fluids and nutrients, daily and seasonally periodic behaviors, and defensive behaviors.

✔ **Activity of two plant hormones (*6 points*):**

- Gibberellins stimulate growth in leaves and stems, but not roots. Gibberellins increase cell elongation and cell division. Some gibberellins cause fruit development, and have been used in agriculture. Plant seeds may contain high levels of gibberellins so that when water is available, the gibberellins are released within the seed and stimulate germination.

- Abscisic acid is produced in terminal buds and inhibits leaf growth. This function is useful in directing plant activity towards dormancy during winter. In seeds, abscisic acid also promotes dormancy, so the hormone acts in opposition to seed gibberellins until the abscisic acid is degraded or diluted during conditions appropriate for germination. Stress conditions such as wilting also involve abscisic acid, which stimulates closure of stomata in order to preserve water.

Grading Outline for Question 4 (*10 points*):

✔ **Properties of living things (*4 points*):** Living things exhibit a high degree of order. Living things grow, develop, and reproduce. Living things respond to their environment, and maintain stable internal conditions.

✔ **Contrasting examples of living and nonliving entities (*6 points*):** A bacterial cell is alive. A chunk of limestone is not alive. Bacterial cells contain atoms arranged within complex molecules, which assemble into functional complexes and systems of interacting molecules that sense, integrate, and perform work. A chunk of limestone is a disordered aggregate of silica, clay, and various other mineral materials. Newly divided bacteria grow, using energy and specific materials to stock themselves with the enzymes and other functional structures needed to sustain their existence. A chunk of limestone does nothing similar, even when freshly cleaved in two. Bacteria frequently replicate their genomes and divide into daughter cells, which eventually go on to acquire the energy and material to replicate themselves. Chunks of limestone remain as they are, until crushed, eroded or melted out of their chunky existence. If a bacterium finds itself immersed in a heterogeneous environment, it will use highly evolved flagella to taxi towards the areas more rich in nutrients. If you drop a chunk of limestone into any kind of environment, it will drop until something stops it from dropping, and then lay still. Bacteria have selectively permeable membranes that preferentially take in nutrients and expel wastes. Chunks of limestone will slowly become permeated with any solution in which you place them.

Chapter 28

Answers to Test 2

*Y*ou came back for a second helping. Well done. Sadly, there are always dishes to be done afterwards. Pile up your dirty answers in the sink and get soapy. Nothing cuts through grease like an answer key.

1. E. Jellyfish, hydra, and some cousins are the major radially symmetric organisms.

2. B. Kinases are part of the army of enzymes that regulate and coordinate the flurry of activity that is cell division.

3. D. When everybody wins, it's mutualism.

4. A. Phloem is the sugar highway through vascular plantland.

5. C. There was Monera and then there were the rest of us.

6. D. A tRNA anticodon with the sequence 3'-UAC-5' complements the mRNA codon 5'-AUG-3', which is the start codon.

7. C. Not all arteries carry oxygenated blood. Just ask the pulmonary arteries.

8. C. The stomach is perfectly happy to let the large intestine take care of water absorption.

9. C. Among those listed, the secondary consumers are the highest trophic level and therefore comprise the least biomass, because energy transfer is highly inefficient between levels.

10. E. Ribosomes are the protein factories.

11. B. Codominance is characterized by simultaneous, unmasked expression of both alleles.

12. A. At rest, neurons maintain low internal sodium ion concentrations — they are polarized. When sodium channels open and sodium rushes down a gradient back into the cell — that's depolarization.

13. D. Cytokinesis (i.e., cell division) follows mitosis in M phase.

14. C. Bird wings and butterfly wings are noticeably similar in structure and are both used for flying, but the two organisms aren't closely related and it is clearly a case of convergent evolution.

15. D. A new cell wall will form between the double membranes of the cell plate.

16. D. The Krebs cycle releases carbon dioxide as the sundered bits of what used to be glucose are split apart to release energy.

17. B. Although root pressure plays a role, the upward tension from evaporation is the major driver of transpiration in this case.

18. C. Insulated from other influences, populations tend to stay steady when parents produce only enough offspring to replace themselves.

19. E. It's scary how close we are.

20. A. All the other pairs of systems are profoundly interconnected in function and regulation.

21. B. A cross between heterozygotes yields 1:2:1 genotypic ratios and 3:1 phenotypic ratios. Know it.

22. D. Although site-directed mutagenesis may use both of the other techniques, that is simply a means to a mutagenic end.

23. E. Insulin is a peptide hormone.

24. D. The blood in pulmonary veins is oxygenated as it returns to the heart from the lungs.

25. E. Soluble proteins have a polar character that is inconsistent with life inside the plasma membrane.

26. B. Though there are others, most life shares the twenty common amino acids.

27. C. Interferon is a chemical messenger sent by virus-infected cells, sounding the alarm of foreign invasion.

28. B. Covalent bonds are the least polar and ionic bonds the most polar.

29. B. Hypertonic solutions have the greater solute concentration; water will move towards the concentrated solute by osmosis.

30. A. Muscle cells require serious ATP for contraction.

31. D. More organisms clustered more closely together increases the likelihood that any given infectious disease will spread.

32. E. All it takes is traits that allow you to reproduce. The game goes on, with variations.

33. E. Though they are important cytoskeletal elements, their role in homeostasis is simply less direct than the others.

34. C. The sequence is correct in this choice, but the direction is wrong; there are valves to prevent that kind of thing.

35. E. Cardiac muscle may be involuntary, but it is striped with sarcomeres and strong; smooth muscle is involuntary, but the smoothness is proof that no sarcomeres lurk within.

36. C. The polar bodies are junior partners in that meiotic division.

37. B. That is essentially the idea behind the sliding filament theory.

38. A. Their precise structural and chemical details may differ, but in any case they carry the genetic information.

39. B. Epistasis is often confused with pleiotropy, in which a single gene controls a number of phenotypes.

40. D. Auxin activity is tied into the phytochrome sensory system.

41. C. Small, isolated populations are classic studies in genetic drift. It doesn't take much of a fluctuation to rock the whole genetic boat, when the boat is small.

42. E. Amide bonds link together the amino acids of a polypeptide.

43. E. Just because excretory and exocrine both start with ex-... it doesn't mean anything...

44. E. Protists are kings of kingdom-wide diversity.

45. C. Populations form communities, not the other way around.

46. A. The other structures may channel the air, but the alveoli is where oxygen and carbon dioxide trade place.

47. B. This is the phosphorylation step of oxidative phosphorylation.

48. E. There are both biotic and abiotic factors in any ecosystem, and permafrost is a defining feature of tundra.

49. C. The androgens are important precursors, but the most direct effects stem from the other choices.

50. E. Cows can do it, thanks to some symbiotic bacterial help. Fungi can do it, even outside themselves. We can't.

51. A. The ribosome takes the presence of the cap as a structural sign that everything is okay, and this mRNA should be promoted to translation.

52. A. Vestigial, you know, as in once-had-a-use-but-no-longer-does-that-we-can-tell. Which is not to say that humans might not have uses for whale hip bones.

53. D. This event happens prior to fertilization.

54. B. Palisade mesophyll are column-shaped cells of the leaf interior.

55. E. Provided nondisjunction doesn't take place, each gamete receives a single sister chromatid representative from each set of homologous chromosomes.

56. E. Glycolysis happens in the cytoplasm.

57. B. Glucose doesn't roll off the photosynthetic assembly line until the light-independent reactions.

58. C. The clincher here is that the goose continues with the rolling motions even when the egg is gone — the action pattern is fixed.

59. C. Stabilizing selection favors the intermediate form of a trait, increasing its frequency within a population over generations.

60. C. There are good reasons for saving it.

61. D. Top of the food chain, feeding on the secondary consumers, few in number.

62. C. The Jan Bradys of the trophic levels.

63. B. The herbivores, feasting on leaves or algae.

64. A. The humble hordes who funnel energy into the system.

65. C. It's obvious once you know the trait is autosomal recessive — which you do know after the next question.

66. B. Based on the appearance of the trait in one of the daughters of I and II, the trait is recessive — neither parent had the trait. It must be autosomal, because it is recessive, so in order for II to pass a sex-linked recessive trait to his daughter, he'd need to have the trait himself, and he doesn't.

67. C. Each was unaffected, but must have carried the recessive allele.

68. E. Come winter, leaves decide to drop dead.

69. B. They're not always hot, but deserts are dry.

70. C. Northern Alaskans' biome of choice.

71. D. The thick canopy leaves little light for the shorter organisms.

72. C. Liver sends bile to the gall bladder. The gall bladder sends the bile to the duodenum to dissolve fats.

73. A. The name really ought to give it away.

74. D. The pancreas sends a digestive hit squad into the duodenum, and chymotrypsin is one of the hydrolytic thugs.

75. B. Gastric juice is an acidic concoction that mixes with chewed food, helping it to break down into chyme.

76. D. Predators depend on prey, and the two adapt in counterpoint.

77. E. Crosses between double heterozygotes always predict this phenotypic ratio.

78. E. Prokaryotes need protein as much as the next cell.

79. D. Only in victim 4's sample can all the bands be accounted for within the lanes of the mother and father.

80. E. The samples from victims 2 and 5 suggest genetic identity.

81. B. It's the closest compromise to the optimal temperature of each enzyme.

82. D. The low pH optimum suggests enzyme III evolved to operate in a low pH environment like the stomach.

83. D. The part of blood sold by many starving college students in order to buy Ramen noodles and beer.

84. B. For completeness, the lymph assists here as well, but B is the best answer.

85. E. Lymph has its own circulation. Edema can result from faulty lymphatic circulation.

86. A. Erythrocytes are lean and hungry for respiratory gases.

87. C. Critical for clotting.

88. A. An inside-negative potential, with sodium pumped out of the cell: that's a polarized neuron at rest.

89. D. The exchange rate is always the same at this border.

90. C. During this phase, no action potentials are possible.

91. D. Pine needles have thick, waxy exteriors to preserve water.

92. A. Remember, plants came to land from the water, just like animals.

93. C. Sporophytes are diploid states within the alternation of generations.

94. E. The ovary may be surrounded by petals and pinned to a lapel.

95. B. Think of them as a sort of Christopher Columbus group, splashing in ignorant triumph onto land that had been discovered by other organisms well in advance.

96. C. Primase gives polymerase a toehold.

97. A. Helicase undoes the helix.

98. E. Polymerase makes the DNA polymer.

99. B. Ligase . . . er . . . ligates.

100. D. It's just fun to say, isn't it?

Part VI
The Part of Tens

The 5th Wave   By Rich Tennant

"I'll have the cheese sandwich with the interesting mold on the bread, and the manicotti with the fungal growth, and that really, really old dish of vanilla bread pudding."

In this part . . .

Finally, in the space between big ideas and little details, you'll find the Part of Tens. This part contains four ten-point summaries of the important stuff, big or little. Use these lists as an anchoring point and compass for your wider wanderings through biology. Use them for review. Use them always for good, and never for evil. Weave them into your very soul. Or, you know, at least look them over when you have the time.

Chapter 29

Ten Terms to Tattoo on Your Brain

In This Chapter
▶ Compacting dense explanations of terms
▶ Getting a better understanding of important concepts

Not all words are equal. Some are packed with more meaning than others. Below are ten dense biological terms. Make sure they're part of that dictionary you carry in your brain.

Hypothesis

The hypothesis is the engine of science, and therefore the engine of biology. A hypothesis is a tentative explanation for how something works. A good hypothesis is one that can be tested. Good hypotheses lend themselves to testing by experiments. Good experiments yield data that either support hypotheses or reveal flaws in them. Revealed flaws generate new hypotheses that generate new experiments. The cycle goes round and round, each turn producing a better model for the way things work.

Energy

Energy is the ability to do work. Energy, supplied overwhelmingly by the sun, infuses the open system we call the biosphere. The energy is trapped by living organisms and used to order matter into structures and systems that support life. Biological functions arise from the ordered structures made possible by the continuous influx of energy. In one sense, death is the degeneration of an ordered biological system such that it can no longer use energy to maintain its internal order. Biological processes consume energy, but also lose energy in the form of heat as a cost of doing business. Metabolism is the collection of chemical reactions used by an organism to convert energy and matter into the forms useful for sustaining life.

Ecosystem

An ecosystem is an interdependent network of organisms and the environment in which they live and with which they exchange materials and energy. Because ecosystems include physical environments, their study encompasses both biotic and abiotic factors, such as temperature, water, and sunlight. The abiotic features of an ecosystem largely constrain the types of organisms that live within it. In any defined environment, organisms of the same species inhabit populations, and different populations form communities. Organisms occupy niches within ecosystems, where a niche is defined as the complete set of resources used by the organism. Ecosystems continually mature into states of equilibrium and adjust to events that throw them into disequilibrium.

Emergent Property

Biological structures and systems are arranged into hierarchical levels, such as atoms, molecules, molecular complexes, organelles, cells, tissues, organs, organ systems, organisms, and networks of organisms. At each increasing level, properties emerge that are not present in the lower levels. In other words, levels of biological hierarchies are more than the sum of their parts. The existence of emergent properties is a defining feature of biological order.

Cells

Cells are the fundamental units of life because they are the lowest level in the hierarchy of systems that possess all the traits of life. Cells use energy, which allows them to maintain a high degree of order and perform work. Cells respond to their external environment and maintain a stable internal environment. Cells grow, develop, and reproduce. Over generations, cells evolve, adapting to their environment.

Evolution

Evolution is the central mechanism by which biology operates. More than that, chemical evolution was the process by which biology came into being. Biological evolution occurs over the generations of an ancestral line, as species adapt to their environments. Adaptations result from the action of natural selection on genetic variations among the members of a species. Variations that are favorable are amplified in subsequent generations because those variations enable their owners to survive and reproduce more successfully. Unfavorable variations are diminished in subsequent generations. What constitutes a favorable or unfavorable variation is largely a function of the environment.

Diversity

Diversity allows biological systems to respond to changes. Populations with greater genetic diversity are less likely to succumb entirely to environmental changes because some members of a genetically diverse population are likely to have variations that are favorable within the new environment. Ecosystems with greater biodiversity are less likely to succumb to disruptions because biodiverse ecosystems have more ways to re-equilibrate; such ecosystems have a greater ability to form new networks that are sustainable in the new environment.

Phylogeny

Phylogeny is the evolutionary development of a group of organisms such as a species, family, class, or kingdom. The aim of modern taxonomy is to categorize species into a family tree that best reflects phylogeny. The tools used in this effort include paleontology, observations of living organisms and, with dramatically increasing frequency, molecular sequence data. A major benefit of well-constructed phylogenies is that, by properly placing a species within one, you immediately know a great deal about that species based on its relatedness to other species.

Homeostasis

Homeostasis is the maintenance of a stable internal state, and is one of the characteristic properties of life. Cells perform homeostasis, as do entire organisms. In cells, selectively permeable membranes are central to homeostasis, because such membranes allow selective entry to nutrients and selective exit to wastes. Networks of interacting molecules within cells support homeostasis by integrating information about the external and internal environments, responding with appropriate signals to alter the properties of cell components and alter gene expression. The same principles of regulation apply to entire organisms. Organ systems responsible for intake and dissemination of nutrients, for excretion of wastes, for sensation and movement — and others — are interconnected by regulatory systems that coordinate their activities in such a way that the internal environment of the organism remains stable. The nervous and endocrine systems in particular participate in a large, interconnected network of sensors, integrators, and effectors that all conspire towards homeostasis.

Feedback

Regulation is a major feature of biological systems, and feedback is a major mechanism of regulation. In negative feedback, the product of a pathway inhibits one or more steps of the pathway that produced it. This arrangement ensures that the product doesn't accumulate excessively. In positive feedback, the product of a pathway accelerates one or more steps of the pathway that produced it. This arrangement enables a rapid and potent response to conditions that require one. In order to exert very sensitive control, biological systems sometimes use negative and positive feedback in opposition within the same pathway.

Chapter 30

Ten Pathways (and Cycles)

• •

In This Chapter

▶ Summarizing important multistep biological showpieces

▶ Getting to know the steps in important biological processes

• •

A then B then C then . . . sigh. In biology, there's no shortage of steps to commit to memory. Fortunately, as you get to know more and more of them, they all begin to make a lot more sense, and you can rely less and less on brute force memorization. Use this list as a bridge to that goal.

Photosynthesis

✔ Light (energy) + 6 H_2O + 6 CO_2 → $C_6H_{12}O_6$ + 6 O_2

✔ Light-dependent reactions: light is trapped within photosystems, water is split, and energized electrons are sent down the electron transport chain, generating ATP and NADPH.

✔ Light-independent reactions: ATP and NADPH are used to fix carbon from carbon dioxide into glucose, the energy-rich product of photosynthesis.

Aerobic Cellular Respiration

✔ $C_6H_{12}O_6$ + 6 O_2 → 6 CO_2 + 6 H_2O + ATP (energy)

✔ Glycolysis: Glucose is split into two molecules of pyruvate, generating a net of 2 ATP.

✔ Krebs Cycle: Pyruvate is the substrate, so there are two rounds per glucose. Each round generates 3 NADH, 1 $FADH_2$, and 1 ATP.

✔ Oxidative phosphorylation: Sends electrons from NADH and $FADH_2$ down an electron transport chain to chemiosmotically synthesize ATP. Oxygen is the terminal electron acceptor and is reduced to water. Per glucose molecule 32 ATPs are generated this way, for a total of 36 ATPs in the entire pathway.

Anaerobic Cellular Respiration

✔ Alcoholic fermentation: Pyruvate from glycolysis is reduced to ethanol, regenerating 2 NAD^+ per glucose, so glycolysis can continue. Releases two molecules of carbon dioxide per glucose, as well.

✔ Lactic acid fermentation: Pyruvate from glycolysis is reduced to lactic acid, regenerating 2 NAD⁺ per glucose, so glycolysis can continue.

✔ Inefficient compared to aerobic respiration — only 2 net ATP per glucose, as compared to 36 ATP.

Cell Cycle

✔ Cell life cycles alternate between long periods of interphase and brief periods of M phase.

✔ Interphase: Growth 1 (G_1), Synthesis (S) and Growth 2 (G_2). G_1 contains rapid growth of a small, newly divided cell. S contains DNA synthesis. G_2 contains intense preparation for division.

✔ M phase: Mitosis and cytokinesis. Mitosis involves even segregation of two sets of chromosomes. Cytokinesis involves physical separation of two new daughter cells into separate cellular compartments.

Mitosis

✔ The process by which eukaryotic cells divide chromosomes into two equal sets for inheritance by two new daughter cells after cytokinesis. Mitosis consists of prophase, metaphase, anaphase, and telophase.

✔ Prophase: DNA condenses from diffuse chromatin state into discrete chromosomes. Centrioles migrate to cell poles, and begin organizing spindle. Nuclear envelope breaks down.

✔ Metaphase: Chromosomes align along the metaphase plate (centerline) of the parent cell. Spindle extends from centrioles at cell poles to the centromeres that join together sister chromatids of each chromosome.

✔ Anaphase: Spindle contracts, separating the identical sister chromatids of each chromosome, one chromatid to either side of the cell.

✔ Telophase: Nuclear envelopes begin to form around each set of separated chromatids. The chromatids begin to unravel into chromatin. A cleavage furrow forms, beginning the process of cell division.

Meiosis

✔ The process of cell division in order to produce gametes (e.g., sperm and egg). Consists of two rounds of division (meiosis I and meiosis II) such that one diploid cell divides into four haploid cells. Each round consists of prophase, metaphase, anaphase, and telophase.

✔ Meiosis I: In prophase I, homologous chromosomes condense and align into tetrads, enabling genetic recombination through crossing over of homologous chromatids. During metaphase I, homologous chromosome pairs independently assort to one side or the other of the metaphase plate. In anaphase I, pairs of homologous chromosomes are separated to either side of the cell. In telophase I, the cell begins the process of division into two haploid cells.

✔ Meiosis II: The stages of meiosis II are similar to those of mitosis, except that only one, haploid set of chromosomes condenses during prophase II, and aligns at the center of each cell during metaphase II. During anaphase II, the chromatids of each chromosome are separated, and the process of division begins during telophase II.

DNA Replication

- ✔ A semi-conservative replication process in which each new DNA double helix contains one parental strand and one newly synthesized strand.

- ✔ Helicase unwinds the DNA to be replicated, creating a replication fork at either side of a single-stranded bubble. Primase synthesizes short RNA primers at the beginning of each replication region. DNA polymerase replicates the DNA from free nucleotides, starting at the RNA primers and using the exposed DNA single strand as a template.

- ✔ On one "leading" strand, DNA replication is continuous and fast. On the opposite, "lagging" strand replication is discontinuous and slow. Discontinuous replication occurs in a series of short Okazaki fragments that must be joined by ligase.

Transcription

- ✔ The process by which an RNA working copy of a gene is made so that it can be processed into an mRNA and exported from the nucleus for translation.

- ✔ Consists of initiation, elongation, and termination. During initiation, RNA polymerase binds to a promoter, unwinds the DNA, and scans to an initiation site. During elongation, RNA polymerase moves along DNA strand 3' to 5', using it as a template to make a complementary RNA, 5' to 3'. Elongation continues until RNA polymerase reaches a termination site, whereupon it terminates transcription.

Translation

- ✔ The process by which a ribosome, aided by tRNAs, synthesizes a polypeptide based on the information genetically encoded within an mRNA.

- ✔ Consists of initiation, elongation and termination. During initiation, a complex of the small ribosomal subunit, mRNA and an initiator tRNA bind to the large ribosomal subunit. During elongation, the mRNA ratchets through the active site of the ribosome as tRNAs move through the A, P, and E sites of the ribosome. tRNAs whose anticodons properly complement the mRNA codon in the active site are retained, and the ribosome catalyzes peptide bond formation between the amino acids served up by successive tRNAs, producing an elongating polypeptide. Termination occurs when a release factor recognizes a stop codon; the ribosome then dissociates, releasing the mRNA and the new polypeptide.

Trophic Relationships

- ✔ Energy is trapped by primary producers (autotrophs). Primary consumers (herbivores) feed on the primary producers. Secondary and tertiary consumers (omnivores and carnivores) feed on the primary producers or on each other. Detritivores feed on dead and decaying material, recycling materials into the ecosystem. Most energy is lost as heat as it moves between trophic levels.

Chapter 31

Ten Organelles to Know

*O*rganelles drive cells (eukaryotic cells, anyway). Cells are the fundamental units of life. The study of life is biology. So, know the organelles back and forth for the AP Biology exam. This summary should help.

Nucleus

✔ The genetic information center of the cell. The nucleus contains the chromosomes, large complexes of DNA and histone proteins. The DNA wraps around histones, forming nucleosomes. Long strings of nucleosomes pack elaborately into the chromosomes.

✔ Transcription occurs in the nucleus. Transcription is the synthesis of the RNA complement of a gene.

✔ Processing follows transcription, and includes splicing, and the addition of a 5' cap and a 3' polyadenosine tail. After processing, a mature mRNA can be exported from the nucleus.

✔ The nucleus contains the nucleolus, a separate, membrane-bound compartment that is the site of ribosome synthesis.

✔ The nucleus is surrounded by the nuclear envelope, a double membrane perforated with nuclear pores. These pores regulate the passage of materials like mRNAs and proteins between the nucleus and the cytoplasm.

Plasma Membrane

✔ The plasma membrane separates the cell's interior from the external environment, which allows the cell to maintain a distinct metabolism and genetic identity.

✔ The major building blocks of the plasma membrane are phospholipids, amphiphilic structures that have distinct polar headgroups and nonpolar tails. When exposed to water, phospholipids spontaneously form bilayer membranes, exposing polar headgroups to inner and outer aqueous regions, and sequestering nonpolar tails within the bilayer.

✔ Plasma membranes enable cellular homeostasis by the action of proteins embedded within the bilayer. By regulating the passage of materials across the membrane, these proteins make the membrane selectively permeable, so that nutrients enter and wastes exit the cell.

✔ The fluid mosaic model describes the plasma membrane as a surface along which embedded proteins and other molecules can freely diffuse.

Cell Wall

✓ Cell walls are found in plants, fungi, and some bacteria and protists. Cells walls are additional barriers that envelop the plasma membrane, providing protection and support, as well as filtering.

✓ Plant cell walls are made from the carbohydrate, cellulose. Many bacterial cell walls are made from the cross-linked peptide-carbohydrate material called peptidoglycan. Other species have cell walls composed of other cross-linked polymers, such as chitin.

Endoplasmic Reticulum

✓ The endoplasmic reticulum is a maze-like network of membranes that resembles a stack of flattened sacs. The ER manufactures various materials for the cell and assists in their transport.

✓ The ER comes in smooth and rough varieties. The smooth ER contains enzymes that participate in the synthesis of lipid-based molecules like phospholipids and steroids. The rough ER contains ribosomes that synthesize certain types of proteins; in particular, ribosomes associated with the rough ER make proteins that need to be sorted or processed, and proteins that will eventually reside within membranes.

Mitochondria

✓ Mitochondria are membrane bound organelles that are the site of aerobic cellular respiration. As such, most of a cell's energy supply comes from mitochondria in the form of adenosine triphosphate, ATP.

✓ Mitochondria possess inner and outer membranes, separated by an intermembrane space. The inner membrane has many folds called cristae, and the fluid-filled interior of the mitochondrion is called the matrix.

✓ Mitochondria have their own genomes, many aspects of which are similar to bacterial genomes. For this and other reasons, mitochondria are thought to have descended from a free-living bacterial ancestor that was enveloped by another cell, the two species subsequently co-evolving; this notion is called the endosymbiotic theory.

Chloroplast

✓ Chloroplasts are membrane bound organelles found only in autotrophic cells. The chloroplast is the site of photosynthesis. Most of the energy used by earth's organisms derives from light energy that was chemically trapped by chloroplasts.

✓ Light-trapping begins with the pigment chlorophyll, that funnels energy from photons into electrons; the energized electrons are relayed into a set of carrier molecules, and eventually used to forge chemical bonds within the energy-rich sugar, glucose.

✓ Chloroplasts are surrounded by a double membrane. The interior of the chloroplast is filled with a fluid called stroma. Within the stroma sit stacks of membranous discs. The stacks are called grana; the discs are made of thylakoid membrane, which contains chlorophyll.

✔ Like mitochondria, chloroplasts are thought to have descended from a free-living bacterium (a photosynthetic bacterium, in this case) that co-evolved endosymbiotically within a larger cell.

Ribosome

✔ Ribosomes are molecular machines that synthesize protein during the process of translation. Ribosomes are built from a large and a small subunit. Each subunit is composed mostly of RNA, with many embedded proteins.

✔ The small subunit of the ribosome, along with tRNAs, deciphers the genetic code in which mRNAs are written. The large subunit catalyzes peptide bond formation between the amino acids specified by an mRNA, and carried to the ribosome by tRNAs.

Golgi Apparatus

✔ The Golgi apparatus is a system of stacked and interconnecting membranes that specializes in sorting, processing, and packing macromolecules — especially proteins and lipids. The stacked membranes of the Golgi are called cisternae. The Golgi is particularly prominent in cells that do a lot of secretion.

✔ Raw materials arrive at the Golgi within membrane vesicles, often sent from the ER. The materials within the vesicles enter the cisternae, and undergo various types of sorting and processing before they are sent out the other side of the Golgi, again within vesicles.

Lysosome

✔ Lysosomes are membrane-bound sacs filled with acidic fluid and digestive enzymes. Lysosomes are made by the Golgi, and function to digest foreign particles engulfed by cells, or other materials that can be broken down and recycled. The digestive enzymes of lysosomes act via hydrolysis, and can break down the major types of biological macromolecules.

Vacuole

✔ Vacuoles are membrane bound compartments that are especially prominent in plant cells. In plants, vacuoles often take up 30 percent and more of the cell volume, and serve as storage reservoirs and as sources of turgor, an internal hydrostatic pressure that gives the plant cell structural rigidity.

Chapter 32

Ten Points on Plants and Animals

. . . .

In This Chapter

▶ Focusing on the features of flora and fauna

▶ Getting better acquainted with systems in your body

. . . .

*P*lants and animals make up a big, leafy, furry chunk of the AP Biology exam. Use this collection of highlights to remind yourself of the big-picture items you need to know. I know we said there were ten points here, but this chapter is more like ten categories with points under each, all of which are worth remembering.

Meristems

Keep these thoughts in mind about meristems:

✔ Meristems are sites of active cell division that give rise to the three major types of germ tissues in plants: dermal, vascular, and ground. All kinds of plant cells develop from these three tissues.

✔ Apical meristems lead to primary growth, the elongation of root, and shoot tips. Lateral meristems lead to secondary growth, the thickening of existing roots and shoots.

Roots and Shoots

You probably never knew you could find out so much about roots and shoots, but what we've listed here are good points to remember when taking the AP Bio exam.

✔ Root shafts consist of an outer epidermis, a middle-layer called the cortex, and an inner layer called the stele. The epidermis has root hairs that aid in absorption. The cortex provides support and can store starch. The stele contains xylem and phloem.

✔ Stem shafts consist of an outer epidermis, an inner pith, and are traversed by xylem and phloem tubes. The epidermis provides protection, the pith provides storage, and the xylem and phloem provide transport.

✔ Leaves develop from leaf primordia that flank shoot apical meristems. Leaves are the sites of photosynthesis, and contain stomata, pores that open and close to regulate the passage of water and respiratory gases.

✔ Monocots have highly branched, shallow root systems. Dicots have a deep, central tap-root. Monocot leaves have parallel veins. Dicot leaves have branched veins.

Plant Vasculature

Like that fancy word? We're basically referring to plants that have special tissues for conducting products, such as water and minerals, through plants. Remember that fancy word as well as the points that follow:

✔ Xylem tubes consist largely of dead cells, and conduct water and dissolved nutrients absorbed at the roots. Xylem transport is driven mostly by transpiration and is aided by root pressure and capillary action.

✔ Phloem tubes consist of living cells, and conduct dissolved sugars both upwards and downwards within plants. Phloem transports sugars from sugar sources to sugar sinks, and is driven by osmosis and pressure.

Photoperiodism

Plants regulate their activities throughout the night and day. The following points highlight some important concepts you should remember about photoperiodism:

✔ Plants regulate their activities in accordance with both daily and seasonal changes in light. These changes can include duration, intensity and quality of light. To sense changes in light, plants use pigment molecules called phytochromes. *Phytochromes* can sense light of different wavelengths, and act as accountants, keeping track of the amount of light at each wavelength.

✔ *Circadian rhythms* are built in biological clocks that help plants regulate periodic activities. Circadian rhythms are initially trained by phytochromes, but later become largely autonomous.

Respirocirculatory System

Study these points about circulation to score some points on your AP Bio exam:

✔ Many animals use a system of double circulation, pumping blood through a series of two circuits. The pulmonary circuit circulates blood from the heart to the lungs and back. The systemic circuit pumps blood from the heart to the body tissues and back. Blood exits the heart through arteries, branching into arterioles and then capillaries. Blood returns from the capillaries into venules, then into veins and back into the heart.

✔ In the lungs, capillaries enmesh tiny sacs called alveoli. Inspiration pulls air into the alveoli, where respiratory gas exchange occurs. Carbon dioxide diffuses from the blood into the alveoli, and oxygen diffuses from the alveoli into the blood. Expiration expels the accumulated carbon dioxide as waste.

✔ Exchange of nutrients and wastes occurs between capillaries and interstitial fluids throughout body tissues. This exchange uses both active and passive transport.

Immune System

No one is immune from questions about the immune system on the AP Biology exam, so be sure to review these points:

- Nonspecific immunity generally prevents or fights off initial infections, buying time for the onset of specific immunity.

- Specific immunity defends against particular infectious agents, and involves humoral and cell-mediated immunity. Humoral immunity includes antibody production, organized by B-lymphocytes. Cell-mediated immunity is organized by T-lymphocytes.

- Both types of specific immunity involve the training of memory cells, which help produce a rapid specific response in case of a second infection.

Musculoskeletal System

You need to know more than just, " . . . the hip bone's connected to the . . ." when it comes to the musculoskeletal system. So, we've given you some points to stew over below:

- The functional unit of bone is the osteon, a circular arrangement of cells served by central nerves and vessels. Bones meet at joints. Joints may be cushioned by cartilage. Bones are attached at joints by ligaments and attached to muscles by tendons.

- Muscles are either skeletal, cardiac or smooth. Skeletal muscle is voluntary. Cardiac and smooth muscle are involuntary. Skeletal and cardiac muscle are striated and contract rapidly. Smooth muscle lacks striations and contracts slowly.

- Striations arise from sarcomeres, the functional units of striated muscle. Sarcomeres consist of overlapping filaments of myosin and actin protein fibers. Action potentials from nerves cause calcium to flow into myofibrils, enabling myosin to pull on adjacent actin fibers so that the filaments slide over one another in a contraction.

Digestive System

There's more to eating than chewing and swallowing. A entire host of things occur in the digestive system, and we've mentioned a few in the following list:

- Digestion is both mechanical and chemical. Mechanical digestion occurs by chewing and churning of the stomach. Chemical digestion occurs by the action of enzymes, stomach acid, bile and other factors.

- Saliva contain salivary amylase, which breaks down starch. The stomach secretes hydrochloric acid and the protein-digesting enzyme pepsin. The pancreas secretes a wealth of digestive enzymes that help to digest protein (trypsin, chymotrypsin, carboxypeptidase), nucleic acids (nuclease) and carbohydrates (pancreatic amylase). The pancreas also secretes bile, which helps emulsify fats. The small intestine secretes lipase, which digests fats.

- Most absorption of digested nutrients occurs in the small intestine, across a large surface area provided by villi and microvilli. The large intestine specializes in water absorption.

Nervous and Endocrine Systems

Okay, so you may be nervous enough about taking the AP Bio exam already that you can't imagine that there's anything more you need to know about being nervous, but there is! Check out what we have to say about both the nervous and endocrine systems below:

- ✔ The nervous system provides rapid electrical communication. Signals travel along the axons of neurons via action potentials. Signals travel across the synapses between neurons via neurotransmitters. Sensory (or afferent) nerves carry information from the peripheral nervous system to the central nervous system. Motor (or efferent) nerves carry information in the other direction. Interneurons connect afferent and efferent neurons.

- ✔ The endocrine system provides slower, distributed chemical communication. Glands secrete hormones into body fluids. Hormones are distributed by circulation throughout the body, but elicit responses only from those cells equipped with receptors for those hormones. Steroid hormones tend to pass directly through cell membranes and exert their effects via complexes with nuclear receptors. Peptide hormones tend to enter cells through the action of membrane protein receptors, and tend to exert their effects via complexes with cytoplasmic receptors.

Reproductive System

Okay, it's time for "the talk." The points below should cover it in case mom or dad never did:

- ✔ Gametes include eggs and sperm. Eggs develop within ovaries, but do not undergo meiosis II until fertilization. Sperm develop within testes, undergoing all phases of meiosis. In egg formation, meiosis involves unequal divisions that yield larger oocytes and smaller polar bodies. In sperm formation, meiotic divisions are equal.

- ✔ Fertilization results from the fusion of haploid sperm and haploid egg, and produces a diploid zygote. Subsequent cell divisions yield a hollow ball of cells called a blastula. This ball folds in on itself as it develops into a gastrula. Gastrulas have outer, middle and inner layers. These layers give rise to the three types of germ tissue from which all other cells develop: ectoderm, mesoderm and endoderm.

Index

BUSINESS, CAREERS & PERSONAL FINANCE

0-7645-9847-3

0-7645-2431-3

Also available:

- Business Plans Kit For Dummies
  0-7645-9794-9
- Economics For Dummies
  0-7645-5726-2
- Grant Writing For Dummies
  0-7645-8416-2
- Home Buying For Dummies
  0-7645-5331-3
- Managing For Dummies
  0-7645-1771-6
- Marketing For Dummies
  0-7645-5600-2

- Personal Finance For Dummies
  0-7645-2590-5*
- Resumes For Dummies
  0-7645-5471-9
- Selling For Dummies
  0-7645-5363-1
- Six Sigma For Dummies
  0-7645-6798-5
- Small Business Kit For Dummies
  0-7645-5984-2
- Starting an eBay Business For Dummies
  0-7645-6924-4
- Your Dream Career For Dummies
  0-7645-9795-7

HOME & BUSINESS COMPUTER BASICS

0-470-05432-8

0-471-75421-8

Also available:

- Cleaning Windows Vista For Dummies
  0-471-78293-9
- Excel 2007 For Dummies
  0-470-03737-7
- Mac OS X Tiger For Dummies
  0-7645-7675-5
- MacBook For Dummies
  0-470-04859-X
- Macs For Dummies
  0-470-04849-2
- Office 2007 For Dummies
  0-470-00923-3

- Outlook 2007 For Dummies
  0-470-03830-6
- PCs For Dummies
  0-7645-8958-X
- Salesforce.com For Dummies
  0-470-04893-X
- Upgrading & Fixing Laptops For Dummies
  0-7645-8959-8
- Word 2007 For Dummies
  0-470-03658-3
- Quicken 2007 For Dummies
  0-470-04600-7

FOOD, HOME, GARDEN, HOBBIES, MUSIC & PETS

0-7645-8404-9

0-7645-9904-6

Also available:

- Candy Making For Dummies
  0-7645-9734-5
- Card Games For Dummies
  0-7645-9910-0
- Crocheting For Dummies
  0-7645-4151-X
- Dog Training For Dummies
  0-7645-8418-9
- Healthy Carb Cookbook For Dummies
  0-7645-8476-6
- Home Maintenance For Dummies
  0-7645-5215-5

- Horses For Dummies
  0-7645-9797-3
- Jewelry Making & Beading For Dummies
  0-7645-2571-9
- Orchids For Dummies
  0-7645-6759-4
- Puppies For Dummies
  0-7645-5255-4
- Rock Guitar For Dummies
  0-7645-5356-9
- Sewing For Dummies
  0-7645-6847-7
- Singing For Dummies
  0-7645-2475-5

INTERNET & DIGITAL MEDIA

0-470-04529-9

0-470-04894-8

Also available:

- Blogging For Dummies
  0-471-77084-1
- Digital Photography For Dummies
  0-7645-9802-3
- Digital Photography All-in-One Desk Reference For Dummies
  0-470-03743-1
- Digital SLR Cameras and Photography For Dummies
  0-7645-9803-1
- eBay Business All-in-One Desk Reference For Dummies
  0-7645-8438-3
- HDTV For Dummies
  0-470-09673-X

- Home Entertainment PCs For Dummies
  0-470-05523-5
- MySpace For Dummies
  0-470-09529-6
- Search Engine Optimization For Dummies
  0-471-97998-8
- Skype For Dummies
  0-470-04891-3
- The Internet For Dummies
  0-7645-8996-2
- Wiring Your Digital Home For Dummies
  0-471-91830-X

* Separate Canadian edition also available
† Separate U.K. edition also available

Available wherever books are sold. For more information or to order direct: U.S. customers visit www.dummies.com or call 1-877-762-2974.
U.K. customers visit www.wileyeurope.com or call 0800 243407. Canadian customers visit www.wiley.ca or call 1-800-567-4797.

SPORTS, FITNESS, PARENTING, RELIGION & SPIRITUALITY

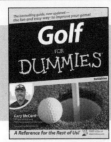

0-471-76871-5

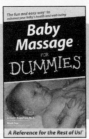

0-7645-7841-3

Also available:
- Catholicism For Dummies
  0-7645-5391-7
- Exercise Balls For Dummies
  0-7645-5623-1
- Fitness For Dummies
  0-7645-7851-0
- Football For Dummies
  0-7645-3936-1
- Judaism For Dummies
  0-7645-5299-6
- Potty Training For Dummies
  0-7645-5417-4
- Buddhism For Dummies
  0-7645-5359-3

- Pregnancy For Dummies
  0-7645-4483-7 †
- Ten Minute Tone-Ups For Dummies
  0-7645-7207-5
- NASCAR For Dummies
  0-7645-7681-X
- Religion For Dummies
  0-7645-5264-3
- Soccer For Dummies
  0-7645-5229-5
- Women in the Bible For Dummies
  0-7645-8475-8

TRAVEL

0-7645-7749-2

0-7645-6945-7

Also available:
- Alaska For Dummies
  0-7645-7746-8
- Cruise Vacations For Dummies
  0-7645-6941-4
- England For Dummies
  0-7645-4276-1
- Europe For Dummies
  0-7645-7529-5
- Germany For Dummies
  0-7645-7823-5
- Hawaii For Dummies
  0-7645-7402-7

- Italy For Dummies
  0-7645-7386-1
- Las Vegas For Dummies
  0-7645-7382-9
- London For Dummies
  0-7645-4277-X
- Paris For Dummies
  0-7645-7630-5
- RV Vacations For Dummies
  0-7645-4442-X
- Walt Disney World & Orlando
  For Dummies
  0-7645-9660-8

GRAPHICS, DESIGN & WEB DEVELOPMENT

0-7645-8815-X

0-7645-9571-7

Also available:
- 3D Game Animation For Dummies
  0-7645-8789-7
- AutoCAD 2006 For Dummies
  0-7645-8925-3
- Building a Web Site For Dummies
  0-7645-7144-3
- Creating Web Pages For Dummies
  0-470-08030-2
- Creating Web Pages All-in-One Desk
  Reference For Dummies
  0-7645-4345-8
- Dreamweaver 8 For Dummies
  0-7645-9649-7

- InDesign CS2 For Dummies
  0-7645-9572-5
- Macromedia Flash 8 For Dummies
  0-7645-9691-8
- Photoshop CS2 and Digital
  Photography For Dummies
  0-7645-9580-6
- Photoshop Elements 4 For Dummies
  0-471-77483-9
- Syndicating Web Sites with RSS Feeds
  For Dummies
  0-7645-8848-6
- Yahoo! SiteBuilder For Dummies
  0-7645-9800-7

NETWORKING, SECURITY, PROGRAMMING & DATABASES

0-7645-7728-X

0-471-74940-0

Also available:
- Access 2007 For Dummies
  0-470-04612-0
- ASP.NET 2 For Dummies
  0-7645-7907-X
- C# 2005 For Dummies
  0-7645-9704-3
- Hacking For Dummies
  0-470-05235-X
- Hacking Wireless Networks
  For Dummies
  0-7645-9730-2
- Java For Dummies
  0-470-08716-1

- Microsoft SQL Server 2005 For Dummies
  0-7645-7755-7
- Networking All-in-One Desk Reference
  For Dummies
  0-7645-9939-9
- Preventing Identity Theft For Dummies
  0-7645-7336-5
- Telecom For Dummies
  0-471-77085-X
- Visual Studio 2005 All-in-One Desk
  Reference For Dummies
  0-7645-9775-2
- XML For Dummies
  0-7645-8845-1

HEALTH & SELF-HELP

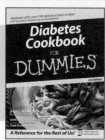

0-7645-8450-2

0-7645-4149-8

Also available:

- Bipolar Disorder For Dummies
  0-7645-8451-0
- Chemotherapy and Radiation For Dummies
  0-7645-7832-4
- Controlling Cholesterol For Dummies
  0-7645-5440-9
- Diabetes For Dummies
  0-7645-6820-5* †
- Divorce For Dummies
  0-7645-8417-0 †

- Fibromyalgia For Dummies
  0-7645-5441-7
- Low-Calorie Dieting For Dummies
  0-7645-9905-4
- Meditation For Dummies
  0-471-77774-9
- Osteoporosis For Dummies
  0-7645-7621-6
- Overcoming Anxiety For Dummies
  0-7645-5447-6
- Reiki For Dummies
  0-7645-9907-0
- Stress Management For Dummies
  0-7645-5144-2

EDUCATION, HISTORY, REFERENCE & TEST PREPARATION

0-7645-8381-6

0-7645-9554-7

Also available:

- The ACT For Dummies
  0-7645-9652-7
- Algebra For Dummies
  0-7645-5325-9
- Algebra Workbook For Dummies
  0-7645-8467-7
- Astronomy For Dummies
  0-7645-8465-0
- Calculus For Dummies
  0-7645-2498-4
- Chemistry For Dummies
  0-7645-5430-1
- Forensics For Dummies
  0-7645-5580-4

- Freemasons For Dummies
  0-7645-9796-5
- French For Dummies
  0-7645-5193-0
- Geometry For Dummies
  0-7645-5324-0
- Organic Chemistry I For Dummies
  0-7645-6902-3
- The SAT I For Dummies
  0-7645-7193-1
- Spanish For Dummies
  0-7645-5194-9
- Statistics For Dummies
  0-7645-5423-9

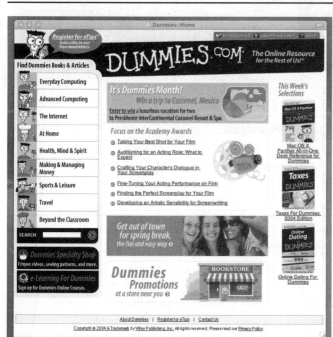

Get smart @ dummies.com®

- **Find a full list of Dummies titles**
- **Look into loads of FREE on-site articles**
- **Sign up for FREE eTips e-mailed to you weekly**
- **See what other products carry the Dummies name**
- **Shop directly from the Dummies bookstore**
- **Enter to win new prizes every month!**

* Separate Canadian edition also available
† Separate U.K. edition also available

Available wherever books are sold. For more information or to order direct: U.S. customers visit www.dummies.com or call 1-877-762-2974.
U.K. customers visit www.wileyeurope.com or call 0800 243407. Canadian customers visit www.wiley.ca or call 1-800-567-4797.